ESCORT TO BERLIN

ESCORT TO BERLIN

By Garry L. Fry and Jeffrey L. Ethell

ARCO PUBLISHING, INC.
NEW YORK

DEDICATION
Fighter pilots exist for one reason—to fly and fight.
To those who lost their lives in performance of that mission.

Published by Arco Publishing, Inc.
219 Park Avenue South, New York, N.Y. 10003

Copyright © 1980 by Garry L. Fry and Jeffrey L. Ethell

Library of Congress Cataloging in Publication Data

Fry, Garry L
  Escort to Berlin.

  1. World War, 1939–1945—Aerial operations,
American. 2. United States. Army Air Forces. 4th
Fighter Group—History. I. Ethell, Jeffrey L.,
joint author. II. Title.
D790.F75   940.54'49'73   79–21070

ISBN 0-668-04768-2 (Library Edition)

Printed in the United States of America

Title page—June 6, 1944: Takeoff of the second mission on the great day, D-Day!
336 gets off first in their freshly AEAF striped kites, as 334 waits on the north apron
of the west runway. 334 is led by CO Mike Sobanski in his new D-model QP-F.
Hofer's QP-L is on the right. (*I. Swerdel*)

Contents

Foreword

BY LT. GENERAL IRA C. EAKER, USAF (RET.)

This book, *Escort to Berlin,* by Garry L. Fry and Jeffrey L. Ethell, is a detailed description of the operation of the 4th Fighter Group of the 8th Air Force in World War II. The authors deserve great credit for the industry they have displayed and the accuracy with which they have reported daily missions.

Escort to Berlin will serve as a valuable source of operational data. Air Force World War II veterans and especially all historical libraries will find it of interest and value in their research.

No one can read this volume without a better understanding of the operations of fighter aircraft in the 8th Air Force, flying out of the United Kingdom, in the dramatic days of World War II. Training, organization, operational methods and the decisive results obtained are faithfully described here.

There are two narrative accounts—one relating the experiences of a pilot forced to ditch in the English Channel, and the other a squadron commander's experiences as a member of the first Shuttle Bombing Operation the 8th Air Force conducted out of England—which will be of a special interest to all readers.

The Eagle Squadrons (those American fighter pilots who voluntarily fought with the RAF prior to our entry), when they transferred to the U.S. 8th Air Force, became the initial nucleus of the 4th Fighter Group, where their experience and early leadership proved invaluable.

I note and commend the many favorable references in this book to the successive group commanders. The 4th Fighter Group was especially fortunate in this regard. Colonel Donald Blakeslee, for example, who served as its commander for the longest period, was a courageous leader in air combat and also skilled in administrative management.

The authors of *Escort to Berlin* have by chance made this book available at a time when I perceive a growing interest in the air operations of World War II. This, hopefully, is a sign of our national recovery from our unfortunate experiences in the Vietnam War.

As the Commanding General of the 8th Air Force from October 1942 to January 1944, I yield to none in admiration for the gallant combat crews who made the story of the "Mighty Eighth" a revelation of the part airpower played in destroying Hitler's territory.

Acknowledgments

Escort to Berlin is the culmination of over ten years' research. Needless to say, it would not have been possible without the kindness and support of the former members of the 4th Fighter Group and the many others who never served with the Group but who shared our fascination.

The following members of the wartime 4th Fighter Group contributed photos, facts, time and effort: Richard Alexander, Donald Allen, Maj. Gen. Edward Anderson, George Anderson, Vincent Andra, Ray Aug, Vincent Baietti, Mickey Balsam, John Barden, Robert Beeson, Walter Behm, James Belcher, William Belcher, Tom Bell, Herbert Blanchfield, Francis Bodner, Vernon Boehle, Raymond Bogusevic, Robert Bolza, Carmine Bonitati, Clarence Bousfield, Beacher Brooker, Carl Brown, Gerald Brown, Paul Burnett, Jerome Byrge, George Carpenter, Van Chandler, Archie Chatterly, Lewis Chick, Joseph Ciciulla, Richard Claspell, Walter Clatanoff, Ray Clotfelter, Virgil Clymer, Ernest Cool, George Cooley, John Cowman, John Creamer, John DeKay, Gordon Denson, Robert Dickmeyer, James DuFour, James Dye, Robert Easton, Louis Engber, Kenneth Ettner, Fred Farington, Francis Farrell, George Fite, Carl Funk, Vermont Garrison, James Gibson, William Gier, Jess Gittinger, Otey Glass, Charles Goodrich, James Goodson, John Goodwyn, Lee Gover, Lawrence Graves, Leslie Graves, Francis Grove, Grover Hall, Dale Hall, Gary Haning, Preston Hardy, Edward Hedrick, Kenneth Helfrecht, Larry Hendel, Howard Hively, David Howe, Gilbert Hunt, Warren Jackman, Elwood Jensen, Waldo Johnson, Robert Kellett, George Klaus, Charles Konsler, Pinckney Lackey, Robert Lewis, Philip Lindsey, Nathan Lippman, Roderic Lonier, John Loy, Paul Lucas, Cecil Manning, Charles Marchinke, Michael Markowitz, Franklin Mason, David Mathies, Raymond Mayorga, Maj. Gen. Carroll McColpin, Thomas McDill, John McFarlane, James McMahon, Charles Mead, Nicholas Megura, Joseph Miller, Brewster Morgan, Edward Nelson, Robert Nelson, Gerald Newton, Leroy Nitschke, Frank Nowak, William O'Donnell, Joseph Patteeuw, Maj. Gen. Chesley Peterson, Steve Pisanos, August Radloff, Alex Rafalovich, Jack Raphael, Edward and Mark Richie, Richard Rinebolt, Baxter Roark, John Romack, Edwin Rowe, William Rushing, George Russel, James Russell, Raymond St. Cyr, Leo Schmidt, Henry Sedmak, Curtis Simpson, Joseph Sills, Frank Speer, William Spencer, Scheley Stafford, John Swan, Herbert Swift, William Taylor, David Van Epps, Steve Vali, Robert Voyles, Willard Wahl, Glesner Weckbacher, Melvin Weddle, Robert Wehrman,

John Wilson, Sidney Woods and Donald Young. A number of these 4th veterans have passed away since the research began. May they find perfect peace.

The widows of other deceased men of the 4th who have aided in this project are Mrs. Ruth (Claiborne) Kinnard, Mrs. Edward Nickerson and Mrs. Isadore Swerdel. To all of you our sincere thanks. A special thank you goes to Mrs. Carl Beeson, mother of deceased 4th ace Duane Beeson.

Fellow aero historians around the world gave aid and advice: Mike Bailey, Allen Blue, Keith Braybrooke, Harley Copic, Fred Dickey, Lou Drendel, Roger Freeman, Frank Gallion, Allan Healy, William Hess, Dick Hill, Tom Ivie, Robert Jones, Art Krieger, George Letzter, Ernie McDowell, Ian McLachlan, David Menard, Gregory Moreira, Danny Morris, Kenn Rust, Jack Spreter, Patrick Stein, Victor Tannehill, and Gerry Zijlstra. All of you were outstanding examples of what our small fraternity is trying to do.

We are truly indebted to the various official agencies who opened their files and resources to us. At the Air Force Museum, Director Royal Frey and Research Director Charles Worman went out of their way to help. The Albert Simpson Historical Research Center, Maxwell AFB, provided microfilm via James Eastman, Gloria Atkinson, Allen Striepe and Judy Endicott. Capt. Rick DuCharme, USAF Magazine & Book Branch, supplied excellent photos from the Aerospace Audio Visual Service. The National Records Center (GSA) opened their stacks to us. The U.S. Army Photographic Agency, through the gracious efforts of Maj. Ray Smith, produced some excellent photographs for us.

A visit to the Ministry of Defense and Air Historical Branch in London was made very pleasant through the kindnesses of the head of MOD PR4, Derek Knight, MBE, and Ronald Kane. We also wish to express our gratitude for documents they supplied and for arranging a visit to RAF Debden.

The present-day 4th Tactical Fighter Wing at Seymour Johnson AFB, North Carolina, provided material and warm hospitality during our visits with them through HQ Tactical Air Command, Wing CO Col. (now Gen.) Bob Russ and Wing Historian Fred Claypoole. Tom Davidson kindly lent the use of his graphics shop lab as a fellow aero historian.

A particular debt is owed to three exceptional airmen, Elmer Ward, George Enhorning and Vern Peterson, who carry history into the present by flying and maintaining P-51 Mustangs. They made it possible for us to experience the almost extinct thrill of flying in the mount that carried the 4th to its greatest triumphs. Finally, a great deal is owed to our fine literary agent, Bill Dean of Sky Books International, for his efforts in making this possible.

To all of you, our warmest thanks. . . .
Cheers!

                                    JEFFREY L. ETHELL and GARRY L. FRY, 1980

Introduction

During the dark days of 1940, when Britain indeed stood alone, sympathetic Americans made their way to England to fly and fight in the Royal Air Force. For various patriotic and political reasons, a number of these American pilots in both the RAF and RCAF were formed into No. 71 Eagle Squadron at Church Fenton on 19 September 1940, flying Brewster Buffaloes. In November the Eagles went operational on Hawker Hurricane Is, seeing action for the first time on 5 February 1941, flying from Kirton-on-Lindsey.

The second Eagle Squadron, No. 121, was formed on 14 May 1941, taking its Hurricane IIbs into combat by the end of July. No. 133, the third of the famous units, began to fly patrols from Fowlmere on Spitfire IIas in October.

While serving with RAF Fighter Command, the Eagles flew convoy patrols, fighter sweeps, bomber escort, air-sea rescue patrols—the full scope of combat operations. A total of eight pilots achieved ace status. A high point in Eagle history came during the air fighting over Dieppe on 19 August 1942 during the unsuccessful Allied landing on the French coast.

Just three days later the U.S. Army Air Force constituted the 4th Fighter Group, chosen to be the parent organization for the Eagles after they exchanged their RAF blues for AAF pinks. When the three squadrons transferred they were credited with 73½ enemy aircraft, a total that would forever remain the property of the RAF. The 4th started out with quite a reputation to live up to.

The Eagles brought a wealth of combat experience and RAF tradition with them. Even with the influx of new personnel direct from the U.S. by early 1944, the 4th would ever retain the manners and unique terminology of those who wore two sets of wings. Aircraft were "kites" . . . one didn't start his kite, he "pressed" . . . an aircraft accident was a "prang" . . . one didn't enter the landing pattern but the "circuit" . . . canopies were "hoods" . . . the Group didn't go on missions, but "shows," called Rhubarbs and Rodeos . . . squadrons were referred to without the "th" on the end, thus "335" went on a show . . . one didn't attend an event, but a "do" . . . or receive a decoration, but a "gong" . . . or get the information, but the "gen" . . . and on it went.

Yet the record of the 4th Fighter Group in World War II bears a stamp all its own. Not until early 1944 did the unit begin to establish itself as the leading AAF fighter group of the war. The slow start was discouraging for men who thought combat great sport. In the great aerial battles over Europe during the last year and a half of hostilities, the 4th achieved a greatness among air fighters that will never be matched.

We have tried to present a factual account, allowing the records to speak for themselves as much as possible within our limitations of space. All source material was first generation; nothing was based on previously published accounts. If we have slighted anyone or omitted something thought important, it was not intentional. Our goal was to give a historical record that reflects those never-to-be-forgotten times when our nation pulled together as a whole.

GARRY L. FRY
JEFFREY L. ETHELL

Glossary and Abbreviations

A-1: Personnel Officer or Section.

A-2: Intelligence Officer or Section.

A-3: Operations and Training Officer or Section.

A-4: Supply Officer or Section.

Abort: Turn back from a mission.

A/C: Aircraft.

A.C.C.: Assistant Crew Chief.

A/D: Airdrome.

APU: Auxiliary Power Unit.

Arm.: Armorer.

Baby: Drop tank.

C.C.: Crew Chief.

CG: Center of gravity on an aircraft.

Chattanooga: Railway strafing in a specific area.

Circus: Large bomber escort mission.

DB: Code name for Debden.

Deck: The ground.

Element: Two aircraft, lead and wingman.

ETO: European Theater of Operations.

Flight: Eight aircraft made up from two sections, designated A, B, C or D.

F.O.: Field Order sent down from 8th Air Force headquarters (Pinetree) outlining mission details and orders.

Gong: RAF slang for decoration or medal.

Group: Normally 48 aircraft; 72 later with "double groups," and over 100 by war's end.

Jackpot: Airdrome strafing in a predetermined area.

KIA: Killed in action.

KIFA: Killed in flying accident.

Kite: RAF slang for aircraft.

M.E.W.: Microwave early warning.

MIA: Missing in action.

MTO: Mediterranean Theater of Operations.

NMF: Natural metal finish.

NYR: Not yet returned.

O/D: Olive drab (color).

Ops: Slang for mission or active duty ("he was off ops"); short for operations; also referred to base operations center.

OTU: Operational training unit.

POW: Prisoner of war.

Prang: RAF slang for crash or damage.

Press: RAF slang for start engines.

PRU: Photo Reconnaissance Unit.

Ramrod: Bomber escort mission.

Rhubarb: Strafing sweep at low level, usually in bad weather, by a few aircraft.

Roadstead: Attack on enemy shipping and port targets.

Rodeo: Bomber escort with bombers as bait to draw enemy up to engage fighter escort.

R/T: Radio/telephone; RAF term for communications radio aboard aircraft.

RV: Rendezvous.

Section: Four aircraft made up of two elements; designated by color.

Show: RAF slang for mission.

Squadron: 12 to 20 aircraft in combat out of 25 total on base; three make up a group.

T/O: Takeoff.

Type 16 Control: Radar vectored mission, normally not very effective, with such call signs as Colgate, Jensen, Snackbar.

W.F.O.: Wing Field Order issued from wing headquarters under VIII Fighter Command (Ajax).

WIA: Wounded in action.

Operational Diary—1942

22 August 1942: The 4th Fighter Group was constituted by the United States Army Air Force as a combat entity. The three Royal Air Force Eagle Squadrons, made up of American pilots, were to be transferred into the new unit and into the service of the U.S. simultaneously.

12 September 1942: Activated at Bushey Hall, Headquarters of VIII Fighter Command, U.S. Eighth Army Air Force, the 4th Fighter Group was assigned a small contingent of lieutenants and enlisted men for each squadron. No. 71 Eagle Squadron would become the 334th Fighter Squadron, AAF; No. 121 Eagle Squadron the 335th Squadron; No. 133 Eagle Squadron the 336th Squadron. For the time being flying control of the Group's three squadrons was to be handled by the RAF and, for a period, the British were to furnish other needed personnel as the Americans acquainted themselves.

21 September 1942: At 1452 hours two 335 Squadron Spitfire Vbs (still on the records as 121 Eagle Squadron aircraft) flew a shipping reconnaissance from Flushing to Haamstede, Netherlands. Crossing Overflakkee, John T. Slater was killed in action, the first casualty recorded for the 4th.

[Box Score: 0 destroyed, 1 lost]

26 September 1942: At 1600 hours twelve 336 Spitfire IXs (still technically 133 Eagle Squadron) took off from Great Stampford to support B-17s bombing Morlaix, France, then sweep the area. After rendezvous in mid-Channel, the formation proceeded to the target. In a tragic combination of navigational error, weather, German fighters and low fuel, 11 of the Spits were forced down on the Brest Peninsula. Four pilots were killed and six taken prisoner. Robert E. Smith managed to escape and return to England. One of the POWs, Edward G. Brettell, was later executed by the Germans for his part in the Great Escape of 76 POWs from Stalag Luft III. He had served as the escape map maker. Another of the captured, Marion E. Jackson, managed to shoot down an FW 190 at 1730 before going down.

[Box Score: 1 destroyed, 11 lost]

133 Eagle Squadron had been using Mark IXs since 4 September but this was the first and only show in the aircraft. By the 28th, when 133 officially became the 336th Fighter Squadron, the boys were flying Spitfire Vbs again.

29 September 1942: In a formal ceremony at Debden, Essex, the Eagles were officially handed over to the USAAF. About 40 miles north of London and 15 miles south of Cambridge, Debden (code letters DB) was listed by the 8th Air Force as Station No. F-356. The nearby village of Saffron Walden would not be losing its boisterous Yanks. On the contrary, the base would take on the frenzied pace of an American fighter group at war.

Air Chief Marshal Sir Sholto Douglas, C-in-C of RAF Fighter Command, addressed the men as they stood at attention in the English drizzle. Maj. Gen. Carl Spaatz, CO 8th Air Force, received the units into his command. Brig. Gen. Frank O'D. Hunter, CO VIII Fighter Command, pinned the first silver wings of the AAF on the three squadron commanders. Col. Edward W. Anderson was present after his trip from the U.S. as the 4th's first commanding officer, although Wing Cdr. Raymond Miles B. Duke-Woolley, RAF, was to retain flying control of the Group for the next two months.

The RAF ground crews and works people remained to acquaint the new AAF crews with the Spitfire Vb's idiosyncrasies. The American ground crews had been awaiting arrival of their parent unit, the 50th Fighter Squadron, 14th Group, at Goxhill when word was received that their familiar P-38s would be remaining in Iceland. These men were assigned to Debden to form the nucleus of the Group's maintenance section until more personnel arrived directly from the U.S.

2 October 1942: Circus (large bomber escort mission) 221. Wing Cdr. Duke-Woolley led a diversionary fighter sweep from Calais to Dunkirk, France. 334 and 335 engaged several FW 190s at 24,000 feet over Calais at 1435 hours, destroying four. Since Duke-Woolley shared his kill with James A. Clark, the Group was credited with 3½. Oscar Coen, Stanley Anderson and Gene Fetrow got one each.

[Box Score: 3½ destroyed, 0 lost]

3 October 1942: Headquarters for all three squadrons moved from Bushey Hall to Debden.

6 October 1942: 335 was sent out on convoy patrol up the coast from the Thames to Oxford.

9 October 1942: Circus 224. Wing Cdr. Duke-Woolley led a Ramrod (bomber escort mission) and diversionary fighter sweep to Euvermon, Abbeville and Fecoup, France, from 0847–1035 hours. The Group rendezvoused with seven Flying Fortresses over Beachy Head at 24,000 feet, then swept in front of the formation. The Forts returned to England before reaching the French coast. FW 190s were spotted in the distance but were too far away to engage.

10 October 1942: Maj. W. J. Daley led a Circus to Le Havre, France. Escort was provided for 12 Bostons without incident.

14 October 1942: Maj. Daley led a patrol of the enemy coast south of Graves to The Hague, Netherlands. Inbound the Spits attacked three flak ships in a harbor close to Noordmal, Holland.

15 October 1942: Maj. Daley led a Ramrod to LeHavre, France, from 1440 to 1615 hours. The Group rendezvoused with 12 Bostons over Selsey and stayed with the bombers until crossing back out at Octeville.

20 October 1942: Two 334 Spits were out on convoy patrol from 1045 to 1455 hours. About 10 miles east of Harwich, at 1430, Anthony J. Seaman's aircraft developed engine trouble, exploded in mid-air and crashed into the Channel, killing him instantly.

[Box Score: 0 destroyed, 1 lost]

21 October 1942: 335 went out on a morning convoy patrol.

Out again in the afternoon, 335 flew a fighter sweep off the French coast.

334 took part in a Circus, escorting RAF Venturas in an uneventful trip to the enemy coast and back.

23 October 1942: 335 was out on another convoy patrol.

24 October 1942: Yet another convoy patrol was flown by 334 and 335. Patrols of this nature were generally very dull. Though pilots were anxious to engage in more than routine missions, they would fly this type of operation well into 1943.

25 October 1942: Circus 232. Wing Cdr. Duke-Woolley led a Ramrod and fighter sweep to LeHavre, France, from 1340 to 1450 hours. The Wing (as the Group was referred to by the RAF) rendezvoused with 12 Bostons over Selsey Bill but 334 and 336 turned back due to poor weather. 335 went on to the target with the bombers.

28 October 1942: 335 went on detached service to Martlesham Heath for air firing practice and later moved to Debden's satellite field at Great Stampford, three miles to the east.

29 October 1942: Two 336 kites were off to Knocke, Belgium, on a Rhubarb from 1435 to 1610 hours, attacking barges in a canal.

31 October 1942: Two 334 aircraft went out on a Rhubarb to Bercks-sur-Mer, France. There was nothing quite like this free-wheeling, anything-goes type of fighter sweep flown on the deck, usually in bad weather. This one resulted in one locomotive destroyed.

4 November 1942: Mrs. Eleanor Roosevelt visited Debden, with Gen. Hunter and Air Marshall Sir Trafford Leigh-Mallory, from 1515 to 1700 hours. The Group performed a Spitfire Fly-by.

6 November 1942: Ramrod 22. Wing Cdr. Duke-Woolley led the Boston escort to Caen airdrome, France, from 1350 to 1550 hours. The Group rendezvoused with the bombers at 1408, flying at 8,000 feet. There were a few breaks in the clouds over Caen but no enemy aircraft showed up.

During this time the RAF was still issuing orders to the Group under the heading "Debden Wing." Though the 4th was indeed an AAF unit much of the operational control over the Group remained with the British.

8 November 1942: Circus 235. Wing Cdr. Duke-Woolley led the patrol and escort to Lille/Fives, France, from 1200 to 1320 hours. After patrolling between Audrico and Gravelines between 22,000 and 24,000 feet, the Group rendezvoused with the first box of 15 B-17s at 21,000. Six FW 190s attacked and 334 tried to bounce with no luck. The wing then split into squadrons to patrol in the Calais/Gravelines area for 15 minutes. Two more Fortress formations were given withdrawal support at 14,000 feet.

9 November 1942: Circus 236. Wing Cdr. Duke-Woolley led an escort to Le-Havre, France, from 1010 to 1500 hours. The Group refueled at Tangmere and then rendezvoused with 12 Bostons over Selsey Bill. 10/10ths cloud over the target forced the formation to Honfleur before turning back for home.

10 November 1942: Circus 237. Wing Cdr. Duke-Woolley led an escort for 18 Bostons to LeHavre, France, from 1420 to 1550 hours. As the bombers approached the target the 4th orbited five miles north at 12,000 to 15,000 feet, then turned for home.

11 November 1942: Two 334 kites were off on a shipping recco, covering Ostend to Knocke, Belgium. No vessels were sighted.

14 November 1942: Another shipping recco, this time by 335, from Flushing to Ostend, Belgium. Again, nothing.

16 November 1942: Four 334 Spits took off on two different Rhubarbs. One section swept south of Cap d'Alprecht to Fret d'Hardelat to Staples while the other two went from St. Valery to St. Aubing, France. Trying to evade flak, James Clark hit the top of a tree and brought back a slightly pranged kite.

17 November 1942: 335 engaged in a fighter patrol of the French coast.

18 November 1942: Two 334 aircraft flew a Rhubarb from Bercks-sur-Mer to Rue, France, staying on the rail line. They managed to beat up a tanker engine with good results. 335 patrolled the French coast again.

19 November 1942: 335 went out on a Rhubarb to attack Flushing airdrome, Netherlands. After so long a lull the enemy came up to fight. Four FW 190s were encountered. With some maneuvering one was trapped 10 miles southwest of Flushing and downed at 1500 hours by Frank Smolinsky.

[Box Score: 1 destroyed, 0 lost]

20 November 1942: Two 335 kites were sent out on a Rhubarb to the Furnes, Belgium, area. Roy Evans caught a wandering Fi 156 and shot it down at 1135 hours three miles southeast of Furnes. Before getting back to England Evans had to bail out into the sea but he was rescued a short time later.

[Box Score: 1 destroyed, 0 lost]

22 November 1942: Two of the three original squadron commanders at the time of transfer into the AAF (Daley and McColpin) were reassigned to the States. A young pilot, Donald J. M. Blakeslee, took his first major command in the service of the United States by assuming leadership of 335.

26 November 1942: Two 335 Spits went out on a Rhubarb northeast of Dunkirk while two 334 kites stayed out on a shipping recco. Robert Sprague was killed in the crash of his Spitfire Vb during a local flight.

28 November 1942: Making a 390-mile round trip, two 335 pilots went on a Rhubarb into Holland.

29 November 1942: After assembling in Atlantic City on 17 October, 800 enlisted men debarked from *RMS Queen Elizabeth* at Grennock, Scotland, and went to Atcham, Shrewsbury, to form the ground echelon of the 4th Fighter Group. Detached units went to VIII Fighter Command at Bovingdon to learn crewing the new P-47 while others went to Great Stampford and some RAF technical schools before being sent on to Debden as the RAF crews phased out.
    Two 335 aircraft went on a Rhubarb into France.

30 November 1942: Again two 335 kites went on a Rhubarb into France.

1 December 1942: From 0855 to 1720 hours 336 sent out its Spitfires in pairs to patrol Clacton without incident. 335 moved back to Debden after detached service at Great Stampford.

4 December 1942: Rodeo 115. Wing Cdr. Duke-Woolley led a sweep and bomber support from 1405 to 1522 hours. The Group followed the coast to Sangatte and Gravelines. A few enemy aircraft were spotted at 27,000 feet without engagement, then the wing flew from Cap Gris Nez to five miles west of Calais before heading back home.

6 December 1942: Wing Cdr. Duke-Woolley was up front again as he led a withdrawal support and fighter sweep to Lille/Fives, France, from 1155 to 1325 hours. After passing over Cap Gris Nez at 1223 the Group swept south to Gravelines and back to Gris Nez where the B-17s were sighted at 20/23,000 feet shadowed by 12 enemy aircraft at 28,000. Approaching the Channel six FW 190s were spotted in straggling pairs five miles north of Calais between 15,000 and 25,000 feet. As the Group orbited over the Channel two more 190s were spotted. Gene Fetrow attacked and damaged one, then shot down what was listed as an unidentified enemy aircraft.

[Box Score: 1 destroyed, 0 lost]
    336 mounted two convoy patrols from 1520 to 1655 and 1610 to 1705 hours off Oxfordness.

8 December 1942: Two 334 kites set out on a Rhubarb to LeCrotoy, France, while eight 335 aircraft flew defensive patrol. Two power houses were set ablaze and one loco damaged. A flak tower was also attacked.

9 December 1942: From 1435 to 1615 hours two 334 Spits went on a fighter patrol over Clacton.

A large batch of AAF enlisted men arrived from the composite group at Atcham while another large group remained on detached service.

11 December 1942: From 0810 to 0920 hours two 334 aircraft went on a Rhubarb from Ghent to Bruges, Belgium. Crossing the Channel at zero feet, Beeson and Anderson made landfall three miles south of Knocke where they attacked enemy troops in physical training. The section went on to Ostend and attacked a staff car. Near Nieuport they came across 150 troops on parade and strafed, inflicting many casualties.

12 December 1942: Circus 242. Maj. Gregory Daymond led a sweep and escort to Abbeville, France, from 1020 to 1200 hours. The Group arrived at the rendezvous point 20,000 feet over Hastings but the 16 B-24s never showed so it was on to Le Crotoy and then to Abbeville. On turning back the pilots saw 12 Liberators and escorted them back to the English coast.

336 was on convoy patrol from 1340 to 1650.

15 December 1942: A Rhubarb was scheduled for two 334 aircraft along the Bruges/Ghent canal area. Five miles west of Walcheren a Ju 52 was spotted at 1,000 feet. Anderson and Boock went after it, getting several strikes. Then enemy flak hit the transport and the port wing broke off. The two pilots were forced to claim a probable, feeling lucky to get out of the intense flak.

20 December 1942: Maj. Daymond led a diversionary fighter sweep and escort to Romilly-sur-Seine, France, from 1045 to 1220 hours. Enemy reaction was heavy and the formation penetrated only eight miles. Thirty enemy aircraft were sighted well up-sun following the B-17s. The Germans attempted to draw the Spitfires away but the bait was not taken.

21 December 1942: Two 334 aircraft went on a Rhubarb along the rail line from Le Touquet to Rue, France. Penetrating to Montruil, they attacked a camp and rail equipment with good results.

Two 336 pilots were out on fighter patrol over Channel shipping from 1415 to 1540 hours.

More enlisted men from the AAF's 131st A&B Group arrived from Atcham to be classified and instructed in their duties by the RAF personnel at Debden. Most of the men learned how to preflight, inspect, arm and maintain the Spitfire Vbs under the watching eyes of the English on base.

29 December 1942: Four 334 kites were out on a shipping recco from Knocke to Dunkirk. Four FW 190s were spotted but not engaged.

Two 336 pilots flew a Rhubarb from 1225 to 1350 hours to Nieuport, Belgium, shooting up a barge and a loco.

30 December 1942: Two 334 Spits flew a Rhubarb against rail targets from Etaples to Capelie, France. After penetrating at zero feet to the Etaples main line, they attacked a train in the yards. It must have been an ammunition train—a violent explosion ripped several of the cars apart. The two fighters crossed back out south of Merilmont.

31 December 1942: Flying in pairs, four 336 pilots flew convoy patrol from 1155 to 1400 hours.

These first operations by the Group were anything but exciting to the pilots. Even though 8½ kills had been scored that was certainly not enough to offset the loss of 14 pilots (13 on ops). Some of the former Eagles had left, while others were needed by VIII FC elsewhere. Several American pilots serving in the RAF, other than with the Eagle Squadrons, came to the Group as replacements, retaining the unique status of an RAF trained unit. The 4th was also scheduled to reequip with the new P-47 Thunderbolt and become the first unit to operate them in the ETO. Ground crews, though maintaining the Spits, were being trained to maintain the 15,000 pound Republic product at the same time. Though pilots were a bit apprehensive about giving up a fighter that weighed half as much for one that was bound to be less maneuverable, sentiment favored increased combat operations regardless of what had to be done to get there. Though 1943 would certainly bring more action the 4th would not break the magic 100 kill mark until late January 1944.

Operational Diary—1943

2 January 1943: 335 and 336 were out on convoy patrol from 1310 to 1425 hours. There was a scramble but no enemy aircraft were found.

3 January 1943: 335 and 336 ran continuous convoy patrols from 0850 to 1400 hours.

4 January 1943: Twenty Spitfires from 334 and 335 ran continuous flights of two on convoy patrol throughout the day.

8 January 1943: 335 flew an uneventful convoy patrol.

9 January 1943: Four 336 kites were on convoy patrol from 0855 to 1100 hours. Two 334 Spits patrolled to Barrow Deep from 1425 to 1545 hours.

11 January 1943: More convoy patrol for 336 from 1615 to 1735 hours.

12 January 1943: Defensive patrol was flown by two 334 pilots from 1425 to 1545 hours.

13 January 1943: From 0855 to 1000 hours two 334 kites were back out on convoy patrol.
  Lt. Col. Chesley Peterson led an escort to St. Omer/Ft. Rouge airdrome, France, from 1140 to 1305 hours. At the rendezvous point near Bradwell two squadrons were unable to sight the 12 Bostons due to the haze. On the way out eight FW 190s were sighted but not engaged.
  Lt. Col. Peterson led the third mission of the day, rear cover for 72 B-17s to Lille/Fives, between 1400 and 1530 hours. Two Spitfires landed at Manston with engine trouble. Initially the 4th patrolled the area from Furnes to Calais at 23/25,000 feet. After sighting the bombers the fighters escorted the Forts back to England.

14 January 1943: Airborne at 1100 hours, three 334 Spits left for a Rhubarb of the Belgian coast, from Knocke to Ostend. After crossing in at 1140 they flew south along the coast until entering a 400 foot overcast and driving rain. After a turn inland Hank Mills got separated and came home alone. Stan Anderson and Bob Boock broke out of the ceiling at Gmisken, getting intense light and medium flak. On the way home at 1155 they saw two FW 190s pass close to starboard and close in on Anderson, who made a violent skidding right turn low over the water while yanking back the throttle. Anderson got on the German's tail and fired—one of the 190s crashed into the sea and the other escaped into the clouds. Two more

8

190s approached from 7 o'clock intent on Anderson. Boock turned into them and fired. The lead 190 climbed 150 feet and then dived into the sea. Boock was forced to climb abruptly into the overcast to avoid colliding with the second 190. Separated, he emerged four miles inland from Ostend where he saw a camouflaged saloon car followed by an open troop-laden lorry. He fired the rest of his ammunition and saw the lead car turn over in a ditch, then turned for home.

[Box Score: 2 destroyed, 0 lost]

336 launched two more Rhubarbs into France and Belgium from 1105 to 1245 and 1110 to 1255 hours. Some successful havoc was wrought in the destruction of locomotives and gun emplacements. Mitchellweiss and Mirsch crash landed after getting shot up. Gover squeaked into North Weald with five gallons of petrol.

15 January 1943: Two 336 kites were out on convoy patrol from 1210 to 1325 hours.

334 officially went off operations to become the P-47 training unit for the Group, pilots being attached to 335 and 336 to continue flying shows in their Spitfires. VIII FC recorded assignment of the first '47s to the Group although 4th records listed it as the 16th.

17 January 1943: From 0915 to 1210 hours four 336 Spitfires were out on convoy patrol.

A number of Group pilots were assigned to the P-47 training squadron at Atcham. 24 pilots in all were to transition into the Thunderbolt.

20 January 1943: 335 and 336 were scrambled to intercept 90 bandits over Dover from 1250 to 1350 hours without result.

335 launched a standing patrol and a Rhubarb while two of 334's detached Spits went on a Rhubarb to LePogue, France, shooting up locos and troops.

21 January 1943: Maj. Oscar Coen led a Ramrod to Caen airdrome, France, from 1140 to 1330 hours. The 18 Venturas were given close escort and some enemy aircraft were sighted but not engaged.

22 January 1943: Circus 253. Maj. Coen led an escort for Bostons to St. Omer airdrome, France, from 1415 to 1550 hours. As the formation crossed the enemy coast it was intercepted by Bf 109s and FW 190s, resulting in a violent dogfight over the Channel at 1515. Boock managed to get his canopy and goggles shot off but downed a 190 before heading back. Four kills were scored while a 335 pilot was downed by flak.

[Box Score: 4 destroyed, 1 lost]

23 January 1943: 336 put up four kites on sea patrol from 1420 to 1535 hours.

25 January 1943: Lt. Col. Peterson led a Ramrod to Flushing, Netherlands, from 1115 to 1200 hours. The escort was recalled.

26 January 1943: Lt. Col. Peterson led a Ramrod for 12 Venturas to Bruges airdrome, Belgium, from 1140 to 1320 hours. Boock was forced to ditch six miles from the coast but he was picked up by Navy vessels.

27 January 1943: 336 flew an air-sea rescue patrol off Oxfordness from 1510 to 1605 hours, sighting nothing.

29 January 1943: Six 335 Spitfires flew standing fighter patrol over the English coast.

Pilots were slowly getting used to flying the new P-47C, but not without some rough moments. Ken Foster crash landed 41-6186 near Chipping Warden—he was not hurt and the aircraft was salvageable. Lee Gover nosed over 41-6190 on take-off due to bad brakes.

1 February 1943: 335 and 336 flew convoy patrol in pairs off Oxfordness from 1315 to 1755 hours. Two 190s were chased twice without result.

John Mitchellweis was off in P-47C 41-6200 over the local area when the aircraft caught fire at 1410 hours, 5,000 feet over Duxford. He bailed out but the opening shock threw him out of the straps and he fell to his death.

On the lighter side, "bubble and squeak" left Debden and a sigh of relief went up from the men. The Officer's Mess changed from British to American rations—farewell to sprouts, cabbage, kipper and imitation sausage. But only the pilots could go to tea at 1630 from this point on—such was life at Debden, as it became known as the pearl of the ETO.

2 February 1943: Maj. Coen led a Ramrod for 12 Venturas to St. Omer, France, from 0915 to 1035 hours, but the mission was recalled at the French coast due to weather.

336 was out on convoy patrol from 1400 to 1740 hours.

3 February 1943: Maj. Coen led a fighter sweep and escort to St. Omer, France, from 1045 to 1130 hours before the mission was recalled.

Maj. Coen led the Group back out on an escort to St. Omer from 1430 to 1610 hours. Escorting the 12 Venturas was uneventful.

336 sent out three Spits on air-sea rescue.

Gun cameras for 334's P-47s arrived for installation. They carried 50 feet of film with a one-foot-per-second exposure rate.

4 February 1943: 335 flew two morning bomber escort shows. 336 launched an air-sea rescue search from 0905 to 1045 hours with three kites and a patrol scramble to Clacton-on-sea from 1025 to 1035 hours with six aircraft.

5 February 1943: 335, out on a shipping recco with six aircraft, jumped enemy ships off Walcheren Island. William Kelly was hit by flak and went into the sea with his Spitfire at 1200 hours.

6 February 1943: 335 was on standing patrol.

11 February 1943: 336 flew convoy patrol from 0810 to 1135 with several relief aircraft, then scrambled to Oxfordness from 1445 to 1630 hours without result.

12, 13, 14, 15, 16, 17, 18, 24, 27, 28 February 1943: Eleven convoy patrols and one scramble patrol were flown by 335 and 336 these days, some patrols lasting as long as six hours through relief. The patrols and readiness alerts were filled with long hours of boredom. One pilot was lost when he bailed out too low and drowned in the Channel after his Spit's engine quit. All in all, the lack of combat was unnerving.

[Box Score: 0 destroyed, 1 lost]

15 February 1943: The mutton and hot milk disappeared from the enlisted men's mess as they went on American rations as well, with great joy.

18 February 1943: At 1909 hours a lost Mosquito with no radio and one engine feathered attempted to land at Debden. As it was about to touch down, the pilot gunned his left engine and swerved off the runway, crashing the Mossie into 334's dispersal hut after going through two P-47s. The two crew members were OK but not until the next day were the four 500 pound bombs found that were aboard the totally disintegrated Mossie. 41-6002 was repairable but 41-6247 went to the salvage heap.

19 February 1943: Maj. Blakeslee led a Ramrod and fighter sweep to St. Omer, France, from 1540 to 1715 hours. 30 bandits were reported but bad fog over the continent prevented contact.

20 February 1943: Even though the Thunderbolt had not entered combat it had been mistaken for an FW 190 (!!). The 4th was ordered to paint a white cowl band on the front of the nose and white stripes on the tail surfaces in addition to placing national insignia on both bottom wings and encircling the fuselage roundel in yellow.

24 February 1943: The RAF brought a captured He 111 and Bf 110 to Debden as a part of their Flying Circus. The P-47s and Spits went up to fly against them. Rides were given in the 110 and the 111 between Debden and one of its satellite fields five miles northeast, Castle Camps.

26 February 1943: Several Roadsteads were flown against armed raiders in Dunkirk harbor by 60 Venturas. Three times 335 and 336 escorted the same 12 Venturas to the target and back. Maj. Coen led the first escort-sweep from 0940 to 1105 and the second sweep and top cover from 1400 to 1530 hours. Maj. Chick led the third escort from 1625 to 1750 hours.

27 February 1943: Lt. Col. Peterson led another Roadstead escorting 24 Venturas back to the same target in Dunkirk harbor from 1345 to 1510 hours.

Lee Gover's 41-6256 threw its engine oil and caught fire. Putting the P-47 into a dive, he put out the fire, landing at Debden dead-stick after considering bailing out three times. During the period the aircraft was not trusted for dead-stick landings and Gover's feat received some attention from VIII Fighter Command.

During the 26th and 27th numerous aircraft visited Debden—the Flying Circus was still on the field with the 110 and 111. Wellingtons, Hudsons, Blenheims, a Lancaster, Mustangs, a Stirling, a Typhoon, a Walrus, Cubs and a Fortress all stopped in.

28 February 1943: On 334's 45th day of non-operational flying P-47C transition was nearing completion. 11 pilots from the three squadrons had almost 30 hours in the new type. The rest of 334 had been flying their Spits with 334 and 336. Now the Spits were to be released and the squadron declared combat ready. Soon the pilots would melt back into their respective units to pass on their knowledge.

Opinion on the '47 varied quite a bit, reflected by 334 calling itself "The Suicide Squadron" during the period. Yet nothing but praise was laid at the feet of the ground crews. T/Sgts. Joe Tabb and Joe Bridges held A and B Flights in 334, responsible for the overall smooth maintenance on the new Thunderbolts.

1–16, 18–31 March & 1 April 1943: On 31 out of 32 straight days the Group endured 29 convoy patrols, 23 scrambles, 1 patrol, 1 shipping recco, one air-sea rescue patrol, one anti-submarine escort—all flown by 335 and 336 with inconclusive enemy contact twice. The pilots were at wit's end with the dull work but the 1 April convoy patrol saw the last of these types of missions.

3 March 1943: The Group P-47s toured area bases to aid in recognition of the new type.

At 2100 hours Debden experienced its first complete blackout. An enemy aircraft dropped a few bombs near the field.

4 March 1943: Aubrey Stanhope undershot the east-west runway in P-47C 41-6238 and skidded to the end of the runway on his belly, badly damaging the aircraft.

5 March 1943: An RAF Polish squadron was on the field for maneuvers, using 336's dispersal while it was on detached service to Martlesham Heath.

8 March 1943: Maj. Blakeslee led a Ramrod and fighter sweep to St. Valery, France, from 1327 to 1450 hours from West Malling. Lt. Col. Peterson, who was to have led the Group, developed engine trouble over the Channel, giving the lead to Blakeslee. The Major must have been gaining in reputation steadily since the boys claimed in fun that Blakeslee gave the old man a bad kite in order to lead. The formation swept the French coast to St. Valery at 25,000 feet and met 12 Liberators four miles inland. Seven FW 190s were making head-on attacks on the bombers—Blakeslee led the Group between the two to block the attack and shepherded his charges home safely. 335 landed at Debden and 336 at Martlesham Heath.

Robert Patterson overshot on landing in 41-6258, went through several hedges and a fence to the road, demolishing the aircraft. John Lutz had engine trouble in 41-6196 and force landed at Great Ashfield successfully.

9 March 1943: Rodeo 177. Maj. Blakeslee led a fighter sweep to St. Omer, France, from 1445 to 1615 hours (335 up from Debden, 336 from Martlesham). The controller ordered Blakeslee to increase altitude as Huns were plotted in the Nieuport area. This caused the two squadrons to fail in rendezvousing. The Group swept on to St. Omer in two formations. Several enemy aircraft were sighted but not engaged.

10 March 1943: Rodeo 179. Lt. Col. Peterson led 14 334 aircraft on the first P-47 show in the European Theater, a fighter sweep from Blankenberge to Ostend, Belgium, from 1515 to 1630 hours. 4th CO, Col. Edward Anderson, participated in A Flight. The Thunderbolts swept the Channel to Walcheren Island at 27,000 feet, swung right and came down the French coast before turning for Debden. The engine electrical systems caused the radios to go berserk.

Drinks that night were on Pratt and Whitney and Republic.

Rodeo 181. Maj. Blakeslee led 335 and 336 in their Spits on a fighter sweep to St. Omer, France, from 1515 to 1650 hours (again 335 from Debden and 336 from Martlesham). The squadrons failed to rendezvous due to weather and 336 was recalled. 335 swept on to Clacton at 500 feet and entered the French coast at Dunkirk at 14,000. Sweeping St. Omer the Group sighted 12 enemy aircraft without engaging them.

11 March 1943: Two 336 Spits were scrambled from Martlesham to intercept two Bf 109s east of Harwich. The Huns were sighted streaking away on the deck but balloons prevented a chase.

12 March 1943: Ramrod 42. Lt. Col. Peterson led a fighter sweep to St. Valery, France, from 1215 to 1345 hours from West Malling. The 28 Spitfires crossed the French coast south of St. Valery at 23,000 feet and met the bombers five miles inland, escorting them back. Three 190s and two 109s were spotted with no engagements.

Rodeo 183. Lt. Col. Peterson led a fighter sweep to St. Omer, France, from 1545 to 1700 hours. 335 from Debden and 336 from Martlesham rendezvoused at zero feet over Bradwell Bay, crossing into France at 16,000 with the two Spitfire squadrons 15 miles apart. 336 was jumped by two FW 190s in the Audruieq area. A break was ordered but Don Gentile left the formation and turned into the Huns, firing away, and got one smoking before turning back. Hazen Anderson was hit 12 miles northwest of St. Omer and went down to become a POW.

[Box Score: 0 destroyed, 1 lost]

13 March 1943: Ramrod 43. Maj. Blakeslee led rear cover for B-17s to Cayeux, France, from 1430 to 1610 hours from West Malling. The bombers were never sighted so the Spitfires patrolled the coast to Dieppe and back to Cayeux at 24,000 feet before turning home.

14 March 1943: Eight 336 Spits scrambled from Martlesham at 1415 hours. Two FW 190s were spotted on the deck but the Spitfires were unable to close. The same thing happened during 336's convoy patrol on 30 March—the Spitfire Vbs were unable to close on two 190s being chased.

16 March 1943: The 4th's Spitfires were officially taken off operations and stored at 336 dispersal, although most of them continued to fly as 336 aircraft until 1 April.

17 March 1943: Pilots attached to 334 for P-47 training returned to their squadrons, taking their Thunderbolts with them. Each would have two pilots in his squadron assigned to him for P-47 instruction.

21 March 1943: At 1545 hours seven P-47s flew to Burtonwood for repairs due to crankshafts not getting enough oil.

22 March 1943: Several 334 and 335 pilots got their first P-47 hops. 335 officially received 18 Thunderbolts this day to begin full transition, though that full number would take a few days to arrive.

27 March 1943: At 1600 hours 12 P-47s and a B-17 flew in from Burtonwood. One of the Thunderbolts was Stanhope's 4 March crash repaired. The Fort took the ferry pilots back at 1700.

31 March 1943: By this day all 334 pilots were engaged in P-47 transition.

1 April 1943: 336 flew their last convoy patrol and transferred back to Debden from Martlesham Heath to begin P-47 transition with six instructors and aircraft from 334.

3 April 1943: As more Thunderbolts arrived on the field new code letters were put on the kites to replace the two-digit serial number codes—QP for 334, WD for 335 and VF for 336.

Frank Smolinsky, returning from a forward base, was killed in 41-6181 as he crashed in flames trying to land. Oscar Coen had a supercharger fire at 25,000 feet during a B-17 affiliation; he bailed out and fractured his shoulder in the chute shroud lines.

6 April 1943: Robert Boock made a dead-stick landing at 1035 hours near Norwich in QP-P from 37,000 feet after getting smoke in the cockpit.

7 April 1943: Marshal of the RAF the Viscount Trenchard visited Debden along with 8th Air Force commander Gen. Ira C. Eaker and VIII FC's Gen. Hunter and some Russian brass.

8 April 1943: Circus 280. Lt. Col. Peterson led a fighter sweep/free lance to St. Omer, France, from 1745 to 1915 hours as all three squadrons put up Thunderbolts. Four P-47s each from the 56th and 78th Fighter Groups also went along to gain some experience, though this was only the 4th's second Thunderbolt combat mission . . . it had taken almost a month to get the radio problems figured out. The formation swept inland 10 to 15 miles from Dunkirk before turning for home.

"Readiness in Spitfires" was still in effect from dawn to dusk at the watch tower for drome defense.

10 April 1943: Two 335 pilots flew the Group's last Spitfire mission, a (what else?) convoy patrol from 1010 to 1140 hours. Before all the Spits left the base one Vb was kept as a hack, the last vestige of a bygone era.

Orders came through not to shoot at enemy aircraft over England. One of the boys saw a Ju 88 but could not fire at it.

11 April 1943: Rodeo 200. Maj. Blakeslee led a fighter sweep to Ostend–Dunkirk–Calais from 1405 to 1515 hours made up of six P-47s from 334 and 335.

The pilots were increasingly unhappy with the P-47 and its teething problems. There was even some relief expressed that there had been no encounters with the Germans in the "seven ton milk bottles."

13 April 1943: Ramrod 50. Lt. Col. Peterson led a joint 4th/78th Fighter Group fighter sweep/free lance to St. Omer, France, from 1145 to 1330 hours. 335 jumped two 190s without result.

Rodeo 202. Lt. Col. Peterson led a fighter sweep/free lance to Berck/Mardyck from 1805 to 1930 hours, rendezvousing with 56th and 78th Group aircraft over Debden. Crossing the enemy coast over Berck at 29,000 feet, the formation found no enemy aircraft. The 78th's Joseph Dickman went down in the Channel after his P-47 suffered engine failure. The RAF picked him up.

15 April 1943: Rodeo 204. Lt. Col. Peterson led a fighter sweep from Furnes, Belgium, to Cassel, France, from 1650 to 1825 hours. Both 56th and 78th Group aircraft participated. After sweeping to Cassel, the formation turned left and reversed course north. At 1701 Blakeslee, with 335 and two dislocated squadrons from the 56th over Knocke at 29,000 feet, spotted three FW 190s at 23,000 feet. He bounced the Huns and stayed with one down to 500 feet, getting numerous hits. The German tried to bail out near Ostend but went in with his machine. The rest of the 4th, five miles off the coast near Ostend, encountered five 190s at 1750. Peterson led the attack—two Focke Wulfs were destroyed and one damaged but two of the Group's pilots went down during the combat. On the way out Peterson developed engine trouble and bailed out into the Channel 30 miles from England to be picked up by a Walrus 45 minutes later.

[Box Score: 3 destroyed, 2 lost]

16 April 1943: Generals and Colonels were all over the base to hear about the first Thunderbolt combat. They were hosted by Col. "Pete" who had two fine black eyes from his dip in the drink. Blakeslee, upon being congratulated at catching his quarry in a dive, flatly said the P-47 ought to dive—it certainly couldn't climb.

17 April 1943: Rodeo 205. Maj. Blakeslee led a fighter sweep from Walcheren to Blankenberge, Netherlands, from 1225 to 1400 hours. The show was uneventful.

Circus 285. Maj. Blakeslee led a diversion sweep from Walcheren to Bruges from 1845 to 2020 hours. While cruising at 26,000 feet the Group sighted enemy aircraft but there were no engagements.

18 April 1943: Rodeo 207. Maj. Blakeslee led a fighter sweep/free lance from 1015 to 1145 hours. The P-47s cruised Nieuport, Dunkirk, Hayebrook, and Sangatte. Two enemy aircraft were sighted, one diving on the formation, but a P-47 turned to meet the attacker which broke off. Nine more enemy aircraft were sighted without engagement.

21 April 1943: Rodeo 208. Maj. Blakeslee led a fighter sweep from 1050 to 1230 hours. The formation flew over Westhoofd, Maaslius and Okenburge at 28,000 feet.

27 April 1943: During a mock dogfight over Castle Camps at 1020 hours, Archie Chatterly sliced off the tail of James Wilkinson's P-47. Chatterly dead-sticked in near New Market. Wilkinson managed to bail out with injuries to his back that kept him in the hospital for months.

29 April 1943: Rodeo 211, F.O. (Field Order) 6. Maj. Blakeslee led a fighter sweep from 1235 to 1415 hours. 40 P-47s were up to sweep Le Crotoy, St. Omer and Ostend. The Group was at full operational readiness now that all of 336's pilots were through transition.

3 May 1943: F.O. 8. Maj. Blakeslee led a Rodeo to sweep Walcheren Island, Knocke, Ostend, Nieuport from 1700 to 1845 hours. Poor weather caused 10 of 11 Venturas to abort and the P-47s came home early.

At 1200 hours the Union Jack was lowered and the Stars and Stripes run up as Debden was officially handed over to the AAF by Gp. Capt. L. G. Nixon. Steve Pisanos became a U.S. citizen. The next day a sign over the bar read, "Free Beer on Steve Pisanos—American."

4 May 1943: Ramrod 68, F.O. 10. Maj. Blakeslee led withdrawal support for B-17s attacking Antwerp from 1750 to 1940 hours. The 4th rendezvoused with the bombers over Flushing at 28,000 feet. The Huns decided to oppose the effort and several combats took place with some damage inflicted on the 190s. John Lutz's engine began to smoke and lose power. Forced to bail out near Flushing, he went into the water and was lost.

[Box Score: 0 destroyed, 1 lost]

7 May 1943: F.O. 12. Lt. Col. Peterson led a Rodeo to Walcheren Island from 1450 to 1630 hours. Cruising at 28,000 feet, the Group sighted many enemy aircraft but did not engage.

13 May 1943: Ramrod 71, F.O. 17. Lt. Col. Peterson led a diversion in support of Forts attacking St. Omer, France, from 1535 to 1720 hours. After rendezvousing with the 56th Fighter Group the formation passed the bombers to sweep inland. Controllers ordered an orbit in the Gravelines/Audruieq area to intercept enemy aircraft but no one showed up for the party.

14 May 1943: Ramrod 73, F.O. 18. Lt. Col. Peterson led support for B-17s going to Antwerp from 1220 to 1430 hours. The Group staged from Bradwell Bay. 50 miles inland numerous enemy aircraft were encountered near Hulst—the FW 190s had yellow noses. 334 remained high cover while 335 and 336 bounced. The combat raged from 1307 to 1325 all the way back out to the coast with the Group claiming two destroyed by Blakeslee and Gover.

[Box Score: 2 destroyed, 0 lost]

15 May 1943: Rodeo 204, F.O. 19. Lt. Col. Peterson led a sweep from Amsterdam to Ostend from 0850 to 1110 hours at 26,000 feet after refueling at Coltishall. Peterson downed a 190.

[Box Score: 1 destroyed, 0 lost]

16 May 1943: F.O. 20. Maj. Blakeslee led a Rodeo into the Walcheren–Bruges–Blankenberge area from 1242 to 1420 hours. Four yellow-nosed 190s were orbiting Noord Beveland, attracting a section from 336. When the P-47s got within 800 yards the Huns went for the deck, so the section rejoined the formation. East of Knocke 15 red-nosed 190s were spotted flying in fours. Several combats resulted in claims but no enemy aircraft were counted as destroyed.

F.O. 21. Maj. Blakeslee led the second mission of the day, a diversionary Rodeo, from 1710 to 1850. Cruising Cayeux–Abbeville–St. Omer–Gravelines, the Group encountered no enemy aircraft.

17 May 1943: F.O. 22. Maj. Blakeslee was at the front of the Group again on a Rodeo to Morlaix-Brest, France, from 1635 to 1810 hours. Staging in and out of Predannack, they were back to Debden by 2050. The boys swore they saw a P-38 on the sweep but have no idea where it came from.

18 May 1943: F.O. 23. Maj. Blakeslee led another Rodeo to Walcheren–Bruges–Nieuport from 1605 to 1745 hours at high altitude. At 1655 three P-47s bounced four FW 190s 5,000 feet below but the Germans got away. At 1702 12 Bf 109s came in astern and the Group turned into them. Two 109s were downed between Blankenberge and Knocke, one the first kill for Duane Beeson, but Robert Boock was shot down during the combat.

[Box Score: 2 destroyed, 1 lost]

19 May 1943: F.O. 24. Maj. Blakeslee led a Ramrod/Circus to Ijmuiden–The Hague, Netherlands, from 1100 to 1240 hours as a diversion for the bombers, which rendezvoused on time. Enemy aircraft were sighted but not engaged.

Don Blakeslee was appointed Group Executive and Operations Officer. Chesley Peterson was assigned to VIII Fighter Command as Assistant A-3, Operations and Training, and taken off ops with 200 sorties.

20 May 1943: F.O. 25. Maj. Blakeslee led a Rodeo to Haamstede and Hamamedorf, Netherlands, from 1115 to 1305 hours. Again enemy aircraft were sighted without engagement.

21 May 1943: F.O. 26. Maj. Blakeslee led a Rodeo to Ostend–Ghent, Belgium, from 1309 to 1445 hours—this route and sweep track formed what was becoming known as "the old bus run." Several groups of enemy aircraft were spotted going west just inland near Bruges. 335 stayed up top as high cover while 334 bounced with 336 blocking the enemy from dashing back to France. The effective quarterbacking got the Group into a tremendous dogfight over the North Sea and Ostend at 1350. Brewster Morgan got a 109 but was promptly shot down in a new P-47D to become a POW. Two more 334 pilots were bested by the 109s and killed.

[Box Score: 1 destroyed, 3 lost]

Under Secretary of War for Air R. A. Lovett visited the base with General Hunter.

25 May 1943: F.O. 28. Maj. Blakeslee took the Group on a Rodeo in France and Belgium from 1049 to 1220 hours. At high altitude they swept Mardyck–Ypres–Swevezeele–Knocke, sighting 20 plus enemy aircraft without entering combat.

26 May 1943: F.O. 29. Capt. Gilbert Halsey led the Rodeo to Belgium and France from 1420 to 1550 hours. At high altitude the Group swept Knocke–Kortrijk–Dunkirk. A section from 335 bounced six to 12 109s southeast of Bruges without making any claims.

27 May 1943: F.O. 30. Maj. Blakeslee led another Rodeo to Belgium from 1625 to 1810 hours. The Group swept Knocke–Roulers–Sangatte, spotting a single enemy aircraft which evaded combat.

28 May 1943: F.O. 32. Maj. Blakeslee took the Group on a Circus to Walcheren–Eekloo–Maldegem, Netherlands-Belgium, from 1710 to 1855 hours. The formation swept the area after an attack by Venturas without incident.

29 May 1943: F.O. 33. Maj. Blakeslee led a Ramrod/Circus to Rennes–Dinant, France, from 1450 to 1656 hours as support for B-17s attacking Rennes. Staging from Predannack, the Group rendezvoused on time with the bombers. Near Dinan six yellow-nosed 190s approached the formation at the same altitude. 335, in the lead, attacked the Huns head-on, then turned and attacked them again without results. The boys were back down at Debden by 1930 after a long round-trip with some badly shot-up P-47s.

31 May 1943: F.O. 34. Maj. John DuFour led the P-47s on a Rodeo into France and Belgium from 1105 to 1240 hours. The formation swept St. Omer–Ypres–Nieuport when poor weather forced them back to St. Omer and home.

2 June 1943: Lt. L. F. Foster led a two-ship weather recco to Dunkirk–Ostend from 0900 to 1100 hours.

6 June 1943: Lt. Foster made a solo weather recco to the Dunkirk area from 1040 to 1140 hours.

The pilots wanted more high explosive ammunition after seeing what it could do to an enemy aircraft, thinking it would give them more destroyed and less damaged claims.

7 June 1943: F.O. 38. Maj. Blakeslee led a Rodeo to Belgium from 1140 to 1320 hours. As the formation hit the enemy coast at Blankenberge the mission was recalled by the controller due to weather.

11 June 1943: F.O. 37. Maj. Blakeslee took the Group out on a Ramrod to Nieuport–Thielt–Eekloo from 1205 to 1345 hours. Sweeping in at 32,000 feet over the Dutch coast, the pilots spotted 10 Focke-Wulfs in the distance which could not be engaged.

F.O. 41. Maj. Blakeslee had the group up for the second show of the day on a Rodeo to France and Belgium from 1610 to 1755 hours. At 28,000 feet, the Group swept Gravelines–Hazebrouck–Courtrai–Ostend, sighting some enemy aircraft in the distance.

Nov., 1940–May, 1941: No. 71 Eagle Squadron pilots run to their Hurricane I's during a readiness scramble at Kirton-on-Lindsey, Lincolnshire. XR is the squadron code of No. 71. (*Keystone Press, London*)

March 17, 1941: 71 Squadron ground crews watch an element of two Hurricanes rip across the Kirton Drome before they start up XR-K with the APU trolley. (*U.P. Photo, London*)

Early Spring, 1942: Pilots of the second Eagle Squadron, No. 121, walk out to their cannon-armed Spitfire VB's at North Weald, Essex. (*Fox Photos, London*)

Spring, 1942: Three Spitfires of 121 E.S. come in with flaps down on their formation landing approach at Southend (Rochford) airdrome. (*Don Young*)

May, 1942: P/O Joseph M. Kelly on the wing of his 71 E.S. Spitfire LITTLE JOE at Debden airdrome, Essex. (*National Archives*)

September, 1942: The third Eagle Squadron, No. 133, has moved into Debden's satellite field at Great Sampford, Essex, where this view of their squadron leader, Carroll McColpin, left, and the indomitable "Dixie" Alexander, right, was taken in their "Mae West" life jackets. (*Carroll McColpin*)

Fall, 1942: The 4TH's "hacks" and communications a/c were ex-RAF types such as this 334th Tiger Moth in the foreground and the Miles Master III by the hangar. (*Nick Megura*)

Fall, 1942: RAF visitors drop in to see the newly installed "Yanks" and park their Spitfire (left) and Hurricane (right) beside the tower. J-P is an individually assigned a/c, probably a wing commander's. (*Nick Megura*)

September, 1942: The changeover to USAAF is shown by this Spit XR-A BM510 (Maj. Daymond's a/c) of 334FS with U.S. star and Lt. Robert Priser in RAF battle dress. It is easier to paint a plane than make a man change his ways. (*Nicholas Megura*)

September 29, 1942: Despite the transfer to the USAAF, Wg/Cmdr. R. M. B. Duke-Wooley, left, will act as the combat leader, and LtCol. Chesley G. Peterson, right, will be his AAF counterpart as Group Executive Operations Officer. (*Illustrated or API, London*)

Fall, 1942: Another RAF a/c retained by the new 4FG was the Wing's Miles Master III W8938, for liaison and communications travel. (*Leroy Nitschke*)

Fall, 1942: Spitfire VB EN853 AV-D was the personal mount of 335FS's new commander, Maj. James Daley. (*Don Young*)

Fall, 1942: AV-F sits on its hardstand of new U.S. pierced-steel plank at 335FS's west perimeter dispersal, all ready for a show with the APU plugged in. (*Leroy Nitschke*)

Fall, 1942: 335's AV-E lands across the south threshold from a test hop. (*Nick Megura*)

Fall, 1942: Ex-Eagles pose by a Spit for the press. *L-R*: R. McMinn, W. O'Regan, S. Anderson, C. Peterson, O. Coen, V. Boehle, and J. Clark. (*Illustrated News*)

Fall, 1942: LtCol. C. Peterson adjusts his sutton-harness in XR-Z while his fellow pilots offer helpful suggestions. The RAF vets were quick to appreciate the immortal rapid-transit "Jeep" of the USA. (*Keystone News Photo*)

Fall, 1942: Lt. Don S. Gentile and his Spit MD-T BUCKEYE-DON. Two swastikas mark two FW190's downed by this experienced RCAF vet at the Dieppe Landing air battles. (*James Du-Four*)

Fall, 1942: Typical of the younger Eagle vets who lacked experience, but who were eager to get into combat with the AAF, is Lt. Duane W. Beeson, here examining the lethal cannon punch of the Spit STINKY. (*Edward Hedrick*)

Fall, 1942: Capt. Donald Willis lent international experience to the 4TH. This 335FS Operations Officer was a graduate of the Finnish Military Academy and he wore Finnish, Norwegian, RAF, and AAF wings. He was shot down in a P-38 in 1944 and into POW status. (*Warren Jackman*)

Fall, 1942: Capt. William "Bill" Kelly, 335FS, was one of the first 4TH pilots to make the supreme sacrifice. A former bus driver, he was KIA on 2/5/43 when his Spit dove into the sea from 1,200 feet after a flak hit. (*Warren Jackman*)

Fall, 1942: Another 335FS flyer who met a cruel end to his war was Lt. Frank Smolinsky. His P-47 crashed and burned on takeoff from a forward base on 4/3/43. (*Warren Jackman*)

January 19, 1943: Lt. Steve Pisanos, left, talks with Lt. Don Gentile, who has just landed from one of the tedious patrols flown over the shipping convoys this Winter. Spit MD-M sits in one of 336's brick revetments. (*Pinckney Lackey*)

January, 1943: "Bill" Chick of 336th in a visiting CG coded Spitfire out front of the squadron HQ. (*Lewis Chick*)

January, 1943: The 4TH is picked to introduce the new P-47 Thunderbolt into combat in the ETO. Some 4TH pilots are sent to Atcham, Shropshire, to train on Jugs like 41-6196, which is warming up here for an air test at one of the depot bases. (AFM)

January, 1943: A seven-ton, eight "Point Fifty" gunned Thunderbolt retracts its wide-spaced undercarriage on takeoff, with the giant Pratt-Whitney R-2800-21 engine behind the 12-foot prop lifting it solidly, but not spritely like a Spitfire, from the runway. (*National Archives*)

February, 1943: The pilots of 334FS's Jug training unit are spending every moment accumulating experience with the a/c, just as these four P-47 pilots are. 6352 and 6267 sport the new white bands on nose and tailplanes given to the Jug by the 8AF to avoid confusion with German FW-190. (*National Archives*)

February, 1943: 334FS training P-47s carry the last two digits of the serial number instead of normal squadron code letters, as shown by Lt. Don Young's 6185 aloft on a practice hop. (*Don Young*)

March, 1943: Don Young watches operations beside John DuFour's MD-E DOREEN I, which is standing readiness alert by the tower. (*Don Young*)

February, 1943: Spit AV-V sits ready for a show, while across the taxi track, one of 336FS's clipped-wing VBs waits with it. The two squadrons carried on regular combat operations while the pilots trained on P-47s between shows. (*Don Young*)

March, 1943: 336FS armorers work on the cannon of MD-C parked in front of the squadron perimeter HQ shack. The beautifully contoured a/c will soon leave the 4TH as the P-47 replaces it. 336 was the last squadron of the group to change over. (*Lewis Chick*)

March, 1943: Lt. Richard McMinn's crewchief checks the gun bay panels of their "04," 41-6204 at their hardstand on the North curve of 334's flightline. The paint-tone difference bespeaks an accident that has occurred to the tailplane previously. (*Edward Hedrick*)

March 5, 1943: The Northolt Wing leader's a/c SZ-S of 316 Squadron RAF carries the Polish insignia, Warsaw Squadron badge, and the Wing Commander's pennant by the cockpit. This squadron used 336's dispersal while they were on DS to Marltesham Heath. (*Edward Richie*)

Spring, 1943: Lt. Bud Castle's QP-E 42-7881 had these "Gremlins" painted on it. They must have done their work, as he was killed trying to do a stall-turn off the end of the runway in this a/c. (*Edward Hedrick*)

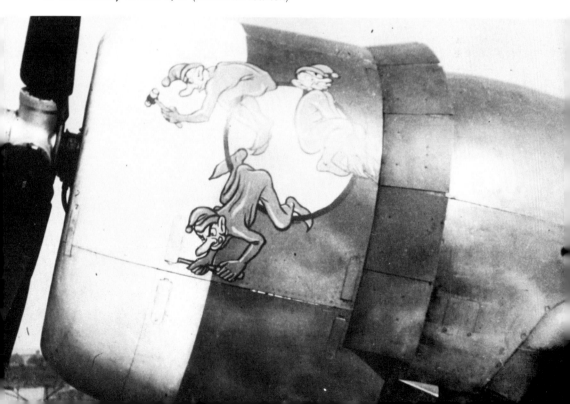

Spring, 1943: C-Model P-47s had four fewer cowl flaps than the later D-Model, as shown here by Lt. Archie Chatterley's QP-G 41-6358. Art by Don Allen. (*Edward Hedrick*)

June, 1943: There is no doubt that Lt. Gerald Montgomery, here on the wing of his QP-H 42-7980 TEXAS, is a native of Dallas. Art by Don Allen. (*Nicholas Megura*)

April-May, 1943: 334FS linecrews take a break as they await a show return beside Chesley Peterson's newly QP-coded "V" for victory 41-6413. (*E. Hedrick*)

Spring, 1943: Pre-mission tasks. Sgt. Paul Louis, 334FS, installs a .50 cal. machine gun fitted with a long blast tube into a squadron Jug after cleaning and inspecting the a/c armament. (*Leroy Nitschke*)

Spring, 1943: The mission "Start Engine" time approaches. Crewchief Don Allen helps his pilot, Lt. Victor France, strap into their MISS DALLAS QP-K 42-7876. Don braces his foot on a fold-out handgrip to stick to the giant fighter. (*Donald Allen*)

Spring, 1943: Taxiing to the active runway for the mission. WD-H 41-6206 rolls by the 335FS Line HQ to takeoff. (*Warren Jackman*)

May, 1943: Twenty-two Jugs bunch up at the west runway for another sweep into France. White ETO bands stand out at a distance, which helped bomber gunners to distinguish friend from foe. (*J. Cowman*)

Spring, 1943: Two sections of four streak across DB to set course over the tower for France. Course out was in close formation to penetrate weather and stay together easily. (*Mrs. W. Nickerson*)

No date: 334th linecrewmen W. Durham and R. Kellett wait for the show to return in their perimeter defense post by the runway intersection. Armament is a water-cooled point fifty calibre. (*N. Lippman*)

Spring, 1943: Post-mission critique. Together and safe on the ground again, 334th pilots discuss the combat. L-R: S. Pisanos, A. Rafalovich, R. Priser, V. France, D. Beeson, H. Mills, O. Coen (Squadron CO), J. Clark. (*Edward Hedrick*)

May-June, 1943: Duane Beeson, 334's later ace, is in the back of the squadron Tiger Moth DE-262, giving hops to the groundcrews between shows. (*E. Hedrick*)

July 10, 1943: The 4TH P-47s regularly visited different bomber bases on affiliation duties to fly with them and acquaint them with the P-47. Here two P-47s visit Ridgewell, home of the 381st Bomb Grp. (*USAF*)

July–August, 1943: Another first for the group. Lt. Kenneth Peterson's VF-F 41-6539 ARIZONA PETE with the new 200-gal. bellytank, which has revolutionized fighter escort tactics. The 4TH flew the first ETO show with the tank on 7/28/43. (*AFM*)

July, 1943: Capt. Deacon Hively in western garb beside his QP-J THE DEACON, which is decked out with a "Baby," the new belly tank coming into use for longer escort range. (*Leo Schmidt*)

July–August, 1943: 334th P-47s wait by the East runway head to takeoff on a bellytank flight, probably to a forward base where they will stay overnight and do a show from in the morning. (*Leroy Nitschke*)

July, 1943: 4TH ace Duane Beeson gets airborne in his QP-B 42-7890 BOISE BEE on an early belly tank show, from the east runway. Often tanks fell off or broke connecting lines on takeoff. (*E. Hedrick*)

August 9, 1943: A 353FG P-47 fitted with a 4TH 200-gal. tank. On this date the 353rd squadron almost flew with 334FS on their first mission, but it was scrubbed after three days of getting the 351st FS a/c ready for it. (*William Rushing*)

July 28, 1943: The first show to Germany is made possible by the tanks, and here Duane Beeson proves his skill at blasting Huns—by getting in close, as he does to this Bf 109. (*J. Romack*)

July 28, 1943: In this frame Lt. Duane Beeson has bored in even closer to finish off a vaunted Bf 109 on the epic show to Emmerich, Germany. (*J. Romack*)

July 28, 1943: Another of the very surprised 109s plunges to earth trailing its lifeblood of glycol, fuel, and oil. Jerry wasn't ready for Allied fighters this far into his Fatherland, a signal of his doomed future. (*J. Romack*)

Late August, 1943: Another mission tomorrow. Lt. Don Young and his chief check out their WD-S 41-6185. The kite carries a new 75-gal. metal belly tank now in use, which is superior to the 200-gal. "bathtub." (*Don Young*)

August, 1943: Mission time has arrived. Groundcrew stand ready to plug the APU into its receptacle to start up, while the pilot receives a last word from the operations officer of 336FS. (*AFM*)

August, 1943: This fine cockpit study shows Lt. Pierce McKennon all set to go in Leighton Read's P-47. His helmet top is painted white to alleviate the effect of the hot sun during the 2-3 hour shows at this time. (*Warren Jackman*)

August, 1943: Lt. Clemens Fiedler, a recent replacement, returns happy but weary, probably from pulling "G's" while sitting on the rock-hard Dingy-pack (left pack) attached to his seat pack parachute (right pack). (*Warren Jackman*)

August 16, 1943: Jim Clark's QP-W displays the result of its part in the big airfight over Paris. The kite has a 3-foot hole blown thru the left aileron and wing. (*N. Megura*)

August 12, 1943: An unusual visitor. Maj. Lewis Chick of 8FC Operations Staff taxies in the first P-51 Mustang to land at DB, after he first buzzed the field. Regretfully, Gen. "Monk" F.O.D. Hunter was a spectator of the buzz and tore a strip out of "Bill" Chick's hide. (*Edward Richie*)

August 20, 1943: Col. Chesley Peterson (right) presents Col. Edward Anderson with a memory album of his 4TH command as Anderson turns the group over to Col. Peterson (*N. Lippman*)

September 7, 1943: Lt. Phillip "Pappy" Dunn's VF-Y 42-7933 MISS SKIPPY with his nickname faintly painted below the cockpit canopy. The a/c has an RAF Spitfire mirror mounted and bears the new red border with white rectangles of the U.S. insignia. These mirrors were much sought after. (*Edwin Rowe*)

September 8, 1943: Two 335FS. "Ace" a/c WD-E 42-74686 in the foreground, bearing the Eagle Squadron emblem of Maj. Roy Evans (335 CO), and WD-C 42-7863, flown by LtCol. Donald Blakeslee, Grp. Ops. Officer. (*C. Manning*)

August, 1943: The 4TH's masterful combat leader on many missions for over two years was the redoubtable "Don Blakeslee," now in the role of Group ops officer. (*4TFW*)

Fall, 1943: Lt. Robert Priser's QP-L 41-6187 with the new 108-gal. paper belly-tank now in 4TH use. Famous 4TH ace, Ralph Hofer, scored his first victory on his first mission with this a/c. (*Edward Nelson*)

September, 1943: The Dogpatch cartoon characters were painted on some 334FS a/c. UNCLE DEN QP-E 41-6187 is Priser's old QP-L flown by Lt. Herbert Blanchfield, shown here ready for a show. (*Nathan Lippman*)

Sept. 26, 1943: S/Sgt. L. Engber poses with his kite, VF-F 41-6539 ARIZONA PETE, which was flown by Capt. Kenneth D. "Blacksnake" Peterson, winner of a DSC for saving bombers' lives. (*L. Engber*)

Fall, 1943: The moment everyone on the ground has worked for arrives; the morning show taxies out for a short range effort with no belly tanks. VF-W 42-7959 was assigned to up-coming ace, James Goodson. (*Edward Hedrick*)

Fall, 1943: A 4TH markings oddity. QP-C carries the whole squadron code forward on the fuselage of the U.S. star, contrary to usual practice. Evidently the urgent need for replacement a/c prevented the Air Depot and the hangar crew of 334 from changing the Republic star position. (*Leroy Nitschke*)

September 6, 1943: Homeward bound over France, Maj. Lee Gover slides in close to a B-17 he is escorting home in his VF-G 42-74688. Note the large star under the left wing for easy bomber I.D. (*Lee Gover/William O'Donnell*)

Fall, 1943: Lt. Jack L. Raphael, 336FS, on the wing of his VF-M 41-6529 EAGER BEAVER-MISS BETH. Note the large blast tubes of the point fifties extending from the wing. (*J. Raphael*)

Fall, 1943: Men of one of the 45th Air Service Squadron's aero repair section mobile units are seen here recovering a crashlanded 4TH P-47. Unloading the ammo was the first step after any crash. (*Francis Bodner*)

Fall, 1943: A 335FS pilot mounts WD-F 41-6214 at Ridgewell AF, Essex. Since he's wearing his Class A cap, it's been a social visit to the 381st BG rather than a mission abort. (*USAF*)

F/O Ralph K. Hofer with his P-47, QP-L 41-6484. The aircraft was destroyed on December 2, 1943, killing F/O John McNabb, 334, near Kenton on a cross-country test. (*Larry Hendel*)

September 25, 1943: P-51B 43-6388 was assigned to 334FS for evaluation for 8FC. All the 4TH leaders and ranking squadron officers got a chance to fly it and they were very enthused about it. (*Edward Richie*)

October, 1943: A Flight of 334FS poses by a Jug. L-R kneeling: V. France, V. Boehle, A. Markel; standing: F. Gallion, D. Howe, I. Moon, R. Hofer, A. Bunte, R. Frazer, H. Blanchfield. (*Edward Hedrick*)

October, 1943: F/O Ralph "Kidd" Hofer did the impossible and astounded his comrades, by scoring his first victory on his very first mission. This was almost unheard of at the time. (*N. Megura*)

October 27, 1943: Capt. Duane W. Beeson became the first 4TH FG WW2 Ace. While others lamented the P-47, he clobbered Huns with his QP-B 42-7890 BOISE BEE. (*Mrs. Carl Beeson [mother]*)

Fall, 1943: Capt. James A. Clark, 334th A Flight CO, just down from a show. Scarce and favored Spitfire mirror has been adapted to his QP-W 41-6413. (*N. Megura*)

Fall, 1943: 336's Lt. Glenn A. Herter and his VF-R 41-6354. He was KIA later in the epic 60-to-9 air battle on 3/3/44. (*N. Megura*)

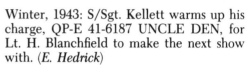

Winter, 1943: S/Sgt. Kellett warms up his charge, QP-E 41-6187 UNCLE DEN, for Lt. H. Blanchfield to make the next show with. (*E. Hedrick*)

November, 1943: Lt. Steve Pisanos (by his QP-D 42-7945 MISS PLAINFIELD) was nicknamed "The Greek" and was the first person to become a U.S. citizen by the modified overseas naturalization law. (*Edward Hedrick*)

Winter, 1943: 334th pilots, *L-R*: H. Blanchfield, S. Pisanos, and unk., walk past QP-S warming up, on their way to the squadron line HQ. (*N. Megura*)

November, 1943: The airwar quickens. Capt. James Clark, 334 Ops. Off., starts up his QP-W 41-6413 as his chief clears the APU before rolling on another show. (*Edward Hedrick*)

Winter, 1943: 336th Jugs leave their frosty hardstands loaded with 108-gal. "Babies" on another early morning show to deep in the Reich. (*D. Hall*)

Winter, 1943: 335th a/c slowly weave-taxi by the tower on the track to the west runway. Vision ahead was blocked by the giant cowling, hence the weave to clear the way. (*D. Hall*)

December 13, 1943: Lt. Louis Norley calms himself after crashing on takeoff for a forward base in his VF-O 41-6183, as armorers remove ammo. A/C was flying again in two weeks. (*Edward Hedrick*)

Winter, 1943: Hit, losing power, starting to smoke, and with his gear dropping from lost hydraulics, this FW-190 pilot is ready to try a bailout if he isn't already dead. (*John Romack*)

Winter, 1943: Former 336 CO, Lee Gover, dismounts upon completing his 100th WW2 mission. His tour over, the former 133 Eagle Squadron RAF pilot returned home and served for over 20 years in USAF fighter units. (*L. Gover*)

Winter, 1943: 4TH a/c often found themselves forced-down on bomber bases due to the lethal English weather, which changed by the second. WD-F 41-6214 is shown on a bomber field with a 108-gal. tank. (*USAF*)

12 June 1943: F.O. 43. Maj. Blakeslee led a Rodeo back to Belgium and France from 1905 to 2055 hours. Flying a diversionary sweep, the fighters covered Noordehoofd–Ypres–Dunkirk without drawing up the enemy.

13 June 1943: F.O. 44. Maj. Blakeslee led yet another Rodeo into France and Belgium from 0850 to 1035 hours. Sweeping Dunkirk–Poperinghe–Knocke, the Group saw 15 Bf 109s but did not attempt to engage due to a lack of advantage. Two 190s followed the formation out to the Channel at 20,000 feet.

The wry comment was made that with all this sweeping, France and Belgium should have been pretty clean by this time. VIII FC's strategy in trying to lure the Luftwaffe up to do battle simply was not working. The Germans were after the bombers and there was no sense in engaging fighters unless absolutely necessary. On the whole these sweeps were fruitless hunting for the 4th's Thunderbolts.

15 June 1943: At 0520 the Group left on a withdrawal support for B-17s, staging from Tangmere. Up at 0807, the formation was recalled 55 miles out over the Channel due to poor weather, getting back down at 0940. Howard "Deacon" Hively was forced to bail out of QP-J due to battle damage and went into the Channel. An hour later he was picked up by a launch from Portsmouth, cold but otherwise fine.

16 June 1943: Generals Eaker, Devers, Hunter, Edwards and Ambassador Winant visited the base to hand out some gongs. From 1105 to 1120 the Group put on a display of formation flying for the event.

17 June 1943: F.O. 47. Maj. Blakeslee was back up front directing the Group on a Rodeo to Ostend–Ypres–Gravelines from 0900 to 1045 hours. Crossing the enemy coast at 0944 at 28,000 feet, the P-47s found nothing to do but wander around for 15 minutes and come home. Without external fuel the Thunderbolt was severely limited in how far it could penetrate. The Pratt & Whitney R-2800 gulped an average of 100 gallons an hour out of the 305 gallons internal fuel the fighter carried into combat.

20 June 1943: F.O. 49. Indefatigable Maj. Blakeslee led a Rodeo to Le Touquet–St. Pol–St. Omer–Calais, France, from 1220 to 1400 hours which proved uneventful.

22 June 1943: F.O. 52. Maj. Blakeslee led a Ramrod to Belgium and the Netherlands from 0827 to 1010 hours in support of the bombers. Due to a last-minute change the rendezvous was changed. When the Group was south of Breskens they saw the B-17s coming out from Antwerp over Zuid-Beveland. Twenty 190s and 109s were attacking the Forts. Blakeslee swung the Group port and came in over the bombers, leaving 334 as top cover. 335 and 336 waded in as four B-17s fell, getting three 190s between 0915 and 0920.

[Box Score: 3 destroyed, 0 lost]

24 June 1943: F.O. 55. Maj. Blakeslee directed a Rodeo into France from 1659 to 1840 hours. The fighters swept Boulogne–Douellens–Berk sur Mer at 25,000 feet without finding anything to shoot at.

The Duchess of Kent bestowed the Royal Badges of 71, 121 and 133 Eagle Squadrons on the corresponding 4th squadrons in the name of the King during a ceremony on the parade ground.

25 June 1943: F.O. 56. Maj. Blakeslee led a Rodeo to the Netherlands from 0820 to 0955 hours. Up from Debden at 0535, the Group staged from Horsham St. Faith. Just after the '47s entered enemy airspace the show was scrubbed due to bad weather.

Wing Headquarters based a Fairchild 24 on the field and new 8th Air Force shoulder patches came in.

26 June 1943: F.O. 57. Maj. Blakeslee was at the front of the Group on a Ramrod to Gisors, France, from 1825 to 1955 hours. Staging from Thorney Island, the fighters were ⅓ the way across the Channel when told the withdrawing bombers were early. After a gradual port turn on the rendezvous point they spotted the bombers northwest of Le Treport with enemy aircraft diving away. As the Thunderbolts arrived six 109s dived under 334 and a combat developed 10 miles off Dieppe at 1859, netting two Messerschmitts downed.

[Box Score: 2 destroyed, 0 lost]

28 June 1943: F.O. 58. Capt. Carl Miley led a Ramrod to Landrodec–St. Brieue, France, from 1605 to 1750 hours. Staging from Warmwell, the Group did not find the Forts at the rendezvous point although four B-17s were spotted on the way back.

29 June 1943: F.O. 59. Maj. DuFour led a Ramrod withdrawal support to Gisors, France, from 1931 to 2120 hours. After staging from Thorney Island, the Group found the bombers at 2022 coming out with another group of P-47s. DeFour led the 4th in front of the formation, coming back in from the rear after a turn at 29,-000 feet. There were no enemy aircraft but flak was heavy south of Dieppe.

1 July 1943: F.O. 60. Maj. Blakeslee led a Rodeo to Le Touquet–Abbe-ville–Cayeux, France, from 1440 to 1620 hours. South of Abbeville the Group entered a wide orbit at 25,000 feet. 335 Red Section bounced several Bf 109s but the Germans shook them off. Two 334 pilots bounced enemy aircraft with no results.

Col. Anderson and Col. Hoyt offered search and rescue assistance to the 78th Fighter Group for the rescue of their CO, Col. Arman Peterson, who had been lost near Ouddorp during a big fight with enemy fighters. In half an hour the mission was underway with 16 aircraft up under Maj. Blakeslee at 2045 hours. Everyone was back down by 2230 with no luck.

2 July 1943: At 1415 hours Bob Hope, Francis Langford, Tony Romano and Jack Pepper gave a USO show on the parade ground.

4 July 1943: F.O. 64. Maj. DuFour led a Ramrod to Le Treport, France, as withdrawal support for B-17s from 1204 to 1330 hours. Just as the Group arrived at the French coast they were recalled due to bad weather.

6 July 1943: F.O. 65. Capt. Halsey led a Rodeo to Ostend–Ghent–Hulst, Belgium, from 1023 to 1210 hours. The sweep netted no enemy aircraft.

9 July 1943: F.O. 67. Maj. DuFour led a Rodeo over Belgium from 0709 to 1850 hours. The formation swept Knocke–Ghent–Courtrai–Ostend from 25/23,000 feet uneventfully, except for much maddening R/T (communications) trouble.

10 July 1943: F.O. 68. Maj. Halsey led a Ramrod general support to Abbeville and Poix airdromes in France from 0650 to 0840 hours. The Group provided withdrawal escort at 28,000 feet to the B-17s without spotting any enemy aircraft.

In order that he might give more attention to his duties as Group Ops Officer, newly promoted Lt. Col. Blakeslee was relieved of his duties as Executive Officer, a spot filled by John Malone.

12 July 1943: Red-bordered white rectangles were ordered added to all national markings painted on the Group's Thunderbolts. They were on by the 19th.

14 July 1943: F.O. 71. Maj. DuFour led a diversionary sweep in general support of bombers attacking Amiens/Glisy airdrome from 0650 to 0840 hours. Ten miles east of Amiens the Group rendezvoused with the B-17s at 29,500 feet in the midst of an enemy attack. 335 headed off five 190s attacking a Fort at 0750, but Ward Wortman was lost in the action.

[Box Score: 0 destroyed, 1 lost]

16 July 1943: F.O. 73. Maj. Halsey led a fighter sweep to Nieuport–Merville–Calais, France, from 1925 to 2050 hours at 28,000 feet. The only enemy encountered was the high pitched R/T whine that drove everyone nuts.

Two things happened that foreshadowed things to come. The new 200-gallon unpressurized belly tanks arrived to be installed on the Group's P-47s ... and Gen. Hunter showed up over the base in a P-51 for a few mock dogfights.

17 July 1943: F.O. 74. Maj. DuFour led a support for B-17s on a diversion to Amsterdam from 0805 to 1000 hours. The bombers were early and already on their way into the target by the time the Group arrived. The Germans didn't show up for the party.

20 July 1943: In a practice escape exercise, 21 pilots were dumped six miles from the field—only seven made it back without being captured. They managed to capture a machine gun post, several rifles and a staff car. The rest got caught due to their impatience.

25 July 1943: F.O. 78. Maj. Halsey led a Rodeo into Belgium from 1410 to 1540 hours without 335. The two squadrons swept Courtrai–Ghent–Flushing without incident.

Instead of going on the show, 335 flew out to the Wash to test drop the new belly tanks.

26 July 1943: F.O. 80. Maj. Halsey led another Rodeo off the Dutch coast from 0930 to 1125 hours. Five miles east of Rotterdam, 334 Green Section bounced four Focke Wulfs at 23,000 feet. Mills got a probable. As the Group swept Schowen to The Hague several more 190s were spotted. 334 Red Section attempted a bounce without luck.

F.O. 81. Maj. Halsey led the Group out for a second Rodeo into France and Belgium from 1657 to 1830 hours. The formation swept Cap Gris Nez–Lille–Nieuport and three different times 190s appeared. Twice they evaded a bounce by ducking into the clouds, and the last time they dived away.

27 July 1943: F.O. 82. Maj. Halsey led a Rodeo into France as a diversionary sweep for B-26s. The group rendezvoused over Etretat at 1754, flying at 18,000 feet, passing over and in front of the bombers for 15 miles, then back over them, covering St. Valery and Dieppe. The P-47s finally had to abort the mission due to lack of fuel, a frustration they would not have to bear much longer.

28 July 1943: F.O. 83. Maj. Halsey, in leading a Ramrod from 1031 to 1300 hours, took the Group to Germany itself for the first time. Carrying the new 200 gallon unpressurized belly tanks, the Thunderbolts provided withdrawal support for the 1st Bomb Wing to Emmerich. In spite of the new tanks being only half filled due to technical problems, the Germans were caught surprised. As the Group arrived over Emmerich there were no bombers. Passing Leerdam, they spotted a different gaggle of Forts being attacked. 335 passed over and in front of the bombers while 336 went port and 335 starboard to get at the 45 to 60 Huns. In a roaring dogfight from 1155 to 1220 from Germany back into the Netherlands the Group downed three 109s and six 190s—Col. Anderson got two 190s for himself. At the end of the combat Henry Ayers bailed out to become a POW.

[Box Score: 9 destroyed, 1 lost]

F.O. 84. Maj. Halsey was back up front for the second time this day on a Circus to Cayeux–St. Omer–Calais, France, from 1805 to 1955 hours. Rendezvousing with the B-26s at 12,000 feet, the Group stayed with the Spitfire escort and the bombers to the enemy coast. After the bombers turned back, the 4th swept on to Hesdin, passed west of St. Omer and came out at 28,000 feet.

29 July 1943: F.O. 85. Maj. Halsey led a Rodeo into Belgium from 1010 to 1155 hours. In a diversionary sweep over Blankenberge–Ghent–St. Nicholas–Knocke the Thunderbolts found no enemy aircraft.

F.O. 86. Maj. Halsey was at the front of a Circus to Nooderhoofd–Sas Van Gent–Ostend, Netherlands–Belgium from 1735 to 1925 hours. After rendezvous and escort with B-26s at 15,000 feet, the Group broke off for a diversionary sweep without result.

Gen. Hunter accompanied Eddie Rickenbacker to the base as "Capt. Eddie" gave a popular speech on the various war fronts.

30 July 1943: F.O. 87. Maj. Halsey led the second belly tank mission, a Ramrod withdrawal support for B-17s to Emmerich, Germany, from 0856 to 1135 hours. As the Group passed Groesbeck two groups of bombers were spotted to the north.

Halsey dispatched 335 under Roy Evans to cover them. Out of everywhere 150 to 200 enemy aircraft attacked as the squadron pulled in. 335 downed five 190s from 1030 to 1040, losing one pilot as the fight ranged over the Netherlands. After the combat, 335 stayed with the bombers until the Dutch coast, breaking off for home at 1053. The other two squadrons continued on to the Rhine, rendezvousing with more Forts at 1015, flying at 27,000 feet. They left the Big Friends at the coast at 1100.

[Box Score: 5 destroyed, 1 lost]

31 July 1943: F.O. 88. Lt. Col. Blakeslee was back up front to lead a Circus from 1525 to 1715 hours. After providing high cover for B-26s, the Group then made a diversionary sweep to Mardyck–Doullens–Sangatte, France, after the bombers left at 1605. The Group came back out at 1638, flying at 26,000 feet.

2 August 1943: Five U.S. Senators, including Jim Mead from New York, visited the base with a gaggle of generals.

W.F.O. (65th Fighter Wing Field Order) 22. Lt. Col. Blakeslee led a Circus to Ghent, Belgium, from 1730 to 1815 hours. Before the sweep reached the target the show was aborted.

9 August 1943: W.F.O. 28. Maj. Halsey led a Rodeo over Le Touquet–Bethune–Lille–Courtrai, France, from 1553 to 1740 hours. Cruising at 25/26,000 feet, the Group made an uneventful sweep with pilots of the new 353rd Fighter Group replacing 334.

12 August 1943: F.O. 98. Lt. Col. Blakeslee led a Ramrod withdrawal support to Sittgard–Bergheim, Netherlands, from 0815 to 1100 hours. The Group rendezvoused with five gaggles of Forts at 0925, flying at 29,000 feet, when four to six FW 190s lined up to attack. As the P-47s came up behind and over the bombers, the enemy aircraft broke, passing under 334. Jim Clark led 334 Green Section down, getting one 109 and damaging another. As the rest of the formation went on, eight Bf 109s jumped the bombers. 334 Red Section engaged, claiming two destroyed and a damaged. Cadman Padgett got a 109 west of Duren as well.

[Box Score: 4 destroyed, 0 lost]

15 August 1943: F.O. 103. Lt. Col. Blakeslee led a Rodeo to St. Inglevort–St. Omer–Knocke, France-Belgium, from 0820 to 1010 hours. The sweep was uneventful.

F.O. 104. Lt. Col. Blakeslee took the Group out again on a Ramrod withdrawal support to Ostend–Brussels–Balcale–Ghent, Belgium, from 1830 to 2045 hours. As the B-17s returned from Brussels/Evre airdrome at 33,000 feet, two 190s tried to attack but 336 forced them to break.

16 August 1943: F.O. 105. Lt. Col. Blakeslee led a Ramrod close escort to Paris from 0805 to 1055 hours. The Group rendezvoused with the B-17s at 0912, flying at 28,000 feet, and orbited to port, coming in behind the bombers, which were being attacked head-on. Blakeslee took the Group up and over the Forts and 334 made the bounce. Soon all sections from all squadrons were involved in the fight, which lasted to and from the target, from 0920 to 1000 hours. The Huns came in from all directions in gaggles of six to eight. Fights ranged all around Paris, giving the partisans quite a show as 18 enemy aircraft were destroyed. Joe Matthews went down but he managed to evade his captors, getting back to Debden in October to confirm his kill. Several aircraft returned with great holes in them from the effective 20mm fire, including Blakeslee's, but the 4th was jubilant. Though they didn't know for sure at the time, the pilots had tied the 56th in kills scored during a single mission.

[Box Score: 18 destroyed, 1 lost]

17 August 1943: F.O. 106. Lt. Col. Blakeslee led a Ramrod penetration support to Eupen–Duren, Belgium-Germany, from 1301 to 1540 hours. The Group rendezvoused with the bombers under attack by six to eight Huns, which broke away and down as the '47s appeared. As the aircraft reached their penetration limit, they turned back past three more bomber boxes under attack by nine enemy aircraft. The fighters scared them off.

Getting back to Debden, the pilots found out the 56th was not going to wait. What was becoming known as Zemke's Wolfpack downed 13 Huns.

19 August 1943: F.O. 108. Lt. Col. Blakeslee led a Rodeo withdrawal support to Woensdrecht–Brecht–Loe, Netherlands, from 1740 to 2005 hours. The Group rendezvoused with the B-17s in mid-Channel at 1840 and left them at Brecht at 1854, flying at 25,000 feet. The bombers were late as usual, and off course.

20 August 1943: F.O. Lt. Col. Chesley Peterson replaced Col. Anderson as Group CO. Anderson went to the 67th Fighter Wing to become a brigadier general.

22 August 1943: 334 took its aircraft off ops for installation of racks and points for a 75-gallon belly tank. Each squadron would get the B-7 racks.

23 August 1943: F.O. 111. Lt. Col. Blakeslee led a Rodeo to Bruges–Goes–Rotterdam–Westhoofd, Belgium-Netherlands, from 1455 to 1655 hours. Sweeping Noord Beveland and Rotterdam in a complete orbit, the Group found nothing to shoot at.

24 August 1943: F.O. 112. Lt. Col. Blakeslee led 336 on a Ramrod to Couches, France, from 1735 to 1926 hours. Rendezvous and escort with the B-17s was uneventful.

334 and 335 remained off ops to get the shackles installed.

27 August 1943: Maj. Halsey led a Ramrod high cover for B-17s to Frevent airdrome, France, from 1845 to 2030. The Group came out with the bombers and their Spitfire escort near Gravelines at 1925, flying at 33,000 feet. The pilots had a rough time landing in almost-dark.

31 August 1943: Maj. DuFour led a Ramrod general support to Romilly, France, from 1635 to 1845 hours. After rendezvous at 1719, the Group covered the Forts to the IP. As the Thunderbolts came out over Beauvais, eight to ten enemy aircraft attacked 336 head on from 27,000 feet. Miley claimed two. As the Group continued on out, a gaggle of Forts was seen over Amiens under attack by 12 to 15 Huns. Stanhope claimed another victory as 336 went to their aid. The claims were never confirmed.

Bad weather had cancelled numerous shows but when the Group did mix it with the enemy they gave a good accounting of themselves during the month.

2 September 1943: F.O. 120. Lt. Col. Blakeslee led a penetration withdrawal support to Beauvais–Tille, France, from 1640 to 1900 hours. After a wide port orbit 20,000 feet over France waiting for the bombers, the Group was ordered to sweep Beauvais. At Formerie the Group made a port turn and climbed to 27,000 feet after sighting four to six enemy aircraft starboard and 16 to 18 west, climbing. At 1750 334 was bounced by these Huns from 3 and 9 o'clock. Dale Leaf was immediately shot down and killed and the rest of 334 felt lucky to have emerged from the effective attack. The fight lasted all the way out at 20,000 feet with both 109s and 190s.

[Box Score: 0 destroyed, 1 lost]

3 September 1943: F.O. 121. Lt. Col. Blakeslee led a Ramrod penetration support to Romilly, France, from 0720 to 1000 hours. As the P-47s neared Abbeville the bombers came in from behind, forcing the Group into a slow orbit to port, then starboard, then port to let them catch up. Rendezvous was at 0826 behind and starboard of the bombers. At 0836 four FW 190s attacked the lead element. 336 engaged. At 0839 another four 190s started an attack but broke away and climbed back for a stern attack. 336 Green Section dispersed the enemy formation. The Group came out at Le Crotoy at 0920, flying at 27,000 feet, having been damaged by the Huns.

4 September 1943: All pilots were taken by transport to Duxford to hear the Chief of the AAF, Hap Arnold, speak.

6 September 1943: F.O. 125. Lt. Col. Blakeslee led a withdrawal support high cover to Epernay, France, from 1000 to 1240 hours. At the rendezvous point over Epernay the Group swung port and came in behind five boxes of bombers as they were being attacked by Focke Wulfs. The Huns broke and dove away. As the Group made a turn, three 190s and a 109 flew 100 feet above 334, apparently not recognizing the P-47s until they skidded and dived away in violent evasive action. Beeson got a few squirts off at them. East of Chalons, 30 to 40 enemy aircraft were seen at the same level, waiting for the fighters to leave. North of Chateau Thierry a 190 attacking a Fort was destroyed by Roy Evans. Near Senlis the 4th was relieved by the 78th's Thunderbolts.

[Box Score: 1 destroyed, 0 lost]

7 September 1943: F.O. 126. Lt. Col. Blakeslee led a Ramrod penetration support to Hulst–Brussels, Netherlands-Belgium, from 0734 to 1000 hours. Rendezvous with the bombers took place near Deynze at 0825. As the Big Friends turned port over the IP at 0840, nine Huns attacked the lead box from the southeast. Blakeslee took 335 and bounced them by diving to 18,000 feet. Aubrey Stanhope found a 190 latched onto his tail in short order. Screaming for the deck, both aircraft were shot down by flak but Stanhope made it out to be captured. 335 zoomed back up and rejoined the lead boxes on the starboard side with 336 and 334 as top cover. The P-47s crossed out at Noordhoofd at 19,000 after leaving the bombers near Hulst. German attacks on the rear boxes were driven off by 334.

9 September 1943: F.O. 128. Lt. Col. Blakeslee led a Ramrod general support to Paris from 0721 to 1030 hours. The Group rendezvoused with the bombers near Elbeuf as attacks were initiated by 30 109s and 190s from up-sun, head-on. 334 and 336 broke up the attacks, then the Group re-formed and continued the escort to Paris. Sixteen enemy aircraft approached from the southeast but 334 headed them off, forcing them to break. Vernon Boehle bailed into the Channel after his P-47's engine failed. He spent two days and two nights in the icy water before he was picked up.

12 September 1943: The First Anniversary of the 4th Fighter Group was celebrated by a Field Day of sports and a dance in the evening.

14 September 1943: F.O. 130. Maj. Miley led a Rodeo to Dunkirk–Roulers–Ostend, France-Belgium, from 1105 to 1250 hours. After rendezvous at 1130 over Bradwell Bay at 14,000 feet, the Group was above and behind the new 355th Fighter Group. The fighters penetrated to the south of Roulers and came out near Blankenberge at 1202, flying at 28/29,000 feet.

15 September 1943: F.O. 132. Lt. Col. Blakeslee led the Group back to Paris on a Ramrod from 1730 to 1955 hours. Up from the forward base at Ford, the 4th met the Forts near Les Chilliers and accompanied them to Paris. Thirty-plus enemy aircraft showed up just west of Paris and the escort was hindered in bouncing them by the bombers' defensive fire. Sobanski led a section in to attack several 190s but, even though there were several individual combats, no claims were submitted. The Group stayed with the bombers to Gournay and came out at Le Treport.

16 September 1943: Night flying practice began in anticipation of late-hour missions in the future.

22 September 1943: F.O. 138. Lt. Col. Blakeslee led a fighter sweep to Calais–Lille–Ostend, France-Belgium, from 1039 to 1220 hours. There were no enemy aircraft but the flak was heavy.

At 1805 the Group was off to Warmwell to stage for the next day's show, landing at 1910.

23 September 1943: F.O. 140. Maj. Coen led a Ramrod target support to Vannes–Brest, France, from 0705 to 1930 hours from Warmwell. This staging base had very poor facilities—it took seven hours to refuel the aircraft and the Thunderbolts could not take off from the field with external tanks. There were several aborts due to mechanical problems. On the way in heavy flak from Guernsey Island damaged a few kites and 336 got separated. 334 and 335 rendezvoused at Cap Berhat at 0807 with the bombers, flying at 25,000 feet. Escort was provided to the target and back, leaving the coast at 0845 over St. Brieuc Bay. A single attack by one enemy fighter was made at the RV point but it quickly broke off. The Group refueled at Warmwell, before returning to Debden.

With barely enough time to breath, the Group was airborne again at 1415, landing at another forward base, Exeter, at 1520 for the second mission of the day.

F.O. 142. Lt. Col. Blakeslee led a Ramrod target support to Dinan–Nantes, France, from 1705 to 1930 hours. Rendezvous relieving another P-47 group was made outside Nantes at 26/29,000 feet as the bomb run started. The Group left the bombers at Dinan to head back for Exeter.

24 September 1943: Blakeslee brought his charges back from Exeter to beautiful Debden from 1105 to 1210 hours.

25 September 1943: 334 received the first P-51 Mustang to come to the Group for operational test and evaluation. It was immediately flown by Coen and Clark the next day, after being officially assigned to the squadron.

26 September 1943: F.O. 145. Lt. Col. Blakeslee led a Ramrod support to Les Andelys–Melun, France, from 1632 to 1855 hours. Rendezvousing over Dieppe at 1721, flying at 25,000 feet, the 4th's Thunderbolts covered three boxes of bombers to Les Andelys where they turned and were picked up by Spitfires. The Group came out near Le Treport at 23,000.

27 September 1943: F.O. 147. Up from Debden at 0630, Lt. Col. Blakeslee took the Group to Hardwick for staging. Blakeslee led a Ramrod support to Emden, Germany, from 0835 to 1135. With 108-gallon belly tanks mounted on the Thunderbolts, the mission was longer than any performed thus far. Dropping tanks at 0926, the Group rendezvoused with the bombers northwest of Ameland Island at 0935, flying at 25,000 feet. Coming out with the bombers over Norderney Island, the pilots saw two FW 190s level with 336 at 27,000, getting ready to bounce 335 in the lead. 336 bounced and Willard Millikan shot down one 190 at 1010 hours. The '47s left the bombers north of Terschelling.

[Box Score: 1 destroyed, 0 lost]

VIII Fighter Command downed 21 enemy aircraft this day—the 78th got eight and the 56th got four. The boys were hacked off about it since they felt they did a better job of escort. The weather in August and September was another factor in keeping the pilots away from the Huns. All in all, the 4th was a very unhappy bunch of boys.

2 October 1943: F.O. 148. Lt. Col. Blakeslee led a Ramrod support to Emden, Germany, from Hardwick, 1455 to 1800 hours. Rendezvous was made at 24,000 feet, 1553 hours, just before Groningen. Six 109s tried to attack the lead box of bombers but 336 White Section diverted the assault. Near Aurich, ten 190s were sighted ahead of the bombers. 334 went after them and Beeson got one. The Group left the bombers near Borkum at 1630.

[Box Score: 1 destroyed, 0 lost]

3 October 1943: W.F.O. 73. Maj. Evans led a Rodeo to St. Valery–Amiens–Pointe-Hautbane–Boulogne, France, from 1455 to 1800 hours. 334 and

335 crossed the enemy coast at 1245 at 26,000 feet and swept Amiens, then headed back and swung north, coming out at 1310.

4 October 1943: F.O. 150. Lt. Col. Blakeslee led a Ramrod withdrawal support to Eupen–Frankfurt, Belgium-Germany, from 1115 to 1400 hours. The Group arrived at the RV point over Eupen at 1224 hours, 27/28,000 feet, but the bombers never showed. After orbiting for 16 minutes, the Thunderbolts withdrew, coming out at 1310 over Knocke.

6 October 1943: The 4th held Open House for 75 aviation personalities and military leaders of the United Nations to view a display of the latest U.S. fighter aircraft, particularly the P-51, in front of the control tower.

8 October 1943: F.O. 151, W.F.O. 74. Lt. Col. Blakeslee led a Ramrod penetration support to Cloppenburg–Oldenburg–Bremen, Germany, from the forward base at Shipdham, 1330 to 1555 hours. Rendezvous was made at 1419 over Texel Island. 334, at the rear of the bombers, saw 30-plus enemy aircraft above and up-sun. As the squadron orbited to gain altitude, it was continually bounced by Hun sections of four to eight fighters, breaking up the squadron and drawing it away from the bombers. Yet no enemy aircraft attacked the bombers, so the purpose was served. Several 334 pilots got into fights over Meppel. Hofer chased a 109 400 feet above the Zuider Zee, trying to get it off another '47's tail. The '47 went in but Hofer got the 109. Beeson got two more, bringing his score up to six, and Evans got a 190, bringing his score up to five. Both shared the distinction of becoming the Group's first aces. Smith and Patterson were shot down, becoming POWs, but not before Patterson kept ahead of the Germans for two months in Belgium and the Netherlands.

[Box Score: 6 destroyed, 2 lost]

10 October 1943: F.O. 153. Lt. Col. Blakeslee led a Ramrod penetration and target support to Munster–Haltern, Germany, from 1345 to 1635 hours. Dropping tanks at 1453, the Group rendezvoused with the last box of bombers at 1506 west of Haltern. The Big Friends were strung out and stacked from 25,000 to 30,000 feet. As the last box reached the IP, the lead box was well beyond the target and under attack by 30 enemy fighters coming in in pairs. Blakeslee led 336 to their aid, preventing further attacks. 334 and 336 then worked up to the lead units near the rally point where more attacks were being made but the bombers were too strung out for effective cover. Beeson claimed a 190 but was denied credit for it later.

Other 8th Air Force fighter groups claimed 21 destroyed.

14 October 1943: Recalled due to fog, the 4th was not able to supply withdrawal support for the bombers coming back from Schweinfurt. On this "Black Thursday" the Big Friends lost 60 of their own.

18 October 1943: F.O. 162. Lt. Col. Blakeslee led a Ramrod to Dinant–Chateaux-D'Ardenne, Belgium, from 1336 to 1555 hours. Reaching the RV point at 1448, the Group orbited for 18 minutes and withdrew after failing to sight the bombers, coming out at Ostend at 1524 and 23,000 feet.

20 October 1943: F.O. 163. Lt. Col. Blakeslee led a Ramrod penetration support to Mons–Duren–Antwerp, Belgium-Germany, from 1315 to 1550 hours. At 1410 the bombers were sighted, being escorted by P-47s near Mons. The 4th relieved this group and at 1447, on the way out, P-38s took over for withdrawal support. 334 Green Section latched onto a straggling Fort which was attacked by two enemy aircraft. "Cowboy" Megura got shot up in the process.

22 October 1943: At 23 years old, Group CO Chesley Peterson was promoted to full Colonel.

The 4th watched the 56th pull into the lead in the ETO score column. It always seemed to be a matter of being in the wrong place at the wrong time for the 4th, while the 56th proceeded to knock down the Huns with effective dive and zoom tactics.

3 November 1943: F.O. 168. Lt. Col. Blakeslee led a Ramrod to Wilhelmshaven, Germany, from 1135 to 1350 hours, using Halesworth as a forward base. Group take-off was fraught with trouble—one '47 crashed but the pilot was OK. 334 was bounced just inside the Dutch coast around 1230, getting one 109 and losing two pilots. As 334 held off the Huns, the rest of the Group went on and orbited the RV point at Hypolitushoef and waited for the bombers in vain. There was also much trouble in getting the belly tanks to jettison.

[Box Score: 1 destroyed, 2 lost]

5 November 1943: F.O. 170. Maj. Evans led a Ramrod target support to Dortmund, Germany, from 1213 to 1505 hours. Rendezvousing east of Borken, 335 took the lead box, 336 the second and 334 the third. On the way in to Gelsenkirchen, 12 FW 190s attacked head-on, line abreast. 335 diverted the Huns. Eight more 190s came in from the north head-on and were into the lead box before Evans could turn the Group into them. The Germans were aggressive and persistant. When the relief fighter escort didn't show up the Group elected to stay with the bombers up to the P-47's recommended maximum endurance limit (Maastricht in this case). Out of the several combats "Snuffy" Smith managed to down a 190.

[Box Score: 1 destroyed, 0 lost]

7 November 1943: F.O. 173. Lt. Col. Blakeslee led a Ramrod withdrawal support to Meulan, France, from 0855 to 1125 hours. At 0935 in mid-Channel the group rendezvoused with 72 B-26s stacked up from 16,000 to 20,000 feet. The 4th provided top cover for the P-38s acting as close escort. Southeast of Rouen, three 109s came in level, head-on to the bombers' first box. Blakeslee led 334 to port, jettisoned tanks and began a bounce but the Huns slipped in, going through the P-38s and the bombers. Three more 109s coming in from below were engaged by the Lightnings. On the way out Blakeslee led 334 to some bandits reported by "Warmsun" (the radar controller) but none were found.

8 November 1943: F.O. 174. Lt. Col. Blakeslee led a Ramrod to Wesel, Germany, from 1305 to 1530 hours. After being vectored extensively by "Warmsun" the

Group never rendezvoused with the Forts. One of the Group's spares, Jack Raphael, bounced two 190s on the way back from the Dutch coast, damaging one.

10 November 1943: F.O. 175. Lt. Col. Blakeslee was back up front to lead a Rodeo to Dieppe–Gournay, France, from 1335 to 1545 hours. The Group made an uneventful sweep in front of the B-26 force.

11 November 1943: F.O. 177. Lt. Col. Blakeslee led a Ramrod support to Wesel, Germany, from 1259 to 1550 hours. As the Group leveled off at 26,000 feet on the way in, 334 was bounced by eight 109s, forcing the P-47s to drop tanks before rendezvous. 335 turned into the sun and climbed to help but it was bounced by four 109s from out of the sun. As 335 turned starboard, eight to twelve more Messerschmitts attacked the squadron. 336 went high to provide top cover. The fighting gaggle made seven wide orbits centering around Hypolituschoef. After 21 minutes the 4th fought to a draw and withdrew at 1250. The bombers were never seen.

13 November 1943: F.O. 180. Maj. Evans led a Ramrod withdrawal support to Visbek–Bremen, Netherlands-Germany, from 1100 to 1400 hours. Staging out of Hardwick, the Group never found their B-24s after finding a formation of B-17s under escort.

15 November 1943: 600 Spitfire mirrors arrived at VIII FC to equip all 8th Air Force fighters. The 4th had found the mirrors installed on its P-47s greatly lacking. Hopefully the English mirrors would remedy the problem.

26 November 1943: F.O. 191. Lt. Col. Blakeslee led a Ramrod withdrawal support to Edenwalt–Bremen, Germany, from 1110 to 1400 hours. Staging from Hardwick, the Group rendezvoused at 1221. The B-17 boxes were well formed but the B-24s were strung out as much as a mile between aircraft, making the formation very difficult to cover. A lone 109 attacking a Liberator was destroyed. East of Pappenburg, three 109s started to attack the rear of the lead box. Blakeslee diverted the Huns which then lined up on the front of the second box. 336 got in the way and the 109s veered away. The Group left the bombers at 1246 as another P-47 outfit came in at 1240. Seven 109s attacked from the south, 500 feet above 334, which was leading, but the Germans dived away as Blakeslee turned to engage. A 56th Group aircraft, coded LM-F, attacked one of the 4th's P-47s without doing any damage.

[Box Score: 1 destroyed, 0 lost]

The 56th shot down 26 Huns, establishing itself beyond question as the top fighter outfit in the ETO.

29 November 1943: F.O. 192. Maj. Edner led a Ramrod withdrawal support to Bremen, Germany, from 1255 to 1555 hours. Staging out of Bungay, the 4th rendezvoused at 1410 with three boxes of bombers. Just prior to reaching the target, six to eight Bf 109s attacked the lead box head-on, then slipped into cloud 500 feet below the bombers. The Germans came out to attack again only to slip back into the cloud. Four FW 190s attacked before the target as well. Some 109s were engaged after the target and "Snuffy" Smith bagged another kill. It was learned that the 56th had arrived on the scene prior to the 4th's picking up the escort, leaving slim pickings after the Germans had been scattered.

[Box Score: 1 destroyed, 0 lost]

30 November 1943: Maj. Evans led a Rodeo penetration target support to the Ruhr, Germany, from 1007 to 1310 hours. Seeing many bombers on the way to the RV point, the Group never found their charges. Turning north to accompany some bombers out, the Group never caught up with the formation. A P-38 group and several P-47 groups were seen.

1 December 1943: F.O. 194. Maj. Edner led a Ramrod to Solingen, Germany, from 1013 to 1315 hours. The Group rendezvoused with the bombers at 1123, 28,000 feet—the Big Friends were late. Edner placed his P-47s on the second box, since another P-47 group and a P-38 group were already with the bombers. At 1145 the 4th broke escort near Sinzig and came home. A Ju 88 was fired on but it escaped into cloud. 336 got into a few scraps as well and John T. Godfrey got his first kill, a Bf 109.

[Box Score: 1 destroyed, 0 lost]

Don Blakeslee went to Boxsted to lead the 354th Fighter Group on its first mission, a sweep of Holland and the French coast. The 354th was the first AAF group to get P-51s. After leading the "Pioneer Mustang" outfit for six missions, Blakeslee came back with a Bf 110 kill, a good impression of a great bunch of fliers, and unbounded enthusiasm for the P-51. He was sure it was the aircraft to carry the 4th into first place could it be obtained.

5 December 1943: F.O. 196. Maj. Evans led a Ramrod penetration support to Bordeaux, France, from 0933 to 1215. Getting airborne from Ford, the Group rendezvoused with four boxes of B-17s at 1023 over a solid undercast. The Forts followed several Liberator formations into the target and at 1053 the 4th withdrew as P-38s had come in at 1050 to take over.

11 December 1943: F.O. 198. Maj. Evans led a Rodeo target support to Leeuwarden–Zoutkamp, Netherlands, from 1025 to 1315 hours. Near Leeuwarden at 1155, eight 109s came out of the east 4,000 feet above in two sections of four, one section on the port and one on the starboard side. The Group and another P-47 squadron turned into them, driving them south. 109s then attacked 335, aided by eight more Messerschmitts that went after 334 and 336. The engagement lasted until 1207 when the Thunderbolt's endurance limit was reached, forcing the Group to break off and come home. The bombers, 25 minutes late, were never seen on their way to Emden.

[Box Score: 1 destroyed, 0 lost]

13 December 1943: F.O. 199. Maj. Edner led a Ramrod general support to Bremen, Germany, from 1025 to 1330 hours. The Group rendezvoused with the bombers at 1200, 20 miles north of Bremen, escorted them to the target and beyond to Groszenkeneten where two more groups of P-47s came in to take over at 1210.

There was some practice dive bombing to prepare for future shows when it would be ordered. There was not great enthusiasm for it, to say the least.

15 December 1943: Ralph "Kidd" Hofer was picked up by M.P.s in London for failing to wear bars on his trench coat and for not carrying an A.G.O. card. As usual, he talked his way out of it.

16 December 1943: F.O. 203. Lt. Col. Edner led a Ramrod withdrawal support back to Bremen, Germany, from 1147 to 1525 hours. After getting to altitude, the Group experimented with a new tactic by spreading the squadrons over a 30 mile front, each squadron being 2,000 feet apart. A fifth section (Purple) was added to each squadron for a total of 20 fighters each. These three new sections flew 500 feet above each of their respective squadrons to report and attack approaching enemy aircraft, thus preventing the Group from being broken up on the way to the rendezvous. The Thunderbolts made the RV point at 1323—the bombers were nowhere to be seen. After orbiting starboard, the Group found the B-17s at 1345 and 27,000 feet about halfway between the target and the coast. A cloud layer had reduced visibility to one-half mile, causing the Group to miss the bombers near the RV point. Escort was broken at 1401 near Den Helder. Gentile, Norley and Garrison teamed up to down a Ju 88 on the way out.

[Box Score: 1 destroyed, 0 lost]

20 December 1943: F.O. 204. Maj. Evans led the Group yet again to Bremen, Germany, on a Ramrod free lance support from 1031 to 1330 hours. Hofer had engine trouble and turned back at the coast only to be bounced by 109s from 30,000 feet. They chased him to mid-Channel where he was able to lose them in the haze. The Group rendezvoused with the Big Friends near Stadskanaal and took them to the target. Just after the Group broke escort at 1156, Millikan downed a 109.

[Box Score: 1 destroyed, 0 lost]

22 December 1943: F.O. 207. Lt. Col Blakeslee led a Ramrod target withdrawal support to Munster, Germany, from 1243 to 1545 hours. Rendezvous was made at 1359 at 26,000 feet 15 miles west of the target area. The Group made a starboard and then a port turn over the target until 1415 and then followed the bombers out, breaking off at 1422. In the Enschede area four 109s were attacked at 10/15,-000 feet by three of the Group's pilots. Three 109s were claimed destroyed but the one shared by Wynn and Godfrey was the only one confirmed.

[Box Score: 1 destroyed, 0 lost]

24 December 1943: F.O. 209. Maj. Clark led a Ramrod area support under Type 16 control to the Margny–Lookcateau area in France from 1221 to 1530 hours. The new "Jensen" Type 16 control vectored the Group toward St. Quentin where the controller reported Huns but they were P-47s. Clark's R/T went out and Maj. Evans took the lead. As it turned out, all vectors were either inaccurate or to friendlies. On a 180° turn the Group split and came home.

28 December 1943: The 4th was finally up to its full strength of 75 Thunderbolts but the 56th was operating with 108 aircraft and the 78th had been at that strength since 5 November. Two days previous, on 26 December, the 56th had also received 21 of the new paddle-bladed props, vastly improving the performance of the heavy P-47. By 28 January 1944 the 56th had 88 aircraft fitted with the new propeller, the only group so blessed in the ETO.

These factors had much to do with the 56th's leap ahead in the scoring race. The situation left the 4th that much more discouraged and disgruntled. Among those most disappointed was Don Blakeslee, who had been convinced he could make the Group the best in the AAF if given command. When Chesley Peterson came back from VIII Fighter Command in August to take command of the Group there was strong sentiment the honor should have gone to Blakeslee. Even though "Col. Pete" was well liked, this feeling was reinforced when he was given his colonelcy back in October.

30 December 1943: F.O. 210. Lt. Col. Edner led a Free Lance and Withdrawal Support to the Beauvais–Soissons area in France from 1248 to 1550 hours. Reaching Lille at 1341, flying at 27,000 feet, the Group orbited until a vector came in from Type 16 "Jensen" to St. Quentin–Soissons where the formation was requested to orbit. Another vector was received at 1348 and at 1402 rendezvous was made with two boxes of Forts and Libs in the Beauvais area. They were in no trouble so the Group orbited the area, returning to Margny to pick up 120 bombers and escort them to Beauvais. Edner broke escort at 1435 and brought the boys home.

31 December 1943: Lt. Col. Blakeslee led a Free Lance and Area Support to Paris, France, from 1030 to 1335 hours. "Jensen" took the Group to Rouen where they orbited from 1124 to 1134. Rendezvous with the bombers was made near Etampes, then the P-47s were vectored ahead of the bombers on to Paris. The Big and Little Friends rejoined a few minutes later on the east side of the city. Escort was broken at 1205 as the Group circled south of Paris, then headed for home, coming out east of Dieppe.

As the year closed, the last two missions were flown under official USAAF terminology. Though the RAF terms such as Ramrod and Rodeo would surface every now and then, the boys would fly Free Lance, Penetration-Target-Withdrawal Support, Fighter Sweep and other familiar missions under an increasingly Army Air Force flavor. The first American-trained pilots would also enter the group during the first month of the new year. Things were changing, but that was fine. Everyone was impatient to get on with it. December 1943 had netted but five kills and the coveted 100 destroyed mark had yet to be reached.

Operational Diary—1944

1 January 1944: Lt. Col. Donald J. M. Blakeslee took command of the Group as Col. Peterson left to serve as Combat Operations Officer for 9th Air Force Headquarters. Blakeslee wasted little time in setting his priorities for the unit. It was clear he wanted to be CO of the best outfit in the AAF and one of the first things he did was twist brass ears to get the 4th re-equipped with North American Aviation's Merlin-engined Mustang.

4 January 1944: F.O. 212. Lt. Col. Blakeslee led a Ramrod Penetration Support to Munster, Germany, from 0900 to 1200 hours. Rendezvous was made in the target area at 1024 at 27,000 feet as the Group flew a port orbit in back of the rear box of bombers. The Thunderbolts flew all the way up the bomber stream and came out over Ijmuiden at 1053, flying at 21,000.

5 January 1944: F.O. 213. Lt. Col. Blakeslee was out front again on a Target Support to Tours airdrome, France, from 1030 to 1340 hours. After rendezvous with the lead bomber units near Vibraye at 1129, escort was provided to the target and on to Laflesche where the P-47s turned for home at 1155. Blakeslee tried to bounce a Do 217 but some other P-47s got it first. Ten to fifteen miles west of the target four 190s were bounced by 336 Blue Section. The Focke Wulfs turned into the attack, allowing 336 Red Section to come in from behind and get two of them.

[Box Score: 2 destroyed, 0 lost]

7 January 1944: F.O. 215. Lt. Col. Blakeslee led a Withdrawal Support under Type 16 Control to Ludwigshafen, Germany, from 1140 to 1440 hours. After being vectored around over France, "Jensen" took the Group to rendezvous with the bomber stream over Lens at 23,000 feet. Near Hesdin, France, 12 FW 190s came down from above and up-sun in finger-fours to attack straggling B-17s in the lowest box. Blakeslee led the bounce, engaging the 190s in combat from 24,-000 to 3,000 feet. With three Focke Wulfs on his tail pumping his Thunderbolt full of holes, Blakeslee shot one down. Goodson and Wehrman came to the rescue, the former downing two of the 190s. That evening 71 holes were counted in Blakeslee's WD-C after a forced landing at Manston.

[Box Score: 3 destroyed, 0 lost]

11 January 1944: F.O. 216. Lt. Col. Blakeslee led a Withdrawal Support to Oschersleben, Germany, from 1109 to 1330 hours. Cloud and haze caused the

Group to split up into sections while continuing on to the Zuider Zee, where "Upper" ordered all aircraft to return at 1212. The bombers were never sighted.

14 January 1944: F.O. 217. Lt. Col. Edner led a Free Lance to Magny–Soissons, France, under Type 16 Control from 1345 to 1630 hours. The formation crossed the enemy coast at 1428 at 25,000 feet, arriving over Magny at 1445. After a port orbit, the 4th flew south when 15 FW 190s were spotted east of the formation, 3,000 feet below. 336 made the bounce, engaging the Huns from 18,000 to the deck. Don Gentile made a head-on run with two of them. They broke, allowing "Gentle" to chase and shoot both of them down, making him an ace. With two 190s still on his tail, he heard numerous strikes all over his Thunderbolt. He turned into them and promptly ran out of ammunition, watching one of the Focke Wulfs stick to him, flown by an old pro. Fifty feet over the forest of Compiegne Gentile let out over the R/T, "Help! Help! I'm being clobbered!" Other 4th pilots radioed back but Don was too rattled to answer. All he could do was keep turning into the expert in the other cockpit. After 15 minutes of reversing turns and head-on attacks, the German ran out of ammunition and both fighters turned for home. Gentile remembered the encounter as his most critical, since he felt he could honestly beat any foe from that point on, having met the best. The Group reformed and was vectored near Soissons where 12 190s were seen 2,000 feet below the P-47s. 334 made the attack, fighting all the way down to 2,000 feet. Near Cambrai another quartet of Focke Wulfs attacked Whalen and Rafalovich but they managed to share in shooting one down. The Group crossed out at 1528, flying at 25,000 feet.

[Box Score: 8 destroyed, 0 lost]

19 January 1944: Col. "Hub" Zemke, the very able leader of the 56th Fighter Group, just back from the U.S., stopped by Debden to give a talk. Respect for the man rivaled that given to Blakeslee.

21 January 1944: F.O. 221. Lt. Col. Blakeslee led a Free Lance Support under Type 16 Control to Soissons–Amiens, France, from 1249 to 1621 hours. The Thunderbolts were vectored to Lille at 27,000 feet to meet the Big Friends, then from Ghent to Amiens–Arras where 12 enemy aircraft were sighted at 10,000. 336 tangled and got one FW 190 at 1504. The Group came out at Cap Gris Nez at 1524 and 19,000 feet.

[Box Score: 1 destroyed, 0 lost]

24 January 1944: F.O. 222. Lt. Col. Blakeslee led an Area Support to Malmedy–Brussels, Belgium, from 1100 to 1415 hours for '17s and '24s going to Frankfurt. "Col. Don" took the Group to the RV point over Malmedy at 25,000 feet and orbited three times as directed by the controller. Three other P-47 groups were there doing the same thing. Blakeslee finally headed for home via Brussels where the 4th orbited once, seeing Spitfires and more Thunderbolts near Lille. The Controller vectored them toward the friendlies before the Group left via Ostend at 1315.

26 January 1944: The first U.S.-trained pilots arrived at Debden, flying on ops three days later. An adjustment? Blakeslee didn't give a flip as long as everyone performed as expected. This could not have been better illustrated this same day when Robert Hills got a week's duty on the control car as punishment for damaging the tail of his kite on a trailer-water tank while parking in the bay after dive-bombing practice.

29 January 1944: F.O. 226. From 0915 to 1230 hours Lt. Col. Edner led a Penetration Support to Maastricht, Netherlands, for Flying Fortresses going to Frankfurt. Rendezvous was made at 1027, at 24,000 feet. Edner broke escort northeast of Malmedy at 1046. Near Maastricht 16-plus Bf 109s were sighted flying 3,000 feet below the Group in staggered line astern. 334 made the bounce at 1105. As the raging combat progressed to Hasselt four FW 190s got in 334's way, flying 5,000 feet under the formation. Six 109s and two 190s went down for the loss of Burton Wyman.

[Box Score: 8 destroyed, 1 lost]

30 January 1944: F.O. 227. Lt. Col. Blakeslee led a Penetration Support to the Lingren area in Germany from 1010 to 1310 hours. No bombers showed at the RV point so the Group continued on to the Lingren area, orbited three times at 27,-000 feet and got bounced by 15 enemy aircraft. 335 took them on and another eight 190s entered the fight from 32,000. After it was all over Charles Anderson downed one while the 4th lost Edwin Mead.

[Box Score: 1 destroyed, 1 lost]

31 January 1944: W.F.O. 85. Capt. Raymond Care led the Group's first dive-bombing show from 1354 to 1615 hours to Gilze–Rijen airdrome, Netherlands. Half of the Thunderbolts flew as "bombers" while the others flew top cover. Crossing the coast at Schouwen at 1442, flying at 25,000 feet, the Thunderbolts turned to enable the formation to make a bomb run from south to north to avoid enemy aircraft. Commencing a 70° dive from 20,000 feet, each pilot released at 8/9,000 feet, pulling out at 5/6,000. After dropping 17 500-pound general purpose bombs, the "bombers" reformed at 16,000 feet and left via Schouwen at 1525. There were numerous hits on the fuel dump southwest of the airdrome with large fires and black smoke rising to 3,000 feet. Three hits were made on the west end of the runway. Meanwhile the "fighters" had been doing their job—15 to 20 Bf 109s bounced the Group at 1455 from 5,000 feet above as it was inbound to the target. More Messerschmitts joined the fight and by the time the airdrome was reached, six more 109s engaged the P-47s from 6,000 feet above. All three squadrons got two each while keeping the Germans away from the dive bombers. After the combat, the "fighters" swept to Lille, coming out at 1540 and 16,000 feet.

[Box Score: 6 destroyed, 0 lost]

2 February 1944: F.O. 231. Lt. Col. Edner led the 4th's P-47s on a Free Lance to Brussels–Mons, Belgium, from 1248 to 1520 hours. Coming in north of Mardyck, the Group was vectored to Brussels, made a port orbit to Mons and came home.

3 February 1944: F.O. 233. Lt. Col. Edner led a Ramrod Penetration Support to Emden, Germany, from 0949 to 1300 hours. The Group arrived at the rendezvous point but the bombers never showed up. At 1056 Edner decided to join on 40 B-17s of the 1st Division. Five minutes later he saw his original charges hitting Emden. The Thunderbolts wheeled over to join this force and bring it home. One pilot was lost in icing and cloud.

[Box Score: 0 destroyed, 1 lost]

4 February 1944: F.O. 234. Maj. Clark led another Ramrod Penetration Support in Duren–Frankfurt, Germany, from 1010 to 1300 hours after Blakeslee aborted due to belly-tank feed problems. Rendezvous was made at 1118 at 25,000 feet. The Group broke off at 1132 for England.

5 February 1944: Lt. Col. Edner led a Free Lance under Type 16 Control to Paris–Rouen, France, from 0943 to 1240 hours. Entering at Le Treport, the Group was vectored to Beauvais. After patrolling Paris to Rouen, the P-47s came out at Etretat.

6 February 1944: F.O. 236. Lt. Col. Blakeslee was back up front again leading his fighters on a Penetration Target Support to Romilly, France, from 0938 to 1235 hours. The Group rendezvoused with the rear bomber boxes at 1048, flying at 25,-000 feet. Fifteen to 20 Bf 109s and FW 190s were engaged in a running battle from 20 miles south to 20 miles north of Paris at 22,000 feet. The fight worked its way down to 12,000 before the thirsty Thunderbolts turned for Debden. Hubert Ballew was shot down by a 190 to become a POW but a 109 and two 190s were destroyed. A few pilots came home with shot up kites.

[Box Score: 3 destroyed, 1 lost]

8 February 1944: F.O. 237. Lt. Col. Blakeslee led the Group on a Penetration Support to St. Vith–Dorsel, Belgium, from 0950 to 1245 hours. The Thunderbolts rendezvoused with the bombers at 1058 at 25,000 feet. P-38s relieved the Group at Dorsel.

10 February 1944: F.O. 239. Lt. Col. Edner led another Penetration Support to Nienburg, Germany, from 0939 to 1255 hours. The P-47s became separated in mid-Channel due to high cloud but contact was made at 1102 with the bombers. The Huns were determined to stop the effort, engaging the formation from Holland to Hannover all the way from 28,000 feet to the deck. Twenty-five to 30 109s and 190s hit the bombers head-on with determined aggressiveness. H. T. Biel and a 78th Group '47 formed to chase several Huns. Vic France joined his Pectin (334) Red Section to Shirtblue (336) Squadron—they were jumped just after crossing the Zuider Zee. Gerald Montgomery spun out after bouncing five 109s east of Zwolle, finally joining four 78th Thunderbolts to come home. Before the 4th broke escort at 1118, three 190s and five 109s were destroyed.

[Box Score: 8 destroyed, 0 lost]

Upon landing at Debden, 334 pilots gathered for a ceremony to pay £30 to the pilot who got #50 for the Squadron. After the 31 January mission, 334 had reached

48 destroyed—all 30 pilots contributed £1 for the lucky winner. Since France, Montgomery and Biel each claimed one destroyed, the prize was split three ways.

11 February 1944: F.O. 240. Lt. Col. Blakeslee led a Withdrawal Support to Frankfurt, Germany, from 1100 to 1415 hours. The Group joined up with the 353rd Fighter Group to search for their Big Friends without success. Blakeslee initiated an orbit and then spotted three boxes of Forts to the south. He met the lead aircraft at 1245 and stayed until 1310 before heading back to the barn.

12 February 1944: F.O. 241. Lt. Col. Clark led a Ramrod under Type 16 Control to Montvider–Frevent, France, from 0905 to 1210 hours. A solid undercast prevailed for the entire mission.

14 February 1944: The first three P-51B Mustangs assigned to the Group arrived, one to each squadron. Sitting out on the grass for all to see, the kites generated a ripple of excitement hard to conceal. Blakeslee made it clear he expected his pilots to check out in them between missions . . . if they couldn't hack it maybe another group would suit them.

15 February 1944: W.F.O. 89. Lt. Col. Edner led a Dive Bombing/Fighter Sweep to Chievres airdrome, France, from 1329 to 1600 hours. The Thunderbolts were divided up into 24 "bombers" with 25 covering fighters. The formation was recalled due to weather but Greenbelt (335) leader swept south to Amiens–Rouen before coming out via Boulogne.

19 February 1944: Debden was the target of an air raid at 0100 hours. Thirty to 40 enemy aircraft dropped 1,100 two-pound incendiary clusters and eight HE bombs in the woods one-half mile south of the field.

20 February 1944: F.O. 245. Capt. Goodson led a Withdrawal Support to Kirkburg, Germany, from 1250 to 1625 hours. The Group rendezvoused with two combat bomb wings of B-24s and five combat bomb wings of B-17s at 1429, flying at 23,000 feet northeast of Koblenz. Five Bf 109s attacked with rockets and 335 engaged. Near Malmedy eight FW 190s attacked the first box from the rear. Mills, Beeson and McKennon each got one. Before Richard Reed was shot down and killed he shared a Bf 110 with Paul Riley. This was the start of what later became known as the 8th Air Force Big Week, 20–25 February 1944.

[Box Score: 4 destroyed, 1 lost]

21 February 1944: F.O. 246. Lt. Col. Blakeslee was back in the lead saddle for a Penetration Support to Dummer Lake–Brunswick, Germany, from 1130 to 1610 hours. The Group rendezvoused with three combat bomb wings of Flying Fortresses at 1314 at 26,000 feet. At 1340, 15 FW 190s were bounced by 334 at 15,-000 feet. David Howe and Raymond Care got one apiece but Care ended up with his hydraulic pressure shot out, landing at Debden without flaps. Raymond Clotfelter got an Me 210. Escort was broken near Dummer Lake at 1346.

[Box Score: 3 destroyed, 0 lost]

22 February 1944: F.O. 247. Lt. Col. Blakeslee led a Withdrawal Support to Aachen–Schweinfurt, Germany, from 1313 to 1700 hours. The Group split up due to weather. 334 and 336 joined up on the Rhine between Koblenz and Bonn with 24 1st Division B-17s at 1503. At 1517 eight FW 190s attacked a circling B-17 at 9,-000 feet and 335 engaged, getting two of them. McKennon got a 109 at the same time. The Group left their charges at 1535 south of Brussels.

[Box Score: 3 destroyed, 0 lost]

23 February 1944: During the 4th's only respite from ops during Big Week, a big batch of Mustangs was delivered to Debden. 335 pilots had to borrow 334 P-47s in order to get enough kites to fly their missions since the "milk bottles" were being shipped out to make room for the P-51s. In spite of daily combat missions, the pilots were getting time in the new fighters—no one wanted to let the Old Man down.

24 February 1944: F.O. 250. Lt. Col. Edner led a Withdrawal Support to north of Koblenz–Schweinfurt, Germany, from 1225 to 1530 hours. The Group rendezvoused north of Koblenz at 1402 with four combat bomb wings of Forts and one wing of Liberators at 25,000 feet. As the P-47s pulled in, four FW 190s attacked the B-24s head-on. The upper squadron drove them off when four more 190s and four 109s were engaged by the other two squadrons. One Focke Wulf was downed but Joseph Sullivan was killed.

[Box Score: 1 destroyed, 1 lost]

Ten more Mustangs were assigned to both 334 and 336, eleven to 335.

25 February 1944: F.O. 251. Lt. Col. Edner led the last Big Week mission, a Penetration Support to Sedan–Stuttgart, Germany, from 1103 to 1425 hours. After joining up with the bombers near Sedan at 1220, the Group saw five FW 190s make frontal attacks on a B-17, shooting out one engine—seven chutes were seen. Gentile, Garrison and Herter got three of the Huns. Then four more 190s were bounced—Beeson and McKennon got one each. The Group broke away for Debden at 1302.

[Box Score: 5 destroyed, 0 lost]

Fifteen more P-51Bs arrived at the field. By this time the ground crews had their hands full trying to get about 50 Mustangs ready for combat. Before morning all of the kites had been painted in QP, WD, VF livery in anticipation of the first Mustang show the next day. The hangars looked like the North American factory.

26 February 1944: Weather scrubbed the 4th's Mustang debut but at least there was time for more familiarization. Mike Sobanski was up at 1135 in his new kite, QP-F, for a weather recce. Coming back in, he put his wheels down and entered the circuit. Thinking his wheels were still up, he flipped the undercarriage lever up, lowered flaps and belly landed the machine. Hell hath no fury like Blakeslee over a pranged kite, particularly over a new Mustang. Why couldn't it have been one of the seven-ton monsters?

27 February 1944: At 1315 a Rolls-Royce technical representative held a briefing on the P-51. Blakeslee held a discussion on flying problems with the Mustang, which had been disappointingly numerous. A plague of mechanical gremlins diminished the pilots' enthusiasm for the highly touted fighter. Jim Goodson, Willard Millikan and George Carpenter had bounced the new paddle-bladed P-47s of the 56th and frustratedly reported that *these* Thunderbolts were a match for the Mustang upstairs and downstairs. This added to the air of uncertainty.

28 February 1944: F.O. 254. Maj. Clark led the first Mustang mission, a Free Lance under Type 16 Control with two 75-gallon drop tanks under the wings of each kite, to Noball targets at Boulogne–Compiegne, France, from 1310 to 1620 hours. Both 334 and 336 got 12 aircraft up while 335 put up 11, but there were several aborts due to mechanical problems. The 4th reached the IP at 1411 at 14,000 feet but no enemy aircraft were found despite much "Jensen" vectoring from England. Northeast of Paris a section went down to beat up an airdrome in the Soissons area—Bill Smith, Cowboy Megura, Duane Beeson and Vermont Garrison teamed up on a single Ju 88 about to take off, blowing it to pieces.

[Box Score: 1 destroyed, 0 lost]

29 February 1944: F.O. 255. Capt. Goodson led a Target Support to Minden–Brunswick, Germany, from 0850 to 1330 hours. The Mustangs rendezvoused with the bombers at 1040 southeast of Minden to travel to the target and back with no encounters. Several pilots dropped down to strafe. The P-51's ugly side reared its head—Mills' prop began throwing oil and his wing tanks would not feed; Biel's cooling system and R/T went out; Rafalovich could not get enough manifold pressure and his R/T also quit. France, Chatterley and Smith could not catch up with the Group. All six were forced to abort the mission.

After everyone got back a bunch of disgruntled pilots went to the briefing room at 1645 to hear a 354th Group pilot talk about mechanical failures with the Merlin engine.

These first two Mustang missions were flown with some pilots having less than an hour in the aircraft. After itching for sleek, inline fighters to replace the bulky P-47, the 4th's pilots were increasingly leery of the P-51. Yet the new kite held great promise for the 4th. Beeson's logbook entry on 28 February read, "First show on Mustangs. VERY SWEET AIRCRAFT!" That it was, when everything held together. Blakeslee was determined to see these teething problems through, even though his P-51B never quite ran the way it should have.

Range also effectively doubled with the Mustang. Shows increased from three to six hours in length and the deeper the Group went in search of the enemy, the more good hunting could be found. Gentile recalled that at last the Group had a fighter that "could go in the front door of the enemy's home and blow down the back door and beat up all the furniture in between." The Thunderbolt's limited endurance had tied it very closely to the bombers but the Mustang opened the way for the most destructive force the Luftwaffe ever faced . . . bands of fighters that would range the Third Reich at will, free to hunt and destroy their prey.

To the credit of both pilots and ground crew, it must be remembered that the

8th Air Force's Big Week maximum effort came smack in the middle of Blakeslee's efforts to get his men operational on the Mustang. The Group flew the Big Week missions in their P-47s while attempting to master what had become a very tough mount to break. Little did anyone know (with the possible exception of Don Blakeslee) that the now wild Mustang would be harnessed and tamed to carry the 4th Fighter Group into the greatest months of its career, March and April 1944.

2 March 1944: F.O. 257. Lt. Col. Edner led a Target Withdrawal Support to northeast of Trier–Frankfurt, Germany, from 1030 to 1450 hours. Rendezvous with the B-17s was made northeast of Trier at 1145 hours, 23/27,000 feet. Other P-51s were with the bombers as well. At 1155 near St. Goar, six enemy aircraft were spotted weaving several miles ahead and parallel to the bomber stream. What turned out to be 109s turned in for head-on attacks. Three were engaged, one destroyed. At 1157 ten FW 190s made a head-on run from above to the lead box and 336 went after them, getting one destroyed and one damaged. One pilot was lost. P-47s joined the bombers at 1300 and escort was broken in stages from 1318 to 1345.

[Box Score: 2 destroyed, 1 lost]

3 March 1944: F.O. 259. Lt. Col. Blakeslee led a Target Support to Berlin, Germany, from 0934 to 1510 hours. The Group rendezvoused with a ragged formation of B-17s and B-24s at 1120 near Neumunster, flying at 28,000 feet. Aborts of several formations due to weather were reported and the 4th left the bombers at 1240 near Terschelling Island on the way back. Deacon Hively successfully directed an air-sea rescue search on the way back, finding the pilot in a dinghy, then directing a Walrus to him. From 1130 to 1150 336 got into a tremendous fight near Wittenberg with 60 plus Huns apparently sent up to deal with bombers that had already turned back. Gentile got two 190s while Carlson, Millikan and Garrison got 110s. Glenn Herter was killed at the beginning of the fight after being lured after the low decoy. Garrison got a 190 but was shot down by flak near Boulogne at 1410 to become a POW. "Pappy" Dunn got a 210 but then got lost on the way home. With no radio, he decided to make for Spain, running out of gas as he shot down an He 111. He bailed out to become a POW eight miles from the border.

[Box Score: 8 destroyed, 4 lost]

4 March 1944: F.O. 260. Lt. Col. Blakeslee led the first full escort mission to Berlin, a Target Support, from 1020 to 1600 hours. The P-51s rendezvoused with 60 B-17s at 1230 north of Kassel. Prior to the IP, 20 109s and 190s were encountered at bomber level. Eight attacked in fours head-on, then dispersed while the rest remained as top cover. Then the last 12 bounced the Group but the attacks seemed half-hearted and the 109s were easily outclimbed. During combat several pilots were hampered by windscreen frost and jammed guns. Hugh Ward went after a Hun only to be pursued by a 109. Megura latched on to give aid as the four aircraft went straight down. At 18,000 feet and 550 mph indicated, Ward's canopy, wing and tail came off, hitting Megura's kite. Ward got out to become a POW and the 109 pilot jumped at 3,000 feet. Paul Ellington had engine trouble and was forced to bail out over the Dutch coast, also becoming a prisoner. Bob Richards was killed when he went in near Framlingham returning from the show. Blakeslee returned fuming—his guns wouldn't fire at all.

[Box Score: 4 destroyed, 3 lost]

5 March 1944: F.O. 261. Lt. Col. Blakeslee led a Target Support to Limoges airdrome, France, from 0859 to 1520 hours. The Mustangs rendezvoused with the lead box of B-24s west of Cognac. Blakeslee was forced to abort due to a rough engine, leaving Beeson in charge. South of Bordeaux two 190s and four 109s made a head-on attack against the bombers—Steve Pisanos got two and two more were damaged. Beeson got a 109 but got his tail feathers all shot up in the process, while Hively got two. Several FW 200s were caught near Bordeaux and three were destroyed. Jim Dye got a 190. At 1330 Pisanos was forced to bail but he was half in and half out when the '51 hit the ground—he survived to become an evader, returning to Debden in September.

[Box Score: 9 destroyed, 1 lost]

6 March 1944: F.O. 262. Lt. Col. Blakeslee led another Target Support back to Berlin, Germany, from 0955 to 1535 hours. Rendezvous was made with the B-17s at 1210, at 23,000 feet. At 1240 the Germans mounted a mass attack. Thirty single engine fighters made head-on attacks from 27,000 while 40 to 50 twin-engine destroyers attacked abeam and astern. The Group engaged on all levels, becoming separated into sections and flights in a mass free-for-all. McKennon's comment was, "Huns? Millions, pal, millions!" Chatterley, closing on a 190 with Mills and two others, asked if they were going to take turns. "Hell no," Mills replied, "first one there gets him." Mills got him. Bernard McGrattan got a Ju 88 but picked up holes in each prop blade, setting up a tremendous vibration. He fought the 300-pound pressure on the stick all the way home by bracing it with his knees. He landed without brakes or trim. It was an incredible day with 17 claimed destroyed, though not all the claims were confirmed.

[Box Score: 13 destroyed, 4 lost]

7 March 1944: New spark plugs were put in all the kites to see if this might improve the engine problems.

8 March 1944: F.O. 263. Lt. Col. Edner led yet another Target Support to Berlin, Germany, from 1055 to 1630 hours. The Group found its charges, B-17s, northeast of Gardelegen at 1330, at 25/27,000 feet, relieving the escorting P-47s. The first German attack by 109s southwest of Brandenburg was intercepted and three destroyed. Then 60-plus Huns approached from the south at the same level and attacked in pairs and fours. Combats ranged from Genthin to south of Berlin at all levels. Several '17s were seen going down with chutes dotting the sky. Allan Bunte knocked down an Fi 156 by hopping over it on the deck, forcing it to crash into the tree tops. Most of the Group got trapped east of Berlin from 1320 to

1420, forcing the pilots to fly toward Russia. Gentile and Godfrey made their first classic team fight over the suburbs of Berlin, downing six 109s between them and bringing Johnny home an ace. Gentile also tied Beeson at 14 to begin their famous scoring race. Megura entered a landing pattern with 190s and 109s west of Berlin and proceeded to blast one of each out of the sky, giving him ace status as well. In spite of claims of 16 destroyed, rough engines and unservicable drop tanks were the order of the day. Seldon Edner also went down to be captured. Regardless of the problems, the P-51 was taking the Group out into the action . . . and could it fight!

[Box Score: 16 destroyed, 1 lost]

9 March 1944: F.O. 264. Newly promoted Col. Blakeslee led a Target Support to Oranienburg, Germany, from 1008 to 1555 hours. Rendezvous was made at 1255 as the Group throttled back to let the stream catch up, then left to join another force at 1330. Leaving them over the target at 1400 and 20/23,000 feet, Col. Don brought his Mustangs past the first force on the way out. Not a single German aircraft rose to challenge the formations.

13–15 March 1944: In spite of the successes against the Germans, the P-51s were mechanical nightmares and they were grounded. Rough engines, props throwing oil, glycol leaks and auxiliary tank feed problems were causing aborts on every mission. These two days all the wing bolts were replaced and the engine mount bolts were magnifluxed, but these precautions weren't effective. On the 17th Burtonwood manufactured new motor mount bolts but even these turned out to be unsatisfactory and by April North American had to rush 250 sets to VIII FC.

Table II prop kits for the Mustang arrived in February and March stripped and useless, so propellers continued to be in short supply until July. V-1650 engines were also in short supply through March and April. All this added up to low mission strengths for quite awhile. Many times a squadron was able to get but 10 aircraft up for a mission. To get 20 up was a minor miracle.

Yet there were the bright notes during the stand-down period. Burtonwood had come up with oxygen kits for the P-51 that would allow pilots to stay at higher altitudes longer. One of the first problems encountered with the Mustang's range was its ability to fly farther and higher than there was oxygen to let the pilot go along with it.

Secondly, on the 15th, what became known as the 4th's trademark was handed down on verbal orders from Group Materiel. Those flaming red noses appeared on the Mustangs as crews busily painted over the white ETO recognition paint that made all groups look the same.

Yet the gloom over losses due to engine problems was hard to dispel. At least five pilots went down during March due to glycol and engine failures, possibly more since several losses are noted as due to unknown causes. The gunnery and electrical systems also failed with regularity, resulting in lost kills. And the installation of the 65-gallon upright tank behind the pilot's seat without baffle plates to prevent violent shifts in the center of gravity was considered a nightmare by several pilots. Peter Lehman's death on the 31st was attributed to this when his P-51 flicked over and spun in during a low level mock dogfight near Duxford.

These were certainly days filled with mixed emotions, since the Mustang was both providing the Group with its finest hour and robbing it of much success and personnel at the same time. Blakeslee's crew chief, Harry East, Jr., never could get the right bank of the Chief Cook's Merlin to quit smoking and missing. Col. Don kept the kite, though, because it was fitted with a better-vision Malcolm hood. 43-6437 was not replaced until a hydraulic line was perforated, much to East's relief. Blakeslee was determined to lead the way in the face of all the mechanical difficulties.

16 March 1944: F.O. 270. Col. Blakeslee led a Target Support to Munich, Germany, from 0940 to 1450 hours. Rendezvous with five combat bomb wings of B-17s was made at 1150 southeast of Stuttgart, 18/20,000 feet. The Group stationed itself as high cover at 26,000 feet since other P-51s were escorting the bombers as well. At 1150 seven Bf 110s engaged the bombers from the rear and the Group swooped down to destroy five. Combats with more 110s went below the cloud deck to 6,000 feet and 12 to 20 Bf 109s joined the fight at 1200. Despite the fighter cover and the loss of Ernest Skilton, the 4th destroyed eight more 110s below the undercast in a hard fight. In spite of several aborts due to rough engines the boys came home happy to a medicinal issue of 60cc (2 oz) of whiskey each.

[Box Score: 13 destroyed, 1 lost]

18 March 1944: F.O. 273A. Col. Blakeslee took the troops back to Munich on a Target Withdrawal Support from 1140 to 1735. At 1335 eight to ten 109s were encountered east of Manheim. Four sections dropped 5,000 feet and bounced, destroying five. Afterwards they dropped down to strafe rather than follow the planned route. The rest of the Group rendezvoused with the B-17s east of Augsburg at 1425 at 20/25,000 feet, only to find them under attack by 60-plus enemy fighters. Aggressive and determined, the Germans gave both bombers and fighters a rough time, yet three 190s were destroyed. The roving sections managed to get three He 111s on the way out as well. There were still rough engine aborts and Woodrow Sooman became a POW after leaving his glycol-spewing Mustang. Ed Freeburger was killed near Nancy at 1435 in a fight with four Huns.

[Box Score: 12 destroyed, 2 lost]

19 March 1944: W.F.O. 71. Capt. Sobanski led an Area Support for 78th Fighter Group dive bombers to Eindhoven airdrome, Netherlands, from 1605 to 1845 hours. The Group crossed in at 1701 over Katwijk Van Zee at 26,000 feet. The Mustangs orbited Eindhoven, then set course south of Brussels, coming out at 1802 without encountering the enemy.

20 March 1944: F.O. 275. Maj. Carpenter led a Target Withdrawal Support to Frankfurt, Germany, from 1000 to 1445 hours. Remaining on course until 1119, the Group found no bombers. Thirty-one Forts were found near Limburg at 1145, at 24/25,000 feet. After escorting these bombers to the target, the Group broke away at 1340 near Amiens. 334 separated to escort eight straggling '17s out to Dieppe.

21 March 1944: W.F.O. 92. Maj. Clark led a Fighter Sweep to the Bordeaux, France, area from 1145 to 1630 hours. Making landfall at 1232 near Fecamp, the Group stacked from 18,000 to 25,000 feet. The 8th Air Force did not have a show laid on for this day but the Group asked to go under Wing approval. The formation swept south until 1330 when 336 turned port as planned. 334 and 335 turned starboard. For about four hours the Group ranged over German fields in France, destroying aircraft in the air and on the ground, from He 177s to FW 190s. But the price was high—two killed, four POWs, one evader. William Hawkins evaded and got back on 16 July; Earle Carlow was captured but he escaped and returned on 10 June. In addition James Dye, hit in the leg by flak, returned to base but did not resume combat.

[Box Score: 20 destroyed, 7 lost]

22 March 1944: F.O. 277. Col. Blakeslee led a Penetration Target Support to Berlin, Germany, from 1000 to 1520 hours. Rendezvous was made 20 miles southwest of Neumunster at 1210, 22/23,000 feet. Only six 190s were seen in the distance near Berlin. After all the action of the previous several days the quiet was a letdown . . . "Ho, hum," came over the R/T and Beeson noted in his log book, "No Huns up today! What's wrong with them?" The Group was getting a real taste for action in their new birds, regardless of mechanical problems. Escort was broken at 1350 north of Steinhuder Lake.

23 March 1944: F.O. 278. Col. Blakeslee led a Target Support to Brunswick, Germany, from 0900 to 1255 hours. Rendezvous was made south of Steinhuder Lake at 1120 and 24,000 feet with P-38s in the vicinity. The bombers were under heavy attack from all directions by 25-plus 109s and 190s. The Group engaged and got into a roaring fight down to 3,000 feet, destroying 10. Before the Group left via Schouwen at 1210 with the bombers, another two enemy aircraft were destroyed. The mission was a cause for celebration—there were no losses. And no aborts for the first time. Duane Beeson was in his prime, noting in his log, "I got 2 109s + dam. a train. Had a hell of a fight with one of them. Lots of fun!" The Blakeslee-inspired spirit of combat being great sport was certainly no myth in the 4th.

[Box Score: 12 destroyed, 0 lost]

24 March 1944: F.O. 279. Maj. Clark led a Penetration Target Withdrawal Support to Schweinfurt, Germany, from 0725 to 1230 hours. Rendezvous was made southeast of Brussels at 0840 over 10/10ths cloud. One Ju 52 was engaged but it escaped into the clouds. Escort was broken at 1156 near Mardyck.

27 March 1944: F.O. 282. Maj. Clark led a Target Support and Free Lance to Pau-Pont Long airdrome, Bordeaux, France, from 1200 to 1750 hours. Rendezvous was made with the B-17s at 1407 over the Bay of Biscay at 20/25,000 feet. The bombers had a P-38 escort so Clark went on to join other B-17s and B-24s at 1419 flying at 12,000 feet. 335 continued on the planned route while 334 and 336 provided escort to Cayaux airdrome. After the field was bombed the two squadrons went down and tore the place apart from 1445 to 1500, destroying 23 on the ground and one in the air. 335 got two 190s at 1520 near Bordeaux during its escort to Pont Long. Archie Chatterley was hit by flak, bailing out to become a POW.

[Box Score: 26 destroyed, 1 lost]

28 March 1944: F.O. 283. Maj. Clark led a Target Withdrawal Support to Chateaudun airdrome, France, from 1221 to 1600 hours. The Group rendezvoused with the B-17s 20 miles southwest of Lisieux at 1348 and 20/23,000 feet. The formation was over the target at 1415 and several dropped down to strafe Dreux/Vernavillet airdrome. One enemy aircraft was destroyed but Raymond Clotfelter had to bail out of his Mustang to be captured. The formation crossed out at Le Havre at 1455 and escort was broken at the English coast by 1520.

[Box Score: 1 destroyed, 1 lost]

29 March 1944: Newly promoted Lt. Col. Clark led a Target Withdrawal Support to Brunswick, Germany, from 1135 to 1645 hours. Rendezvous was made with the B-17s at 1315 near Nienburg with more bombers joining up at 1325 south of Celle as the two middle wings cut across north of the target. At 1330, near Gifhorn, 30-plus enemy aircraft approached the bombers from the northeast at 18,000 just as 15 single-engined fighters made a rear attack on the first wing from the south. The Group bounced both formations from 24,000 feet, breaking into numerous engagements all the way to the deck. By 1350 four more fighters attacked the lead boxes near Celle. H. T. Biel chased several FW 190s that came through at 1330. After getting a few strikes on one, Biel was chasing it around a small town. Closing to 200 yards, he severely damaged the 190 and started a fire after the belly tank blew up. The German flew into a snow storm and when the two adversaries emerged, Biel was alongside looking the German in the face. Biel slid back and did more damage to the cockpit area with his .50s, then came up and flew wing tip to wing tip on the FW's starboard side to see if the German was still alive. The Focke Wulf pilot looked at Biel much to the latter's amazement. More firing away until the German fighter was on fire from nose to tail. The canopy flew off but the German was too low to bail out. Biel pulled up alongside again and flew wing, right down to the German's perfect belly landing into a snow covered field. Biel did not see if his opponent got out of the flaming wreckage since flak was coming up all over the place. Kenneth Peterson and William Newell both became POWs—Peterson after attacking 12 enemy aircraft alone to rescue a B-17. He got two 190s before having his rudder shot away, which threw his '51 into an inverted spin but he bailed out at 10,000. Gentile got three himself and the Group racked up another 20-plus destroyed.

[Box Score: 24 destroyed, 2 lost]

By the end of March the Mustang was somewhat tamed—at least she wasn't biting as many pilots. But what an incredible jump in the Group's fortunes—an ETO record of 156 kills in one month. Blakeslee made it clear he thought the

Group was only beginning to get to work. He stated he wanted 200 destroyed in April and that people better start getting ready for the celebration.

1 April 1944: F.O. 286. Col. Blakeslee led a Fighter Sweep/Withdrawal Support to Ludwigshafen–Mannheim, Germany, from 0735 to 1305 hours. The sweep netted nothing until south of Stuttgart and north of Lake Constance—two boxes of Liberators were under attack by four to six 109s at 19,000 feet. The Group engaged down to 7,000 feet and came home with four destroyed, bringing the Group total to over 300 destroyed. Beeson and Gentile each got one, placing them at 21 and 22 kills respectively in their scoring race. The 56th Group was still ahead at 400 destroyed.

[Box Score: 4 destroyed, 0 lost]

5 April 1944: F.O. 288. Col. Blakeslee led a Jackpot Operation to several airdromes in Germany from 1237 to 1750 hours. The Group descended through cloud near Berlin at 1500 to attack Friedersdorf and did not stop until the P-51s had blasted Stendal, Plaue, Brandenburg and Pottsdam. The 4th came home with two air and 43 ground kills, 336 getting a record 26 for itself. Four pilots were lost—Carr, Bunte and Beeson, who all became POWs, and Robert Hobert, who died of exposure after going down in the North Sea. Gentile came home with five to bring him up to 27 kills but Beeson's loss damped the celebration.

[Box Score: 45 destroyed, 4 lost]

7 April 1944: Malcolm Ltd. delivered three blister canopies to Lieston for VIII FC tests on the P-51B series fighter. Blakeslee had wangled a "Malcolm hood" for his WD-C long before VIII FC began to test the improved canopy and he pushed to get the 4th re-equipped. By late September 1944 all VIII FC P-51B/C aircraft had them, but by then the 4th was getting as many P-51Ds as possible.

8 April 1944: F.O. 291. Maj. Carpenter led a Free Lance/General Support to Ulzen–Brunswick, Germany, from 1135 to 1620 hours. Southwest of Bremen the Group heard bombers calling for help. The Mustangs turned south and rendezvoused at 1300 near Nienburg with four combat bomb wings of B-24s at 22/25,-000 feet. Another group of P-51s was present so Carpenter broke escort east of Nienburg by pulling ahead of the formation. At 1320, near Celle, 75 to 100 190s and 109s were spotted coming for the bombers from the northeast at 21,000 in gaggles of threes and fours. The Group attacked and got into a fight that ranged over a 30-mile area from 23,000 to the deck, getting 33 and damaging nine. Gentile, Norley and Millikan each got three. The boys saw four to six '24s go down with chutes everywhere. Two pilots were killed and two taken prisoner.

[Box Score: 33 destroyed, 4 lost]

9 April 1944: F.O. 292. Col. Blakeslee led a Withdrawal Support to Tutow airdrome, Germany, from 1050 to 1505 hours. After a late take-off due to weather, the mission changed from a Target to a Withdrawal Support. Rendezvous was made with three wings of B-24s near Ulzen at 21/22,000 feet, 1250 hours. P-38s,

P-47s and P-51s were all escorting the formation so the 4th left to strafe two grass airfields near Osnabruck. Two Ju 88s and an Me 410 were destroyed but David Van Epps was hit by flak. Pulling up to 1,000 feet, he bailed, with his chute opening just before he landed between two houses.

[Box Score: 3 destroyed, 1 lost]

10 April 1944: F.O. 293. Lt. Col. Clark led a Jackpot under Type 16 Control to several airdromes in France from 0755 to 1150 hours. The Group swept Boissons, Melun, Cien, Tours, seeing bombers at 0950. Swinging east, the Group flew to Romorantin airdrome, making ten passes on the lightly defended training field. At 1005 the Group left the field, which was burning furiously with 28 destroyed aircraft for the loss of Clemens Fiedler.

[Box Score: 28 destroyed, 1 lost]

This mission put the Group at 405½ destroyed . . . ahead of the Wolf Pack! Debden's boys were, at last, to be reckoned with and slowly the term "Blakesleewaffe" began to emerge.

11 April 1944: F.O. 295. Maj. Carpenter led a Withdrawal Support to Cottbus–Sagan from 0935 to 1640 hours. Rendezvous was made ten miles southeast of Zielenzig with six wings at 12/18,000 feet, 1225 hours, as other '51s and '47s were leaving. At 1225 six Bf 110s at 10,000 came in from 5 o'clock to attack the low lead box. One section jumped them, destroying three. An Me 410 and a Do 217 were also bagged. Two Mustangs went down to strafe a grass field near Stargard, getting three on the ground and a Ju 88 at 8,000 which had taken off from the attacked field. The Group left the bombers between Kiel and Pellworm at 1430.

[Box Score: 9 destroyed, 0 lost]

Supreme Allied Commander Gen. Dwight Eisenhower visited the base with Doolittle, Spaatz, Auton and Kepner. Blakeslee staged a mock briefing, then narrated some combat film. Both Gentile and Blakeslee were awarded D.S.C.s, then "Ike" took a ride in a 55th Fighter Group P-38J Droopsnoot, CL-*X*.

12 April 1944: F.O. 296. Col. Blakeslee led a Target Support to Oschersleben–Magdeburg, Germany, from 1205 to 1645 hours. Ten miles northwest of Brunswick, at 1410, four 109s were bounced and destroyed by 335 at 15,000 feet. Magdeburg was made by 1420 but no bombers so the Group came home via Brunswick.

[Box Score: 4 destroyed, 0 lost]

13 April 1944: F.O. 298. Col. Blakeslee led a Target Withdrawal Support to Schweinfurt, Germany, from 1140 to 1640 hours. On the way cries were heard from the bombers under attack south of Aschaffenburg, so Blakeslee pushed up the speed to the RV point. Arriving at 1345, the boys found 20-plus FW 190s approaching from the northeast at 23,000 feet and engaged. In vigorous combat from 24,000 to 10,000 feet, the '51s broke up the enemy formation, causing the 190s to scatter. Georgia Wynn was shot down by one of the Focke Wulfs but

Cowboy Megura then shot the German down. Another four 190s were downed before the Group attached itself to four combat wings, providing cover for the rear two as P-38s covered the lead two. Escort was broken at 1557 east of Ghent. Ralph Saunders went down somewhere over Holland.

[Box Score: 5 destroyed, 2 lost]

Gentile came in low for the press cameras as the Group returned . . . and flew into the ground, totaling VF-T. Blakeslee could have fried him alive. Good thing it was Gentile's last mission before returning to the States—Ole Man River's law was that anyone who pranged a kite while stunting was immediately kicked out of the Group.

15 April 1944: F.O. 299. Capt. Care led another Jackpot to Juterbog airdrome, Germany, from 1130 to 1605 hours. The primary target was abandoned due to weather and the Group became split-up into sections. Three airdromes were attacked by small groups of aircraft—Magdeburg, Fassburg and Hagenow—and 13 aircraft were destroyed. Ray Care bailed out near Celle at 1445 to become a POW and Bob Siefert was killed after bailing out into the North Sea on the way in.

[Box Score: 13 destroyed, 2 lost]

16 April 1944: The 400 victory dance was held on base to the merriment of all. 334 also had it's callsign changed from Pectin to Cobweb. The three squadron callsigns were changed throughout the war, as were those used to designate the Group leader. Horseback became the trademark for Blakeslee in the air, although the term applied to whoever was leading the Group.

18 April 1944: F.O. 304. Col. Blakeslee was up front on a Penetration Target Withdrawal Support to Berlin, Germany, from 1200 to 1730 hours. Rendezvous was made at 1409 with five combat wings of B-17s southwest of Wittenburg at 25,000 feet. Other P-51s were already with the bombers. Near Rhin Canal 25-plus 109s and 190s attacked from 24/28,000 feet, from the northeast. The Group engaged and chased them into cloud at 1425 but not before three were destroyed. George Carpenter got two of these before going down near Rathenow to be captured. Escort was broken near Stendal at 1450 when P-38s came in. 334 dropped down to strafe Juterbog and Fassberg, getting several kills. North of Genthin four 109s were caught landing. France, Seims and Megura teamed up to get one but France flew into the ground and was killed chasing another 109. Lloyd Henry was killed in the same fight that claimed Carpenter.

[Box Score: 19 destroyed, 3 lost]

19 April 1944: F.O. 305. Capt. Sobanski led a Target Withdrawal Support to Eschwege, Germany, from 0815 to 1250 hours. The Group joined up with five combat wings of B-17s at 21/24,000 feet northeast of Eschwege at 1023. Over 50 enemy fighters attacked the rear boxes at 1025, going through the formation in sixes and eights. The Group bounced and fought the Germans from 25,000 feet to the deck, destroying several. There were no further attacks and escort was broken at 1103 over the Rhine River as '47s and '38s provided close escort for the Big

Friends' journey home. Some of the guys were a bit disconcerted that the Forts fired on them when they were cutting off the enemy attacks.

[Box Score: 6 destroyed, 1 lost]

20 April 1944: F.O. 307. Capt. Sobanski led a Fighter Sweep under Type 16 Control to Paris–Epernay–Rouen, France, from 1700 to 2040 hours. The Mustangs were over Cisors by 1803 at 25,000 feet. "Snackbar" vectored the boys over the three cities but no enemy aircraft were sighted.

New, water-filled G-suits arrived for the pilots to get used to. Five hours practice in the "Zoot suits" were required before taking them into combat, but, as it turned out, they were never used in combat.

22 April 1944: F.O. 309. Col. Blakeslee led a Fighter Sweep from 1620 to 2030 hours to Kassel–Hamm, Germany, in support of the bombers. Several aborts resulted from problems with the new paper "babies" hung on the wings. Though these external tanks would later become standard equipment, they caused headaches at first. By 1757, as the Group passed Kassel at 18,000, 20-plus Messerschmitts formed up 12,000 feet below. Losing altitude by orbiting, the Group bounced the Germans and fought them to Warburg and south to Eder Lake. Several 109s attempted to shake off the Mustangs by aerobatics right on the deck but the boys destroyed one after the other. Robert Nelson's engine failed in the middle of a fight but he bailed out and ended up in a tree. The Germans didn't catch him until four days later. In 25 minutes Willard Millikan managed to shoot down four 109s near Sachenhausen . . . with only 666 rounds. Godfrey got three, Blakeslee two.

[Box Score: 17 destroyed, 1 lost]

At 1400, before the mission, Blakeslee gathered his squadron commanders and flight leaders to tell them that there would be flying from dawn to dusk, especially for the newer pilots.

23 April 1944: In keeping with his firm talk of the day before, Col. Don wrote a stern letter to what he considered his increasingly lax men: They were to wear proper uniform, eat at specified times, show up for duty on time, control dogs, salute, participate in athletics, have no unauthorized use of Group vehicles . . . "I want to say that we are just beginning to work—the busy season is at hand. We have been living under very easy conditions for a long time and some of us still want to 'be babied.' Already I hear complaints of overwork, references to rotation, promotions and petty problems. For these I have no sympathy. The next few months will test the 'guts' of a lot of people. I hope you stand the test. Let's get to work and keep the finger out—way out! (signed) Donald J. M. Blakeslee, Colonel, Air Corps, Commanding." Blakeslee expected as much from his men as he did from himself . . . and no less. That night the Group flew practice until after midnight.

24 April 1944: F.O. 312. Col. Blakeslee led a Free Lance Support to Munich, Germany, from 1055 to 1520 hours. The Group arrived over Frankfurt at 1233 at 18,000 feet, then turned south and let down to 10,000. Just north of Worms, 34

190s and 109s were spotted heading down the Rhine. The 4th engaged at 1245 hours and clobbered the Huns. Three pilots were lost—two became prisoners and H. T. Biel was killed in aerial combat. Jim Goodson got two 109s this day, while over Wiener Neustadt with the 31st Fighter Group in the MTO.

[Box Score: 16 destroyed, 3 lost]

25 April 1944: F.O. 313. Col. Blakeslee led a Penetration Target Withdrawal Support to Mannheim–Ludwigshafen, Germany, from 0740 to 1300 hours. The Group found three gaggles of B-24s at 21/23,000 feet near Sarrebourg at 0925 and escorted them to the target. Escort was broken at 1130. Intense, heavy flak appeared all around the fighters over Stuttgart.

26 April 1944: F.O. 315. Lt. Millikan led a Fighter Sweep to Cologne–Trier, Germany, from 0730 to 1120 hours. Before landfall word was received the bombers had aborted but the Group swept Trier, orbited east of the Ruhr and came out at Walcheren Island at 1040 at 25,000 feet.

27 April 1944: F.O. 317. Col. Blakeslee led a Ramrod Support to Blainville/Toul airdrome, France, from 1645 to 2120 hours. Rendezvous was made with two wings of B-24s at 20/22,000 feet. After the bombing, 335 attacked the drome with Blakeslee while 334 and 336 stayed with the bombers to Dunkirk before breaking escort at 2024. One aircraft was destroyed on the ground.

[Box Score: 1 destroyed, 0 lost]

29 April 1944: F.O. 320. Capt. Sobanski led a Penetration Target Withdrawal Support to Berlin, Germany, from 0830 to 1430 hours. At 1015 the boys joined with the bombers at 24,000 feet—P-47s were also with the Big Friends. No enemy aircraft were sighted on the way in to the target although contrails appeared to head toward the formation until turned into. 334 Blue Section and 336 Red Section strafed Nordhausen, blasting a bunch of Ju 52s and a Do 217 to junk. They also strafed some marshalling yards. Two pilots went down to become POWs. The bombers were left at 1250 east of Osnabruck.

[Box Score: 7 destroyed, 2 lost]

30 April 1944: F.O. 321. Col. Blakeslee led a Free Lance General Support to Lyon, France, from 0715 to 1315 hours. The Group swept Lyon–Valence and back up to 20,000 feet by 1040. A 110 was bounced by three pilots and easily destroyed. A section from 334 strafed Lyon/Bron airdrome and got one while Blakeslee led three others in blasting three seaplanes. Freddie Glover was hit by flak but he bailed out to be picked up by the French Resistance, eventually getting back to England.

[Box Score: 5 destroyed, 1 lost]

Blakeslee returned home thinking his promise of 500 destroyed by the end of the month was not a reality, but since Ajax (VIII FC) had promised an afternoon mission if needed, Col. Don was ready to get another show on. As it turned out the Group's total had been pushed to 503½. The party that night was a roaring celebration. The Wolfpack was trailing far behind and Ajax wired, "You are a scourge to the Hun." Final figures for the Group as of 30 April 1944 were 207–4–111 for the month (another Blakeslee "order" carried out) and 505½–39–232 since September 1942. The Group was later awarded its first Distinguished Unit Citation (on 29 July) for destroying 323 enemy aircraft from 5 March to 24 April 1944, losing 44 pilots.

1 May 1944: F.O. 323. Col. Blakeslee led a Penetration Target Withdrawal Support to Rohrback–Saarbrucken, Germany, from 1625 to 2050 hours. Rendezvous with two wings of B-17s was made at 1757. By 1805 the Group broke off east to join up with two wings of bombers over Nancy at 20,000 feet. North of Luxembourg, 12 to 20 Bf 109s, flying in fours, came in from Cologne to make a stern attack on the second box. Four were destroyed between 1830 and 1850. Escort was broken at 2005 east of Dunkirk.

[Box Score: 4 destroyed, 0 lost]

4 May 1944: F.O. 326. Lt. Col. Clark led a Penetration Target Withdrawal Support to Rheine, Germany, from 0848 to 1145 hours. The Group was recalled at 1010 northwest of Rheine due to weather.

The official 500 victory party was held in the gym with free beer. . . . Cheers, mite!

7 May 1944: F.O. 329. Capt. Millikan led a Target Withdrawal Support to Berlin, Germany, from 0815 to 1420 hours. The initial plan was abandoned in favor of contacting the 2nd Air Task Force to provide escort. Rendezvous was made with six wings of Forts near Pritzwalk at 27,000 feet, 1045 hours. The Lightnings providing escort at the RV point left before the target and the Group broke escort on the way out northwest of Lingen at 1302. The works had been gummed up when the Field Order arrived late, delaying take-off by 45 minutes and causing an inadequate briefing.

8 May 1944: F.O. 331. Col. Blakeslee led a Penetration Target Withdrawal Support to Berlin, Germany, from 0800 to 1355 hours. The Group rendezvoused with five combat wings of B-17s at Nienburg at 0959, 23/26,000 feet. By the time over target there was a 10/10ths undercast. P-38s came in at 1123 and the Group left northwest of Dummer Lake at 1220 when Thunderbolts joined up. North of the Ruhr a straggling Fort at 10,000 was attacked by three 109s and a 190. 334 Red Section attacked, damaging two and forcing the Germans to duck into the cloud deck.

Two 334 sergeants were assigned to Farnborough to learn maintenance of the new K-14 gyro gunsight. Two days previously Deacon Hively had returned from Southend with favorable reports on testing the sight.

9 May 1944: F.O. 333. Capt. Millikan led a Jackpot to St. Dizier airdrome, France, from 0740 to 1200 hours. After two port orbits over Troyes at 25,000 feet, the Group met 72 B-17s at 0920 and provided escort to St. Dizier. Orbiting starboard twice to let the bombers finish, the Group lost altitude and attacked. Only one aircraft was seen on the ground. Reforming northwest of the drome, the P-51s flew over Juvincourt, Laon/Athies, Laon/Couvron at 5,000 but saw only fires. One section from 334 attacked Reims/Champagne three times, destroying a Ju 88 and damaging two more, but it wasn't worth it. Robert Sherman's prop hit the ground as he strafed and he bellied in to become a POW. Herb Blanchfield was shot down by flak and Vernon Burroughs bailed out—both became prisoners. Lloyd Waterman also went down to be captured.

[Box Score: 1 destroyed, 4 lost]

10 May 1944; F.O. 334. Maj. Goodson led a Ramrod to Brunswick, Germany, from 0850 to 1015 hours. On the way in the show was aborted.

11 May 1944: F.O. Weather Recce. Capt. Hively led seven other 334 Mustangs to Strasbourg, France, from 0555 to 0945 hours.

F.O. 336. Maj. Goodson led a Free Lance and Target Withdrawal Support to Saarbrucken, Germany, from 1640 to 2025 hours. The Group swept to Bonn–Koblenz at 25,000 feet, then received word the bombers were being attacked by 60-plus bandits ten miles east of a certain control point. Goodson tried to find the Big Friends but the Field Order did not specify such points to the fighters during briefing. Goody found five wings of bombers east of Metz at 1845, flying at 23,000, but there were no enemy aircraft. Escort was broken near Brussels at 1930. Robert Tussey died after bailing into the North Sea.

[Box Score: 0 destroyed, 1 lost]

12 May 1944: F.O. 337. Maj. Goodson led a Penetration Target Withdrawal Support to Brux, Czechoslovakia, from 1015 to 1540 hours. Arriving in the Kassel area at 1214, the Group heard the bombers were under attack in the Frankfurt area. Goodson brought his Mustangs south and rendezvoused with five wings northeast of Bad Nauheim at 1220, 23,000 feet. Just afterwards more than 30 bandits were seen on the deck heading northeast to Giessen—the 4th bounced and fought the Germans all the way to Mannheim, getting several kills. The 4th then climbed back up and continued escort to Coburg. At 1335 Goody decided to withdraw due to dropping tanks earlier than expected. Several sections stayed with the bombers beyond the target, which was bombed at 1340. Eight more 109s were encountered attacking the bombers east of Sonneberg at 20,000. The red-nosed Mustangs broke up the thrust.

[Box Score: 10 destroyed, 0 lost]

13 May 1944: F.O. 338. Capt. Millikan led a Withdrawal Support to Poznan, Poland, from 1230 to 1835 hours. At 1443 the bombers reported they were without escort northeast of Stettin. The Group turned north and rendezvoused with two wings at 1529 and 25,000 feet, which turned out not to be the Poznan force. Millikan turned the Group back out and found the rear boxes of the other formation at 1540 over the Baltic Sea. Passing Westerland at 1650, the P-51s left the Big Friends. As the 55th Fighter Group came in to take over with their P-38s, a single FW 190 appeared near Kadet Channel but a section engaged and the Focke Wulf disappeared into the haze. One pilot was killed after going down in the North Sea at the beginning of the show.

[Box Score: 0 destroyed, 1 lost]

14 May 1944: All aircraft were grounded until the 18th to fit permanent lines for the new British Thermostat Co. 108-gallon paper tanks, which replaced the metal 75-gallon teardrop external tanks.

15 May 1944: Col. Blakeslee announced new tours for pilots would be 300 hours rather than 200 hours, with the possibility of an unlimited tour.

A Station Defense plan went into effect. Four pilots were to be at continuous readiness from 15 minutes before dawn to 15 minutes after blackout at dispersals. The three squadrons would alternate. This meant that the mechanics assigned to the aircraft had to be up at 0300 to get them ready.

It just so happened that three years previously, to the day, Don Blakeslee had arrived in the United Kingdom to fly with 401 RCAF Squadron and he had not been off ops since. Another of his famous nicknames, Ole Man River, began to take on meaning as the tour duration was upped. He was also miffed at unnecessary flying and taxiing accidents. If they continued, he said, more pilots would face fines or permanent grounding . . . and the uniforms were generally poor and there was too much loose talk before missions. The CO would have the best or none at all.

19 May 1944: F.O. 342. Col. Blakeslee took the Group back to Berlin, Germany, on a Target Withdrawal Support from 1110 to 1725 hours. The Group arrived over the predetermined Control Point ̀3 at 1302, then changed course to orbit northwest of Berlin at 25,000. At 1343 Blakeslee reported the weather to the bombers and led his boys in an orbit east and south of the city. Rendezvous was made with five wings of Fortresses at 25/27,000 feet west of the target at 1400 in the midst of intense, accurate heavy flak. Escort was provided to Warnemunde, two squadrons leaving at 1445. 334 returned to the control point to escort the rear boxes, breaking off over the Baltic coast at 1453. West of Weimar the squadron bounced three 109s, destroying one. West of Lubeck at 1530 six more were bounced; the rear three dove away, but five were destroyed, three by Hively, along with an unidentified single-engine enemy aircraft. Two of the Messerschmitts were destroyed when they collided as a ̀2 made a violent port turn, cutting the tail off ̀3. Twelve 109s jumped 335 but nothing developed. One 336 pilot was downed by rocket flak to become a POW.

[Box Score: 7 destroyed, 1 lost]

20 May 1944: F.O. 343A. Maj. Goodson led a Free Lance Support to Liege, Belgium, from 0830 to 1250 hours. On the way in bandits were reported near Soesterberg but none were spotted. The Mustangs swept southwest to the edge of the Ruhr, near Cologne, then to Aachen and Namur, where bandits were reported southeast; again, nothing. Rendezvous was made with four wings of B-17s northeast of Liege at 1045, 18/25,000 feet. The bombers were left west of Breda at 1130 to search for more reported bandits near Eindhoven but it turned out to be another wild goose chase.

Air Sea Rescue. Capt. Megura led three other 334 P-51s from 1555 to 2150 hours in search of a downed B-17 crew. The downed men were found, and managed to struggle into a dropped raft before rescue.

21 May 1944: F.O. 344. Col. Blakeslee led the Group's first Chattanooga Free Lance (attack on railway) from 1030 to 1555 hours to the Berlin–Stendal area, Germany. North of Stendal at 1244, the Group separated into squadrons and led down from 26,000 feet through holes in the undercast. 334 went west, Blakeslee took 335 east and 336 stayed in the center. Everyone latched onto the main rail lines—tugs were strafed on the Elbe; trains, warehouses, vehicles all got roughed up. Rathenow airdrome was beat up as well, netting four destroyed and a Bu 131 shot down. The Group left the area by squadrons at 1330. Some 500 AAF fighters were out this day to strafe, with the most distant targets assigned to the 4th. William Hunt was killed strafing a marshalling yard.

[Box Score: 5 destroyed, 1 lost]

22 May 1944: F.O. 346. Col. Blakeslee led a Free Lance Target Support to Kiel, Germany, from 1040 to 1525 hours. Sweeping Bremen to Hamburg, the 4th rendezvoused at 1300 with B-17s over Kiel at 26,000 feet. 334 and 335 stayed with the Big Friends while 336 swept south to Lubeck and engaged ten Bf 109s above 30,000. Millikan got one. The escort left the bombers west of Heide at 1340. Four pilots spotted over thirty 190s at 18,000 flying north from Hamburg. The attack was blocked as P-38s joined in the fight. Cowboy Megura was attacking three 109s when one of the Lightnings raked him with gunfire, puncturing his glycol system. His section escorted him to Laaland, Denmark, and broke off as he headed for Sweden, where he belly landed at Kalmar to be interned for a few weeks. He was back to Debden by 28 June but did not reenter combat. Ironically, he shared one-half a 109 with the unknown P-38 pilot.

[Box Score: 2½ destroyed, 1 lost]

23 May 1944: F.O. 348. Capt. Sobanski led a Ramrod Escort to Chaumont–Troyes, France from 0715 to 1210 hours. Rendezvous was made at 0834, 20 miles north of Orleans, with two wings of Forts. These bombers turned out to be the wrong '17s so the Group orbited. 334 and 335 Red Sections escorted the formation to Chaumont with 334 Green and Blue Sections taking a force to Troyes.

24 May 1944: F.O. 349. Col. Blakeslee led a Penetration Target Withdrawal Support to Berlin, Germany, from 0815 to 1355 hours. Six combat wings of B-17s were joined ten miles west of St. Peter at 26,500 feet. Blakeslee took eight Mustangs and flew via Bremen to Berlin as a fighter control section and rendezvoused with the bombers at 1100. He then took the '51s parallel to the bomber stream south of the formation to St. Peter and left them at 1233. Col. Don found the experiment frustrating and unsuccessful due to all the R/T chatter. The rest of the Group, with Goodson up front, sighted over 40 Germans in two gaggles at 1025 in the Hamburg/Lubeck area at 31/35,000 feet, coming from the southeast. The rear enemy gaggle bounced the rear box escort by fours while the lead gaggle attempted to attack the bombers. 334, which had climbed to 36,000, bounced the latter attack and fought the 109s and 190s all the way to the deck. Before long the entire Group was in combat, chasing 109s and 190s, destroying ten for the loss of one pilot.

[Box Score: 10 destroyed, 1 lost]

W.F.O. 99. Maj. Goodson led a Glide Bombing show to Beaumont-sur-Oise, France, from 1640 to 2010 hours. Two sections from each squadron carried bombs while a third acted as fighter escort. After a port orbit at Gisors, the bombers let down to 5,000 feet and bombed the primary target, a rail bridge, at 1757 from the northwest in 30° glides. Bomb release was at 100 to 150 feet with fair results.

25 May 1944: F.O. 350. Maj. Goodson led a Penetration Target Withdrawal Support to Chaumont–Sarreguentines, France, from 0705 to 1140 hours. Rendezvous was made with eight wings of B-17s at 0836, 20/22,000 feet west of Chaumont. The Group covered the three lead boxes over the target. 336 got into a big scrap with 109s and 190s, destroying five and losing two pilots (POWs). Escort was broken north of Dunkirk at 1045.

[Box Score: 5 destroyed, 2 lost]

27 May 1944: F.O. 351. Capt. Sobanski led a Penetration Target Withdrawal Support to Karlsruhe, Germany, from 1030 to 1545 hours. Rendezvous was made 30 miles east of Epinal at 1235 with two combat wings of Forts at 26/28,000 feet. On the way in, Elliot Shapleigh aborted due to problems with his kite and went down to become an evader. Escort was broken at 1500 near the English coast.

[Box Score: 0 destroyed, 1 lost]

28 May 1944: F.O. 352. Maj. Goodson led a Penetration Target Withdrawal Support to Ruhland–Dessau, Germany, from 1145 to 1710 hours. The P-51s found their Forts at 1350 near Gardelegen at 22/23,000 feet. Just after joining up, the pilots saw 20-plus 109s and 190s approaching from the southeast at 26,000 to attack the wings that had split off for Magdeburg. 334 bounced, breaking up the attack, scoring seven and one-half kills—the half was Lang's share with a P-38. Two more pilots went down to be captured. Continuing on to the target, the bombers left at 1505 west of Saalfeld; the Group broke escort at 1534. Though Hofer got a 20mm hit in his QP-L's rudder, he did a victory roll over Debden, feeling the oats of getting six kills so far in May. It was only a prelude to the next three days.

29 May 1944: F.O. 353. Col. Blakeslee led a Withdrawal Support to Poznan, Poland, from 1020 to 1730 hours. Northwest of the target area the Group found their three wings of Flying Fortresses at 21/22,000 feet. Hofer and Frank Speer attacked Mackfitz airdrome near Stargard and destroyed seven He 177s between them before Speer was hit by flak. He was captured after bellying in near the field. Oren Snell shot the tail off a 109, and two seaplanes were destroyed at Dieuenaw seaplane base, along with 12 damaged. 335 and 336 downed four more Germans.

[Box Score: 14 destroyed, 1 lost]

30 May 1944: F.O. 354. Capt. Hively led a Free Lance Withdrawal Support to Stendal–Dessau–Halberstadt, Germany, from 0850 to 1400 hours. The Mustangs made Arendsee Lake by 1110 and turned southeast. In the Genthin area 30 to 40

109s and 190s were seen at 25,000 feet, covered by another 20 to 25 at 30,000 approaching from the southeast. The 4th, at 26,000, engaged the enemy aircraft below and was promptly bounced by the covering German fighters. Two Germans were destroyed in dogfights from 34,000 to the deck along the Elbe River. Two sections from 334 strafed Oschersleben airdrome, getting six aircraft, before climbing back up at 1220 to join 335 in escorting B-17s to Dummer Lake. Escort was broken at 1302 over the enemy coast. Near Wittenburg, Willard Millikan and Sam Young collided as Young tried to avoid a flak burst. Both bailed out OK to become POWs.

[Box Score: 8 destroyed, 3 lost]

31 May 1944: F.O. 355. Maj. Goodson was in the lead again, taking the Group on a Free Lance General Support to Mulhouse–Colmar–Strasbourg, France, from 0855 to 1245 hours. Towering cumulus split the Group into squadrons southeast of Namur; the bombers faced the same problem. The controller, "Colgate," told the Group to abandon the briefed mission and remain with the bombers. 334 was vectored to Charleroi to escort a small box of bombers out to the coast. Kidd Hofer continued on and joined up with the 357th Fighter Group escorting bombers to Luxeuil airdrome. After the bombing, Hofer went down with his newfound buddies and destroyed three Bu 131s. In the last four missions Hofer had destroyed 10½ to tie him with Goodson at 15 aerial and 15 ground kills. Homuth and McElroy aborted together; the former was never seen again and the latter became a POW.

[Box Score: 3 destroyed, 2 lost]

Air Sea Rescue. Four kites were sent up to look for Hofer, who had not been heard from since 0950 when it was thought he had aborted at the enemy coast. The Kidd came gleefully in at 1430.

2 June 1944: F.O. 359. Maj. Blanding led a Fighter Sweep under Type 16 Control to Compiegne, France, from 1815 to 2145 hours. Landfall was made at Dieppe at 1909 and 20,000 feet. Nothing but flak was encountered before coming out at 2125 over St. Valery.

4 June 1944: F.O. 365. Lt. Col. Clark led a Free Lance Sweep to Cap Gris Nez–Abbeville, France, from 1120 to 1405 hours. Though supporting the heavies, the mission was uneventful.

F.O. 368. Maj. Blanding led a Withdrawal Support to Bourges–St. Avord, France, from 1855 to 2205 hours. Rendezvous was made at 2025 east of Caen. The formation came back out at 2101 and the Group left the Big Friends in mid-Channel as the bombers broke into small groups.

5 June 1944: F.O. 369. Lt. Col. Clark led a Type 16 Control to Tournai, Belgium, from 0820 to 1100 hours. The Mustangs passed Lille at 0912 and 16,000 feet, then patrolled the line from Ghent to Cambrai, coming out at Gravelines at 1005. Two unidentified aircraft were seen near Lille/Venderille airdrome but intense flak kept a section from closing.

F.O. 370. W.F.O. 104. Capt. Hively led a Dive Bombing show to Lille–Pont-a-

Marcq, France, from 1345 to 1535. A motor convoy was spotted on a road between the two cities at 1435. Two out of the 30 to 40 trucks were destroyed by dive bombing.

All crews reported to the hangars at 1750 hours to paint black and white stripes around the fuselages and wings of the Group's Mustangs, finishing at midnight. The aircraft were taken back to the flight lines, refueled, and two bombs were set aside for each kite.

At 2000 Blakeslee announced the invasion of the Continent and by 2300 all pilots were briefed on the general invasion plan. Several missions were to be flown on D-Day, often using one or two squadrons at a time rather than the entire Group.

6 June 1944: F.O. 371-Part 1. At 0130 everyone was awakened after only a couple of hours sleep. Col. Blakeslee led the first mission of the day, a Fighter Sweep by 334 and 335 of the Rouen, France, area from 0320 to 0945 hours. Landfall was made over Dieppe at 0409 but dense cloud prevented pin-pointing and claimed Thomas Fraser, who went down after 0642 east of Rouen to be captured. Changing winds caused the formation to drift east of Paris and come out at various points east of Calais. Hofer strafed a couple of locos after blurting over the R/T, "Whoo, a train!"

[Box Score: 0 destroyed, 1 lost]

F.O. 371-Part 1. Lt. Col. Clark gathered 336 for a Type 16 Control to the Rouen, France, area from 0635 to 1150 hours. Coming in behind the other two squadrons, 336 faced the same conditions.

F.O. 371-Part 2. Capt. Hively led 334 only in a Fighter Bombing show back to the Rouen, France, area from 1120 to 1400 hours. The Squadron made landfall at 1206 over Dieppe and arrived in the Rouen area at 1215 to search for communications targets. A 15-car troop train was bombed with poor results but the boys ran into 10-plus FW 190s preparing to land at Evreux airdrome. From 1230 to 1245 everybody took turns and four Focke Wulfs were shot down.

[Box Score: 4 destroyed, 0 lost]

F.O. 371-Part 2. Maj. Happel took 335 out for a Dive Bombing mission to Fleury marshalling yards, France, from 1220 to 1500 hours. After dropping their bombs, the boys came back out without incident.

F.O. 371-Part 2. Maj. Goodson took 336 out for a Fighter Bombing show and Free Lance to Rouen, France, again from 1335 to 1615 hours. Roaming the countryside was uneventful until flak hit Harold Fredericks near Evreaux at 1445. After crash landing, he managed to evade capture and make it back to England. Oscar Lejeunesse was shot down by flak at the same time and bailed out.

[Box Score: 0 destroyed, 2 lost]

F.O. 372. Col. Blakeslee took 334 and 335 back out on a Fighter Patrol to the Rouen–Dreux, France, area from 1820 to 2340 hours. Landfall was made at Dieppe at 1915. Near Rouen a 20-truck convoy was attacked by 335 Blue Section at 1840 but over fifteen 109s and 190s then bounced the Mustangs—all four pilots were shot down and killed. At 2035 Edward Stepp was heard over the R/T talking to Mike Sobanski, "Watch those behind you White Leader!" after Sobanski had requested a visual check of his aircraft after hitting some wires. Both men were killed. As if this wasn't enough, Mike McPharlin reported over the R/T at 2100 that his left magneto was out and he was aborting. On loan from the 339th Fighter Group in his 6N-Z, he had come back to Debden to fly the big one with his old 334. He was never heard from again. The boys came out at 2220.

[Box Score: 0 destroyed, 7 lost]

7 June 1944: W.F.O. Col. Blakeslee led a Fighter Bombing show to Rennes–Dol Deb, France, from 1430 to 1805 hours. As the Mustangs were getting off, Kenneth Smith and Lt. Pierini collided a mile south of the field. Smith was killed. Landfall was made west of Dieppe at 1525. The Group followed the rail line to Fougeres without finding any targets until sighting a road bridge and four small locos. There were two fair hits out of six on the bridge and one out of 12 on the locos. No question the boys were better fighter than bomber pilots. O. R. Jones crash landed after being hit by flak near Dol Deb. He was captured after running into the woods. The Group came out at 1715 over St. Valery-en-Caux.

[Box Score: 0 destroyed, 2 lost]

The 1770th Ordnance S&M Co. sent two convoys to depots for badly needed bombs and ammunition, which arrived back at 0030 hours. The men worked through the night unloading, then reported for work in the morning cheerful and ready to get on with it. Convoys continued through the month carrying 100, 250 and 500 pound bombs and frag clusters. All the gun belts on hand had to be reworked due to shortages in the types of ammunition used. Support of the invasion was tough both on the ground and in the air.

8 June 1944: F.O. 377-Part 1. Lt. Col. Clark led a Ramroad Area Support to Nantes, France, from 0555 to 1110 hours. The P-51s reached Rennes by 0728, then patrolled the area south to the Loire River for two hours. On the way home a vector was given to bandits at Fecamp but they turned out to be P-51s. The boys came out east of Fecamp at 1013 and 18,000 feet.

F.O. 377-Part 2. Col. Blakeslee led another Fighter Bombing mission to Le Mans–Montfort, France, from 1245 to 1615 hours. Landfall was made at St. Valery-en-Caux. Flying at 14,000 feet, the Group swung west, attacking a marshalling yard. Fifty percent of the rolling stock was destroyed, the main double tracks were severed in three places and five sidings were severed. Two bridges were also bombed. Over Le Mans at 1430, Eacott Allen sliced the tail off James Scott's Mustang at 2,500 feet. Scott went straight in and was killed but Allen bailed out onto a rooftop to become an evader, getting back to Debden on 23 August. The formation came out west of Le Havre at 1520, flying at 17,000 feet.

[Box Score: 0 destroyed, 2 lost]

10 June 1944: F.O. 379. Lt. Col. Clark led a Ramrod Area Support to Morlaix airdrome, France, from 0550 to 1115 hours. Landfall was made at 0725 over Painpol at 17,000 feet. The Group orbited and patrolled. Two sections from 334 attacked a train and armored car at 0900. Another three trains were attacked and

Monroe and Gillette orbited Morlaix to report bombing results to the B-17s but the bombers never showed. Coming out at 0925, the Group was flying at 7,000 feet.

F.O. 380. Col. Blakeslee led a Type 16 Control to Rouen–Paris–Oisemont, France, from 1240 to 1700 hours. After crossing Dieppe at 18,000 feet at 1320, a vector was received to bogies that were never found. The next vector was to the bombers but P-51s were already providing escort so Blakeslee took the boys back to the assigned area. At 1500 everyone went down on the deck near Poix and strafed motor targets and trains before coming out over Coutray at 1540. Two pilots went down; one was killed, the other captured.

[Box Score: 0 destroyed, 2 lost]

F.O. 381. Maj. Goodson led a Fighter Bombing show to Le Mans–Leval, France, from 1830 to 2115 hours. After crossing Dieppe at 2050, the '51s let down from 18,000 to 3,000 feet below the cloud deck and orbited starboard. Goodson went port and located a previously bombed marshalling yard. Before finishing, the 4th damaged over 40 boxcars and several locos, then exited via Coutray at 2050 at 8,000 feet.

11 June 1944: F.O. 382-Part 1. Col. Blakeslee led a Fighter Bombing mission to Bernay, France, from 0720 to 1030 hours. Northwest of Contes, the Group let down to 3,000 feet and bombed a rail intersection with fair results. East of Dreux over 20 boxcars were bombed. Hofer and Siems strafed two armored cars at Epinay, then Siems bombed a rail bridge southeast of Contes and destroyed it. 334 White and Red Sections set several heavy trucks on fire. The Group came out via St. Valery-en-Caux at 0935 and 8,000 feet.

F.O. 382-Part 2. Lt. Col. Clark led more Fighter Bombing to the Vire area, France, from 1155 to 1510. Ten miles southwest of Vire the P-51s bombed and strafed 70-plus trucks. Both Harry Noon and Leon Cole were killed, the former hitting some trees with his two bombs still attached and the latter by flak. Enemy air support was sent in but there was too much ammunition gone to stay and fight. Thirty-two trucks were left destroyed. Hofer's oil system was punctured by small arms fire and he was forced to land at a forward air strip in Normandy. Maj. Gen. Ralph Royce, 9th Air Force CO, met him and escorted him on a tour of the front.

[Box Score: 0 destroyed, 2 lost]

13 June 1944: Pilots were ordered to learn quick refueling and rearming of their Mustangs in addition to how to make daily inspections of the kites. Contests were held among the pilots in drills, 334 CO Hively giving a bottle of whiskey to his A & B Flights, the tied winners. Speculation was that this meant a shuttle escort mission to Russia or Italy.

F.O. 382. Col. Blakeslee led an Area Support for B-26s to a forest east of Dombront, France, from 1930 to 2255 hours. Landfall was made east of Fecamp at 2038 and 15,000 feet. The assigned area was patrolled but the bombers never came into the target. A small convoy of trucks was attacked at Brettville at 2130 and nine were destroyed. The Group came out at Cap D'Antifer at 2210, flying at 10,000 feet.

15 June 1944: F.O. 390. Maj. Goodson led a Penetration Target Withdrawal Support to Nantes, France, from 0605 to 1015 hours. Nine to ten groups of B-17s were met at 0722, 18/20,000 feet and escort was broken west of Guernsey at 0915.

After extensive tests, which began on 10 February 1944, all VIII FC bases started getting 100/150 octane fuel. It was noted that these tests could have been responsible for several of the Mustang losses of the past 3½ months. Later in the month new kits arrived for the installation of new bob weights, dorsal fins and landing gear uplock systems in the P-51s. During March and April some 4th kites lost wings and tails in combat and after modifications there were no further problems of this type.

Everyone was restricted to the post due to plans for a Russia shuttle mission for the next day. At 1800 35 enlisted men left for bomber bases to make the trip with the Big Friends and detailed maps were prepared for all pilots. The next day the show was scrubbed due to weather.

18 June 1944: F.O. 398. Col. Blakeslee led a Fighter Sweep into France from 1930 to 2320 hours. Landfall was made at Grandcamp at 2030 hours and 8,500 feet. The Group was vectored to Avranches where it orbited and swept to east of Dinan, Evreaux and Rouen. 334 covered as 335 and 336 beat up a horse-drawn convoy near Combourg after visiting VIII FC Col. Ben Kelsey called out a suspicious horse and cart. Two P-51s were downed by rifle fire, one pilot becoming an evader, the other a POW, while another pilot was killed.

[Box Score: 0 destroyed, 3 lost]

19 June 1944: F.O. 399. Capt. Hively led a Ramrod to Cholet, France, from 0655 to 1010 hours. After crossing the coast near Bayeux at 0800 and 20,000 feet, the '51s encountered dense haze and icing. Hively took the Group up to 25,000 before calling it off near Vire when the bombers were supposed to go under the 8/10ths cloud. 334 Blue Section bounced a 190 but it evaded into the cloud at 5,000 feet. Dean Hill was killed after disappearing into the overcast. The 4th came out at Cherbourg at 0835.

[Box Score: 0 destroyed, 1 lost]

20 June 1944: F.O. 402. Lt. Col. Clark led a Target Withdrawal Support to Politz, Germany, from 0635 to 1230 hours. The mission was laid on so fast the ground crews were not able to get the kites properly serviced. Form up was confusing and there were numerous aborts. Landfall was made over Den Helder at 0743 at 23,000 feet. Near Griefswald Bay over 25 enemy aircraft were seen going south at 10,000 feet. 334 Red Section dropped babies to bounce when five-plus 109s were spotted at 15,000 swinging around to attack the Group. Two were destroyed before a milling fight developed with over 50 German fighters. Several enemy aircraft were engaged with success. 336 then attacked Neu Brandenburg airdrome and destroyed a few but Jim Goodson's glycol system was hit, forcing him to belly-land his brand new P-51D. After he got out and walked to nearby woods with his hands in his pockets, the boys strafed the Mustang to junk. The Group reformed and rendezvoused with B-24s east of Stettin, giving support to Husum where the formation came out at 1057 and 20,000 feet. Vol Harris went down near Lubeck to be captured.

[Box Score: 15 destroyed, 2 lost]

The base was alerted again for the Russia shuttle mission . . . much work was done all through the night.

21 June 1944: F.O. 407. Col. Blakeslee led a Ramrod Shuttle to Ruhland, Germany, and Leszno, Poland, from 0755 to 1450 hours, landing in Piryatin, Russia. Blakeslee was all business in the briefing—there would be no fighting on the way over, no dropping of tanks and no R/T chatter. "No one will abort because of lack of oxygen. You'll be at 15,000 feet. You don't need it. You have no business in the group if you have to have oxygen at 15,000. If you get dizzy, go down under the bombers for awhile. . . . This whole thing is for show. That's why everything must be pansy. It's not what you do, but what you seem to do." Blakeslee wanted to lead the show bad enough to have an extra Mustang standing ready in case his WD-C had to abort. He stuffed 16 maps into the cockpit with him to assure a "pansy landing" at Piryatin. Hofer was giving his CO, Hively, a headache since the Kidd refused to take his shots, even on orders. Hively flatly told Hofer he wasn't going. Hofer relented at the last minute but the Deacon sent him packing to fly with another squadron and gave "Salem Representative" to Preston Hardy.

Forty-five Mustangs of the 4th along with 16 P-51s of the 486th Fighter Squadron, 352nd Group, crossed Overflakkee at 0903 at 20,000 feet. Cruising over a solid undercast half way to Berlin, the fighters rendezvoused on time with three wings of B-17s over Leszno at 1113 after Ruhland had been bombed. At 1240, 25 Bf 109s came in for a head-on attack against the bombers. The enemy fighters were engaged but the advantage could not be pressed due to fuel restrictions. Two were destroyed for the loss of Frank Sibbett. Disregarding orders, Hofer continued to chase the Germans on the deck. He was listed as MIA until word filtered in later that he had landed at Kiev. S/Sgt. Robert Gilbert, a 336 crew chief who had served Goodson, was forced to bail out of one of the B-17s the 33 enlisted men were flying in. He fought for 36 days with Polish guerrillas against the Germans before returning to Debden on 17 August. The Group escorted the Big Friends beyond Russian lines for a total distance of 580 miles. Upon sighting the Russian field, on time to the minute, Blakeslee threw all 16 of his maps into the air within his cockpit.

[Box Score: 2 destroyed, 2 lost]

That night, as the bomber base at Poltava was severely pounded by German bombers, Piryatin became a madhouse with chandelier flares and anti-aircraft going off all over the place. 4th pilots spent an uneasy night in the trenches. Siems and Blanding couldn't get out of their sleeping bags so they hopped all the way to the trenches.

22 June 1944: The Mustangs were flown to Zaporozhe, Odessa and Chingueue in the wake of the German success at destroying numerous Forts the night before. The Russians turned out to be warm hosts. Deacon Hively and Bill Hedrick visited the Russian general in command of the Air Army at Stalingrad, drinking numerous toasts with Vodka, Stadka and wine. Deacon and the general, before going completely mindless, exchanged belts. A few pilots found beds but most slept on boards.

24 June 1944: The P-51s were flown back to Piryatin where wing tanks were installed. No missions were laid on so the pilots flew back to their respective bases. At 1900 Joyce, Monroe, Gillette and Simon scrambled from Chingueue to intercept a reconnaissance aircraft but they gave up after 2hrs. 15min.

25 June 1944: It was back to Piryatin where the ground crews pulled an inspection to get serviceability up for next day's anticipated flight to Italy.

26 June 1944: Col. Blakeslee led a Penetration Target Withdrawal Support from Piryatin, Russia, to Drohobycz, Poland, from 1405 to 1935 hours, landing at Lucera, Italy. Hofer, Gillette, Callahan and Lane were forced to abort and head back to Russia. Rendezvous was made at Brodye, east of Lvov, Poland, at 1607. Escort was broken at 1851 over the Yugoslavian coast and the Group flew across the Adriatic. 15th Air Force pilots greeted the 4th and 352nd with champagne. Everyone partied into the wee hours.

27 June 1944: The Group's Mustangs were dispersed to Lesina, Madna and San Severo with other '51 groups of the 15th. The 5,000-foot steel planking, dust, cots and tents weren't Debden but hospitality was warm. 334 stayed with the 325th Fighter Group, the Checkertail Clan, and some of the 325th pilots remember the 4th's initial attitude as condescending, as though the real war were taking place from England.

28 June 1944: F.O. 421. Lt. Col. Clark led 11 of the Group's P-51s on a Penetration Target Withdrawal Support to Saarbrucken, Germany, from Debden from 0620 to 1030 hours. Forming a squadron of the 352nd Group, the boys rendezvoused with the other Mustangs over Bodney and headed out to join six B-24 wings at 0738. Escort was broken near Namur and the P-51s came out at 0945, flying at 11,000 feet.

29 June 1944: F.O. 422. Lt. Col Clark again led a composite squadron of 12 kites with the 352nd Group on a Penetration Target Withdrawal Support to Leipzig, Germany, from 0700 to 1220 hours. Rendezvous was made with the Liberators at 0833 and escort was broken near Dummer Lake at 1035 and 30,000 feet.

Meanwhile, the four aborts of the 26th left Poltava to rejoin the rest of the Group in Italy. Hofer, again on strict orders not to bounce the enemy unless bounced, went off chasing bandits. Callahan broke and covered him; both ran short of fuel. While Gillette and Lane made it safely to Foggia, Hofer overshot Italy and was guided to Malta by Spitfires, where he spent the night. Callahan ran out of fuel and crash landed on the beach at Sampieri, Sicily. He was picked up uninjured by the British and taken to Catania. The next day Hofer flew from Malta to Catania to see Callahan, then on to land at Foggia. Callahan was flown to Algiers, Rabat and England by the British.

2 July 1944: F.O. 15th AF. In concert with the 52nd and 325th Groups, Col. Blakeslee led the 4th on a Fighter Sweep to Budapest, Hungary, from 0740 to 1250 hours. Forming up over Lake Lesina, the Mustangs went on to the target where 75 to 80 109s were encountered. The Huns were very aggressive, pressing attacks at all altitudes. Hively, after destroying a 109, was jumped and shot up, losing his canopy which gave him a good crack on the skull and wounded an eye. Grover Siems shot the Hun off Deacon's tail but Siems was then jumped and severely wounded. Despite his dazed condition, Hively downed two more 109s while Siems nursed himself back to Foggia, severely wounded in the shoulder, neck and chin. With his left side paralyzed, he had to kick down the gear handle with his right foot but after getting down he was so weak he couldn't get the canopy open—he kicked the gun switch on, fired his guns to attract attention and was pulled from his ship. He was returned to the States in serious condition. During the roaring dogfight at 1045 four of the Group's pilots were shot down, two killed and two POWs. One was Kidd Hofer, who was last seen over Budapest climbing to engage 20-plus 109s. The wreckage of his Mustang, QP-X, and his body were later found at Mostar, Yugoslavia.

[Box Score: 8 destroyed, 5 lost]

The mission had been rough. The returning pilots were thereafter much more cordial to their 15th Air Force hosts, deciding there was a war going on after all in southern Europe.

3 July 1944: F.O. 15th AF. Col. Blakeslee led a Penetration Target Withdrawal Support for 8th Air Force shuttle bombers to Arad, Rumania, from 0930 to 1435 hours out of Foggia, Italy. The 8th and 15th Mustangs formed up over Lake Lesina at 1008 and rendezvoused with the bombers southwest of Belgrade. Escort was broken at 1335.

4 July 1944: F.O. 427. Lt. Col. Clark led the Debden composite squadron of 12 Mustangs on a Penetration Target Withdrawal Support to Gien–Sully-sur-Loire, France, from 0600 to 0955 hours. Rendezvous was made with two combat wings of B-17s at 20/23,000 feet and escort was broken at 0906 near St. Valery-en-Caux.

5 July 1944: F.O. 430. Lt. Col. Clark had 16 Mustangs up from Debden for a Penetration Target Withdrawal Support to LeCulot, Belgium, from 0710 to 1030 hours. The bombers were 20 minutes late so the Group orbited and rendezvoused at 0819 with B-24s at 20/23,000 feet. After passing over the target at 0850, the 4th left the bombers at 0935 over the coast.

F.O. 431. Col. Blakeslee led his charges from Silinas, Italy, on a Ramrod Shuttle to Beziers, France, from 0940 to 1630 hours, landing at Debden. Col. Ben Kelsey was at the head of the formation until Blakeslee could catch up over France— seems Col. Don and the Deacon had talked their way out of the hospital to end up leading the Group back to home base. Rendezvous was made with B-17s at

1235 over the Mediterranean south of Toulon at 20,000 feet. The target was crossed at 1330. One enemy aircraft was sighted but it got away. At 1500 escort was broken near Chateauroux as more 8th Air Force fighters showed up to relieve the shuttlers. Debden dispersals were charged with excitement as Old Man River led the weary bunch in. VIII FC CO William Kepner was on hand to greet Blakeslee, who was given a seven-day furlough along with Deacon. Everyone else got the next day off and that night free beer and much food was consumed as the pilots rejoiced in returning to the luxury of Debden.

The enlisted men, some of whom had never flown before, returned with souvenirs and stories of being gunners while watching their own pilots in action on 21 June. Several got to fire at enemy aircraft. Since their shuttle bombers had been, for the most part, destroyed at Poltava, the crews came home via Teheran, Cairo, Tripoli, Algiers and Casablanca—except for Don Allen, who went with the bombers to Italy by mistake, the only enlisted man in the Group to make the entire shuttle mission. Everyone arrived home between the 6th and the 10th.

The entire tour covered 6,000 miles, 10 countries and 29¼ hours of operational flying for 10 destroyed and seven lost.

6 July 1944: As everyone took time to relax, nine P-51s took off from Madna, Italy, at 0740 hours for England led by Maj. Jackson of the 486th Fighter Squadron, 352nd Group. These Mustangs were the 5 July aborts and the four repaired late arrivals from Russia (five from the 352nd and four from the 4th). A total of 13 fighters was lost by both groups and the 352nd lost two pilots on the shuttle.

7 July 1944: F.O. 436. Lt. Monroe led a Penetration Target Withdrawal Support to Bernberg–Aschersleben, Germany, from 0535 to 0945 hours. The Group met their B-24s west of Dummer Lake at 0845. Near Nordhausen over 70 German fighters approached from the northeast at 20,000, crossed close in front of the bombers and prepared to make a beam attack. 334 broke up the attack and destroyed three. John Scally destroyed his Me 410 by running into it, losing a wing; he got out and was captured. About 75 more enemy fighters approached from the southwest without attacking. Preston Hardy and Willard Gillette bounced 14 109s, getting two. 335 and 336 also claimed kills. The Group escorted the bombers over the Dutch coast at 1045.

[Box Score: 7 destroyed, 1 lost]

9 July 1944: F.O. 438. Lt. Col. Clark led a Penetration Target Withdrawal Support to Saumur–Tours, France, from 0535 to 0945 hours. Rendezvous was made at 23,000 feet over St. Pierre–Eglise with B-17s at 0652. Escorting over a solid undercast, the Group came back out at 0905.

11 July 1944: F.O. 441. Lt. Col. Clark led a Penetration Target Withdrawal Support to Munich, Germany, from 1000 to 1600 hours. Rendezvous with the B-17s was made at 1130 with a wide swing to avoid heavy flak. The bombers were left at 1442. One pilot went down to become a POW.

[Box Score: 0 destroyed, 1 lost]

12 July 1944: F.O. 442B. Lt. Col. Clark led another Penetration Target Withdrawal Support to Munich, Germany, from 1045 to 1655 hours. The Group picked up the Fortresses at 1216 and provided escort until the formation came out over Dunkirk at 1558 and 22,000 feet.

13 July 1944: F.O. 444. Maj. Blanding led the third Penetration Target Withdrawal Support to Munich, Germany, in as many days from 0710 to 1320 hours. After rendezvous with the Forts at 0850, stacked from 21,000 to 26,000 feet, the formation headed for the target where the most intense flak ever encountered by the 4th was thrown up. Before the formation came out over Calais at 1230, Wilson Edwards was shot down by flak over Metz and was captured.

[Box Score: 0 destroyed, 1 lost]

With Blakeslee and Hively back from a week in London, the CO wasted no time in calling a 1630 briefing for all pilots. A new Operational Training Unit was to be formed on the field for many newly arrived pilots . . . and for any pilot not meeting the best operational standards. Accidents were more expensive than pilots and they would not be tolerated. Any pilot not saluting Col. Blakeslee would be grounded for two weeks. The flavor of the briefing was to rebuild the Group to its former status as the best outfit in the AAF.

14 July 1944: F.O. 446. Lt. Col. Clark led a Penetration Target Withdrawal Support to Lyon–Grenoble–Tulle, France, from 0615 to 1230 hours. At 0744 the Mustangs joined up with the B-17s. Near Bourges the bombers began to let down in heavy cloud until everyone was below 1,000 feet in the target area. Then the Big Friends released containers with parachutes onto a plateau where Marquis partisans ran out to get them, waving wildly—it happened to be Bastille Day. The formation came out at 1130 and 20,000 feet.

16 July 1944: F.O. 450. Col. Blakeslee had the helm back on a Penetration Target Withdrawal Support to Munich, Germany, from 0645 to 1250 hours. Near the Rhine, after picking up the B-17s at 0752, the escort was joined by more P-51s. 10/10ths cloud forced the formation to climb to 26/29,000 feet while Blakeslee perched up at 34,000. On withdrawal the 56th joined escort north of Mulhouse and the bombers were left at 1145.

17 July 1944: F.O. 451. Lt. Col. Clark led an Area Support to Nevers–Moulins–Montargis, France, from 0855 to 1410 hours. As the Group arrived at Auxerre at 1037, several boxes of Libs passed under. Then the P-51s went down on the deck and strafed over 20 rail cars. Roving sections strafed an ammo train that blew sky high. The Mustangs left the Montargis area at 1230, coming out at 1315 at 17,000 feet after more strafing.

F.O. 453. Maj. Blanding led a Type 16 Control in support of B-24s to Rouen–Beauvais, France, from 1935 to 2230 hours. After landfall at 2037, rendezvous was made with B-24s. The Group was vectored to bogies at Beauvais without result and everyone came out 23,000 feet over Fecamp at 2140.

18 July 1944: F.O. 454. Col. Blakeslee led a Penetration Target Withdrawal Support to Kiel, Germany, from 0620 to 1100 hours. Rendezvous was made at 0804 with B-17s stacked at 18/23,000 feet over 10/10ths cloud. After escorting the bombers to the coast, the Group turned to 095˚ for 14 minutes and picked up two boxes of Forts at 0910, escorting them out and leaving for home at 0923.

19 July 1944: F.O. 456. Maj. Blanding led a Penetration Target Withdrawal Support to Munich, Germany, from 0649 to 1240 hours. Enemy aircraft were reported south of Munich. 334 saw nine after becoming separated and bounced two without scoring. The rest of the Group engaged 10 to 15 109s at 1015, getting four for the loss of Kermit Dahlen. At 1045 Curtis Simpson said he was going down with a glycol leak. (After being interned, he evaded back to Debden by 15 October.) Escort was broken near Aachen at 1140.

[Box Score: 4 destroyed, 2 lost]

20 July 1944: F.O. 457. Maj. Blanding led a Penetration Target Withdrawal Support to Leipzig–Kothen–Dessau, Germany, from 0810 to 1410 hours. After landfall over Zeebrugge at 0859 and 20,000 feet, rendezvous was made with the Forts as scheduled. The Group split up and went different ways with various boxes of bombers to the three different targets. The flak over Leipzig and Dessau was very intense up to 35,000. Lester Godwin was hit by flak over Aachen but he got back to Antwerp before bailing out and becoming an evader. The Group came out at various points over the Dutch islands around 1345, from 20,000 to 25,000 feet.

[Box Score: 0 destroyed, 1 lost]

21 July 1944: F.O. 458. Lt. Col. Clark led a Penetration Target Withdrawal Support to Munich, Germany, from 0735 to 1310 hours. At 0921 the Group joined the B-24s at 25,000 feet. Fifteen to twenty 109s attacked the lead box and 335 gave chase without engaging. Escort was broken near Liege at 1220.

22 July 1944: F.O. 459. Col. Blakeslee led a Ramrod Escort to Kiel–Hamburg–Bremen, Germany, from 1615 to 2055 hours. Rendezvous with seven B-17s was made over the North Sea at 18,000 feet, climbing to 31,000, with landfall over Cuxhaven at 1852. The Forts then proceeded to drop propaganda leaflets dealing with the 20 July attempt on Hitler's life. The 4th left the bombers at the English coast at 2015. Takeoff for this mission was pretty much a nightmare. Lloyd Kingham spun in and was killed. Gillette and Brown collided but both made it back down. On the way back in at 2130 from aborting, James Ayres crashed in a potato patch with a faulty engine.

[Box Score: 0 destroyed, 1 lost]

24 July 1944: F.O. 461. Col. Blakeslee led a Strafing show to the Weingarten area, Germany, from 0935 to 1510 hours. Landfall was made over Ostend inbound for the assigned target, Lechfeld airdrome. By 1115 the formation should have been over Augsburg but 10/10ths cloud from the coast inland prevented pinpointing, so Lechfeld was scrubbed. Blakeslee brought the Group starboard to find a hole at 1210. The Group went down and attacked a power station at Weingarten, badly damaging it. Splitting up to attack targets of opportunity, the P-51s roamed from Weingarten to Tuttlingen and along the north shore of Lake Constance. Near

Stockach several sections attacked trains. Numerous cars and locos were destroyed. The Group came home split up.

25 July 1944: F.O. Weather Recco. Lt. Emerson led two 336 sections to Lake Constance, Germany, from 0640 to 0940 hours.

28 July 1944: F.O. 469. Capt. Van Wyck led a Penetration Target Withdrawal Support to Merseburg, Germany, from 0725 to 1300 hours. After rendezvous with the B-17s at 0928, the Group skirted the target due to intense, heavy flak. The flak was the same over Koblenz. Escort was provided to the coast, where the bombers were left at 1200, 21,000 feet over Walcheren. At the beginning of the mission Deacon Hively inadvertently dropped his tanks on take-off. Coming back, he traded QP-J for QP-W and got off again but he was unable to catch the Group. He joined the 355th Fighter Group, which encountered what were thought to be new Me 209s near the RV point. Hively claimed a probable.

29 July 1944: F.O. 470. Col. Blakeslee led another Penetration Target Withdrawal Support to Merseburg, Germany, from 0715 to 1135 hours. After landfall at 22/23,000 over Schiermonnikoog, the Group was unable to find the Fortresses, even with vectoring. The Mustangs orbited near Emden over 10/10ths cloud but still no Forts, so they left the area at 0945 and went home.

31 July 1944: F.O. 472A. Col. Blakeslee led a Penetration Target Withdrawal Support to Munich, Germany, from 1010 to 1630 hours. Landfall was made at Zeebrugge at 1101 and 16,000 feet. Rendezvous with the Big Friends took place south of the briefed point and the fighters provided cover for the lead box of the first task force. The Group orbited until the bombers left at 1320, then dropped down near Heilbronn to attack a small airdrome with four FW 200s and several single-engine aircraft. Blakeslee tried to ignite his dropped tanks in a wooded area without success. The fighters came out at 1527, flying at 20,000 feet.

Even though the Group passed the 600 destroyed mark in July (623–38–282 as of 5 July), morale was generally low due to the letdown from the 4th's small role in the invasion . . . and there was no increase in activity as expected. While the Russia shuttle was taking place there was virtually no activity at Debden and when the Group was up in force again the Luftwaffe would not come up to do battle. The general sentiment was why not go somewhere the 4th was needed, possibly even another theater. Some of this was surely reflected in the fire of Blakeslee's 13 July briefing.

At least the tactical dive bombing would be pretty much left to the 9th Air Force as the Group got back to flying strategic escort shows to Germany. 336 also installed seven K-14 computing gyro gunsights in some of the kites in July. They were told they were the first in the 8th to fly ops with them and they would prove to be great aids in destroying enemy aircraft. 336 also had a laurel hung on its armorers: VIII FC acceptable average for ammunition per stoppage was 800 rounds, but in July the squadron was getting 6,904 rounds per stoppage.

1 August 1944: F.O. 473. Maj. Hively led a Penetration Target Withdrawal Support to Paris, France, from 1322 to 1755 hours. As the Group rendezvoused with the Big Friends at 1433 and headed in at 22/25,000 feet, Blakeslee, Godfrey and Glover flew with RAF Wing Commander Wickham (in QP-Z) to hunt for enemy aircraft. The patrol netted nothing and the boys left for home at 1630.

2 August 1944: F.O. 475. Maj. Blanding led a Type 16 Control for Strafing to Beauvais airdrome, France, from 1735 to 2250 hours. After landfall over Dieppe at 1818 at 22,000 feet, the Mustangs orbited Rouen, swept Beauvais, then went back to Rouen a total of three times. There was some strafing and Gerald Chapman was killed after leaving Beauvais.

[Box Score: 0 destroyed, 1 lost]

3 August 1944: F.O. 476. Capt. McFarlane led a Penetration Target Withdrawal Support to Joigny, France, from 1345 to 1805 hours. After landfall at 1454, the 4th joined on five boxes of bombers—the wrong ones. The Group turned back and rendezvoused with two boxes of Forts and escorted them to the target and back. Snuffy Smith failed to return, ending up a POW.

[Box Score: 0 destroyed, 1 lost]

4 August 1944: F.O. (?). Capt. McFarlane led a Penetration Target Withdrawal Support to Rostock, Germany, from 1140 to 1710 hours. Rendezvous with the bombers was ten minutes late over Husum, south of course. The airdrome was bombed at 1452 and the formation came home.

5 August 1944: F.O. 483. Col. Blakeslee led a Penetration Target Withdrawal Support to Brunswick, Germany, from 1025 to 1535 hours. Rendezvous was made northwest of Cuxhaven at 1220. Several free lance sections hunted for enemy aircraft and did some strafing. Glover got a 109 while Godfrey, back from the States since 24 July, got a 109 in the air and three Ju 52s on the ground.

[Box Score: 5 destroyed, 0 lost]

F.O. (?). Lt. Patteeuw led a Type 16 Control to Lens, France, from 1310 to 1450 hours. After some vectoring, the P-51s escorted returning bombers out to the coast.

6 August 1944: F.O. (?). Maj. Blanding led a Penetration Target Withdrawal Support to Berlin, Germany, from 0920 to 1555 hours. Rendezvous was made at 1135 with bombs away at 1237. Several sections roamed for prey, destroying three on the ground and two in the air. After getting an Me 410, Johnny Godfrey was hit by flak, crippling his fuel system. He jettisoned the canopy and got ready to jump when Glover talked him into using his hand-pump primer to keep the kite up. After 2½ hours and a bloody primer hand, Godfrey landed at Beccles, Norfolk.

[Box Score: 5 destroyed, 0 lost]

7 August 1944: F.O. 492. Col. Blakeslee led a Strafing show to Dijon–Chalon–Meaux, France, from 1425 to 1850 hours. Landfall was made over Treport at 1510 and 17,000 feet. By 1630 the formation was down to 2,000 over Chalon-sur-Saone. As was almost normal when beating up ground targets (this time locos, vehicles and other moving things), flak claimed some of the Group's pilots. Sidney

Wadsworth emerged from a terrible crash to be captured. Donald Malmsten went down at Dijon, suffering burns and wounds, to become an evader. He made it back to Debden on 12 September.

[Box Score: 0 destroyed, 2 lost]

8 August 1944: F.O. 494. Col. Blakeslee led a Ramrod for RAF Beaufighters attacking convoys off the Norwegian coast from 1200 to 1755 hours. The Mustangs joined on the 30 Beaus at 1245 at North Coates, 300 to 500 feet off the water. The formation attacked 14 merchant vessels near Verhaug at 1445. 334 Blue Section stayed with the Beaus to bring them home while the rest of the Group went north to Stavanger/Sola airdrome. Only one Ju 88 was destroyed there. A sweep of three more locations revealed bad hunting so the P-51s headed for home. On the way out of Norway at 1550, the Group was hit by murderous flak. Robert Fischer headed for Sweden in his crippled P-51B but was never seen again. Frank Jones ditched but apparently did not get out—it was his last mission and he was to have been married in ten days. Leon Blanding's kite was hit square in the canopy and he received severe injuries to his head and side. Tearing his trousers to bandage himself, he was led by Kolbe and Berry to wobble into Acklington, Northern England. Blood was streaked all the way back to the tail but he recovered. Earlier in the mission Thomas Underwood bailed out of his flaming kite to become a POW.

[Box Score: 1 destroyed, 3 lost]

9 August 1944: F.O. 496. Col. Blakeslee led a Penetration Target Withdrawal Support to Stuttgart, Germany, from 0900 to 1315 hours. There were no bombers at the RV point and no R/T communication so the Group followed the briefed course. As they crossed the Rhine the boys saw the bombers hitting targets of opportunity. The Group took up escort from 1050 to 1120, then went northwest to Zweibrucken to join up with 100 B-24s and 300 B-17s, the original charges. Before leaving the bombers at the coast at 1210, some of the '51s dropped down from 18,000 to strafe a train.

F.O. 497. Col. Blakeslee led a Fighter Bomb/Sweep to Chalons-sur-Marne–Chaumont, France, with 250-pound bombs from 1700 to 2040 hours. At 1816 the Group split up—336 to Verdun, 335 to Troyes, 334 with Blakeslee to Vitry. Results were listed as good against rail tunnels and other targets.

10 August 1944: F.O. 498. Maj. Hively led an Area and Withdrawal Support to Sens-St. Florentine, France, from 0900 to 1320 hours. Rendezvous was made five minutes late with bombs away at 1045. Some strafing was done with good results.

11 August 1944: F.O. (?). Capt. Van Wyck led a Penetration Target Withdrawal Support to Coulommiers airdrome, France, from 1010 to 1435 hours. Rendezvous was made with the Libs at 23,000 feet. The bombers then left the briefed course and bombed Chateaudun airdrome at 1230. Escort was broken at 1324 at the coast on the way out. Needham force landed at A-2 Cricqueville on the beachhead at 1335. The engine was changed on his QP-N and he flew home on the 13th.

12 August 1944: F.O. 506. Capt. Brown led a Penetration Target Withdrawal Support to Mourmelon and LeGrand landing grounds in France from 0730 to 1210 hours. After forming up with B-24s at 0909, the formation turned off the briefed course for targets northwest of Rheims. The Group was vectored to bandits without success, then to a train of buzz bombs with the same results. Crossing Charleroi airdrome, the roving Mustangs found no aircraft to shoot up but they strafed it anyway along with several targets on the way out.

F.O. 507. Capt. Brown took the Group out again with 500 pound bombs on a Fighter Bomb/Sweep to Chalons–Troyes–St. Dizier, France, from 1525 to 1925 hours. From Boulogne, the Mustangs dropped from 17,000 to 2,000 feet north of Troyes at 1640, then split into squadrons. 334 swung port and mistakenly got into the area assigned 335, then went back starboard and strafed locos before going port to Chalons to drop bombs on targets of opportunity with poor results. 336 got on a marshalling yard after missing their assigned target and 335 had to jettison most of its bombs before destroying a few targets. Jahnke, on climbout in QP-T, was forced to bail out due to an in-flight fire at 1600 near Lashendon–Bradwell Bay. The kite blew up with its bombs.

[Box Score: 0 destroyed, 1 lost]

13 August 1944: F.O. 511–512. Capt. Van Wyck led a Fighter Bombing mission with 500-pound bombs to Beauvais–Compiegne–Paris, France, from 0825 to 1150 hours. Arriving in the target area at 0930, the Group split up into squadrons, then into sections to hit communications targets. Results in both bombing and strafing were generally good.

F.O. 511–512. The Group went on a Penetration Withdrawal Support to St. Malo, France, from 1230 to 1525 hours. Rendezvous was made over Grandchamp at 1334 and escort was broken on the way back in mid-Channel.

F.O. 511–512. Capt. Van Wyck led the third mission of the day, another Fighter Bombing with 500 pounders, to the area west of Paris, France, from 1720 to 2035 hours. By 1820 the Group went into the target area from Nantes to Druex, with heavy flak over the latter. Results were again good in strafing and bombing. Stephen Boren was killed near Troesnes at 1925 after hitting a tree while strafing.

[Box Score: 0 destroyed, 1 lost]

14 August 1944: F.O. 513. Capt. Van Wyck led a Penetration Target Withdrawal Support to Lyon/Brun airdrome, France, from 0900 to 1435 hours. Rendezvous was made three minutes late at 15,000 for an uneventful escort.

15 August 1944: F.O. 516. Capt. Emerson led a Penetration Target Withdrawal Support to Bad Zwischenahn, Germany, from 1015 to 1355 hours. Rendezvous was made six minutes late at 1154 north of Battrum, crossing the airdrome at 17,000 feet in moderate "golf ball" flak. Leaving 334 to take the bombers back out to the Zuider Zee, 335 and 336 went down and strafed on the way out. Norman Achen was downed near Zwischenahn Lake and was captured.

[Box Score: 0 destroyed, 1 lost]

16 August 1944: F.O. 518. Capt.Van Wyck led a Penetration Target Withdrawal Support to Dessau, Germany, from 0820 to 1340 hours. Everyone joined up on time at 22,000 feet and made a starboard orbit. The 355th Fighter Group rendezvoused on time at 1030 and finally the 353rd Group picked up the rear of the bomber formation to bring them home. Ira Grounds downed a single Bf 109.

[Box Score: 1 destroyed, 0 lost]

17 August 1944: F.O. 519. Capt. Van Wyck led a Penetration Target Withdrawal Support to Les Foulens, France, from 0820 to 1415 hours. Weather made the "sightseeing cruise" uneventful for both the Forts and the fighters. Near Chartres the 4th was vectored to enemy aircraft that weren't there. As it turned out, ten bombers ended up being escorted by both the 4th and 355th Groups so the 4th stooged all over the beachhead, leaving the bombers at Bayeux at 1305.

It was found out that Blakeslee had to go out and get a new logbook—no doubt to continue doctoring it in order to hide his actual amount of combat time (various estimates placed it at 1,300 hours at this time). He was asked when he was going to quit. . . . "Hell, I'm just learning to fly!"

18 August 1944: F.O. 523B. Col. Blakeslee led an Area Support for fighter bombers of the 56th and 356th Groups to Beauvais, France, from 1225 to 1545 hours. The Group entered the target area at 17,000 feet and was vectored north, then west of Paris. 335 and 336 went down on the deck at Montdidier as 334 provided top cover under Type 16 control.

F.O. (?). Capt. McFarlane led a Dive Bombing and Strafing show to Beauvais–Gisors, France, from 1745 to 2140 hours. Arriving in the Gisors area at 1850 and 4,000 feet loaded with 500-pound bombs, the Group headed south for targets of opportunity. At 1930 fifteen Bf 109s bounced 334 south of Beauvais, downing three Mustangs (one pilot killed, one a POW and the other an evader who made it back to Debden in September). Arthur Cwiklinski, the evader, managed to get two of the Messerschmitts before going down. At 2000 the Group was bounced by over 50 more bandits. 335 and 336 tangled with the 109s and 190s, losing six pilots (all were killed except Otey Glass who managed to evade back to Debden by 2 September). Three 109s were shot down. Overall it had been a rough day.

[Box Score: 7 destroyed, 9 lost]

24 August 1944: F.O. 527. Col. Blakeslee led a Penetration Target Support to Misburg, then a Target Withdrawal Support to Merseburg, Germany, from 0825 to 1455 hours. Rendezvous with the B-24s was made at 1018, flying at 23,000 feet, and the target was bombed at 1129. 334 then went to Merseberg and swept south, returning to Merseburg for rendezvous with the Forts by 1213. As 335 was escorting stragglers at 1255, Ted Lines shot down two 109s southeast of Emden. John Godfrey and a few other 336 pilots strafed an airfield northeast of Nordhausen. Godfrey got four Ju 52s, Melvin Dickey got three and Pierce Wiggin got one. As the Mustangs worked the field over, Godfrey's kite was hit and he was forced to belly in and spend the rest of the war as a POW. It was later determined that Dickey, Godfrey's wingman, shot his leader down by accident.

[Box Score: 10 destroyed, 1 lost]

Two 336 kites flew an Air Sea Rescue from 1030 to 1520 hours.

25 August 1944: F.O. 528. Capt. Brown led a Penetration Target Withdrawal Support to Schwerin, Germany, from 0840 to 1430 hours. The Group rendezvoused with B-24s at 1046 south of Husum at 22/25,000 feet. West of the target 11 Bf 109s tangled with 336 at 1220 and three were destroyed. 334's Kenneth Rudkin went down to become a POW, presumably due to flak.

[Box Score: 3 destroyed, 1 lost]

F.O. 531. Lt. Glover led a Penetration Target Withdrawal Support to Liege, Belgium, from 1630 to 1950 hours. Rendezvous with 18 B-24s was made from 1719 to 1725 over Westhoofd at 23,000. Escort was uneventful and the Mustangs left the bombers over Walcheren between 1840 and 1849.

26 August 1944: F.O. 532. Capt. Brown led a Penetration Target Withdrawal Support to Rheine–Salzbergen, Germany, from 1050 to 1425 hours. The Group joined up with one wing of Liberators at 1210 northwest of Meppel at 21,000. The target was bombed at 1245 and the trip home was a milk run.

27 August 1944: F.O. 535–537. Col. Blakeslee led a Penetration Target Withdrawal Support to Basdorf–Orienburg, Germany, from 1205 to 1630 hours. Rendezvous with the lead wing of B-24s was made at 17/21,000 feet, 20 miles west of Nordstrand. Just inland a solid front rose to 26,000 so the Libs turned north and came out after a wide orbit over the Danish peninsula. Escort was broken at The Wash at 1620.

28 August 1944: F.O. 538. Col. Blakeslee led a Strafing show from Strasbourg to Sarrebourg, France, from 0650 to 1105 hours. 334 made Sarrebourg by 0840 but weather prevented the formation from going farther east. The Group strafed several trains and motor transport, losing three killed and two evaders. Pierce McKennon and Archibald Thomson both got away from the Germans for awhile. After a month with the Maquis, McKennon got back but Thomson was captured. Two-thirds of the Group landed at forward bases due to bad weather.

[Box Score: 0 destroyed, 5 lost]

30 August 1944: F.O. 541. Col. Blakeslee led a Ramrod Escort to Pas de Calais, France, from 1005 to 1300 hours with 16 kites from 335. Flying to the French coast, the Group saw neither bombers nor enemy aircraft before coming back home.

Strafing was taking its toll as the most dangerous form of combat for the 4th. Hofer turned out to be the only major 8th Air Force ace to be lost in aerial combat during the war. Everyone else went down while attacking things on the ground. Blakeslee wrote a treatise on strafing for VIII Fighter Command use released this day and he offered the following advice: "Once I hit the drome, I really get down on the deck. I don't mean five feet up; I mean so low the grass is brushing the bottom of the scoop." This may have sounded hot rock to many but the lower one came in, the harder it was for flak crews to get a good tracking solution. Skilled flying at zero feet was better insurance than sitting up higher.

1 September 1944: F.O. 543. Capt. Brown led a Penetration Target Withdrawal Support to Foret de Haguenau, Belgium, from 0925 to 1325 hours. At about 1040 the bombers aborted and were seen returning. Brown led the Group in a 180°turn for home but after crossing the coast a vector was received to head back on a fighter sweep. Ranging as far as Halle, the Group destroyed four, including a 109 by newly arrived Lt. Col. Claiborne Kinnard.

[Box Score: 4 destroyed, 0 lost]

F.O. (?). Capt. Joyce led a Penetration Target Withdrawal Support for 12 B-24s to Grave, Holland, from 1800 to 2100 hours. Rendezvous was made near Lowestoft for another uneventful escort.

Blakeslee was officially placed on leave for the States for the month, leaving Jim Clark as acting Group CO and former 355th Group Commander Claiborne Kinnard as deputy Group CO. Within a few days Kinnard assumed Clark's position when Jim was transferred. While gone, Col. Don made the famous remark "women and fighter pilots don't mix" to the New York press, much to the merriment of the guys at Debden. During his absence Blakeslee was secretly married.

2–4 September 1944: New air pressure G-suits were test flown by the Group's pilots for possible use in combat. Steve Pisanos, missing in action since 5 March, returned to Debden on the 3rd with stories of crash landing his kite while standing on the wing and evading to Paris where he fought with the Maquis until liberation.

5 September 1944: F.O. 550. Lt. Glover led a Penetration Target Withdrawal Support to Karlsruhe, Germany, from 0920 to 1435 hours. The P-51s found the B-24s at 1055. 334's Jerry Brown was forced to bail out of his ailing Mustang but he was picked up and toasted by the French, returning to Debden the next day via C-47 from Amiens.

6 September 1944: Four 334 and two 336 kites flew to Northholt where they staged a Special Escort to Amiens, France, for three C-47s from 1630 to 1900 hours. One of the Gooneys carried the Prince of Holland.

8 September 1944: F.O. 556. Capt. Norley led a Penetration Target Withdrawal Support to Ludwigshafen, Germany, from 0935 to 1355 hours after initial leader Lt. Glover aborted. When the primary B-24s aborted, the Group rendezvoused with several wings of B-17s near Saarbrucken at 22/28,000 feet. Towering cumulus made join up and escort difficult. The Group left the bombers at 1315 in the Paris area.

9 September 1944: F.O. 558. Capt. Brown led a Penetration Target Withdrawal Support to Gustausburg–Mainz, Germany, from 0848 to 1305 hours. Near Brussels the Group joined up with 72 B-24s at 0952. The bombers missed their briefed turn for the target but came back and got on the proper run-in heading, bombed, then came back home.

F.O. 560. Lt. Col. Kinnard led a Dive Bombing mission to the Dutch Islands from 1646 to 1910 hours. Communications targets were bombed at Schouwen, 336 hit Overflakkee and transport ships were attacked at Walcheren. Several boats were strafed but there were no bomb hits.

10 September 1944: F.O. 561. Capt. Brown led a Penetration Target Withdrawal Support to Ulm, Germany, from 0845 to 1410 hours. Two wings of Libs were joined at 20/22,000 feet and P-38s joined the escort just before the target. Brown took two sections toward Strasbourg at 1115 in reply to Ted Lines, who R/T'd, "I've got seven of them cornered." Trying to catch up with the Group after landing for quick repairs at an advanced base, Lines attacked seven 109s and a Ju 88. Some P-47s arrived to help with the 109s but Lines did OK—he got three along with the Ju 88. Brown finally quit looking and rejoined the bombers as they dropped near Ludwigshafen at 1120. On the way back from the show Robert White crashed near Boxted and was killed.

[Box Score: 4 destroyed, 1 lost]

11 September 1944: F.O. 563. Lt. Col. Kinnard led a Penetration Target Withdrawal Support to Halle, Germany, from 0918 to 1445 hours. The Group orbited at the RV point until the Forts caught up north of Koblenz at 23/25,000 feet. In what many pilots considered the first good fight since May, the Germans put up over 100 fighters to stop the 8th Air Force. By 1120 combats were raging all over the route into Germany. Several 109s were caught in landing patterns and much strafing was done at Langensalza airdrome, netting several ground kills in addition to the aerial kills. 334 rejoined the bombers and took them to Aachen, then broke off at 1335. Two of the 4th's pilots were killed and three captured.

[Box Score: 14 destroyed, 5 lost]

12 September 1944: F.O. 565. Capt. Brown led a Penetration Target Withdrawal Support to Brux–Ruhland, Germany, from 0833 to 1440 hours. Rendezvous was made over Hagenow at 22/25,000 feet with B-17s. A jet was observed to pass close by but it was gone before anything could be done. After the secondary target was hit at Ruhland, another jet was seen. Near Frankfurt 336 R/T'd 14 enemy aircraft spotted and the Group got into a fight, destroying several by the time the fight worked its way to Wiesbaden. Two pilots went down to be captured.

[Box Score: 9 destroyed, 2 lost]

A Field Day was held on the athletic field to celebrate the Group's second anniversary. Several 4th kites were also loaned to the 355th at Steeple Morden to make an extra squadron for a Russia shuttle show.

13 September 1944: F.O. 566. Lt. Col. Kinnard led a Penetration Target Withdrawal Support to Ulm, Germany, from 0836 to 1345 hours. The assigned bombers aborted so the Group picked up several combat wings of B-17s over the Rhine River. 334 Blue Section strafed Schwabisch Hall airdrome at 1145, getting one by William Smith, who was then hit by flak and killed. 335 strafed Limburg and

Gelcheim airdromes, getting 11 destroyed. The bombers were escorted until Ostend at 1300.

[Box Score: 12 destroyed, 1 lost]

Upon returning to Debden it was found the 4th had once again taken the scoring lead back from the 56th's Wolfpack, 687 to 684 victories. A party was held in the mess to celebrate.

15 September 1944: F.O. 571. Capt. Brown led a Penetration Support to Warsaw, Poland, from 0905 to 1235 hours. On what was supposed to have been a shuttle to Russia, three wings of B-17s turned back after the 1035 rendezvous. The Group orbited and then came home after passing over the Frisian Islands.

16 September 1944: A V-1 hit near the water tower in Saffron Walden at 0610, shaking things up quite a bit.

17 September 1944: F.O. 576. Lt. Col. Kinnard led an Area Patrol under M.E.W. control from Harderwijk, Netherlands, to Wesel, Germany, from 1025 to 1545 hours. The Group provided escort during the mass paratroop and glider assault phase of Operation Market Garden to Arnhem. The Mustangs then patrolled as a screen for the area east of the landings. Near Bocholt the '51s were bounced by 15 FW 190s at 1345. In fights from 10,000 feet to the deck, 335 got six of them but Nicholas Vozzy was killed and Clifford Holske captured.

[Box Score: 6 destroyed, 2 lost]

18 September 1944: F.O. 577. Lt. Howe led a Penetration Support to Warsaw, Poland, from 0715 to 1440 hours. At 0910 rendezvous was made with three wings of Fortresses near Heligoland at 14,000 feet. Escort was broken at 1117. On the way back the Group passed the 355th's Mustangs on the way to pick up the escort near Neustettin for a shuttle to Russia; some of the 4th's borrowed kites were in the formation. Bogies were called but never found and after Schwerin 336 Lt. Smith was bounced by an Me 262. Four of the boys tried to engage without success.

19 September 1944: F.O. 579. Maj. Brown led an Area Patrol from Eindhoven to Nijmegen, Netherlands, in support of Market Garden from 1500 to 1815 hours. Visibility was very poor in the assigned area. The Group ended up contacting some empty C-47s going southwest and followed their track until recalled at 1720.

20 September 1944: F.O. 580. Lt. Col. Kinnard led an Area Support for the 1st Allied Airborne Army at Eindhoven, Netherlands, from 1505 to 1925 hours. Entering the area at 1620, the Mustangs climbed to 12,000 feet and orbited to port and starboard, working southwest, before going home.

23 September 1944: F.O. 585. Lt. Col. Kinnard led another Area Support back to the 1st Allied Airborne Army slogging through Market Garden. The Group patrolled from Zwolle to Apeldoorn, Netherlands, and back from 1405 to 1910 hours at 6/8,000 feet.

25 September 1944: F.O. 586. Capt. Glover led a Penetration Target Withdrawal Support to Koblenz, Germany, from 1005 to 1505 hours. Rendezvous was made with one wing of B-24s at 1122 near Ghent at 23,000 feet. The Group was relieved by P-47s on the way out, freeing the Mustangs to strafe. 334 returned on track to the target area, then went on to Frankenberg, shooting up a train and several trucks. Warren Williams of 336 destroyed a Ju 88 on the ground at Bad Lippspringe and visiting SAAF Capt. Henwick was lost, but he evaded back by the 28th.

[Box Score: 1 destroyed, 0 lost]

26 September 1944: F.O. 588. Lt. Col. Kinnard led a Penetration Target Withdrawal Support to Hamm, Germany, from 1240 to 1720 hours. At 1355 the Group joined up with two wings of Libs over Texel at 22,000 feet. Controllers vectored the fighters without result; the P-51s returned to the bomber track. Escort was broken near Vic Almelo and the P-51s stooged toward Bremen before turning for home.

27 September 1944: F.O. 590. Maj. Brown led a Penetration Target Withdrawal Support to Kassel, Germany, from 0745 to 1300 hours. By 0850 the P-51s rendezvoused with three wings of B-24s at 22,000 feet. 334 and 335 swept south of the bomber stream on withdrawal and at 1030 heard 336 calling 100 bandits attacking the bombers near Giessen from the northeast at 26,000. The squadron got four of them and 334 got one. This put the Group over the 700 destroyed mark.

[Box Score: 5 destroyed, 0 lost]

28 September 1944: F.O. 591. Lt. Col. Kinnard led a Penetration Target Withdrawal Support to Magdeburg, Germany, from 0850 to 1515 hours. At 1025 rendezvous was made with four combat wings of Flying Fortresses at 25/28,000 feet. Shortly after Hersfeld 60-plus FW 190s approached the last formation of bombers in two tight gaggles. 334 Green Section attacked broadside and the 479th Group's P-38s came in from behind to get two. Five B-17s were seen to go down as the Group fought off the attackers. Escort was broken near Malmedy at 1345.

[Box Score: 1 destroyed, 0 lost]

30 September 1944: F.O. 592. Maj. Brown led a Penetration Target Withdrawal Support to Hamm, Germany, from 1145 to 1600 hours. The P-51s joined on their B-24s over Turnhout at 24,000 feet and broke an uneventful escort by 1505.

2 October 1944: F.O. 594. Maj. Brown led a Penetration Target Withdrawal Support to Hamm, Germany, again from 1140 to 1555 hours. As the Group made landfall at 1251, rendezvous was made with two combat wings of B-24s at 21,000 feet. During the otherwise uneventful escort, George Logan spun out and was killed near Apeldoorn.

[Box Score: 0 destroyed, 1 lost]

3 October 1944: F.O. 596. Maj. Brown led a Penetration Target Withdrawal Support to Baden-Baden, Germany, from 0930 to 1425 hours. Rendezvous with one wing of Liberators was made at 24,000 feet and broken by 1310.

5 October 1944: F.O. 598. Lt. Col. Kinnard led a Penetration Target Withdrawal Support to Paderborn, Germany, from 0935 to 1410 hours. The P-51s joined up with 80 B-24s as landfall was made at 1052 and 23,000 feet. A few sections dropped down to strafe before escort was broken at 1300 near the coast.

There was a V-1 alert that night at Debden and two exploded nearby before the all-clear at 2006.

6 October 1944: F.O. 599. Capt. Glover led a Penetration Target Withdrawal Support to Berlin, Germany, from 0900 to 1435 hours. The Group found one wing of B-17s at 22/24,000 feet northeast of Bremerhaven at 1100. As the Group was on the way in, two 335 pilots downed an Me 410 over Heligoland. Near Nauen eight Bf 109s came in from the north at 1205 and three sections tried to catch them without success. 334 Green Section, lost in the overcast, turned back to the last box of bombers as it was attacked by 40 to 50 109s from the cloud layer above. Leonard Werner chased one down at 600 mph and as the 109 attempted to turn port it shredded into tiny pieces, the victim of a tenacious pilot flying the product of North American's engineering genius. Werner noted that his new G-suit was a great help. Another 109 was destroyed 15 miles east of Berlin by Joseph Joiner.

[Box Score: 3 destroyed, 0 lost]

The score wasn't quite enough, though: This day the 56th again passed the 4th in the number of aircraft destroyed.

Forty-seven Mustangs of the 354th Fighter Group arrived from A-66 in St. Dizier, France, due to fog covering their home base. Each 4th squadron played host to one of their counterparts until the 11th, flying two missions together. Line and hangar personnel serviced all the fighters, and were greatly overworked.

7 October 1944: F.O. 600. Lt. Col. Kinnard led a Penetration Target Withdrawal Support to Magdeburg, Germany, from 0915 to 1455 hours. On the way out at 1035 Lt. Foster bailed out of QP-T as it blew up; he was fished out of the Channel after half an hour. Rendezvous with two combat wings of B-24s was made near Alkmaar at 1110 and 24,000 feet, joining the 56th Group in providing escort. Eleven 355th Fighter Group aircraft were with the Group on this mission. Escort was broken at 1350.

Another Buzz Bomb alert was sounded at 2018 and two exploded before the all-clear at 2046.

9 October 1944: F.O. 603. Maj. Brown led a Penetration Target Withdrawal Support to Giessen, Germany, from 1245 to 1705 hours. The Group joined the B-24s at 1450 and 21,000 feet. The Big Friends bombed by PFF near Frankfurt. Ted Lines got two 109s at 1515 southwest of Gedern, one just airborne, the other on the ground. The bombers were left south of Liege at 1554.

[Box Score: 2 destroyed, 0 lost]

10 October 1944: Four RAF Gloster Meteor jets arrived at 1200 hours to work with the 4th in developing German jet countermeasures for 8th Air Force fighters.

11 October 1944: Capt. Glover led an Air Sea Rescue Support with eight kites from 336 between 1500 and 1855 hours.

12 October 1944: F.O. 1235A. Capt. Norley led a Penetration Target Withdrawal Support to Rheine–Salzbergen airdrome, Germany, from 0955 to 1350 hours. 334 was cut loose to free lance while the other two squadrons provided escort. Much strafing was done by two of 334's sections.

At 1500 the Meteors and Mustangs tangled in dogfights over Debden in a very clear sky much to the delight of everyone on the ground.

At 2345, 15 minutes after 334's party let out, there was a Buzz Bomb alert and once again it was not meaningless, as one exploded nearby.

13 October 1944: At 1600 the four Meteors were up to joust again with the Group's P-51s. The next day they were up again. Pilots found the mock dogfights very valuable since the jets provided a first-hand experience with how to get at their German counterparts. All in all, the Meteors were the victors since they could easily outrun the '51s if cornered.

There was another Buzz Bomb alert at 2145 and yet again one exploded nearby. People were wondering if Göring didn't have specific orders to launch his V-1s at the "Red Nosed Gangsters" before they did any more damage in the air to his hard-pressed Luftwaffe.

14 October 1944: F.O. 1239A. Lt. Col. Kinnard led a Penetration Target Withdrawal Support to Kaiserslautern, Germany, from 1045 to 1455 hours. The Group joined up with two wings of B-24s at 1200 and 23,000 feet. Shortly thereafter a formation of B-17s flew into the Liberators and Mustangs head-on, giving some anxious moments. Then control reported bandits but nothing was sighted and the bombers were diverted to a target of opportunity near Mannheim. Joseph Lang got separated and at 1310 he R/T'd, "This is Lang. I am down below clouds with ten 109s; I got two; I don't know where I am and I need help." He was seen to crash by ground troops in his QP-Z.

[Box Score: 2 destroyed, 1 lost]

Yet another Buzz Bomb alert from 0330 to 0400 got everybody up.

15 October 1944: F.O. 1240A. Capt. Glover led a Penetration Target Withdrawal Support to Cologne, Germany, from 0835 to 1210 hours. Rendezvous was made at 0920 with two combat wings of Liberators at 18,000 feet. The uneventful escort was broken at 1145.

17 October 1944: F.O. 1245A. Capt. McKennon led a Penetration Target Withdrawal Support to Cologne–Leverkusen, Germany, from 0815 to 1210 hours. As the Group made landfall over Dunkirk at 0900, they joined the B-24s at 18,000 feet. Another uneventful escort was broken at 1140.

18 October 1944: F.O. 1246. Capt. Glover led a General Support to Cologne, Germany, from 0930 to 1405 hours. At 1055 the Big and Little Friends were just about to rendezvous when the controller called bandits near Koblenz for a goose-chase. At 1115 the Mustangs picked up 12 B-17s and escorted them to Brussels, then left them near Lille as they headed toward Boulogne. The Group came out over the coast at 1305.

19 October 1944: F.O. 1249A. Lt. Col. Kinnard led a Penetration Target Withdrawal Support to Mainz, Germany, from 1050 to 1520 hours. After rendezvous at 1145 south of Brussels with B-17s at 16,000 feet, escort was provided to the target. The red nosed P-51s broke off at 1420 near Ghent.

20 October 1944: Blakeslee arrived on the field from his Stateside leave, minus his ribbons, saying soldiers on the home front were hostile to overseas men. He was happy to be "home" and in addressing 336's enlisted men he said, "You are not missing anything by not being in the States." The men's reaction was "Bull!"

22 October 1944: F.O. 1254A. Capt. McKennon led a Penetration Target Withdrawal Support to Hamm, Germany, from 1155 to 1635 hours. Rendezvous was made with the wrong box of bombers at 18,000 feet. The Group turned back and found its five wings of B-17s at 1335 over the Zuider Zee. Several sections went on a strafing spree on the way out from Groningen, getting locos and other targets of opportunity. The remainder of the P-51s left the bombers at 1510.

23 October 1944: Another alert was called as four Buzz Bombs exploded in the area between 1938 and 1950 hours.

25 October 1944: F.O. 1263A. Col. Blakeslee was happily leading the herd for the first time in almost two months on a Penetration Target Withdrawal Support to Neumunster, Germany, from 1105 to 1535 hours. Rendezvous was made with two combat wings of Libs at 1310 over Jutland at 24,000 feet. An uneventful escort was broken at 1415 north of the Frisian islands.

26 October 1944: F.O. 1264A. Col. Blakeslee led another Penetration Target Withdrawal Support, this time to Minden, Germany, from 1230 to 1640 hours. The Mustangs joined on two wings of B-24s at 1400 over 10/10ths cloud at 22,000 feet. Ted Lines, trying to catch up, encountered six FW 190s at 1425 and got two. Then a rocket-powered Me 163 made two passes at him from 200 yards and left. Escort was broken at 1530.

[Box Score: 2 destroyed, 0 lost]

27 October 1944: Rudder colors were applied to all three squadrons, aiding in both unit recognition and individual color. 334 was red, 335 white with a red outline and 336 blue.

30 October 1944: F.O. 1273A. Col. Blakeslee led a Penetration Target Withdrawal Support to Hamburg, Germany, from 1030 to 1530 hours. One wing of B-24s was found at 1240 over 10/10ths cloud. The formation became separated from the main force, rejoined it near Heligoland, then the Group broke off from 1400 to 1420 north of Texel.

After getting back from the show, Blakeslee received news he had been dreading for well over a year—he was grounded. Col. Hub Zemke, the 56th's famous and able tactician and former Group CO, had been downed in bad weather and captured this day while flying with the 479th. VIII Fighter Command had no desire to lose Ole Man River in the same way. Before leaving again for the States on 19 November, Col. Don made several leisurely trips in WD-C to the old bases he had frequented during his 3½ years in the U.K., as well as a trip to Paris. But he was very dispirited. In many ways Debden would always be home and he hated to leave, but leave he did without his decorations or his RAF wings . . . or the silver beer mug his men gave him.

1 November 1944: F.O. 1278A. Capt. Glover led a Penetration Target Withdrawal Support to Gelsenkirchen, Germany, from 1210 to 1550 hours. At 1310 the Group rendezvoused with B-24s at 22,000 feet. An Me 262 was seen to make a dart at the bombers before escort was broken at 1510, 19,000 feet over Alkmaar.

Lt. Col. Kinnard assumed command of the Group from Blakeslee.

2 November 1944: F.O. 1281A. Capt. Glover led a Free Lance/Target Withdrawal Support to Merseburg, Germany, from 0925 to 1530 hours. The Group swept in over Ijmuiden at 1040, doing much strafing, and by 1200 bogies were reported north of Wernigerode. The Group turned and encountered 15 Bf 109s and five rocket-powered Me 163s at 1215. 335 and 336 engaged southeast of Leipzig. Glover and Norley each got a 163 and two 109s were destroyed. The Mustangs escorted the bombers back out to the Channel and broke off at 1420 and 14,000.

[Box Score: 4 destroyed, 0 lost]

4 November 1944: F.O. 1286A. Lt. Col. Kinnard led a Penetration Target Withdrawal Support to Hannover–Misburg, Germany, from 0945 to 1450 hours. South of Hamburg, the bombers arrived at 1145 late for rendezvous—the Group had been flying back down the briefed track to find them. A few suspected jet contrails were investigated, yielding nothing. Escort was broken at 1327 over the northeast Polder.

5 November 1944: F.O. 1288A. Maj. Carlson led a Penetration Target Withdrawal Support to Karlsruhe, Germany, from 0915 to 1455 hours. Shortly after landfall over Calais at 1000, rendezvous was made with B-24s at 23,000. After making the target at 1126, the Group left the bombers near Luneville shortly after 1200 to strafe rail and road traffic to the limit of their endurance. Before passing out over Dunkirk at 1400, the Group wreaked much havoc and destruction, but lost Russell Anderson, who became a POW.

[Box Score: 0 destroyed, 1 lost]

6 November 1944: F.O. 1291A. Lt. Col. Kinnard led a Penetration Target Withdrawal Support to Minden, Germany, from 0845 to 1310 hours. When not able to find the bombers at the RV point, the Group went on and found them north of Munster at 19/20,000 feet. Time over target was 1045. The Group destroyed a 109 and a 190 for the loss of two pilots (KIA and POW) in a fight before leaving the bombers over Ijmuiden at 1215.

[Box Score: 2 destroyed, 2 lost]

8 November 1944: F.O. 1296A. In an effort to avoid the Germans' outnumbering the escorts, the 4th flew its first A and B "Double" Group mission, eventually working up to 36 fighters per Group. On a Penetration Target Withdrawal Support/Free Lance to Merseburg, Germany, Maj. Carlson led A Group from 0855 to 1450 hours and Capt. Montgomery led B Group from 0910 to 1450 hours. B rendezvoused with B-17s near Minden while A flew south, inside of the route of the bombers, to join up at 1040 with the Forts near Wernigerode at 25/27,000 feet. The bombers were left from Lingen to the Zuider Zee between 1230 and 1245, both Groups turning back to strafe locos and trucks near Vechta. Both Groups came out at 1350 near Ijmuiden. An Me 262 was chased near Dummer Lake but the '51 couldn't catch up even though going all out at 450 mph IAS. Earl Quist went down to be captured.

[Box Score: 0 destroyed, 1 lost]

9 November 1944: F.O. 1299A. Capt. Montgomery led a Penetration Target Withdrawal Support to Saarbrucken–Thionville, France, from 0800 to 1250 hours. Rendezvous was made at 0915 with B-17s at 23,000 feet. Both targets were bombed. Near Neufchateau three sections left the bombers to strafe northeast and east of Saarbrucken while the rest of the Group left between Lille and Dunkirk at 1200. Several trains and barges were destroyed by the roaming Mustangs.

10 November 1944: Lt. Werner led 334 on a Photo Reconnaissance of targets in the Halle, Germany, area from 0935 to 1400 hours. Landfall was made over Holland at 1030 and 22,000 feet over 10/10ths cloud. Over Erfurt airdrome the Squadron let down below the cloud deck. Snow, rain and scud made reconnaissance impossible near Halle. At 1145 the formation climbed back up and came home at 24,000 feet, crossing out over Dunkirk at 1330.

F.O. 1301A. Maj. Carlson led a Penetration Target Withdrawal Support to Hannover–Langendiebach–Hanau, Germany, from 1020 to 1550 hours. Rendezvous was made at 1131 with the B-24s at 22/23,000 feet. The milk run was broken near Malmedy at 1345 to head for home.

11 November 1944: F.O. 1306A. Lt. Col. Kinnard led a Penetration Target Withdrawal Support to Munster–Osnabruck–Gladbeck, Germany, from 0950 to 1310 hours. The Group found their B-17s at 1105, flying over the Zuider Zee at 25/28,000 feet. Several task forces mingled and separated on the way to the target and back. The fighters left the bombers at Alkmaar at 1225 and 24/26,000 feet.

18 November 1944: F.O. 1317A. Lt. Col. Kinnard led a Strafing show to Leipheim airdrome, Germany, from 1000 to 1605 hours. After landfall at Dunkirk at 1042, the Group climbed from 3,000 to 12,000 feet, then orbited Colmar to wait for the 355th Group. The two Mustang groups rendezvoused at 1210 and headed for Leipheim, arriving at 1245. 335 and 336 tried to deal with the flak defenses as the rest went in. Me 262s were all over the place and the boys, making an average of four passes each, destroyed 12 of the vaunted jets and a single 109 on the ground. Fitch and Creamer teamed up to get one in the air a mile south of the field. After

January, 1944: Lt. Nicholas "Cowboy" Megura and his ILL WIND QP-P before a morning show with 108-gal. tanks. A wingman with Capt. D. Beeson, he went on to triple Acedom and the DSC when he got a lead slot of his own. (*Nicholas Megura*)

Winter, 1944: A rising star of 336th is Lt. John T. Godfrey, shown here with his VF-P 42-7884 LUCKY–REGGIE'S REPLY. Lucky is his dog's name and Reggie was his brother killed in the North Atlantic sea war. (*J. Raphael*)

January, 1944: LtCol. Don Blakeslee checks times and compass headings for the mission he is leading today as the new 4TH commander. He has been leading the Group for a long time in the air as operations officer. (*4TFW*)

January, 1944: 334FS weaves up the perimeter track for takeoff on a crisp morning with tanks for a long ride into Germany. They will soon catch up with the long-outbound bombers. (*Leroy Nitschke*)

January, 1944: Maj. Lee Gover marks a milestone takeoff on his 100th mission. Soon after, his tour was completed and he returned to the U.S. as a P-47 instructor and tactician. (*Lee Gover*)

February 24–March 13, 1944: Sgt. Mynard Bartels, 334 IO section, in front of Maj. Jim Clark's new Mustang QP-W 43-6560. As squadron CO, Clark had one of the first Malcolm hood canopies at DB. His uncle, Tommy Hitchcock, had been a crusader of the P-51 development with the Rolls Royce engine. (*Edward Hedrick*)

January, 1944: Lt. J. L. Bennett, Capt. W. Millikan, and two 336th armorers check out the first bomb to be hung on a squadron a/c. (*J. Raphael*)

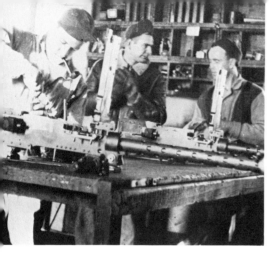

March, 1944: 334th armorers work to get the guns of the new Mustangs into shape for the heavy fighting now going on. The P-51 guns had troubles that needed urgent solutions. (*Leroy Nitschke*)

Feb. 27–Mar. 13, 1944: Lt. H. Blanchfield's brand new QP-E 43-6746 ready on the hardstand for a show with 75-gal. metal wing tanks. (*E. Hedrick*)

March, 1944: An early P-51B show gets off. Lt. W. Sooman in VF-D 43-6936 were both downed on 3/18/44 near Frankfurt, Germany. White-nosed a/c denote a pre-March 13th show. (*J. Raphael*)

Feb. 25–Mar. 13, 1944: Capt. K. D. Peterson and his VF-F 43-6696 were shot down on 3/29/44 when he won his DSC saving bombers from attack single-handedly. (*J. Raphael*)

Feb. 28–Mar. 3, 1944: Lt. G. Villinger has the scoop radiator door full open on takeoff with his VF-C 43-6985. Both disappeared into the bright blue sky forever on 3/2/44 (*J. Raphael*)

Winter, 1944: This 4TH pilot has deflection, which means destruction for this FW 190. (*J. Romack*)

Winter, 1944: Having pulled deflection on the FW 190, the 4TH pilot's hits of high explosive show as white spots on its wing root. (*J. Romack*)

March 5, 1944: Lt. Bob Wehrman, 336, looks over his just crashlanded VF-N 43-7005 at Heathfield, UK, after the plugs fused on the way home and he made a long glide to a total "prang." (*R. Wehrman*)

Vinter, 1944: Enemy FW 190 has dumped s canopy, wheels drop from damage, prop nd engine quit, smoke and debris trail its lunge towards the frozen earth. Another TH victory. (*J. Romack*)

February 28, 1944: Capt. Duane Beeson's QP-B 43-6819 just down from the first P-51 mission. Squadron line crew flock around to learn how it went and what problems they have to fix before tomorrow. (*Leroy Nitschke*)

April 1–5, 1944: Maj. Duane W. Beeson gives the mission news to anxiously waiting groundcrews as his prop stops and he begins to unhook from QP-B. Note his "Bee" emblem on helmet. (*N. Megura*)

March 4, 1944: Lt. Albert Schlegel went to Berlin and back in his WD-O 43-6770, only to have the gear collapse at the end of his landing. (*William Rushing*)

March 5, 1944: Capt. Duane W. Beeson by the flak-damaged fin of his QP-B 43-6819. He was hit on the record length show to Bordeaux, France, not far from the Spanish border. (*Larry Hendel*)

March, 1944: 336th pilots report their claims to the squadron I.O., Capt. Lloyd Benjamin. L-R: L. Norley, R. Hughes, W. Millikan, L. Benjamin, N. Gallagher (Millikan's crewchief), F. Blankschaen, unk., and E. Briel, on wing. (*Illustrated or News Photo*)

March, 1944: 336th pilots try to relax between operations in the Flt. Line HQ of the squadron. L-R: R. Simon, J. Godfrey, R. Nelson. Copies of the girlie art on the wall could be seen on bomber noses all over the 8AF, used as models by dozens of artists. (*Illustrated Press Photo*)

March 21, 1944: One of the dangers of strafing, now being done by 8AF fighters, was hitting a powerline cable. Lt. Vasseure Wynn's a/c on a long-range airfield beat-up to Bordeaux in southern France. (*Leroy Nitschke*)

Late March, 1944: Per new 8FC orders the Mustangs got red noses and the white ETO tail bands were removed to avoid confusion of the P-51 with the Bf109. The painting was done while the a/c were in hangar being checked for defective motor mount bolts. (*Leo Schmidt*)

April, 1944: Five top-hands of 336th in front of John Godfrey's VF-P 43-6765. L-R: D. Emerson, R. Hughes, D. Gentile, K. Carlson, and D. Patchen. Their combined victories came to 46. (*Popperfoto*)

April, 1944: Lt. John T. Godfrey and his dog, Lucky, on his VF-P. He and Gentile became a dual scoring element combination. They put red/white checkered panels on their a/c to aid form-up. (*Illustrated News Photo*)

March, 1944: The famous aces relax at a DB party. Front row, the three squadron COs: James Goodson of 336, George Carpenter of 335, and Jim Clark of 334. Back row: John Godfrey, Charlotte Fredericks, Don Gentile, and unknown date. (*N Lippman*)

April, 1944: Another show rolls out. QP-Z carries two 75-gal. metal tear-drop wing tanks now in P-51B use. This B Flight kite is probably flown by Lt. J. Lang. (*William Rushing*)

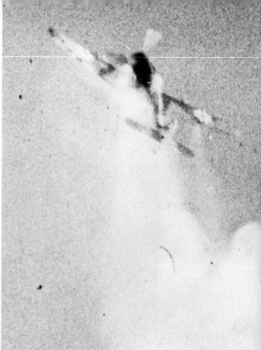

April, 1944: Capt. Nicholas "Cowboy" Megura pulls up to a bomber in his ILL WIND QP-N 43-6636 bearing his current 15 victories on the cowl. Ortho film makes red nose color light. (*Tom Boyle via Nicholas Megura*)

March, 1944: An FW 190 streams smoke and flame as it is pounded by hits from a 4TH pilot. (*J. Romack*)

April, 1944: Famous 4TH Ace, Don Gentile, makes an authorized low approach "buzz" north up the N-S runway past 334th HQ. This was about the time he was close to tying Rickenbacker's score. (*USAF*)

April, 1944: Capt. W. Millikan's VF-U lies on the runway with collapsed landing gear, a casualty of lesser nature in combat ops. (*John Romack*)

April 29, 1944: A mission return mishap of a human failure. Lt. Monroe in QP-C has taxied into a 336th a/c, VF-Q. (*William Rushing*)

April, 1944: 336's Capt. Kendall "Swede" Carlson happily holds up a finger to show that one Hun pilot less will be back tomorrow to shoot at him. (*N. Megura*)

April, 1944: Lt. Robert F. Nelson of 336th is welcomed back by his pooch and his crewchief, S/Sgt. F. Blankschaen. (*R. Nelson*)

April 29, 1944: This is what it looked like from the 4TH's position as top cover as 453rd BG Forts hit Berlin. Note Tempelhof airport to the left with several aircraft, both multi-engine and single-engine. (*USAF*)

April, 1944: The mobile repair units of the 45th Air Service Squadron work hard to have LtCol. Jim Clark's QP-W 43-6560 ready for the next show. The engineering feats of the 4TH maintenance echelons made much of the unit's success possible. (*William Rushing*)

April, 1944: Heavy combat and losses meant fitting-up new planes by the hangar crews. 43-6489 is being gun-bore sighted on the hangar door pattern, while a Malcolm hood and whip antenna are put on and the nose is painted red. (*Joseph Ciciulla*)

April, 1944: The new look in 4TH kites is the natural metal finish as the AAF deletes camouflage. WD-A 42-106911 is flown by Capt. Pierce McKennon and named YIPEE JOE!! A/C has a practice bomb hung on each wing for training in dive-bombing. (*Joseph Sills*)

May 1, 1944: VF-T 42-106686 ANN III was shared by Capt. J. H. Bennett with his squadron junior, Lt. F. "Pappy" Grove. Their CC was S/Sgt. John Ferra, Gentile's old chief. (*F. Grove*)

May 1, 1944: S/Sgt. John Ferra on the wing of his kite VF-T 42-106686 ANN III, bearing 8 kills of Capt. J. Bennett, who later became a POW on 5/25/44. (*F. Grove*)

April, 1944: A famous "Old Head" of 335th will be Capt. Pierce McKennon, the squadron CO thru VE-Day. He will successfully evade twice and live thru 26 months of combat and 22 victories. (*Joseph Sills*)

April, 1944: Capt. Louis Norley is another new ace who will serve on thru the remainder of the war with the 4TH, see combat in all three squadrons, and will be the inspiring commander of 335 and 334 before VE-Day. (*4TFW*)

April, 1944: A brave 335th ace who fell victim to airdrome flak and crashed to his death on April 10th, 1944, was Lt. Clemens Fiedler, seen here with his crewchief and their SNAFU. (*Leo Schmidt*)

April, 1944: Capt. Albert Schlegel in his WD-O 42-106464 with ten of his 15 victories on the cowl. He was 335th operations officer when he was lost on 8/28/44 to unknown causes on a strafing show. (*Woody Jensen*)

April 11, 1944: Col. Jesse Auton, 65FW CO, shows Gen. Eisenhower the 4TH's P-51 punch. He is firing the guns of Lt. F. Glover's VF-C 43-12214 REBEL QUEEN into the butts at 334th hangar. (*Leo Schmidt*)

April 24, 1944: A visiting Spit VB BM512 parked by DB tower. Wearing AAF stars and no codes, it is probably flown by some 8FC Brass staying over for a DB party night. (*Glesner Weckbacher*)

Spring, 1944: Capt. L. "Red Dog" Norley and a victory flourishing VF a/c. Both have seen long and heavy action by this date, as the kills and scruffy paint job denote. (*F. Grove*)

May, 1944: Lt. Joseph Higgin's VF-D 43-6942. The kite bears the standard Mustang colours now in use, without the name MEINER KLEINER later put on the nose by Lt. Higgins. (*Glesner Weckbacher*)

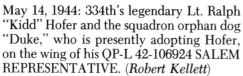

May 14, 1944: 334th's legendary Lt. Ralph "Kidd" Hofer and the squadron orphan dog "Duke," who is presently adopting Hofer, on the wing of his QP-L 42-106924 SALEM REPRESENTATIVE. (*Robert Kellett*)

May, 1944: Don Allen's 334th artwork flourished on the squadron B models. QP-M 43-6957 TURNIP TERMITE was the assigned a/c of Lt. Donald Malmsten, later belonged to Lt. Frank Speer. (*Leroy Nitschke*)

May, 1944: QP-J 43-6898 THE DEACON taxies past the 334th AA emplacement from which this view was taken. A/C now has a Malcolm hood and carries 108-gal pressed-paper tanks for the long show. (*Leo Schmidt*)

May, 1944: Lt. Dave Howe rolls past in his QP-S 43-6717, as 334th B Flight approached in the background. (*Leo Schmidt*)

May, 1944: A rare photo. "Kidd" Hofer's flamboyant QP-L 42-106924 SALEM REPRESENTATIVE. Note whitewall tires, OD topsurfaces, red tail fin band; his nickname is also painted on the black ETO band of the gear cover. (*Leo Schmidt*)

May, 1944: 336th heads for the runway on another show as D-Day nears and the tempo speeds up. The kite has VF in small letters under the nose and the polished air filter covers unique to 336FS OD 51B's. (*Joseph Ciciulla*)

May, 1944: VF-A carries 75-gal tanks as it follows a NMF 336th a/c to the runway. (*Joseph Ciciulla*)

May, 1944: The group rolls on takeoff with each a/c toting two 500-lb. bombs destined for enemy communications and transport in France. (*Edward Hedrick*)

May, 1944: Two of 336's NMF birds. Capt. W. Millikan in his VF-U 43-24769 MIS-SOURI MAULER, leads his wingman off in VF-T. Milly's P-47 emblem is repeated on the leftside cowl with 14 kill crosses. (*Edward Hedrick*)

Spring, 1944: Hits splatter on this Bf 109 as the 4TH pilot has an excellent position, dead aft at approximately 50 yards. (*J. Romack*)

Spring, 1944: The 109 begins its final dive pouring smoke, glycol, oil, and hydraulic fluids. (*J. Romack*)

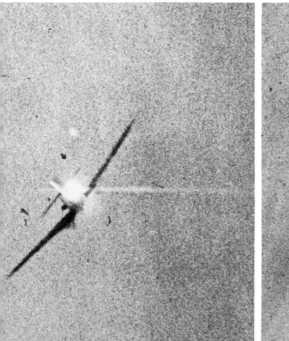

May 9, 1944: Shells explode among a GO-242 glider and HE-111 on Juvincourt A/D, France. This 336th pilot just misses trees and a hangar. The Group comes back from escort on the deck shooting up dromes. (*William O'Donnell*)

May 22, 1944: Another combat loss. Swedish AF crew raise Capt. N. Megura's QP-F 43-7158 from its belly on Kalmar A/D, Sweden, where "Cowboy" crash-landed it. He was shot up by a P-38 near Berlin and made it to internment. (*Swedish Air Force*)

May 31, 1944: Lt. R. Hofer touches the flak-hit rudder on his QP-L 42-106924. He awed line crews by victory-rolling the a/c in this state before landing. (*Leroy Nitschke*)

Spring, 1944: Arizona's future 4TH ace, Lt. Ted Lines, casts a pensive look at a near-run-thing by the damage on his tail fin. (*J. Cowman*)

May, 1944: Lt. T. McDill and his chief, Tony Cardella, with their VF-N LITTLE MAC after installing a new Spit mirror and Malcolm hood. A couple of days later they were both shot down in a fight with a superior number of enemy fighters. (*Thomas McDill*)

May, 1944: Capt. W. Millikan and his chief, Neal Gallagher. On 5/30/44 Milly and VF-U 43-24769 MISSOURI MAULER were downed in a mid-air collision with his wingman while dodging flak over Germany. (*F. Grove*)

May, 1944: Repairs and inspections pile up on 334th hangar crews as the ops roll on. Lt. Hofer's QP-L gets a Malcolm hood and check-out. Note gun bore-sight pattern on hangar door. (*Joseph Ciciulla*)

May, 1944: Maj. James Goodson in his VF-B here is vying for top Group ace during this period. The 336FS CO is just back from MTO where he instructed 15AF units in P-51 procedures and employment. (*4TFW*)

May, 1944: Smoke of a distant plane crash rises behind Maj. M. McPharlin's 339FG 6N-Z 42-106909. He returned often to his old 334FS to fly with his pals on 4TH shows. He died in "Z" with the 4TH on D-Day. (*Waldo Johnson*)

Spring, 1944: Lt. Ralph Hofer's a/c, before the famous emblem of the boxing mule was on it, carried his nickname on the gear cover, left side. Dark paint on wing, topside, is 8FC scheme for a/c possibly to be based in France after D-Day. (*Leo Schmidt*)

May, 1944: Lt. T. Fraser's QP-G 43-24825 JERRY waits in a B Flight bay with full 108-gal. tanks, ready for a show to go out. On D-Day, he and the a/c will be downed. He became a POW. (*Leo Schmidt*)

June, 1944: The 4TH planes, such as QP-N seen here in a B Flight bay, carry the flashy black-and-white stripes of Allied Expeditionary AF now that D-Day has arrived at last. (*Leroy Nitschke*)

June, 1944: The Invasion meant heavy workloads for ground crews. Here 335th armorers take ammo out of wing trays for return to the shop for repositioning, linkage checking, cleaning, counting, and resequencing of the loading. (*Baxter Roark*)

Pre-June 6, 1944: A 4TH alumnus returns. Maj. "Wee Michael" McPharlin of the 339FG with his 6N-Z 42-106909 WEE GINNY, in which he was KIA on D-Day while flying with the 4TH. (*Leroy Nitschke*)

June 20, 1944: 334th pilots (in leather jackets) learn to armor their own guns in readiness for the Russia Shuttle mission. They will be on their own with no ground crews at times. (*Edward Hedrick*)

June 6–20, 1944: Third ranking 4TH WW2 ace, Maj. James A. Goodson, is rightfully proud of his 30 victories displayed on his new VF-B 44-13303 D-model. On 6/20/44 he was downed in it to become a POW. (*F. Grove*)

June 21, 1944: Russia Shuttle day. Flying with the 4TH for added strength is the 486FS of the 352FG "Bluenoses." A/C have their in-squadron letter moved to the nose because of D-Day stripes on fusilage. GIGS-UP II pilot, Maj. Gignac, was killed several days earlier. (*John Romack*)

June 21, 1944: Famous firsts. Col. Blakeslee wears a flying scarf and the 4TH flys to Russia off the map to the right. It will be a ½-hour ride to Piryatin, USSR, on the extra mapboard by Don's knee. (*Cecil Manning*)

June, 1944: Col. Don Blakeslee straps in for the long ride to Russia while he checks his 16 maps carried to cover the route. (*4TFW*)

July 5, 1944: Gen. "Bill" Kepner, 8FC CG (left), watches the 4TH land home from the Italy leg of the Russia Shuttle. With him is Jim Clark, 4TH Deputy CO (center), and Col. Lawrence Callahan, 8FC IO and famous WW1 Ace (right). (*J. Cowman*)

July 5, 1944: 334th crews and no-go pilots gather around squadron CO Deacon Hively upon his return from Italy leg for the news of the great trip. QP-L (background) survived the trip, but Kidd Hofer was killed. (*N. Megura*)

July 5, 1944: PENROD "69" 877 is one of the P-51s swapped to the 4TH by the MTO 325FG, so that pilots with damaged a/c could get back to the UK. "69" formerly belonged to the 325's Maj. Roy Hogg. (*F. Grove*)

July 6, 1944: 44-13641 is a brand new D-model replacement for 335th to make up for their Shuttle losses. Depot-applied black ETO nose color will be removed before the Group Red goes on. (*F. Grove*)

June, 1944: Another in the endless parade of visitors is the P-47 of the commander of the 356FG at Martlesham Heath, LtCol. Philip E. Tukey. The NMF a/c has dark green applied over all of topside. (*Glesner Weckbacher*)

Summer, 1944: ETO HAPPY, the Group Fairchild 24 reflects the fact that the unit is approaching its second anniversary in the European Theatre of Operations. A/C 43-14442 has a yellow nose and 1943 red-bordered star. (*Francis Grove*)

Summer, 1944: The 4TH's heavy communications and liaison a/c is this red-cowled Airspeed Oxford AS-728. It was used to haul parts from the 8ASC depots during this time of hectic operations. (*Glesner Weckbacher*)

July–Aug. 1944: Lt. "Pappy" Grove's VF-T 43-103603 stands fueled, armed, plugged into its APU, and awaiting its pilot on the PSP hardstand. A chief's screwdriver stuck into the ground next to the wheel was a silent symbol that the a/c was ready for flight. (*F. Grove*)

August, 1944: Lt. Ayer's QP-F showing the result of being taxied over from behind. It is thought that "F" is the late Lt. Hofer's famous QP-L 42-106924. (*Leo Schmidt*)

Summer, 1944: 4TH kites led by Col. Don Blakeslee in WD-C airborne over Essex with 108-gal. tanks. Capt. Bob Church and Capt. Bob Mabie tuck in close. (*Pinckney Lackey*)

August, 1944: Free of escort duty, the 4TH hits deck strafing German fields. This wise FW-190 pilot turns his guns into the 4TH pilots flight path, about all he can do after being caught on the ground at his field in France. (*Isadore Swerdel*)

July, 1944: John McFarlane leads Preston Hardy on the same flight. (*Pinkney Lackey*)

August, 1944: The show returns. Col. Don's old WD-C 42-106726 lands into the south wind as WD-S, with Lt. John Goodwyn at the controls. (*Edward Hedrick*)

August, 1944: The ground echelon's work rolls on. Capt. J. MacFarlane's VF-L 44-13961 sits in 336th hangar for inspection. (*Glesner Weckbacher*)

August, 1944: 2A-B 43-9202 of the 9AF's 416BG parked by DB tower. Possibly the white-banded A-20G has dropped off a 4TH pilot forced down on the continent. (*Glesner Weckbacher*)

September, 1944: MAN-O-WAR QP-A 44-14292 is the flashily-painted a/c of Lt. Col. Claiborne Kinnard, who is the new Dep. CO to acting CO Jim Clark, while Col. Blakeslee is on Stateside leave. (*Leroy Nitschke*)

September 23–on, 1944: WD-A 44-14570 RIDGE RUNNER is the first known a/c to carry P. McKennon's famous emblem. S/Sgt. J. Sills warms up his kite for another mission by the once-evader. (*Pinckney Lackey*)

September, 1944: S/Sgt. G. Anderson has pulled the tarps, preflight inspected, warmed up, checked mags, and topped off the tanks of Capt. F. Young's VF-A 44-14276 MARTHA JANE, readying it for the morning show. (*Melvin Weddle*)

45 minutes of pounding the field, the ravenous Mustangs left and came out over Calais at 1515 at 4/5,000 feet. Ralph Lewis was killed though he was not seen to go down.

[Box Score: 14 destroyed, 1 lost]

19 November 1944: W.F.O. 114. Maj. Hively led a Photo Reconnaissance to Leipheim airdrome, Germany, from 1205 to 1710 hours. The 12 Mustangs made landfall on the deck over Ostend at 1242 hours, then climbed to 7,000 upon nearing Leipheim and on to Schwabisch-Hall. Several Me 262s were spotted and the formation came out over Calais at 1624.

20 November 1944: F.O. 1320A. On a Penetration Target Withdrawal Support to Duisburg, Germany, Maj. Hively led A Group from 1000 to 1400 hours and Maj. Montgomery led B Group from 1010 to 1410 hours. A had been scheduled for the first of the B-24s and B for the last but after the Groups became airborne the bomber escort was cancelled and the formations were told to go to Koblenz. A and B rejoined and made landfall over Knocke at 1105 and 18,000 feet when an unknown voice began to give false vectors. The Mustangs tried to climb through the clouds but on reaching the second base at 20,000, the formation came back down to 14,000. The fighters arrived around 1200 and orbited the only hole in the lower layer. They proceeded on to Aachen and north along the west side of the Ruhr where A Group went west near Zwolle and came out at Ijmuiden at 1304, flying at 27,000. B Group continued north and left via Terschelling at 1300 and 25,000. Donald Bennett and Leonard Werner went down under unknown circumstances at 1245; the first was killed, the second captured.

[Box Score: 0 destroyed, 2 lost]

21 November 1944: F.O. 1323A. Capt. Glover led a Penetration Target Withdrawal Support to Merseburg, Germany, from 0920 to 1500 hours. Rendezvous with the B-24s was made at 1100 over Dummer Lake with a badly scattered bomber formation. Glover called bandits at 1140 and he got three 109s while Douglas Groshong got two. At 1230 John Kolbe got a 109 while Carmen Delnero was shot down and killed in a fight. George Klaus was shot down by flak and captured. Several sections strafed on the way out, damaging several locos and trains.

[Box Score: 6 destroyed, 2 lost]

25 November 1944: F.O. 1333A. On a Penetration Target Withdrawal Support to Merseburg, Germany, Maj. Hively led A Group from 0910 to 1505 hours and Maj. McKennon led B Group from 0920 to 1515 hours. As B followed A throughout the mission, the 4th came in behind the Forts and rendezvoused with them at 1045 and 23,000 feet. A 109 was claimed by 335 but disallowed. The Groups left the bombers at 1400 and did some strafing.

26 November 1944: F.O. 529B. Capt. Glover led a Penetration Target Withdrawal Support to Bielefeld, Germany, from 1005 to 1405 hours. At 1127 the Group rendezvoused with the B-24s at 22/25,000 feet over the northeast Polder. Some strafing was done and the bombers were left over the Zuider Zee at 1245.

27 November 1944: F.O. 1343A. Capt. Glover led another Penetration Withdrawal Support to Offenburg, Germany, from 1010 to 1535 hours. At 1135 the Mustangs rendezvoused with their Liberators at 24,000 feet. The Group broke escort over Mirecourt at 1300 when bogies were reported near Koblenz but no enemy aircraft were spotted. The formation came out near Walcheren at 1500.

29 November 1944: F.O. 1348A. Maj. McKennon led A Group in a Free Lance/General Support to Altenbecken, Germany, from 1050 to 1505 hours while Maj. Carlson led B Group in a Close Support to the same target from 1045 to 1455 hours. At 1204 the Group joined up with B-24s at 22,000 and by 1358 escort was broken.

30 November 1944: F.O. 1354A. On a Penetration Target Withdrawal Support to Halle–Merseburg, Germany, Maj. Hively led A Group from 1015 to 1610 hours and Capt. Glover led B Group from 1015 to 1620 hours. Rendezvous was made at 1125 with B-17s over Liege at 18,000 feet. Escort was broken at Brussels–Ghent and the P-51s left the coast at 1531, flying at 8,000 feet.

During November the Group Operational Training Unit (OTU) was established. At "Clobber College" 4th veterans transitioned new pilots from the U.S. or from other units into the Group's way of doing things with the P-51.

2 December 1944: F.O. 533B. Capt. Montgomery led a Penetration Target Withdrawal Support to Bingen, Germany, from 1050 to 1450 hours. Rendezvous was made at 1145 with B-24s near Brussels amidst several layers of cloud. After the target, "Nuthouse" vectored the Group to bandits southwest of Koblenz. The bogies were spotted at 3 o'clock level and reported as P-47s by Montgomery but a few 4th pilots turned into them to find 30-plus FW 190s. The 361st Fighter Group broke up the main attack but Jack McFadden destroyed one at 1245 near Hottenback. Escort was broken at 1345 near Brussels at 15/18,000 feet.

[Box Score: 1 destroyed, 0 lost]

4 December 1944: F.O. 1370A. On a Penetration Target Withdrawal Support to Bebra, Belgium, Maj. Hively led A Group from 1035 to 1533 hours while Capt. Glover led B Group from 1030 to 1555 hours. A rendezvoused with the B-24s near Ghent at 1135 and 22,000 feet while B joined up east of Brussels at 1145. At 1235 A left B and turned starboard to sweep Gotha, Mulhausen and Kassel before rejoining the formation at 1330. Near Brussels the Group dropped to the deck to avoid high winds, coming out at Knocke at 1453.

5 December 1944: F.O. 1374A. On a Penetration Target Withdrawal Support, Capt. Glover led A Group to Hertford, Germany, from 0840 to 1235 hours and Maj. Hively led B Group to Munster, Germany, from 0845 to 1300 hours. A rendezvoused with B-24s 22,000 feet over Alkmaar. Bogies were called but they turned out to be P-47s. The formation swept the target area, then turned west, coming out at Katwijk. Flying north along the coast, A rejoined the bombers near Egmond to go back into the target by 1020. A broke escort at 1135, 15,000 feet over Egmond. B rendezvoused with two Aphrodite B-17s, one robot and one mother ship, near Enkhuisen. The mother was at 20,000 with its baby at 10,000. Another mother was picked up over the northeast Polder at 10,000 with a baby at 2,000 escorted by two PRU Lightnings. On penetration both sets of bombers orbited near Dummer Lake and the higher parent came down to 14,000, lowering its baby in spirals. The baby then headed east at 1,000 feet, nosed down and exploded with a tremendous blast in woods a mile southeast of Steinfeld. The Group felt the concussion at 14,000. The other baby crash landed in a field ten miles southeast of Dummer Lake. The request to strafe the robot was emphatically rejected by the 4th's pilots. Both parents turned west and disappeared in the haze, causing escort to be broken. B Group then strafed on the way out, getting several locos and barges. Near Lingen, Charles Harre was engaged by an Me 262 after getting lost but he got away. Hively got a 190 at 1115 northwest of Nordhorn.

[Box Score: 1 destroyed, 0 lost]

At 2026 a V-1 fell in the vicinity of Stanstead, shaking buildings on base. It had been downed by a Mosquito.

6 December 1944: F.O. 1383A. On a Penetration Target Withdrawal Support to Halle, Germany, Capt. Glover led A Group from 0955 to 1455 hours and Capt. Norley led B Group from 1000 to 1525 hours. Bad weather hampered take-off but there were no accidents. B was more fortunate in setting course, spotting the bomber stream in mid-Channel. They rendezvoused with the B-17s at 1100 over the northeast Polder. A joined up at 1145 over Lingen, giving high cover while B acted as close escort. A left the bombers near Meppel at 1400 and B broke off at 1425 over the coast.

7 December 1944: Lt. Col. Harry Dayhuff, formerly of the 78th Fighter Group, took command of the Group from Lt. Col. Kinnard. For the past several days, first Lt. Col. William Trippet and then Lt. Col. Jack Oberhansly had served as Acting Group Commander in Kinnard's absence.

9 December 1944: F.O. 1397A. On a Penetration Target Withdrawal Support, Capt. Glover led A Group to Stuttgart, Germany, from 1000 to 1515 hours while Capt. McKennon led B Group to Schwenningen, Germany, from 0920 to 1400 hours. A rendezvoused with the main force of B-17s at 1120 at 25,000 feet over St. Dizier, making the target by 1226. Escort was broken at St. Menehoued at 1355. B rendezvoused with their force at 1014 near Schwenningen at 15,000 feet. Escort was broken at Nancy by 1230.

10 December 1944: F.O. 1404A. On a Penetration Target Withdrawal Support to Bingen, Germany, Maj. Hively led A Group from 0840 to 1300 hours and Capt. Howe led B Group from 0835 to 1310 hours. A rendezvoused with the main force east of Brussels at 0955 and 24,000 feet. Hively led his Group away from the bombers at Liege and swept Trier to the target, on to Augsburg, and then below to Strasbourg before swinging northwest to rejoin the bombers near Ghent. Escort was broken between 1200 and 1215 from Ostend. B made a large orbit at the RCM force RV point at 17,000 but the bombers didn't show up and there was no response on the R/T. The Group proceeded enroute, searching ahead of the 1st Force through the target before coming back out north of Ostend at 1150 and 6,000 feet.

11 December 1944: F.O. 1408A. On a Penetration Target Withdrawal Support to Hanau, Germany, Lt. Col. Dayhuff led A Group from 0945 to 1525 hours as Capt. Howe led B Group from 0955 to 1535 hours. With A acting as free lance and B as close support, rendezvous was made at 1120 with Liberators at 20,000 feet. The Big Friends unloaded from 1148 to 1215 and the Group gave general area support before leaving near St. Dizier. Several stragglers were escorted from the Rhine into friendly territory. Michael Kennedy went down as an evader or a very late return while Lt. Dickmeyer was forced to land in France on an Allied airstrip with his ailing Mustang.

[Box Score: 0 destroyed, 1 lost]

12 December 1944: F.O. 1412A. On another Penetration Target Withdrawal Support to Hanau, Germany, Maj. Hively led A Group from 0950 to 1545 hours and Capt. McKennon led B Group from 1000 to 1450 hours. Both Groups rendezvoused with their B-24s from Brussels to Mayen between 1100 and 1125, at 20/22,000 feet. One section from B went down and photographed three targets with K-25 cameras, then withdrew. A turned back at 1240 to pick up B-17s near Fulda at 25,000. B left the bombers in the Malmedy area at 1310 while A escorted their Forts back to Mayen. At 1340 MEW vectored A onto bandits attacking Lancasters bombing the Ruhr. The Mustangs swept up the west side of the Ruhr and across to Dortmund, then down the east side and out via Duisberg and Eindhoven. Several sections strafed.

Lt. Payne's brother landed at Debden with his B-24 and spent a good part of the day taking 30 or so of the enlisted men for a ride. (Ah, those were the days when one could go joyriding in a four-engined bomber.)

13 December 1944: Lt. Col. Dayhuff formally introduced himself to the pilots as the new CO. He announced a change from current RAF flight standards to regular AAF standards and introduced Lt. Col. Oberhansly as new Deputy Group Commander.

14 December 1944: A new terror struck when a V-2 impacted southwest of Debden at 0500 with the worst explosion felt thus far in the war.

15 December 1944: F.O. 1422A. Capt. Glover led a Penetration Target Withdrawal Support to Kassel, Germany, from 0955 to 1500 hours. 335 and 336 got off ahead of 334 and form-up was difficult. The average rendezvous time with the B-17s was 1115 over the Zuider Zee at 20,000. The Task Force had to plow through high cirrus before the P-51s left the bombers and stragglers at 1300 near Murlbach.

18 December 1944: During two Buzz Bomb alerts three V-1s were seen after 0355 hours. One was hit by a British night fighter and it came over the field on fire before falling and exploding a few miles away.

F.O. 1430A. Lt. Col. Dayhuff led a Free Lance Fighter Patrol to the Kassel–Frankfurt area from 1100 to 1645 hours. Climbing up through 10/10ths cloud, the Group had to go to 34,000 feet to get on top. The P-51s swung south and let down in an area believed to be east of Dortmund, splitting up. Seven Bf 109s were encountered climbing northeast from 5,000 when the Mustangs broke out at 1430. Two were destroyed along with an FW 190 but Charles Hewes was killed. The formation came out over the Dutch islands at 1510, flying at 15,000.

[Box Score: 3 destroyed, 1 lost]

23 December 1944: F.O. 1443A. On a Penetration Target Withdrawal Support to Ahsweiler, Germany, Maj. Hively led A Group from 1050 to 1500 hours and Capt. Montgomery led B Group from 1105 to 1505 hours. After take-off the Group had trouble forming up. B was unable to locate the bombers. A crossed in over Ostend at 1117 and saw B-24s but the combat group assigned to the 4th had aborted. Some B-26s were mistaken for enemy aircraft and bounced, causing the Group to drop tanks. MEW control vectored the 4th all over the target area and after awhile pilots were beginning to think they were chasing each other since the squadrons were separated. The Mustangs came out over Calais/Ostend at 1430, flying at 10,000.

24 December 1944: F.O. 1446A. On a Penetration Target Withdrawal Support to Giessen, Germany, Lt. Col. Dayhuff led A Group from 1135 to 1700 hours while Capt. Norley led B Group from 1140 to 1700 hours. The Groups rendezvoused with B-17s ten miles east of Liege at 1307 and 20,000 feet. The time over target was 1450 and the Mustangs left the Big Friends at 1555 over Ostend at 16,000. Just a few minutes before scheduled landing time Debden was completely socked in, forcing all but one of the P-51s to land at Raydon, Wattisham, Warmingford, Castle Camps and even Belgium. The mess, planning a big Christmas dinner, was undaunted, dispatching turkeys, whiskey and cigarettes to the stranded pilots.

25 December 1944: F.O. 1451B. Lt. Col. Dayhuff led a Penetration Target Withdrawal Support from Raydon to Kassel–Bonn–Trier, Germany, from 0842 to 1340 hours. Rendezvous with the B-24s was made at 22,000 feet over Ghent by 1050. At 1200, over 30 FW 190s and Bf 109s were engaged from 26,000 to the deck ten to 15 miles south of Bonn, blocking the Germans from attacking the bombers out of the sun. In a fight that lasted well over half an hour, the Group got 12, including some of the new FW 190Ds. Charles Poage was downed by one of the Focke Wulfs but he bailed out and was captured. Donald Emerson's last R/T message said he was starting home on the deck after downing two out of six 190s. He was found dead in the wreckage of his VF-D by the British in Belgium, a victim of ground fire. The action gave 334 the distinction of being the first squadron in the ETO to destroy 300 enemy aircraft. Escort was broken over Ostend at 1240. The fog continued to hover over Debden, forcing Dayhuff to take his charges back to Raydon.

[Box Score: 12 destroyed, 2 lost]

Debden had been covered with a frozen white fog, decorating it for 300 local children attending a Christmas party.

27 December 1944: F.O. 1454A. Maj. Hively led a Free Lance Support to Bonn, Germany, from 1155 to 1530 hours. Landfall was made 20,000 feet over Flushing at 0959. North of Aachen the Group was vectored by MEW control to sweep the Rhur from 22/24,000 feet. After an uneventful cruise the Mustangs came out over Flushing at 1430.

28 December 1944: F.O. 1458A. On a Penetration Target Withdrawal Support to Bingen, Germany, Capt. McKennon led A Group from 1045 to 1500 hours and Lt. Col. Dayhuff/Capt. McFarlane led B Group from 1045 to 1500 hours. Rendezvous was made with the B-24s at 18/23,000 feet over Mons at 1155. The milk run escort was broken near Sedan at 1345.

29 December 1944: F.O. 1463A. On a Penetration Target Withdrawal Support to the Schleiden–Ruhr area, Germany, Maj. Hively led A Group from 1040 to 1530 hours while Capt. Joiner led B Group from 1050 to 1525 hours. A rendezvoused with the B-24s near St. Hubert at 1200 and 23,000 feet while B joined up at Neuchaten. Bombs away was at 1234. B broke escort at 1300 over Hammut, then headed back for the target area for 15 minutes before coming home. A stayed in the target area until 1310 when it was vectored to the Ruhr and then north to Rheine, the Zuider Zee and back. Before coming out at 1440 11,000 feet over Ostend, A bounced some Spitfires.

30 December 1944: F.O. 1467A. Maj. Hively led a Free Lance Withdrawal Support to the Kassel–Rheine area, Germany, from 1015 to 1535 hours. The Group arrived in the Rhine area at 1200 and patrolled before heading for the target area to orbit during bombs away at 1243. As the Forts headed out north of Koblenz, the Mustangs went south to Kaiserslautern, then picked up the rear bomber box south of Malmedy before breaking escort at 1415 over Brussels.

31 December 1944: F.O. 1471A. On a Penetration Target Withdrawal Support to Misberg, Germany, Maj. Hively led A Group from 0915 to 1425 hours and Maj. McKennon led B Group from 0925 to 1425 hours. Take-off was delayed due to ground fog, then the formation was blown off course due to strong winds. As the Group joined up at 1120 with B-17s at 30,000 feet over Sharhorn, the bombers orbited to collect their straggling formation. Time over target was 1205 and escort was broken 25,000 feet over Alkmaar at 1355.

Operational Diary—1945

1 January 1945: F.O. 1476A. On a Penetration Target Withdrawal Support to Derben–Stendal–Genthin, Germany, Maj. Glover led A Group from 0925 to 1440 hours and Maj. McKennon led B Group from 0930 to 1445 hours. A rendezvoused with B-17s northeast of Heligoland at 1125, flying at 25,000 feet. After the leader sent two flights to stay with the bombers, 336 made a bounce at 1230 in the Ulzen area, downing four Bf 109s. Donald Pierini, after getting one of these 109s, shot down an Me 262. Escort was broken at 1330 west of the Rhine at 22,000. B Group made landfall near Sylt, following the bomber track, but the P-51s never caught up. They went to the target area and then came back out over Walcheren at 1402, 25 minutes early.

[Box Score: 5 destroyed, 0 lost]

2 January 1945: F.O. 1479A. Maj. McKennon led a Free Lance under MEW control to Aachen–Cologne, Germany, from 1035 to 1610 hours. The formation came in near Knocke at 16,000 feet, then flew east to Aachen over an undercast. "Nuthouse" vectored the Group to Duren, Cologne and Limburg. At 1400, two 109s were bounced 5,000 feet over Westerburg and destroyed. One of the pilots sharing in the victories, Arthur Senecal, was shot down by flak and killed. The Group crossed out at 1440.

[Box Score: 2 destroyed, 1 lost]

3 January 1945: F.O. 1485A. Lt. Col. Oberhansly led a Penetration Target Withdrawal Support to Neukirchen, Germany, from 0915 to 1340 hours. At 1025 the Group joined up with B-24s near Liart at 22,000 feet. Bombs away through 10/10ths cloud was made at 1126 and escort was broken at 1210 before coming out at 14,000 feet.

At 1900 there was a Buzz Bomb alert and three exploded in the vicinity. At 1935 there was another alert and another V-1 exploded nearby. By 2007 the third alert was sounded and yet another V-1 exploded. Through the sleepless night there was speculation as to what the Huns were after.

5 January 1945: F.O. 1491A. Maj. Glover led a Free Lance Support to the Metz area, France, from 1005 to 1520 hours. The P-51s came in south of Dunkirk at 1045 and 18,000 feet over 7/10ths to 8/10ths cloud. Rendezvous was made at 25,-000, then the formation was vectored north to the Cologne area, to Koblenz, then to Mannheim and back to Cologne before crossing out 24,000 feet over Walcheren at 1440.

Lt. Malmsten led four 334 kites on a PRU escort to Hannover, Germany, from 1125 to 1445 hours. Heavy cloud cover prevented photos in the target area so the formation diverted to Dortmund and got a few pictures.

6 January 1945: F.O. 1496A. On a Penetration Target Withdrawal Support to Limburg, Germany, Lt. Col. Dayhuff led A Group from 0945 to 1420 hours while Maj. McKennon led B Group from 0955 to 1405 hours. At 1042 the Group joined on B-24s at 23,000 feet 15 miles southwest of Brussels—the bombers were nine minutes late. At 1158 bombs were away through 10/10ths cloud and the Mustangs left the Big Friends south of Ghent at 1245.

7 January 1945: F.O. 1499A. Maj. McKennon led a Penetration Target Withdrawal Support to Landau, Germany, from 1015 to 1515 hours. Rendezvous was made with the B-24s at 1118 in the Mons area at 16,000 feet. Time over target was 1235 and escort was broken south of Luxembourg at 1410.

8 January 1945: F.O. 1503A. Maj. Hively led a Penetration Target Withdrawal Support to Alzey–Frankfurt, Germany, from 0920 to 1440 hours. At 1033 rendezvous was made with B-17s at 30,000 feet over Perrone with 10/10ths cloud below. After passing the target at 1101, 334 went to Frankfurt, Fulda, then back to Frankfurt and on to Mannheim, Karlsruhe, Strassbourg and home. Due to a last-minute change 334 had not been with the bombers as briefed. The Group came out at 1339, 16,000 feet over Boulogne.

10 January 1945: Noel Coward's USO show of *Blythe Spirit* did a two-night run at the base theater.

11 January 1945: Capt. Bell led four 334 and two 336 aircraft on a PRU escort to Dortmund–Hamm, Germany, from 1215 to 1435 hours. The formation left Debden with one F-5 Lightning. Icing and solid cloud prevented completion of the mission. The formation turned back from the target area at 1330, leaving the Lightning over the English coast at 1415.

It snowed most of the day on base so a few pilots took the time to give Piper Cub hops to the men.

13 January 1945: F.O. 1513A. Lt. Col. Dayhuff led a Penetration Target Withdrawal Support to Kaiserslautern, Germany, from 1120 to 1535 hours. After pushing through 10/10ths cloud on the way out, the Group rendezvoused with B-24s at 1235 and 20,000 feet. East of Trier, "Colgate" issued a recall and the Group left the continuing bombers at 1345. "Colgate" suggested landing at Brussels due to weather but Dayhuff decided to press on for home, coming out at 1400 7,000 feet over Dunkirk.

14 January 1945: F.O. 1515A. On a Penetration Target Withdrawal Support to Braunschweig–Stendal–Ehmen, Germany, Maj. Hively led A Group from 1035 to 1540 hours while Maj. McKennon led B Group from 1040 to 1545 hours. The Mustangs made the RV point on time without sighting the Big Friends. The Group proceeded to south of Hamburg where at 1300 B joined up with B-24s at from 22,000 to 24,000 feet. A Group swept on to Berlin and then back to the target area. After bombs away at 1350, B went down on the deck in the Steinhuder area when control reported bandits west of Dummer Lake. Finding nothing, the P-51s climbed up to 15,000, then left the bombers at 1430 to go prowling on the deck again. The fighters came out at 1500 hours at 18,000 feet over Alkmaar.

16 January 1945: F.O. 1521A. Maj. Glover led a Penetration Target Withdrawal Support to Ruhland–Dresden, Germany, from 0905 to 1515 hours. Rendezvous with the B-24s took place northwest of Dummer Lake at 18,000 feet between 1035 and 1040 hours. After bombs away at 1210, the Group descended to strafe. 334 came upon Neuburg airdrome, destroying an He 177 and an Me 262 on the ground for the loss of Victor Rentschler who was captured after being downed by flak. 336 flew over Neuhausen to find it literally packed with aircraft from one end to the other. Glover led his troops in one run after the other on the parked Huns. Twenty FW 109s, two Bf 109s, two Ju 87s, a Ju 88 and an He 177 were destroyed. As the Group came back over England, ground fog forced the Mustangs to land at several advanced bases on the continent. Frederick Hall, trying to land at Folkstone, dove into the ground and was killed at 1515. Some of the pilots did not get back to Debden until the 19th.

[Box Score: 28 destroyed, 2 lost]

17 January 1945: F.O. 1525A. Maj. Hively led a Penetration Target Withdrawal Support to Hamburg, Germany, from 1008 to 1455 hours. At 1138 rendezvous was made with B-17s south of Heligoland at 23,000 feet. On the way across the North Sea Robert Stallings was lost after he bailed out. Bombs were away at 1156 and escort broken by 1255.

[Box Score: 0 destroyed, 1 lost]

18 January 1945: Maj. Norley led 335 in an Air Sea Rescue search for Lt. Stallings, finding only his dinghy in rough weather. Lt. Rinebolt made a lucky escape from his shredded aircraft after an attempted landing in bad weather.

20 January 1945: F.O. 1535A. On a Penetration Target Withdrawal Support to Heilbronn, Germany, Maj. McKennon led A Group from 0920 to 1400 hours and Capt. McFarlane led B Group from 0930 to 1410 hours. A rocket had exploded near the field at 0845 and another exploded just after take-off. Rendezvous was made at 1039 with B-17s at 27,000 feet over Sedan. A Group left the Big Friends at 1240 and B Group broke escort at 1309 at Sedan.

21 January 1945: F.O. 1539A. On a Free Lance Patrol from 0950 to 1520 hours, Maj. McKennon led A Group while Capt. Joiner led B Group. Landfall was made at 20,000 feet over Knocke at 1045, although everything was covered with 10/10ths cloud. The Group crossed over Frankfurt by 1145, then headed southeast. At 1200 the two Groups became separated due to weather. Two 334 sections bounced 336 and then stayed with them to strafe coal cars and dummy He 111s. B Group strafed rail targets near Donausworth before coming out over Dunkirk at 1430. Several other sections came out separately after strafing several targets of opportunity.

Four Mustangs each from 335 and 336 escorted two PRU Lightnings to Heilbronn, Germany, from 1200 to 1600 hours. The formation crossed the coast at 1250 near Knocke, making the target by 1325. The P-51s turned for home at Brussels where they left the Lightnings.

29 January 1945: F.O. 1566A. On a Penetration Target Withdrawal Support to Lahnstein–Hannover–Koblenz, Germany, from 0930 to 1420 hours, Lt. Col. Dayhuff led A Group and Maj. Glover led B Group. The previous eight days of noshows weather was still hanging on as the Group formed up over 10/10ths cloud on the way out. Rendezvous was made with Flying Fortresses at 1110 northwest of Dummer Lake and the target was bombed through a solid undercast. The P-51s left the bombers at 1210 near Frankfurt to head east for 15 minutes and do some hunting. Finding nothing, B Group rejoined the bomber stream from 1245 to 1300 and left near Charleroi at 1300. A Group went home on the deck after an orbit of Wiesbaden.

1 February 1945: F.O. 1575A. Maj. Norley led a Free Lance Support under MEW control to Mannheim–Giessen–Wesel, Germany, from 0925 to 1430 hours. The Group was vectored to Giessen, but found no enemy aircraft. Course was set for Mannheim via Wiesbaden but cloud up to 29,000 feet forced the Group to turn back north. The Mustangs left the Frankfurt-Koblenz area at 1215 for home.

3 February 1945: F.O. 1586A. On a Penetration Target Withdrawal Support to Magdeburg, Germany, Maj. Glover led A Group from 0920 to 1445 hours and Lt. Col. Dayhuff led B Group from 1930 to 1445 hours. At 1040 rendezvous was made with Liberators east of the Zuider Zee at 19,000 feet. As the Big Friends hit the target at 1140, the Group left to head toward Berlin before swinging north to pick up Fortresses at Pritzwalk. The boys withdrew with them and broke escort 22,000 feet over Bremervord at 1305.

4 February 1945: Lt. Savage led an Air Sea Rescue escort by four 334 P-51s from 1244 to 1530 hours. The Mustangs rendezvoused with six B-17s at 1315 and searched the Texel area for downed crews.

6 February 1945: F.O. 1595A. On another Penetration Target Withdrawal Support to Magdeburg, Germany, Maj. McFarlane led A Group from 0915 to 1430 hours while Lt. Col. Oberhansly led B Group from 0905 to 1425 hours. As the Group crossed over the North Sea, William Bates went down and was killed. Rendezvous was made with B-24s over the coast at 1020 and by 1128 bombs were away. On the way out the Group left the bombers at various places in sections, the last breaking off near Venlo at 1310 and 17,000 feet. As 335 was strafing motor transport at Torgau, Paul Santos was killed. More strafing was done on locos and trucks. Due to bad weather several of the pilots had to land at other fields.

[Box Score: 0 destroyed, 2 lost]

9 February 1945: F.O. 1605A. Maj. Norley led a Penetration Target Withdrawal Support to Magdeburg, Germany, from 0930 to 1455 hours. Though hampered by mud on the taxi strips, the Group got off to rendezvous with B-24s at 1030 off the coast from 14,000 to 24,000 feet. Bombing was done from 1205 to 1210. The Mustangs tried to find reported bandits without luck, leaving the target area at 1240 to rejoin the bombers near Celle at 1310. Escort was broken at 1354 hours at 24/25,000 feet over Alkmaar.

11 February 1945: F.O. 1612A. Maj. McKennon led a Fighter Sweep and Strafing mission to Osnabruck–Hannover–Soest, Germany, from 0745 to 1210 hours. At 0844 the formation crossed in at 15,000 feet over Katwijk before letting down at 0910 hours to strafe. At 0940 Henry Kaul was killed trying to drop his wing tanks on a truck. Numerous locos, barracks, tugs and motor transport were strafed before the Group started to come out in sections from 1015 to 1022 between Den Helder and Ijmuiden at 15,000 feet. Weather again forced some landings at other bases. Morton Savage made it into Wattisham, took off again to try and reach Debden, but was forced back due to bad fog. His QP-W struck a radio tower at Nuthhampton and he was killed.

[Box Score: 0 destroyed, 2 lost]

12 February 1945: Col. Rozanoff of the Free French Air Force visited Debden. Col. Dayhuff loaned his Mustang to the Frenchman for a short hop.

14 February 1945: F.O. 1622A. On a Penetration Target Withdrawal Support/Free Lance to Magdeburg, Germany, Maj. Norley led A Group from 1030 to 1610 hours while Lt. Col. Dayhuff led B Group from 1035 to 1545 hours. Entering the continent as a Free Lance, the formation was vectored to bandits without luck before being sent to join the B-24s at 1139. The Mustangs then swept Bad Frankenhausen up to the target area. On the way out the Vechta–Oldenburg area was strafed to get locos, buildings and other targets. The P-51s came out at Alkmaar by 1450 hours.

18 February 1945: A new two-seater conversion was completed on one of the Group's older, war weary P-51Bs. 336's VF-4 ended up with a Malcolm Hood for the rear seat, beautiful powder blue color overall (336's rudder color) and the bright swept red nose.

19 February 1945: F.O. 1638A. Maj. Norley led a Penetration Target Withdrawal Support to Meschede, Germany, from 1155 to 1640 hours. The Group joined on the B-24s at 1315 hours at 20,000 feet over the North Sea. After bombs away through 10/10ths cloud, the Group broke off at 1545 and 13,000 feet. As a part of the mission two 334 aircraft escorted an VIII FC Mosquito. Ground fog at Debden once again forced the pilots to proceed to several other stations in England, primarily Wattisham.

20 February 1945: F.O. 1642A. On a Penetration Target Withdrawal Support to Nurnburg, Germany, Maj. Norley led A Group from 1000 to 1550 hours and Capt. Carlson led B Group from 0950 to 1540 hours. A and B rendezvoused over Wattisham at 1015 and headed out over 10/10ths cloud until 15 miles west of the target. All the assigned B-24s aborted so the Group dropped down through breaks in the cloud deck to strafe a factory, oil storage centers, wagons and other targets in the area. At 1318 Joiner and Carlson teamed up to jump two 190s on the deck, destroying both. John Fitch's Mustang was hit by flak at 1335 hours, forcing him to bail out; he was captured.

[Box Score: 2 destroyed, 1 lost]

21 February 1945: F.O. 1647A. On a return Penetration Target Withdrawal Support to Nurnburg, Germany, Capt. Montgomery led A Group from 0910 to 1440 hours and Capt. Carlson led B Group from 0915 to 1455 hours. At 1000 the Group joined on B-24s at 15,000 feet over Ostend. A then went around the target ahead of the bombers, which dropped their bombs at 1151. The Mustangs then went on to Donauworth where they strafed trains, wagons and other targets. Carlson and Brooker strafed 50 German soldiers. Two pilots, August Rabe and Andrew Lacy, went down to become POWs, the former after hitting a tree and the latter after being hit by flak. The Group came out north of Dunkirk at 1400.

[Box Score: 0 destroyed, 2 lost]

Col. Everett W. Stewart assumed command of the Group after coming from the 352nd Fighter Group.

22 February 1945: F.O. 1651A. Maj. Glover led a Penetration Target Withdrawal Support to Hildesheim–Peine–Stendal, Germany, from 1015 to 1555 hours. Rendezvous with the Liberators was made at 1118 hours at 15,000 feet over Ijmuiden. Escort was provided to north of Einbeck where the Group left to strafe the autobahn between Brunswick and Hannover. Roaming over to the east, the Group caused a traffic jam on the Berlin to Leipzig autobahn. Glover led several pilots over Halberstadt airdrome to destroy eight on the ground. During the strafing a 479th Group P-51 was accidentally shot down by a 4th pilot. The Group came out 10,000 feet over Egmond at 1515.

[Box Score: 8 destroyed, 0 lost]

23 February 1945: F.O. 1654A. On a Penetration Target Withdrawal Support to Naumburg–Gera, Germany, Maj. McFarlane led A Group from 0905 to 1510 hours and Capt. Howe led B Group from 0915 to 1445 hours. After climbing out over 10/10ths cloud, the Group rendezvoused from 1030 to 1035 with B-24s at 15/18,000 feet east of the Zuider Zee. One box bombed at 1145 through the undercast, then the Big Friends broke into small groups. B Group left the bombers to strafe Schweinfurt airdrome but the warm anti-aircraft reception prevented their getting at over 30 multi-engined aircraft. Some strafing was done before coming out at The Hague at 1345 hours and 15,000 feet.

24 February 1945: F.O. 1658A. Maj. Norley led a Penetration Target Withdrawal Support to Herford, Germany, from 1015 to 1535 hours. The Mustangs joined on the B-24s at 1126 north of Alkmaar at 19,000 feet, making the run over the target from 1255 to 1300. The boys then left the bombers near Dummer Lake and swept towards the Zuider Zee, strafing barges, locos and targets of opportunity, coming out at 1421 at 11,000 feet over Alkmaar. Alvin Hand was hit by flak and captured.

[Box Score: 0 destroyed, 1 lost]

25 February 1945: F.O. 1662A. Maj. McKennon led a Free Lance Fighter Sweep to the Dessau area, Germany, from 0800 to 1420 hours. Mac led the Group in over the Hook of Holland at 0900 and 10,000 feet. Tanks were dropped to bounce four FW 190s that had been called in as friends. By 1010 the Group was in the target area. Rohrensee and Kothen airdromes were hit. Kendall Carlson, while strafing Kothen, mushed in and hit the ground. He got out, stood on the wing and directed the beat up on the R/T before being captured. He got Brooker and Morgan onto the tail of a landing 190 piloted by the German station CO, Hoffman; they shot him down. Before 336 pulled off Kothen around 1100 they left four destroyed, one credited to Carlson before he went in. 334 Blue Section (Bell, Payne, Bowers, Denson) destroyed seven on the ground at Rohrensee and Carl Payne downed an Me 262 in the air four miles southeast of Naunburg. Malmsten and Bryan shared a 190 destroyed in the air. As the four pilots from Blue Section were on the way out at 1115, they were bounced by seven 190s and 109s at 11,000 feet . . . but no one fired. Both formations were out of ammunition. The 11 fighters joined up as the German leader looked over and waggled his wings. Everyone flew on until the Germans broke off. The four amazed pilots landed in France to refuel, getting back to Debden by 1735. The rest of the Group came out at 1223 north of The Hague at 12,000.

[Box Score: 13 destroyed, 1 lost]

This mission ran the Group score over 800—not only was there a continuing race with the 56th's Wolfpack but also a race toward the 1,000 destroyed mark.

Two 334 aircraft provided escort for a PRU Lightning from 1055 to 1540 hours.

26 February 1945: F.O. 1665A. Maj. Glover led a Penetration Target Withdrawal Support to Berlin, Germany, from 1020 to 1635 hours. After rendezvous with the B-24s at 1145 at 21/23,000 feet, the formation was forced to penetrate in large S-turns to avoid overtaking Fortresses ahead. Berlin was covered by a solid cloud deck. Two 334 aircraft again covered the Air Task Force Commander's Mosquito. The bombers were left at Dummer Lake and the Mustangs came out at 1550, flying at 10,000 feet.

27 February 1945: F.O. 1670A. Maj. Glover led A Group on a Free Lance to Leipzig, Germany, from 1020 to 1700 hours while Col. Stewart led B Group on a Penetration Target Withdrawal Support to Halle, Germany, from 1020 to 1615 hours. B joined up at 1135 with B-24s at 19,000 feet southeast of Brussels, making the target by 1300. The B Group aircraft then left the bombers at 1310 to strafe trains and troops before hitting Weimar airdrome. Strafing the drome from one end to the other, B was joined by A at 1335, the latter having swept Erfurt after leaving the bombers. In all the confusion of strafing and flak, Harold Crawford and Robert Voyles went down to be captured, but the 4th destroyed over 40 aircraft, including a C-47, before leaving at 1345, coming out over Ostend.

[Box Score: 43 destroyed, 2 lost]

28 February 1945: F.O. 1675A. Maj. Glover led a Free Lance Fighter Sweep to Steinhuder Lake–Weimar–Ingolstadt, Germany, from 1210 to 1715 hours. The Group crossed in over 10/10ths cloud at 1315 at 15,000 feet over Alkmaar. The weather was too poor to let down below 8,000 near Weimar, so Glover continued around Nurnburg. A single 109 bounced the formation but then evaded into the cloud deck. At 1630 the Mustangs came out at Walcheren, still over a solid undercast.

1 March 1945: F.O. 1679A. On a Penetration Target Withdrawal Support to Neuburg–Ingolstadt, Germany, Maj. Norley led A Group from 1100 to 1710 hours and Maj. McFarlane led B Group from 1105 to 1715 hours. Rendezvous with the B-24s was made after bombs away at 1320. A Group left to strafe between Ingolstadt and Nurnburg from 1400 to 1445; B Group joined in the strafing as well.

2 March 1945: F.O. 1683A. On a Penetration Target Withdrawal Support, Lt. Col. Woods led A Group to Genthin, Germany, from 0820 to 1350 hours while Col. Stewart led B Group to Magdeburg, Germany, from 0815 to 1405 hours. Rendezvous was made with the B-24s at 23/24,000 feet above Lingen at 0946. Several aircraft let down in the Dummer Lake area to 8,000 feet searching for bogies, then rejoined the bombers. A Group swept ahead of the bombers in a general free lance escort and B left the bombers at 1305 over Alkmaar.

3 March 1945: F.O. 1690A. On a Penetration Target Withdrawal Support to Magdeburg–Brandenburg, Germany, Lt. Col. Woods led A Group from 0740 to 1315 hours and Col. Stewart led B Group from 0745 to 1320 hours. South of Heligoland at 0940, the Group found the B-24s at 20/25,000 feet. As the formation approached the IP, five Me 262s bounced, and the 4th turned into them, getting strikes on two. As the Allied stream progressed from the IP to the RP a total of 15 Me 262s made feints at the Group. A Group broke escort northwest of Goslar at 1040, sweeping to Dummer Lake before coming out at 1215 west of the Zuider Zee at 18,000 feet. B Group gave area support to Brandenburg from 0955 and came out by 1210. Kenneth Green and George Davis both went down to be captured.

[Box Score: 0 destroyed, 2 lost]

Col. Jacobson, Swedish Royal Air Force, Maj. Cernel, Air Attaché Swedish Embassy, and Mr. Wassgres, a Swedish engineer, visited Debden with the probable intent of looking over the Mustang for Swedish purchase.

4 March 1945: F.O. 1697A. Maj. Glover led a Penetration Target Withdrawal Support to Schwabisch Hall airdrome, Germany, from 0750 to 1235 hours. The Group took up escort with B-24s at 0935, flying at 23,000 feet. The uneventful milk run was ended by 1115 over Metz at 18,000 feet.

5 March 1945: F.O. 1704A. Maj. McKennon led a Penetration Target Withdrawal Support to Hamburg, Germany, from 0740 to 1220 hours. The Group joined the Liberators at 25,000 feet north of Baltrum Island. Preceding the bombers to the target, the Mustangs picked up much flak and never managed to rejoin the bombers. The Group crossed Ostend on the way out at 1150.

8 March 1945: F.O. 1721A. Maj. Norley led a Penetration Target Withdrawal Support to Dillonburg–Siegen, Germany, from 1125 to 1625 hours. The bombers and fighters joined up at 1330 near Dummer Lake and the boring escort was broken at 1505 hours at 10,000 feet over Louvain.

10 March 1945: F.O. 1731A. Lt. Col. Woods led a Penetration Target Withdrawal Support to Paderborn, Germany, from 0930 to 1450 hours. Rendezvous with the B-24s was made over 10/10ths cloud at 1040 and 20,000 feet. Nothing eventful again—the bombers were left at 1257 hours, flying at 18,000 feet.

11 March 1945: F.O. 1738A. Maj. Glover led a Penetration Target Withdrawal Support to Kiel, Germany, from 1050 to 1540 hours. Rendezvous was made with the Libs over the IP at 1310 and escort broken at 1425 north of Terschelling.

12 March 1945: F.O. 1742A. On a Penetration Target Withdrawal Support to Swinemünde, Germany, Col. Stewart led A Group from 0900 to 1510 hours while Maj. McFarlane led B Group from 0905 to 1500 hours. At 1055 the Liberators and Mustangs joined up at 20,000 feet over Husum. The target was bombed at 1205 through 10/10ths cloud. B Group attempted to go under the cloud deck and take pictures, but by the time the P-51s were down to 500 feet over the water north of Swinemünde they were still in the soup. A Group withdrew while B flew lower and to the south of course. A left the bombers north of Borkum at 1400, flying at 10,000 feet. B chased three enemy aircraft on top of the clouds near Bremen before coming out. John McFarlane was forced to bail out due to coolant trouble, evading to Sweden.

[Box Score: 0 destroyed, 1 lost]

14 March 1945: F.O. 1752A. Col. Stewart led A Group on a Free Lance Support to Holzwickede, Germany, from 1315 to 1820 hours while Lt. Col. Woods led B Group on a Fighter Sweep to Warstein–Kassel–Steinau–Marsburg–Koblenz, Germany, from 1330 to 1830 hours. A Group rendezvoused with B-24s at 1441 east of Blankenheim at 22,000 feet. Escort was broken by 1555 and the Group swept east to Fulda, coming out north of Bruges at 1730. B Group, approaching Nordhorn, was vectored southeast to sweep in bad haze at 8/10,000 feet. B finally headed out north of Koblenz by 1665.

15 March 1945: F.O. 1761A. On a Penetration Target Withdrawal Support to Berlin, Germany, Col. Stewart led A Group from 1130 to 1815 hours and Lt. Col. Woods let B Group from 1140 to 1720 hours. At 1250 rendezvous was made with Liberators over the Zuider Zee at 20/22,000 feet. With A acting as a fighter sweep to Berlin and back, and B providing close escort, the uneventful escort was terminated by B Group at 1630 at the Zuider Zee. A crossed out at 10,000 feet over The Hague at 1715 hours.

17 March 1945: F.O. 1774A. Capt. Howe led a Penetration Target Withdrawal Support to Hannover, Germany, from 1205 to 1640 hours. Rendezvous with the Liberators and Mosquitoes was made at 1314 hours at 22,000 feet over the northeast Polder. The formation crossed back at 20,000 feet over Alkmaar at 1540.

18 March 1945: A Buzz Bomb alert at 0256 was followed by a big explosion and an all clear at 0304.

F.O. 1779A. On a Penetration Target Withdrawal Support to Berlin, Germany, Maj. McKennon led A Group from 0925 to 1530 hours and Capt. Howe led B Group from 0930 to 1435 hours. The Group rendezvoused with B-24s north of Ijmuiden at 1033 and 20,000 feet. While B stayed with the bombers, McKennon led A down to strafe Neubrandenburg airdrome. As Mac went across the field to test for flak, he was hit, bailing out three miles west of Prenzlau into a plowed field. 335 covered as George Green R/T'd he was going to land and pick up the CO. Green put "Suzon" down into the field, threw out his parachute and let McKennon get in. Green then got on his lap and after a very short take-off over trees the two of them flew back to Debden sharing oxygen, amid cheers and whoops over the R/T. McKennon calmly suggested to Col. Trippet that Lt. Green be made a general at once. Technically, records list McKennon as a loss and evasion back to base!

[Box Score: 0 destroyed, 1 lost]

19 March 1945: F.O. 1785A. On a Free Lance/Target Withdrawal Support to Ingolstadt–Donauworth, Germany, Maj. Norley led A Group from 1145 to 1810 hours and Capt. Alfred led B Group from 1150 to 1820 hours. The Mustangs were forced to penetrate through bad weather to sweep Stuttgart and Munich before rendezvousing with the B-24s at bombs away between 1450 and 1500. At 1615, near Frankfurt, Norley bounced a 109 and shot it up until the pilot bailed out from 11,000 feet. Lt. Ayer's section became separated and was bounced by two Me 262s near Lechfeld. The P-51s tried to give chase but they were left behind by the jets.

[Box Score: 1 destroyed, 0 lost]

20 March 1945: F.O. 1794A. Capt. Monroe led a Penetration Target Withdrawal Support to Hamburg, Germany, from 1410 to 1845 hours. Rendezvous was made at 1530 with B-17s at 26,000 feet east of the Frisian Islands. Just after bombs away, ten Me 262s were encountered at 1605 flying at 22,000 feet. There were no claims but two of the jets were damaged before they left the Mustangs.

21 March 1945: F.O. 1801A. Maj. Montgomery led a Penetration Target Support to Hesepe and Ahlhorn airdromes, Germany, from 0750 to 1240 hours. Rendezvous with the B-24s was made at 0900 20,000 feet over Alkmaar. The bombers split up to bomb numerous targets. Due to intense flak, the Group did not strafe Hesepe, turning for Achmer where the 353rd Fighter Group was strafing with good results. After the 353rd withdrew, the Group strafed from 1000 to 1030, destroying nine for the loss of Robert A. Crammer and Albert J. Davis. Crammer's Mustang was hit in the cooling system—making it for the Allied lines, he was forced down and captured. Davis went in on fire and was killed.

[Box Score: 9 destroyed, 2 lost]

From 0825 to 1155 hours, two 334 aircraft escorted a Mosquito out on the mission as Command ship.

Three 336 and one 334 aircraft escorted a Catalina search and rescue aircraft over the North Sea off the Hook of Holland from 0825 to 1230 hours. After rendezvous at 0930, the formation proceeded out to look for a man in a dinghy. After spotting the downed airman, the men helplessly watched as shore batteries scored hits on the Catalina. The P-51s were forced to leave, calling on relief cover to get back to the PBY.

At 2130 a V-2 exploded near Debden and during the night another six exploded within a 50 mile radius of the base.

22 March 1945: F.O. 1810A. On a Penetration Target Withdrawal Support to Ruhland, Germany, Lt. Col. Woods led A Group from 0955 to 1540 hours while Maj. McKennon led B Group from 1000 to 1600 hours. At Brussels B was vectored to Frankfurt in search of bandits. Not making the rendezvous, B went on to sweep Leipzig to Bremen, crossing out at Egmond by 1510 at 15,000 feet. A Group arrived at Brux to see their 15th Air Force B-24 stream passing in front at 1220 hours. Several Little Friends were around so the Group chased some jets headed for Berlin. At 1300 a large gaggle of FW 190 Jabos (fighter bombers) was seen forming up over Furstenwalde and the Group bounced. Combat took place from 5,000 feet to the deck for 40 minutes as the heavy bomb-laden FWs were pounded. The Group destroyed 11 without loss. In 20 minutes Sid Woods had knocked down five of them. The Mustangs crossed out at 1458.

[Box Score: 11 destroyed, 0 lost]

23 March 1945: F.O. 1819A. Maj. Norley led a Penetration Target Withdrawal Support to Munster, Germany, from 0845 to 1300 hours. The Group joined on their Liberators at 20,000 feet over Alkmaar at 0950, providing a milk run escort until coming out at 1458.

Two 334 and two 336 aircraft provided a PRU escort to Wurzburg and Schwabisch Hall airdromes from 1200 to 1620 hours.

Fifteen 8th Air Force fighter group commanding officers met at Debden to plan fighter cover for the Rhine River crossing.

24 March 1945: F.O. 1826A. On an Area Support to Lingen–Rheine–Munster–Osnabruck, Germany, Lt. Col. Woods led A Group from 0805 to 1150 hours and Col. Stewart led B Group from 0810 to 1200 hours. The Group arrived in the area at 0945, flying at 10,000 feet. Near Wesel, support was given to paratroops and gliders taking part in the Rhine crossings. The Mustangs were vectored to Rheine airdrome, where B-17s were bombing, before leaving at 1050.

F.O. 1826A. Heading back to the same area to continue support of the Rhine crossings, Maj. Glover led A Group from 1225 to 1805 hours while Capt. Alfred led B Group from 1430 to 1920 hours. A arrived in the area by 1430 at 11,000 feet and patrolled a 900-square-mile area near Osnabruck until relieved by B Group at 1605. B left the area at 1835.

25 March 1945: Another rocket exploded near Debden during the night.

26 March 1945: F.O. 1843A. Maj. McKennon led a Free Lance Fighter Sweep to Worms–Plauen–Weimar–Crailsheim, Germany, from 1105 to 1645 hours. Arriving in the area at 1300 and 6,000 feet, the Mustangs patrolled until 1415 before leaving near Mannheim. Earl Hustwit developed coolant trouble at this time and was killed going in with his Mustang. 336 went to Plauen to rendezvous with bombers at 1250. On the way back in, Harry Davis was seen coming out of low cloud at 1503 with his port wing in fire. He was killed in the crash of his fighter at Woodbridge, Suffolk.

[Box Score: 0 destroyed, 2 lost]

28 March 1945: F.O. 1857A. Maj. Glover led a Withdrawal Support to Berlin–Hannover, Germany, from 0945 to 1345 hours. Rendezvous was made at 1130 with B-17s over Hannover. Jets were reported but none were spotted. Escort was broken in the Dummer Lake area.

30 March 1945: F.O. 1863A. Maj. Norley led a Free Lance Fighter Sweep to Hamburg, Germany, from 1115 to 1630 hours. By 1253 the Group arrived over Hamburg at 12,000 feet through bad weather. Near Lubeck five Me 262s passed under the Group but the Mustangs could not catch up with them. Everyone came out 10,000 feet over Ijmuiden at 1529.

31 March 1945: F.O. 1847A. On a Penetration Target Withdrawal Support to Hassel–Berlin, Germany, Lt. Col. Woods led A Group from 0715 to 1155 hours and Maj. Norley led B Group from 0720 to 1340 hours. The Group rendezvoused with B-24s at 20,000 feet over the Zuider Zee at 0815 hours. B Group then let down to 12,000 and continued under the bomber stream until the target, where the Mustangs swept toward Gorlitz. Near Breslau three Russian P-39s bounced the P-51s, putting a cannon shell through Lt. Payne's prop. One 336 pilot got hits on a P-39 but the two formations pulled apart at 1100 before any more damage was done. Ken Foster went down to become a POW in Germany. A Group crossed out at 1055 for home with B following almost two hours later.

[Box Score: 0 destroyed, 1 lost]

From 0530 hours on, Group pilots (flying singly, in pairs and in threes) acted as cover for a Catalina that had been trying to get a B-17 crew off the enemy coast for over 24 hours, with a Warwick leading the way out at times. The boys saw an Me 262 strafe the PBY east of the Frisian Islands. One of the PBY's engines had a broken oil line, making take-off impossible. By 1210 the 4th's part in covering the rescue effort was over, with the PBY still down.

By month's end the 4th had 867 victories, quite a way from 1,000 considering that the Luftwaffe was all but extinct . . . and the Mustang was still bucking mechanically at times. During March several magneto failures were traced to bad bearings in the distributors after 150 hours; several losses were attributed to the problem.

2 April 1945: F.O. 1882A. On a Penetration Target Withdrawal Support to Aalborg West airdrome, Denmark, from 1355 to 1835 hours, Capt. Alfred led A Group and Maj. Montgomery led B Group. At 1450 the Group rendezvoused with B-24s at 18,000 feet off the Frisian Islands. The escort was made over 10/10ths cloud, the Group breaking off at 1715 north of Terschelling.

3 April 1945: At 1215 hours the Group continued to give cover for the downed Catalina crew off the Frisian Islands. As the Mustangs circled over the scene from 1430 to 1800, a Warwick tried to get a launch to the crew unsuccessfully. When the boys left, two Warwicks were circling over the PBY.

4 April 1945: F.O. 1896A. On a Penetration Target Withdrawal Support to Parchim airdrome, Germany, Lt. Col. Woods led A Group from 0725 to 1245 hours while Col. Stewart led B Group from 0730 to 1235 hours. Arriving at the RV point by 0840, the Group rendezvoused with B-24s at 0847, flying at 18,000 feet. As the formation approached the target area at 0940, eight Me 262s attacked the bombers from 5 o'clock low. Pilots from 334 engaged, downing two. Three more 262s attacked the stream at 0955 near Stendal and four pilots teamed up to shoot one down. A broke escort at Wittenburg by 1030 and B left the bombers over Breda at 1120.

[Box Score: 3 destroyed, 0 lost]

5 April 1945: F.O. 1903A. Maj. McKennon led a Penetration Target Withdrawal Support to Hof, Germany, from 0815 to 1425 hours. By 1030 the Group had joined up with their Liberators north of Frankfurt. An Me 262 was chased but it easily got away. Escort was broken near Giessen at 1230.

6 April 1945: F.O. 1909A. Lt. Young led a Penetration Target Withdrawal Support to Halle, Germany, from 0710 to 1300 hours. At 0820 rendezvous with the Libs was made at 17,000 feet east of Duren. The formation crossed over the target, covered by solid cloud, at 0937 and escort was broken by 1130 near the Rhine River.

7 April 1945: F.O. 1914A. Maj. Glover led a Penetration Target Withdrawal Support to Duneburg–Krummel, Germany, from 1010 to 1550 hours. At 1140, south of Leeuwarden, the Mustangs joined on the B-24s at 18,000 feet. North of Steinhuder Lake four jets attacked the bombers, destroying one. By 1215 piston-engined fighters entered the bomber stream—two FW 190Ds approaching from the west. Norley chased one down through the Liberator formation but the 190 collided with a B-24, chopping its tail off; both aircraft went down. Several 109s approached and three were downed. It was clear to the Group that the jets and the piston-engined fighters were operating in concert. 335 broke escort at 1345 west of Meldorf and swept Cuxhaven to Dummer Lake. At 1245 six German operated P-51s attacked a box of B-17s from above in the Hamburg area. 334 and 336 left their B-24s at Neumunster at 1320, latching onto Fortresses until breaking off at Bad Oldosloe.

[Box Score: 6 destroyed, 0 lost]

Three Group Mustangs escorted a PRU Lightning to Berlin, landing by 2110.

8 April 1945: F.O. 1918A. Maj. Norley led a Penetration Target Withdrawal Support to Bayreuth, Germany, from 0855 to 1510 hours. Rendezvous with the Liberators took place at 1105, flying at 22,000 feet. Several sweeps were made away from the formation without result and escort was broken by 1345 near the Rhine.

Four pilots escorted a PRU Lightning to Kassel and Leipzig from 1405 to 1835 hours.

9 April 1945: F.O. 1929A. Maj. McKennon led a Penetration Target Withdrawal Support to Neuburg airdrome, Germany, from 1315 to 1900 hours. Rendezvous was made at 1525 with Forts 16,000 feet over Bad Kreuznach, escort being broken by 1700. 335 left early, at 1600, led by McKennon. Sweeping over Munich–Brunnthal airdrome, they found the field crammed with enemy aircraft and destroyed one after the other. Two Mustangs, flown by Herman Rasmussen and Robert Bucholz, were hit by flak and went down; both pilots were killed.

[Box Score: 14 destroyed, 2 lost]

10 April 1945: F.O. 1936A. Lt. Col. Woods led a Penetration Target Withdrawal Support to Rechlin airdrome, Germany, from 1205 to 1750 hours. The Group joined on their Liberators at 1320 west of the Frisian Islands at 15,000 feet. At 1445 Wilmer Collins shot down an Me 262 and by 1600 334 descended to strafe Wittstock airdrome, destroying four after the 355th Group got through with the field. Robert Miller was wounded seriously enough to force his leaving ops after an emergency landing at Eindhoven.

[Box Score: 5 destroyed, 1 lost]

11 April 1945: F.O. 1944A. Going to Regensburg, Germany, Lt. Col. Woods led A Group on a Free Lance Fighter Sweep from 1015 to 1655 hours while Col. Stewart led B Group on a Penetration Target Withdrawal Support from 0715 to 1625 hours. As A Group swept ahead of the bomber stream to Ingeltheim, Dresden, Proba and Munich, B Group rendezvoused with the B-24s at 1215 hours at 18,000 feet. B then broke escort by 1445 hours at 10,000 feet over Ingelheim. A crossed out over Ostend at 1605 after a very frustrating mission. The 4th had been ordered to stop strafing and the boys saw loads of parked aircraft but were able to do nothing.

13 April 1945: F.O. 1962A. Lt. Col. Woods led a Penetration Target Withdrawal Support to Neumunster, Germany, from 1325 to 1650 hours. At 1500 the Mustangs joined on their Fortresses northwest of Heligoland. Two squadrons broke off at Ratzburg by 1548 and descended to find the 479th Group shooting up seaplanes on the lake; an Ar 196 and an He 115 were destroyed. The fighters then swept to Hamburg before turning for home, coming out at 1803.

[Box Score: 2 destroyed, 0 lost]

When the Group got back they received word that the 56th Group hit Eggebek airdrome and destroyed 90 on the ground, pushing the Wolfpack's score to 1,002½. The first part of April found the 4th with a good chance of beating the 56th to the magic 1,000 destroyed mark. On 4 April the Group was ahead of the 56th by 15½. On the 7th both Groups stayed about even in the day's tally but on the 10th the Wolfpack destroyed 41 on the ground to pull their score up to 911, leaving the 4th behind at 893. The 11 April order not to strafe was agonizing and the subsequent lifting of the restriction went in favor of the Group's rivals. Now the race was on to top the Wolfpack's score before the Germans surrendered.

15 April 1945: F.O. 1989A. Capt. Bell led a Ramrod Escort to Ulm, Germany, from 1210 to 1740 hours. At 1355 the Group picked up their A-26s southwest of Strasburg at 10,000 feet. The boys enjoyed being with these fast 9th Air Force medium bombers since their cruise speeds almost matched. Escort was broken at 1505 over the RV point and the Group swept back to Reutlingen, then to Lake Constance before turning and coming out south of Knocke by 1703. While on R/T relay, Edward Wozniak's P-51 developed engine trouble. He crash landed ten miles north of B-53 at Wattau, Belgium, and his injuries kept him from returning to the Group for combat.

[Box Score: 0 destroyed, 1 lost]

16 April 1945: F.O. 1997A. Lt. Col. Woods led A Group on a Free Lance/Strafing to Prague, Czechoslovakia, from 1200 to 1740 hours while Maj. Norley led B Group on a Penetration Target Withdrawal Support/Strafing to Rosenheim–Gablingen airdrome, Germany, from 1255 to 1940 hours. As A Group swept into the Prague area at 1500 they found three fields crammed with German aircraft that had been pulled back from the front. For what seemed an eternity, the Mustangs made run after run in the midst of heavy flak to destroy 61. Multiple kills were numerous—Douglas Pedersen got eight—but the intense flak claimed eight pilots—two killed and the rest captured. Among the POWs was mission leader Woods. Norley's B Group rendezvoused with their B-24s at 1440 southwest of Stuttgart at 15,000 feet, leaving by 1600 to strafe. The boys found Gablingen airdrome crammed with aircraft as well and strafed from 1700 to 1745 to get 44 destroyed without loss. Most of the Group had to land and refuel on the continent before coming back to Debden. The Group was back in the running to beat the Wolfpack.

[Box Score: 105 destroyed, 8 lost]

17 April 1945: F.O. 2006A. Maj. Glover led an Area Support/Free Lance to Karlsbad–Prague–Linz–Salsburg, Germany, Czechoslovakia, Austria, from 1145 to 1840 hours. The Group crossed in at 1242 and headed for Prague. An Me 262 was chased and went in wheels up, but no claim was made. The Mustangs then swept south at 6,000 with 334 flying top cover as 336 tested for flak. Pilzen airdrome had a few aircraft and four were destroyed. Robert Davis' coolant system was hit and he bailed east of enemy lines; although he was seen to hit the ground OK near Eger–Marienbad, he was killed. The Group crossed out over Knocke at 1730.

[Box Score: 4 destroyed, 1 lost]

18 April 1945: F.O. 2017A. Maj. Norley led a Penetration Target Withdrawal Support to Passau, Germany, from 1105 to 1715 hours. The B-24 escort, from 1311 rendezvous near Meidelberg to 1530 break off south of Koblenz, was a milk run.

20 April 1945: F.O. 2039A. On a Penetration Target Withdrawal Support to Klatovny, Czechoslovakia, Col. Stewart led A Group from 0900 to 1440 hours while Maj. Norley led B Group from 0910 to 1535 hours. Rendezvous with the B-24s was made at 1049 southeast of Frankfurt at 12,000 feet. A Group broke escort at 1210 near Barnau and swept from Munich to Durlag before coming out at 1450 over Ostend. B Group left at 1315 and swept back past Frankfurt. Three 334 aircraft stayed with the Bomber Command Mosquito from 0900 to 1435.

21 April 1945: F.O. 2053A. Maj. Glover led a Target Withdrawal Support to Salzburg, Austria, from 0725 to 1330 hours. As the Group got off, Glover was forced to abort, leaving Lt. Frederick in charge. Rendezvous with the B-24s was made at 0944 southeast of Frankfurt at 6,000 feet. The Libs aborted but the Group caught up to other Big Friends at 1105, leaving five minutes later to sweep the area. The P-51s set course for Debden at 1045.

22 April 1945: John Godfrey, having returned the day before after his time as a POW, gave a talk at 1100 hours in the briefing room about his adventures away from Debden. Over the next month several more POWs returned.

23 April 1945: A B-24 took the first batch of enlisted men to Paris for 48-hour passes.

25 April 1945: F.O. 2054A. Col. Stewart led a Fighter Sweep to Linz–Prague–Dresden, Czechoslovakia, Germany, from 0510 to 1415 hours. The P-51s arrived over Linz by 0830, flying at 10,000 feet, before swinging north to Prague. William B. Hoelscher bounced an Me 262 at 0945 near the Prague/Ruzyne airdrome, getting several strikes before he was hit by flak; the coolant system was punctured and 40mm hits smashed the left wing root and elevator. He bailed out and made it back as an evader. Four to six other 262s came in from the same direction as the first but the flak was too intense to attack. The mission extended so far that several pilots had to land on the continent and refuel before coming on back to Debden.

[Box Score: 0 destroyed, 1 lost]

As things went, this mission turned out to be the last for the 4th Fighter Group in World War II. Without POW tallies and pending claims, the score stood at 1,008½ for the 56th Group and 1,003 for the 4th.

7 May 1945: The first Trolly Mission was flown by four B-24s holding eight to ten enlisted men each. From 1400 to 2045 hours the bombers took the men on a sightseeing tour to Ostend, Belgium, Mannheim, Dusseldorf and deeper into Germany to get a look at what Allied airpower had done.

8 May 1945: VE-Day was officially proclaimed. All the Mustangs were grounded and ammunition removed. At 1400 hours 4th personnel stood formation on the parade ground as Chaplain Brohm led in prayer. From 1500 to midnight free beer was served and all work was suspended. The Flying Eagles dance band was going full tilt. By 2230 a victory bonfire started on the ball field and Very pistols got heavy use. The celebration lasted into the next day.

The Group's victory tally came in officially as 1,016, putting it ahead of the Wolfpack. VIII Fighter Command subsequently reappraised all the claims and credited the Group with 1,058½ destroyed although the earlier figure is considered closer to the final count. Regardless, it placed the 4th Fighter Group, for so long made up of AAF "wash-outs," as the leading fighter outfit of the USAAF in World War II.

13 May 1945: 720 fighters of VIII FC flew around London and southern England in a giant victory review from 1800 to 2000 hours at 2,000 to 2,500 feet. High Wycombe, 8th AF HQ, and Gen. Jimmy Doolittle's home on the Thames were on the counter-clockwise route that circled London 20 miles out.

17 May 1945: At 1700 hours word was given to ground all 4th Mustangs again until black ID letters (the squadron codes) could be painted under the port wings. Low flying was making the English a bit jumpy.

23 May 1945: No. 453 Squadron, RAAF, arrived from Manston with their Spitfires to fly in mock combat with the Group. Word was out that the 4th would be going to the Pacific in P-47Ns and the Spits were to serve as Zeros. Everyone enjoyed getting their hand back in.

From this date through most of June at least eight war weary P-47s of the 5th Emergency Rescue Squadron, Boxted, were based at Debden. These aircraft were most likely to be used to convert 4th pilots to the Thunderbolt. But VJ-Day came along too fast and the Pacific adventure was cancelled.

29 May 1945: As things slowly wound down, most of the Group's P-51s with less than 100 hours were transferred to Speke Air Depot near Liverpool. At 1000 hours twelve 336 aircraft airborne for the Depot encountered bad weather after climb out. While letting down from 7,000 feet near Manchester, Barnaby Wilhoit and Harold Fredericks were killed when they flew into the ground in dense fog. Beacham Brooker hit the ground, after being thrown by the explosion of Fredericks' crash, tearing the wingtip from his '51. He made it back to Debden. A few other pilots turned back but most reached Speke.

June 1945: The Group gradually disbanded internally as plans for the Pacific were cancelled and men began to leave. The beautiful red-nosed Mustangs were gradually flown out to other bases.

7 July 1945: Fred Glover's P-51D, repainted to represent John Godfrey's VF-P, was flown to Paris and displayed with other 8th Air Force aircraft under the Eiffel Tower.

10 July 1945: The 14-piece Flying Eagles band left Debden for a 30-day tour of the UK, proving to be the most popular attraction around.

27 July 1945: Fair Debden saw the last of the 4th as men and equipment transferred to Steeple Morden.

15 August 1945: The announced surrender of Japan produced no great rejoicing. Everyone just wanted to get home.

Throughout September the last of the original 4th members departed England and the Third Anniversary of the Group, on the 12th, was almost forgotten. The

P-51s were flown to Burtonwood and other depots and pilots with less than 62 points for rotation home were assigned to the Occupational Air Force to fly, of all things, UC-64s. By 9 November the *RMS Queen Mary* docked in New York bearing all that was left of the Group, and on 10 November 1945, the 4th was inactivated at Camp Kilmer, New Jersey.

Cheers!

Post-VE-Day, June, 1945: The wreckage of 336's VF-M joins the litter of Luftwaffe aircraft in France. The shot was taken by a 78th FG officer while on a visit to Paris. (*Russell Hunter*)

The Hively Accounts

Howard D. "Deacon" Hively was one of the genuine "characters" inhabiting the environs of Debden during the war years. In September 1942 he transferred from 71 Eagle Squadron into the newly formed 4th Fighter Group. With exception of a two and one-half month leave, "Deac" flew with the Group until things were winding down in 1945. He saw it all.

Due to the scope of this book, the authors were forced to limit much anecdotal material, with regret. A natural choice to remember the "flavor" of the Group, "Deac" enthusiastically sent page after page of first-hand material when asked to help. Herein are those recollections by one of the few surviving insiders of the "Blakesleewaffe."

15 JUNE 1943
MISSION ALMOST IMPOSSIBLE

In the summer of 1943 the 4th Fighter Group was often assigned advanced base missions. We had been recently equipped (the previous March) with America's answer to the Hot War, P-47s, or as the British called them, Thunderbolts. Fighter pilots were then and always will be a breed of their own, and in their language this over-sized, short-ranged, cumbersome fighter plane was most often referred to as the "Jug." No doubt the most dominant question in the minds of all those who flew them was, "Do you think the airplane is here to stay or will the P-47 take its place?"

Anyway, on the occasion of 15 June 1943 we had been ordered to an advanced base, Tangmere, on the south coast of England to cover an air strike against the submarine pens at St. Nazaire. The only question in all our minds (concerning the order) was that part stating, "Class A uniforms will be worn!" There was no question about the advanced base—we had to shorten the range in order to reach St. Nazaire—but can you imagine wearing that dress uniform in the close confines of a fighter cockpit? Just picture yourself all dressed up in a tuxedo sitting in an outdoor john with tight straps across your lap and shoulders, then hang on your person 80 pounds of equipment, including Mae West, back pack chute, oxygen tube, mask, bail-out bottle, dinghy, escape kit, a large knife, Colt .45 and God only knows what other sundries that each fighter pilot personally believed was necessary to complete his mission. Needless to say, a fighter pilot's life is no bed of roses at any time, but the narrow, greasy confines of fighter cockpits do not lend themselves to Class A uniforms. Where do you put your hat, let alone the bottle of rum?

When we arrived at Tangmere in our dress pinks, sponged of grease with 100 octane gas, our British allies were completely impressed. Their oft amazed question of, "Do you always wear those uniforms on a mission?" were invariably answered with, "What else?" Sooo, before first light we had completed our briefing, climbed into our "Jugs" and set off to do battle with the wily Hun.

The facts of that particular day have never been quite clear, or perhaps they have only been forgotten in the aftermath of a long war and what followed on that day. We did go round and round—I do believe the submarine pens were clobbered by the bombers, though I never established this. But when our leader's long awaited order of "Let's git the hell out of here" rang across the airs, all 48 intrepid fighter pilots turned as one and headed home. After all, that's where the rum came from.

It did not take long, however, to ascertain that something was not just quite right. First thing I noticed were two small streams of blue smoke jutting forward over my shoulders and somewhat of an increased cockpit temperature. Everything else was all right though . . . all my buddies were close by, the sky was beautiful, clear and blue. We hadn't really had a tough "Do"; the opposition had been less than meager, and after all, we were headed home.

Then, all of a sudden, the fit hit the Shan! When my boots got too hot to be comfortable, I spied all at once a fire beyond the firewall on the cockpit floor. Gauges went haywire, temperatures out of the green into the red, and the rudder pedals became so hot my feet were burning up. All fighter pilots are quick of mind, along with righteous, able and loveable, so with all my inherent perspicacity, it only took five or ten minutes to come to the complete realization that this cockpit was no longer tenable.

Someone pulled alongside. I think it was Pierce Winningham McKennon, God rest his soul. He said, "I think you'd better get out of there, Deac." "I been thinking about it Mac, but it looks awful wet down there; maybe I can hold on for a little while longer." "We'll follow you down, don't worry," said Mac. "O.K." said I, "but I'm gonna wait for awhile, if I can. That's one helluva step!"

At that time, we were at about 27,000 feet. I know I had not yet even considered the possibility I would have to leave the securities of that small cockpit for isn't it true that God takes care of fools, drunks and fighter pilots? Nevertheless, it wasn't long before that possibility became more than apparent even to this God-fearing fighter pilot . . . all of a sudden the propeller stopped, frozen in a four-bladed apparition. The fire grew hotter and hotter, 'till I had to tuck my feet up under the seat. My boots were burning and it became damned uncomfortable in there.

Decisions, decisions, decisions! How to get out? Should I merely climb out, step off the wing and hope or should I just roll it over and fall out or should I "pop out"? All of these methods had been discussed over and over amongst us fighter drivers. Next to women, hangar flying was the most valued of all conversational subjects. To "pop out" meant to wind all nose trim forward 'till one had to exert a great deal of back pressure on the stick in order to keep the plane level. Then, much like pulling a tooth, count three, shove the stick forward and virtually "pop out." Actually, all one had to do is push the plane away, but the appearance was as if the pilot popped out.

I decided I'd take the easiest of the three methods and just roll the '47 over and fall out. Meanwhile, back in the cockpit, I had switched the radio over to our emergency channel (D for dinghy). I had all the Maydays going I could muster in my best devil-may-care manner, "Mayday, Mayday, Mayday, Heyday, Payday," which it was. Control kept calling for a fix and a long count. I started off in the proper manner, like "1 . . . 2 . . . 3 . . . 4 . . . 5 . . . 6 . . . 7 . . . 8 . . . 9 . . . 10," but it got shorter and shorter as my house got hotter and hotter. Finally, at about 7,000 feet, I figured the time had come so I unhooked all the straps, laid my hat down on the floor and started to roll it over. "Damn it!" I just couldn't do it. Every time I'd get halfway over I'd let loose of the controls and grab the sides to hold on. It wasn't easy to let myself go, in any way, let alone to just give up and fall upside down out of an airplane. Besides, I came to the conclusion right then and there, "It ain't fittin' or proper for a fighter pilot to leave in such a manner." Something had to be done! About that time control called once again for a long count. I hurriedly rolled all the trim forward, gave the count, "12345678," said goodbye, popped the stick forward and left.

Never before or since have I had such a feeling. I certainly didn't pop out, but seemed to float up over my airplane and just hang there. I could look down and see all the straps hanging straight up . . . there was my hat (helmet) hanging straight up from it's cord. I could see the fire and counted seven bullet holes in the left wing. I remember being quite concerned about those for I hadn't even known any Huns had gotten close. 'Course, as the old adage goes, "It's always the one you don't see that gets you!" I just seemed to hang there, then—W H I S H—I was free, falling! The feeling was one of freedom, total unattachment, softly suspended, free of machines and ties of any sort. It was wonderful. I've always meant to jump on purpose some day—never have. 'Bout the only feeling I've had that came close was with a nurse I once knew—she made me float for a night or two!

"Wake up Deac!" I found myself yelling, "Wake up Deac!" Frantically I reached for the D-ring and couldn't find it. It was supposd to be just over my heart but it wasn't. It was clear around almost in the middle of my back. I could hardly reach it. Wouldn't you know I had borrowed the chute while mine was being repacked. I got two fingers around it and jerked as hard as I could. It came loose but slipped through my fingers and went sailing off into space. "Damn!" And then I watched the chute coming out. Surprisingly, it came out sideways, not up; and what's more it looked old and dirty. I kept thinking, "I hope it opens." I don't know what I would have done if it hadn't, but as it kept running out, I kept thinking, "I *hope* it opens." It did . . . Whoomp!! I looked up and it was beautiful. I look down and there, right below me and just out of reach, was my D-ring. "Damn!" I thought again, "there goes a pound." In those days that was $4.04. Looking down again, I found my airplane some distance away, heading straight down. I watched fascinated, then Boom! It exploded, sending the tail section sailing end over end, off to the left, as the nose went straight down and kersplashed into the water! There was a helluva rush of hot air that almost seemed to stop me in mid-air. I came down again with a smaller Whoomp, looked up at my chute and found it had collapsed on one side.

Then I started to swing. I'd go sailing way up, almost horizontal, and the other side of the chute would collapse before I'd start down in the other direction. Way up, then the other side would collapse, and down I'd go again. What a ride! It was, to say the least, a bit breezy. I tried to pull on the risers but that only made it seem worse. I must have been pulling on the wrong ones—anyway, I quit that. I looked down again and my dinghy was hanging on a strap attached to my Mae West about six or eight feet below. With the water getting close, I knew I was going to have to swim. "One last cigarette" popped into my mind. Though the chute straps were so tight I could hardly get at the case, I somehow got one out and got it lit. I knew it would be the last for awhile.

Since I didn't want to be weighed down with anything unnecessary if I was going into those cold waters, I started to unload. I pulled out my knife and threw it away—hated to see it go—dumped my cigarette lighter and case, reached in and pulled out my .38 revolver. It was a beauty—pearl handles and everything. My father had given it to me to take to the wars and I'd carried it for years. I started to throw it away and then I thought, "Hell, I've never fired it." So I let loose with all six shots and gave her the old heave-ho. "Damn!!" I hated to see that go too.

I turned the release dial on the chute harness, ready to drop out just above the water. I was close, but it was real hard to tell exactly 'cause I was still swinging in a pretty good arc. Then—swish—across the top of one wave, through the next wave and S P L A S H into the next.

Man! I hit the release dial so hard it almost knocked me out. I hadn't realized how hard the wind was blowing. The waves were enormous and I hit in almost a horizontal position with the chute directly behind me. As I felt the harness leave, I reached over my shoulder to grab it, but that thing was traveling straight across the water like a speedboat. There wasn't a chance and that was the last I ever saw of it.

Down I went. I don't know how deep the Channel is at that point, but I've sworn over and over again I couldn't have been far from the bottom. Paddle—paddle—paddle. I paddled and kicked 'till I reached the top, took a big breath, and down I went again. That uninflated dinghy was worse than a 180 pound anchor. I couldn't get my Mae West inflated as the pull strings were stuck behind the CO_2 bottles. They had gotten wet and swelled up. I was frantic! The third time I surfaced, I said to myself, "Deac, you got to do something!" As I went down for the fourth time, I deliberately opened my eyes, took a careful look at the CO_2 bottles, held my breath 'till I thought I would bust and managed to free one. When I came up that time, I found that I could stay up. What a relief! I took my time and got the other one undone . . . then it was great.

I don't know how long I laid there just floating and breathing, but all I could think of was how high the waves were. They sure look different when you're in them than they do when you're above them. Anyway, I finally hauled the dinghy up and started to open it. I got the canvas cover off real easy (all I had to do was unsnap it), but then came the fun. All of us had sat on those damn things for years. Never had I ever looked one over before. The only thing that any of us had ever done was cuss and complain about the position of the CO_2 bottle in them, for that was always placed in the most uncomfortable spot anybody could have picked, especially after sitting on it for hours at a time in a cramped cockpit. Nevertheless, I found I knew exactly where it was and I knew how to open it . . . just twist the knob. But twist as hard as I could, I couldn't get it open. Then I had a bright idea—"If all else fails, read the directions." Sure enough, it said, "Remove safety pin, twist cap." I did! The dinghy went W-h-o-o-f and almost exploded.

It filled up—but my hand froze to the bottle! Damn it was cold . . . not only my hand, but all of me. They say the Channel is colder in June than in December due to water cooling more slowly and consequently heating more slowly than air or land. This I will assure you, it's damned cold in June! I thought to myself, "Don't pull your hand off that bottle." I remembered touching my tongue to my sled runner when I was a kid and the disastrous results. I just lay there 'till the bottle came loose on its own accord.

"Now, to get in that dinghy." Boy, that was a problem, especially in rough water. I have no idea how many times I tried. If that thing hadn't been attached to me, I would have lost it many times over. Finally, I think I just reached out and pulled it under me—I think—but once in, I felt the battle was over. It was dryer than the Channel, not much, but it was dryer and what's more, it was a real treasure trove.

The first thing I found was a little package of six red flares. All my buddies were buzzing around, every once in a while coming straight over the dinghy at less than zero feet. I was positive they saw me, but I knew that I should let them know I was all right, so out came a flare. It was about as big around as my thumb and say, eight inches long. There were directions all over the case. They read, "Two red flares—unscrew cap—lift tab—hold at arm's length." I did and nothing! I couldn't read the rest at arm's length so I brought it back and it said, "Pull tab sharply toward you." I did and quickly stuck my hand out to its fullest extension. The thing went buzzzzzzzzzzzzzz and all of a sudden BOOM!

I watched it go sailing up. A big, bright, red ball of fire made a high, beautiful arc. But, damn it, all I got was one red ball when there should have been two. My hands were wet and the recoil shot it right out of my hand into the water. "I'll fix that," I thought to myself. "This time I'll get two." I held my hand at arm's length all right, but rested it firmly on my knee, unscrewed the cap, lifted the tab and pulled it sharply toward me. Again, it went buzzzzzzzzzzzz, BOOM! The recoil was tremendous . . . it damn near busted my knee. Honest, I limped for weeks afterward, and that undoubtedly was the worst injury I received in the whole mission.

Then it became a game. I had four left so I tried to hit the guys as they came thundering over me. I never did, but I came real close. I missed Jim Clark by a foot or less. Afterwards, when we talked about it, none of the guys ever saw a flare. Fact is, they didn't even see me or the dinghy, but I didn't know that then and was as happy as a bug in a rug, thinking all the while that everybody saw me and that a boat would soon be there. Little did I know!

The flares were fun, but pretty soon they were all gone and so were all the guys. They just disappeared, as if by magic, and there I was, all alone. It was a lonesome old feeling. That dinghy seemed to get smaller and smaller, the waves bigger and bigger as I got colder and colder. I paddled and paddled and paddled. That kept me a little warmer, so I paddled and paddled some more. Then I got brave—when I reached the top of a wave, I would stand up to see how far I had gotten. In the distance I could see the coast of England but right behind me, and even closer, was France. I just wasn't making any headway. Every once in awhile, as I would stand up on top of a wave, I would fall in.

That little dinghy acted more like a cork than a boat. Each dunking brought a lot of water with it, both into the boat and into me. Eventually I found that it was warmer with the water in the dinghy than it was to bail it out, so I stopped bailing. My body temperature heated up the water.

I got sort of adept at standing on that thing without falling in. I could ride it like a surfboard but I was tired, bored and I was getting sleepy. I knew this was a bad sign. I had to stay awake or freeze. I looked through the dinghy for something to keep me awake and that's when it became a treasure trove. First, I found a sea anchor. How it was supposed to work was beyond me. At the time that little funnel didn't look as though it would anchor anything, but I threw it out anyway.

I found a sail with directions all over it. Finally I got it all rigged up with the aid of the detailed directions and had a ball sailing for over an hour. It was bright red and gave quite a feeling of security with all its color. Then I found a fishing line and hooks—no bait. A nice little waterproof package contained malted milk tablets, a chocolate bar, dry matches (no cigarettes), halazone tablets, two compasses, a sawblade, first-aid kit . . . and, what's more, 2,000 francs in French money. More rummaging produced plugs (two sizes), a band pump, a bailer and scads and scads of things I can't recall. It was a genuine treasure trove but I began to feel sad that I had used up all my flares because I was wondering when somebody was going to come and get me.

I heard an airplane! Could it be the Nazis come to strafe? They did that, you know! Was it one of ours? And there it was, coming right toward me . . . a Walrus! Not one of the animals, but a Walrus airplane, a British seaplane. Round and round it went just above me. I thought, "I know it's rough, but couldn't they even attempt a landing?" Really at heart I knew they couldn't but all of a sudden it leveled off and came right at me. There was a bomb hanging under each lower wing—one of them let loose and came sailing right at me! I hit the drink! When I came up, there it was six feet away and smoking like a fiend. Down I went again! The next time I came up for air, I realized it was a marker, a smoke bomb. And smoke it did, a thick, voluminous, greenish-yellow cloud.

I crawled back in the dinghy and watched the Walrus disappear behind the waves. It was gone. "Must be a boat around here some place," but I couldn't find one. I stood up again on the dinghy and looked all around—but no boat. Damn, it was cold. I knew I couldn't last much longer. All I wanted to do was lie down and sleep. I paddled some more, but that didn't last long either. I was just too tired. I stood up again—a BOAT!? Yes, by God, a boat! But it was going in the wrong direction! I yelled! I yelled at the top of my lungs. I yelled louder than anybody had ever yelled before. I stood up and waved the little flag I had found in the dinghy as hard as I could. I waved that little flag so hard that it went sailing off its stick like a newly launched bolo. I waved frantically, forgot where I was, jumped up and down, and fell in once again. I was back in that dinghy and up again before you could say Eisenhower . . . and behold! it was coming to me.

"They're not close enough. They ought to get closer." They stood off what looked to be a mile, but maybe it was only 50 yards or so, still in the water. There were a whole bunch of guys standing up on deck looking at me. One of them had a rope in his hand and started swinging it like a cowboy. "What are they going to do, lasso me?" The guy let loose of that rope—it came sailing across the water like a shot out of a cannon. I watched it come on and on until I had to duck. It would have hit me right on the head.

What a toss! I'll never forget that one. I bet that guy would have had a great future with the Cincinnati Reds. When I got ahold of that rope, it was all she wrote. I cut a swath through that water like a Gar Wood speed boat. They pulled so hard and fast I had a time holding on.

Then another problem arose. How did one get aboard one of these boats? They were well over 80 feet long (87 I think) but the closer I got, the bigger it got and the waves were bigger still. I let loose of that rope in a hurry, for all of a sudden the boat went up on one wave and I went down. Then the boat started down and I started up. I thought the boat would crash down on me. I paddled backward as fast as I could as the boat went rushing past. Up, up, up I went 'till I looked down and saw the white faces of the guys on board looking up at me. Down I went and up they came. This continued several times. Finally they lowered a sort of net over the side, and as that boat went by for the ninth time, I reached out and caught hold of the net. Just to give some idea how high those waves were . . . I'm almost six feet, must be eight feet with my arms outstretched. The dinghy was four feet long and attached to me by a strap eight feet long, so eight and four and eight is 20. As I hung onto that net, I looked down and we were all out of the water. I swear, at that time the waves seemed not 20 but more like 50 feet high.

That was it, however. Those guys took over completely. As my head came over the gunnel, hands reached from somewhere above and grabbed me by hair, shoulders, arms, back of the neck, anywhere they could get a hold, and up I came to have a cigarette stuffed in my mouth. When my feet hit the deck, out came the cigarette and someone threw a shot of rum down my throat. I promptly threw up all over the guy in front of me. I was just too full of salt water to accommodate anything else at the time, let alone 180 proof Navy rum. It didn't seem to bother them, though, as I was whisked down below and stipped of all my clothes. I tried to help, like unbutton my shirt, but I was so cold and shaking so hard that finally I just tore them off and relaxed.

They came at me with towels and 44 hands, rubbing and rubbing 'till I was raw on both sides. I kept screaming and finally they stopped. Then came long underwear, a pair of soft, flannel grey trousers and a beautiful white turtleneck wool sweater, tennis shoes and blanket after blanket. I just lay there getting warmer and warmer. The feeling was incredible. The warm started in with a speck clear down in the middle of my bones and then slowly started out millimeter by silly millimeter. I could feel it reach the outer edge of my bones and start into my flesh 'till finally it permeated my whole being. That nurse I mentioned could never compete, and I mean never!

I looked up and there were six happy, smiling faces looking down. "How do you feel? Would you like some medicine?" The medicine was a whole gallon of what I knew to be that Navy rum, but I remembered my experience with that on deck a few minutes before. I wasn't about to be caught again. "No thanks," I said and every face fell. I got the message. It *was* medicine, medicinal rum, and could only be broken out if there was a patient aboard. "O.K.," I said, "I'll try it once more." A GI water glass appeared and was filled to the brim. I tasted it very carefully. It was good, real sweet, heavy and didn't burn at all. I took another sip, every move followed by those quizzical fallen faces. I smiled, "Would you guys care for one?" *UP* went all the faces, round went that glass in a flash, and back it came empty. "Could I have another?" I ventured. The smiles grew bigger and every face beamed. We were buddies! Several sips later, it came to me all of a sudden, "Who's driving the boat?" "The Captain," they said. "Could I?" said the fighter pilot. "Sure!" said the crew, in one voice like an a cappella choir.

What a ball! What a ride! What a piece of machinery! That thing had three big Rolls Royce engines. It would do a mile a minute and that's how we completed the crossing all the way to Portsmouth, through hell and high water, spurred on by a fighter pilot's enthusiasm and several sips of good ole Navy rum.

We were greeted in Portsmouth with everything but a Navy band. I felt like a prize sail fish or something. They even had a flag flying to show they had captured me. There were three ambulances on the dock plus a great crowd of people, all with the same question, "Where's the patient?" I was helping them dock, all dressed up in the turtle-neck and grey flannel pants, three sheets to the wind—one flapping due to Navy rum, no doubt—after having swum most of the English Channel and in Class "A" uniform at that.

That 'bout winds up the story, except, as you might have guessed, the cigarettes and chocolate bars and respect and admiration and comradeship that passed from one fighter pilot to that crew and the whole RAF rescue service.

THE RUSSIA SHUTTLE MISSION

It wasn't long after D-Day in June 1944 that we received word we were going to Russia. Once before during Eagle Squadron days we had been booked to go, and at that time we were to have put our Spitfires on a convoy and headed for Murmansk, but this time the word was we were going to fly. There is no way to recount the hours that Don and I devoted to cussing and discussing the ifs and possibilities of that sort of mission. Those sessions started after every mission almost, and carried on far into the nights, even after the bar was closed and most of the guys were long in bed. For sure there were many mornings we had time only to change clothes, throw a little water on our faces, and make the morning's briefing. We figured, for some reason, that we would probably go to Moscow, maybe because that was about the only city we knew about there. And be-sides, according to what maps we could obtain then, that would be the longest extension of our range possible, unless we went over Finland to Leningrad. Anyway, the apparent terminals looked like either Leningrad, Moscow, or Kiev. We picked Moscow.

I can't remember the exact day we received word of the mission and the details, but when we found we had over 200 bombers to escort over 2200 miles of enemy territory, we knew this was a big one. We were assured that special bases had been provided for us, built by GIs and maintained by GIs and that they had been there for some time get-ting everything ready. Our base in Russia was to be at Piryatin—about half way be-tween Kiev and Karkov—and the bombers were to have two bases close by at Poltava and Mylograd. Our base at Piryatin—the last to be built—had only one metal strip, North and South, but we were assured there would be adequate facilities for mainte-nance and quarters, and that we wouldn't be there long, for we were to escort the bombers back as soon as they could be rearmed and refueled. The new term applied was "Shuttle bombing." The whole concept was that we were to bomb on the way in, then bomb on the way out. In that way we would have the Hun boxed in, so to speak, so that we would be hitting him from all directions. In other words, we'd have him coming and going with bases in England, Russia, and Italy. The attacks then could eventually begin from three different directions, three different countries. We could combine the efforts, personnel, and equipment of the two major air forces, the 8th and the 12th, with all the advantages thereof. It was a hell of an idea! We were more than enthusiastic, even though the problems were great. Don Blakeslee will never gain the credit due him. He was a doer. Let somebody think of it and Don would do it. He knew he had the confi-dence of all his men. He had the ability to see the heart of a problem. He had the air sense that few ever attained, he had the guts and he had the command presence. Con-sequently his group, the 4th Group, was constantly called upon to do the firsts, to do the difficults, to do the unprobables, and they had achieved the experience.

It was decided that this one was to be a maximum effort do, so we were to take four squadrons of 16 aircraft per squadron or 64—normally we flew 48 on a mission—and the powers that were then assigned to us one squadron of the 352nd group—Joe Mason's group. Joe and I had been Boy Scouts together—Troop 10, Columbus, Ohio. It was great fun kidding Joe. He was comparatively new to the theatre at that time, so Don and I concocted many a fine story and tale that kept Joe in a constant state of flux. He kind of thought we were kidding, but he couldn't be sure and besides nobody could, or even would, argue with Blakeslee. I know—I used to try, but I never won. I remember one time in a staff car going to a meeting in London at Fighter H.Q. I was expounding on what we should do on future operations. His answers were short, to the point and went something like: "That's being taken care of," "Started that yesterday," "Claiborne is taking care of that," "We'll get that done as soon as," "I already did it." Finally I blew and yelled, "How come you're always ahead of me! You're no smarter than I am. I can outfly you. How come?" He grinned and said very quietly, "I get my information three days ahead of you!"

Joe Mason, however, had inadvertently caused us another problem, and that was—who would go? We had at that time almost 150 aircraft in the group and 125 well qualified pilots. Only 48 of them could make it. I shan't go into how we picked the ones that made it—and needless to say, Blakeslee left the final decisions to the squadron commanders—but some guys had to be left out. It may seem odd to the layman, and surely it doesn't go with all the movie scripts, but of the 125 guys available, 126 were chomping at the bit to risk their lives on a damned difficult and dangerous do. That was Blakeslee's fault. He had so instilled in every soul the will and want to fly, that the competition in the group had exceeded all bounds. With some reluctance I was forced to scratch Kidd Hofer from the mission. However, I did post him and his wingman as alternates. It was some sort of disciplinary action and as I remember it was because he had on several occasions broken formation and gone on his own. That we couldn't use. A squadron is a team and must act like one; individual efforts could and would not be tolerated by Blakeslee or me. Don had fined Gentile for just that thing and sent him back to the States. Hofer was a good kid; he was hot, but like all kids thought he knew more than the CO—or the CG for that matter. I should have set him all the way down, but like I said he was a personable young man, and finally after a lot of pleading I gave in and made him alternate. I took Siems as my wingman—he had good eyes—I made Shell Monroe deputy sqd. CO and assigned him No. 3 in my flight, with Hedrick as No. 4. Hedrick was not the best pilot, but he had been a Master Sgt. pilot prior to the war, now a Capt., and had been in for a long time. I knew we were going to be seeing the Russians and I figured I would need him for protocol and things like that. McKennon was not yet back from leave in the U.S., so Blakeslee took 335 squadron and Lum Blanding took 336. I forget who Joe Mason assigned to lead his squadron—for a long time we thought maybe he would go himself, but it didn't happen. Don had designated me as second in command with the position of high cover for my squadron.

We were the second squadron off. The form-up was routine and we set course for Russia. Our route was as direct as possible. There was quite a large diversion laid on from the north approaches to bomb Berlin. We flew almost directly over the northern part of the Ruhr—with flak like you have never seen—and in the midst of violent evasive action there was a yell from Siems, my No. 2, "I've been hit!" He had been, but not badly, for when he pulled up alongside I couldn't see any serious damage—no vapor trails, no glycol leaks, no oil, no fire—so when I asked, "Can you make it?," I received a timid, "I think so," and he tucked back into formation.

We picked up our 200-plus bombers on the other side of the Ruhr and took them on into their target. They bombed well, it seemed to us, but fighter pilots are hardly ever looking at the ground—'cause the sky was our charge and we were there to defend it. It was reported to us afterward that after they finished bombing they dropped leaflets saying they were going on to Russia and would be back. Somehow, to most of us that seemed somewhat foolish—kinda advertising what you were doing and where you were going, and that night sort of confirmed it. From Frankfurt on navigation was the big problem. I had been to Poznan, Poland, once before, but although the weather was beautiful, all landmarks were strange to us. The diversion had worked and we had no opposition over the target. However, over Poland, south of Poznan, there was a little scuffle with some FW190s, but not by us in 334 Squadron, for we were flying top cover. It was here that Hofer was supposedly hit. He had again disobeyed orders and instead of

September, 1944: 336th marshalling on the south edge of the west runway while waiting for 335th to takeoff on the show. (*John Romack*)

September, 1944: FRANKIE lands from the south on show return. Q is an early D-model lacking the stabilizing strake to the vertical fin. (*John Romack*)

September, 1944: Lt. Darwin Berry's WD-K FEISTY SUE just about to strike rubber on touch-down over the south threshold. (*John Romack*)

September, 1944: A QP kite back home with throttle cut back. Oxide trail on cowling, caused by a long ride at low fuel, a lot of air, and lean mixture to extend range. This often caused hot running, blown coolant, and loss of pilot and a/c. (*John Romack*)

September 1944: 334th armorers line up for the group photog for one of those picture magazine poses seen so often. A few minutes later they were back at the serious business of having record fewer stoppages than most groups. (*John Cowman*)

Fall, 1944: Lt. G. Ceglarski (l.) sits on his SWEET STUFF 335th D-model with pals, G. Cooley (cntr.), and J. Kolbe (r.), relaxing and glad to have added another show to their tour. (*George Cooley*)

October 10–on, 1944: Col. Blakeslee's mount WD-C 44-13779. The new white 335th rudder color has been added and a wing root fillet has been borrowed from a 336th a/c to keep the Col.'s kite flying. (*Philip Lindsey*)

October, 1944: Maj. P. McKennon (r.) and his chief, S/Sgt. Joe Sills with the original RIDGE RUNNER bearing 11 of Mac's total 22 victories. The 335th commander is back from a month of evading Germans in France. (*John Cowman*)

October, 1944: Even if the Germans are hard to find in the air, the job of flaming them on the ground is as perilous as ever. This 4TH pilot skims the ground to avoid flak as he hits a FW-58C and the hangars behind. (*Isadore Swerdel*)

October 10–12, 1944: Five Top-secret RAF Gloster Meteor jets visit DB to help work out tactics against the new German Jets. Station letters and landing tee by tower in foreground. (*Joe Sills*)

November 1, 1944: A legend leaves the 4TH. Col. Don Blakeslee, with his silver mug farewell gift, congratulates LtCol. Claiborne Kinnard for assuming command of the 4FG. Don was grounded after another valuable leader was lost. (*Cecil Manning*)

November, 1944: The 4TH's first two-seat Mustang, an old War-weary OTU a/c conversion by T/Sgt/E. Jensen, lands on the west runway. (*J. Sills*)

December 26, 1944: Ready for combat in the cold dawn is Lt. J. Hileman's VF-C. 44-15191 MARY BELLE was often borrowed by 336th CO Maj. F. Glover as his chief John Wilson crewed it. (*Glesner Weckbacher*)

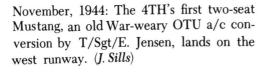

December 25, 1944: VF-S-(slash) 43-6975 sits alone in 336th area. The Group operated overnight out of Raydon. The old B-model has the peculiar frozen "Fog" on it first seen that day. (*Isadore Swerdel*)

December, 1944: The new Group nose marking is carried under the cowl to the front of the wing root. Capt. George Davis' VF-D 44-63233 INKYS DINKY was lost with Lt. H. A. Kaul on 2/11/45. (*William O'Donnell*)

December, 1944: Capt. Francis "Pappy" Grove's chief checks the hydraulic fluid before the morning show. VF-*T* is retro-fitted with Malcolm hood, dorsal fin fillet, and bears 336th's red depth-edged codes and squadron blue rudder color. (*Francis Grove*)

December, 1944: The only olive drab D-model of the 4TH was Maj. H. Hively's QP-J 44-15347, parked before the 334th HQ shack. The kite was painted by the hangar crew and had NMF undersides. (*Edward Hedrick*)

January, 1945: Winter halts ops today, but the open canopy means the chief is still working. QP-F has the December 24-in. nose color while Lt. R. A. Dyer's QP-VV 44-14323 LAZY DAISY has the new January swept-under look. (*William Rushing*)

January, 1945: Lt. W. Dvorak's QP-I ZOMIN ZOMBIE waits for the weather to lift over the UK and Germany. Black-lettered name with red capitals. (*William Rushing*)

January, 1945: QP-X 44-11661 IRON ASS seen here on 334th line was the kite of LtCol. Jack Oberhansly, acting 4TH CO in December and now Deputy CO to LtCol. Harry Dayhuff, the current Group & Station commander. (*Edward Hedrick*)

January, 1945: LtCol. Harry J. Dayhuff, the 4TH commander now, signs the Form 1 for his crewchief in 336th as the winter daylight wanes after the show return. (*H. Dayhuff*)

After January 26, 1945: New 334th CO, Maj. Louis "Red Dog" Norley, takes off in QP-O, former CO's QP-J. He soon traded 44-15347 for a newer NMF bird. (*Edward Hedrick*)

January, 1945: After escort this 4TH pilot found an He-177 to fill his sight at the proper grasstop strafing altitude. The film came back so he didn't buy a POW by hitting the trees as some did. (*John Romack*)

January, 1945: The safe return and break as Capt. William O'Donnell leads his 335th Flight into the left-hand pattern over the runway junction. (*William O'Donnell*)

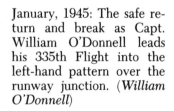

January, 1945: Lt. Fred Farrington's QP-N shows the style of "Name" art currently popular in 334th. (*John Romack*)

January, 1945: Winter clamps down again as Capt. Dave Howe's QP-G 44-13884 has just landed and sits chocked on the hard ground across the taxi track. (*William Rushing*)

February, 1945: Armorers Sgts. (*L-R*) Thomas Lockner, Albert Wendt, and Waldo Johnson make last-minute repairs to Lt. J. McFadden's QP-Q 44-14202. Gun-heater blocks hang over the raised bay door. (*Leroy Nitschke*)

February, 1945: Crewchiefs ready their a/c for the show on the 334th line. Sgt. V. Andra in Maj. Norley's QP-O 44-72196 out front of squadron HQ. (*Edward Nelson*)

February, 1945: Leading the mission will be the new 4TH CO, Col. Everett Stewart. The new "Horseback Leader" is a Pacific vet and later 355FG CO, now at DB. (*Francis Bodner*)

February, 1945: Lt. Melvin Dickey's VF-R 44-13630 BETTY JANE II gets a bath to improve its speed and lose drag. Propwash on the line produced much grime on the kites. Three of Dickey's victories are recorded on canopy. (*Waldo Johnson*)

February, 1945: Lt. Melvin Dickey takes Harry Hagan's VF-Y 44-72053 up for an air test. A/C has newly painted flat black glare-panel and canopy frame seen on some 336th a/c at this period. (*John Romack*)

February, 1945: Ops are over for the day and Lt. C. Willruth's WD-Y 44-15028 DOTTY sits quiet. A/C was used as WD-O by Capt. L. Norley in Fall, 1944. (*John Romack*)

March, 1945: First two-seat P-51 of 4TH. The kite was converted by T/Sgt. Woody Jensen in Fall, 1944, for use by the Group "Clobber-College" OTU to transition new pilots in 4TH tactics. Red/White/Blue rudder denotes OTU status. (*James Gibson*)

March, 1945: Another stand-down day. QP-H SIZZLIN LIZ belongs to Maj. G. Montgomery, 334th Ops Officer. In line-up is Howe's *G*, J. Ayer's *K*, Norley's *O*. Radio mast in front of HQ allowed R/T combat chatter to be picked up sometimes. (*Edward Nelson*)

March 21, 1945: A new replacement a/c puffs its tires in a "wheel" landing as it arrives from the depot. 44-72265 will finish the war with 335th. Depot-fresh a/c are now devoid of theatre markings when issued. (*Shelly Stafford*)

March, 1945: Lt. D. Peterson's WD-H- 44-13977 COOKIE is second "H" of squadron. Another tension-filled show deep into the Reich rolls out weaving on the perimeter track. (*James Gibson*)

March, 1945: The pilot of WD-U 44-14438 LITTLE NAN intently watches the flagman (a pilot disciplined for an infraction) for the "go" permission. Radiator door is dropped for maximum cooling of glycol to prevent "popping it." (*William O'Donnell*)

March, 1945: The flagman gives Maj. Norley the green in "O," as his wingman, W. Dvorak in QP-I ZOMIN ZOMBIE follows. No. 3 element leader, C. Payne, in QP-J 44-72381, brakes till his turn. (*Edward Hedrick*)

March, 1945: Lt. M. W. Miller in VF-S- 44-14527 MARY leans into the acceleration as he rushes past with the tail lifting. (*Francis Grove*)

March, 1945: WD-B out for a practice hop "Balboa" (squadron formation flight) with other 335th birds. Nearest is No. 4 of other section in WD-3 JOE'S JUNK, a war-weary OTU B-model. (*Paul Lucas*)

March, 1945: Two 336th kites tuck in close. Lt. W. Hastings is in "E" and Lt. Clarence Bousefield in VF-M 44-15613 PEACHES. Name is faintly seen under exhaust manifold of "M." (*Clarence Bousfield*)

March, 1945: Lt. C. Bousfield in VF-M cruises over broken cloud on a test hop over Essex. Red nose appears light due to film type. (*Francis Grove*)

March 22, 1945: Third generation 4TH pilots led by LtCol. S. Woods surprised a Gruppe of FW 190s taking off near Berlin and clobbered them in true form. Woods got five himself. (*J. Romack*)

February 27, 1945: With the Reich shrinking, the fields are now loaded with a/c targets as this field west of Leipzig shows. Smoke of 4TH-claimed strafing rises as the Group departs for DB. (*Tom Bell*)

March, 1945: A fine aerial perspective of Debden from the South. 334th area loops around North end of runway. 335th area goes from West end of runway South thru the looped taxi track to trees meeting taxi track. From there 336th's double bays are on Southwest corner and the rest of 336th area loops around South end of runway up to control tower in front of the hangars. (*Richard W. Waters [D. Beeson logbook]*)

March 17, 1945: The moment waited for, the show is back. A section banks into the pattern as another one passes low over 334th area. Tanks still on denotes a recall or an uneventful trip. (*Glesner Weckbacher*)

Spring, 1945: Rare drama caught by camera. The pilot of VF-X 44-73061 BLOOD AND GUTS at the moment of contact in a gear-up bellylanding. Gear fairing doors droop from no hydraulic pressure. In a second the prop blades will shower sparks (*Edward Hedrick*)

March, 1945: Capt. E. Wozniak taxies his QP-T 44-63583 HELEN. Exhaust oxide and oil streak of the crankcase overflow denote a long and acrobatic show. (*Waldo Johnson*)

March, 1945: All hands pitch in to replace radios in Maj. Norley's QP-O 44-72196 for the second show of the day. New tanks are hung and the a/c is topped off at 480-gals of 150 octane. (*Edward Hedrick*)

March 19, 1945: 335's Lt. George Green (left) shows how he shared his oxygen mask with his CO Maj. Pierce McKennon when they flew home from a German field where Green landed and picked up McKennon. (*J. Cowman*)

Spring, 1945: VF-4 is a war-weary up-dated P-51B/C which 336th is using to train their "Clobber-College" OTU boys fresh from the U.S. Note tail-tow bar attached to lift-point by "4." (*Edwin Rowe*)

Spring, 1945: Down from the show and ready for a re-arm is WD-U 44-14438 LITTLE NAN (left nose). Chief is Geo. Lee in C Flight out on West squadron perimeter. (*Phillip Lindsey*)

Spring, 1945: Another nose-art in current 334th theme of a Don Allen cutie and a big red and black name is MY ACHIN' BACK. A/C serial is 731?5. Code and pilot unknown. (*Mrs. E. B. Nickerson*)

Spring, 1945: Just back from the show is Lt. Kenneth Helfrecht, who explains his emblem GEORGIE to his CC S/Sgt. Robert Lewis. Their a/c is QP-R 44-14110. (*R. Lewis*)

March, 1945: A clear day and West wind finds VF-H 44-14277 JERSEY BOUNCE III (popular song title) on the South perimeter. CC S/Sgt. Frank Mason has the kite tanked and set for the morning show. (*Henry Sedmack*)

Spring, 1945: This P-51B bears the red and white nose bands of the Flight Section of the 65FW based on the field's NW edge. 43-6542 is coded in all likelihood J-A, after the 65FW CG Jesse Auton's initials. (*J. Cowman*)

Spring, 1945: Some of the 336th pilots put in time with the T-6 when not on ops. Lt. C. Shilke in cockpit is probably off for a forward base to pick up a forced-down pilot or for spare parts from the depot or giving hops to ground crew. (*Francis Grove*)

Spring, 1945: Lt. Paul Lucas' WD-F 44-11200 on the West line waits for the next show in 335th red canopy and 335th red-bordered white rudder colors. (*Paul Lucas*)

Spring, 1945: Ops are done as WD-W 44-72241 rests across the taxi track from the bomb dump in the twilight. Shortly the chief will tie on the canopy tarp, plug the header pipes, and ride his cycle back to the living site in the distance. (*Woody Jensen*)

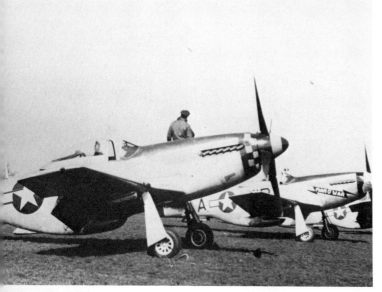

March 23, 1945: 15 CO's of the 8AF fighter groups come to DB for the planning of the air cover of the Rhine River crossings. LtCol. Elwyn Righetti's CL-P 44-72296 (55FG) in foreground. LtCol. Claiborne Kinnard's WR-A 44-15625 MAN-O-WAR (355FG) 2nd in line. (*Glesner Weckbacher*)

March 23, 1945: 20FG CO Col. Robert Montgomery, poses in his LC-D 44-72519 GUMPY after the Rhine Crossing meeting. Then he took off for Kingscliffe, Northampshire, home of the black-striped Mustangs. (*John Romack*)

March, 1945: The newly opened "Pioneer Club" for non-com's at DB. Club Sec/Treas. Bob Lewis downs a "Mild & Bitter" to inaugurate it. Decorative art is by the ever-popular Don Allen. (*Edward Hedrick*)

April, 1945: Takeoff for the morning show. Possibly on 4/9/45 when Lt. Robert Bucholz was lost as a KIA in this a/c WD-T 44-14389 at Munich. (*Edward Hedrick*)

April 16, 1945: Maj. McKennon ready to lead his troops on the last big show of WW2 for the 4TH. He scored three victories, had a 20mm shell explode on his canopy, limped to a forward base behind allied lines, and had fragments removed from his temple and forehead. Then he flew home to DB. (*James McMahon*)

April 16, 1945: Capt. W. O'Donnell ready to go on the big "Jackpot" show to Prague. Inked circles mark flak hits on his WD-B 44-14557 THE DUCHESS upon return. (*William O'Donnell*)

Spring, 1945: Wild black skip marks spell out the groundloop performed by this 335th a/c on the west runway. A/C slumps on its damaged gear as the mobile repair unit heavy wrecker arrives. (*T. Bell*)

April, 1945: 335th squadron dispersal area on a non-ops day. View N/W from AA emplacement. Windsock flies over "Narvik" underground squadron HQ. Woods across West runway behind HQ mark the 65FW Flight Dispersal. P-51B in foregrd. is 335th OTU WD-3. (*Francis Grove*)

Spring, 1945: The hardstands in front of 336th HQ. VF-R is Lt. Dickey's BETTY JANE II. VF-ZZ and VF-SS (right of Capt. Grove's VF-T) are a/c in squadron with 2nd issue of that letter. Off right is VF-Y, and two double bays are out-of-sight to right. (*Francis Grove*)

Spring, 1945: 336th line South around perimeter from the tower. VF-B 44-64153 is Maj. Glover's a/c, VF-F 44-73021 CLARINE, VF-I 44-15647 JOHNETTA IV, VF-G 44-64142 TIGER BABY. Glover's a/c has a powder blue glare-panel and canopy frame. (*Francis Grove*)

Spring, 1945: 336th dispersals opposite 335th hangar hold VF-F 44-73021 CLARINE, VF-I 44-15647 JOHNETTA IV, VF-G 44-64142 TIGER BABY. Long building in background is the EAGLE'S NEST base theatre/motor pool garage. *Francis Grove*)

Spring, 1945: Visitor by the tower is a P-47M LM-P of the 56FG which the 4TH has just outscored to become the top WW2 AAF fighter unit. 44-70392 is the Group's red nosed UC-64 Norseman. P-51B's unit is unknown. (*F. Grove*)

Spring, 1945: A fine side-view of Group "Hack" AT-6 42-84602. A/C has red Group nose color, red wheel covers, wingtips, tail tips, and fin tip. Army engineers emplaced wood hardstands where the PSP ones were ruined. (*Francis Grove*)

Spring, 1945: Capt. Francis Grove's chief warms up and tests the engine of their VF-T 44-72767 out front of 336th HQ. D-Day bands and ETO theatre bands had been deleted from a/c by early 45. (*Francis Grove*)

Spring, 1945: This sunny afternoon finds the chiefs in 336th pulling cowling for inspections. VF-Y 44-72053 is Lt. H. Hagan's a/c. Earth wall of bay is also an air-raid shelter. (*Edwin Rowe*)

Spring, 1945: Lt. James McMahon on his VF-A 44-14276 MARCY, which had seen much action as Capt. Frank Young's MARTHA JANE. Indicators on top of wing are glide/dive-bomb sighting marks. (*James McMahon*)

April, 1945: The nose art carried by 335th CO Maj. Pierce McKennon on his WD-A RIDGE-RUNNER III by the end of the war in Europe. Twin RAF Spitfire mirrors adorn the canopy. (*Francis Grove*)

Spring, 1945: The last 335th pilot to die was Capt. Richard L. Tannehill (center), who was killed in a training accident on 5/17/45. He passed out from oxygen loss and spun-in in North Wales. (*Victor Tannehill*)

May, 1945: VE-Day saw large ID letters given to 8AF to prevent low flying a/c (on their underwings). WD-P 44-72416 MAN-I-ACK has such letters. Lack of operations is shown by lounging crews, empty ammo boxes, and unhung wing tanks. (*Ernest Cool*)

May, 1945: The Champagne express. The 334th acquired a Martin Marauder B-26 after VE-Day. Its main use was to fly leave/furlough men to Paris and to haul back wines and delicacies unobtainable in England. (*Francis Grove*)

May 23, 1945: Spitfire IXs of No. 313 Squadron (Czech) RAF flew in from Manston to simulate Japanese fighters for the 4TH. The Group was in training to go to the Pacific Theatre. (*Francis Grove*)

May, 1945: Yet another visitor was this Beaufighter IIF. (*Francis Grove*)

Spring, 1945: This Vultee Vengeance A-35B parked near the 65th Fighter Wing HQ revetment on the N/W side of the field was used for hack and target-tow duties. FD196 WW41-31385 MISS BEVERLY retains RAF roundels. (*Francis Grove*)

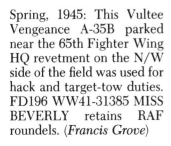

Spring, 1945: A 65th Fighter Wing HQ P-47D-22RE. War-weary 42-26059 carries code of A-J, presumably for *Jesse Auton* (B/Gen. OIC 65FW). In the distance is the West runway and 335th dispersal. (*Francis Grove*)

Spring, 1945: AH-OY is a Piper L-4 Grasshopper used by the 65FW HQ. It has the red/white nose bands of 65th a/c. The little tiger-mouth a/c is minus a propeller at this instant. (*Francis Grove*)

Spring, 1945: Another red/white cowled 65FW a/c is this Cessna UC-78 Bobcat 42-58515. The hack-communications a/c is tied down on the infield between the runway and the N/W perimeter. (*Francis Grove*)

July 10, 1945: The 4TH's famous Flying Eagles dance band departs via 94BG B-17 for a 30-day tour of bases, hospitals, rotation centers, etc. A tour on the continent was cancelled by VJ-Day. (*Frank Nowak*)

July, 1945: A tour of Debden starts at the South Main gate from Elder Street. Dodge staff car pulls up to Base HQ inside the gate. (*Francis Grove*)

July, 1945: Debden tour: Jeeps parked in front of Station HQ on the left past the South gate. An underground command post was built behind this one. (*Francis Grove*)

July, 1945: DB panorama from the base water tower. View N/W. Counter-clockwise from lower right: coal bunkers, 334th hangar, control tower, briefing rooms left of hangar, supply warehouses left center. (*Leroy Nitschke*)

Summer, 1942–45: As the time for return to the U.S. nears, 4th men paid last visits to their old haunts. One was the Rose & Crown Hotel in Saffron Walden, four miles north of DB, where many a visiting sweetheart and wife stayed. (*Henry Sedmack*)

Date unknown: An after-show let-up to relieve the tensions, in Col. Blakeslee's room. *L-R* front: P. McKennon, H. Hively. *L-R* rear: C. Ingold, L. Norley, F. Glover, D. Blakeslee, and L. Benjamin (336 IO).

Mar. 9–Apr. 9, 1944: The club bar buzzes after a tough show in the new Mustangs. Smiles of 23 pilots in photo denote good scoring. (*N. Lippman*)

November 21, 1942: Lt. Richard "Dixie" Alexander, 336FS., models the flight gear worn on ops . . . DIXIE MKIV is probably his Spit VB BL-773 coded MD-?. (*U.S. Army photograph*)

September 14, 1942: These hangarcrewmen work on the powerplant of a Spitfire VB in the dark of night readying it for a show the next day. Note the vulnerable coolant piping (large pipe) and tank which, if hit, meant the loss of plane/pilot. (*U.S. Army photograph*)

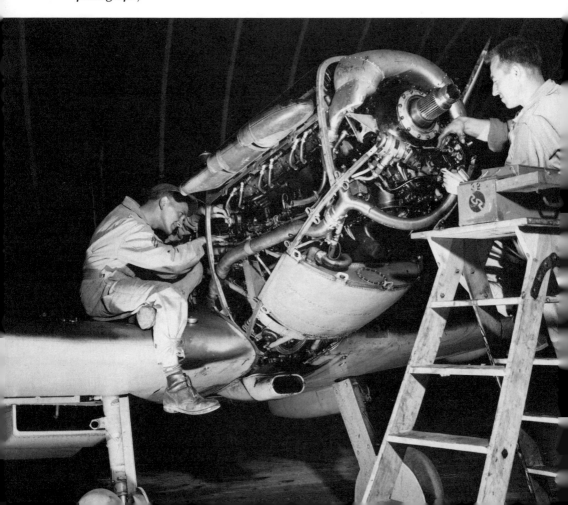

turning back as alternate when there were no aborts, had tagged on and followed us across. I've often wondered if the Germans had not jumped him for lagging behind. I never knew, for I never saw him again. There was some radio conversation about bogeys but I really can't remember or recall exactly what was said or who was talking 'cause Don and I were busy confirming our landmarks and positions. We stayed right with the bombers all the way and when we sighted Kiev they started letting down at a pretty good rate. We broke off from them about there, for they were going to Mylograd and Poltava, which was quite a bit north of our base at Piryatin.

When we hit about 17,000, maybe 15,000, we were met head on by a whole flock of P-39s with Russian insignias. They seemed to have no formation of any sort, but what we assumed to be a recognition signal of a series of sharp dips with one wing. Don and I responded and I think most everybody did, but there were short warnings from Blakeslee's cockpit as to "Don't shoot! They are friendly." "What the hell are they doing." "Dumb bastards—I almost hit him!"

I noticed a whole bunch of flares off to the right about one o'clock and pulled up beside Don and pointed! With that he threw every map he had up in the air. You couldn't see him for all that paper flying around in the cockpit and I'm sure he couldn't see either—but we were only one minute off our ETA after that whole trip and, by gosh, if that doesn't impress you . . . I *know* it impressed the Russians. I've kidded Don for years: "Hell, you could never make an ETA, you were one whole minute off to Russia!"

Our landing was something else. The runway was perforated metal strips and the grass had grown up through the perforations. The first guys were all right, but each successive 51 that landed squashed the grass and pretty soon it was slicker than a cat's ass. I certify I closed my eyes there once 'cause P-51s toward the end were sliding sideways, like they were landing on ice. Everybody had kept their drop tanks and that didn't make it any better; but we were lucky, only one accident and he busted a tail wheel. Later we wired a 2x4 on in place of the wheel and I've got to give that kid credit, he flew that thing all over Russia, Italy, and back to England with wired-on 2x4s for a tail wheel.

We were greeted by a bevy of Russkies. Before I could get the engine shut off there was a Russian GI cleaning the windshield. We landed with clean windshields and canopies, but when we left Russia we had the *cleanest* windshields in the world, for they never—and I mean never—quit cleaning the windshields, and that was their total maintenance. Later one day I found a Russian GI trying to clean my cockpit, I think; anyway, I didn't want him in there and I made the mistake of yelling and making frantic motions for him to get out and leave. That caused a hell of a commotion and one Russian officer actually drew his gun and led that poor guy off by the ear—I don't know whether they shot him or not—I know there was a story going around that . . . But you know fighter pilots! Not that they are likely to exaggerate or anything.

Anyway, when I got out of the airplane I was greeted with a bouquet of roses! Yes, roses, no less. Fortunately no one kissed me then—that came later—but I couldn't get away. I wanted to see Blakeslee, but try as I could, I couldn't make them understand and I was herded, pushed, and led with all my guys up a hill to a shack type building where we met the first American GI. He issued each of us a regulation sleeping bag, another roll of toilet paper, more soap, tooth paste, etc. We had all been briefed before about what to take and what not to take. For instance, nobody was allowed to take any weapon of any kind—not even a knife. That didn't go over with the guys. We didn't mind giving up the pistols but I don't think any one of us went without a knife. I had two—one in my boot and one in the airplane. We all had toilet paper, soap, tooth paste, cigarettes, booze, and, at HQ insistance, delousing powder. Our toilet paper was the most valuable item we had—every Russian wanted some and we bartered it a few sheets at a time for our entire stay. You know what they wanted it for? Even the officers? They rolled cigarettes in it!

I couldn't find Blakeslee anywhere. Finally there appeared an American Colonel—

not a flyboy. I think he was an engineer who had built the base. He informed me that Don had gone on to Moscow—this had not been planned—and that I was in charge. My first duties were to assign quarters. That was easy. There was a tent line of GI pyramid tents up the hill, so I designated the top tent as HQ with each of the four squadron commanders in it and told everybody else to choose up sides and take a tent. We had from four to six in a tent; everybody had a cot and a GI sleeping bag—no blankets—and a buddy to yak with.

By the time we got settled in our quarters, it was getting time to eat. Remember, the time difference was three to four hours and we had been in the airplanes enroute for over eight hours.

The mess hall was a communal one in a real large tent. GIs were everywhere. There would be two or three of us and six to eight GIs at every table. I was led to one in the middle of the tent and was greeted very friendly by all the GIs. Lot of questions by both sides and a real jolly atmosphere. Our table was served by a good-looking Russian broad, and I mean good looking. She had long hair, an officer's jacket—no insignia—good-looking boots up to her knees and a short skirt, shorter than I had ever seen at that time. It was a good four or five inches above her knees. Her name was Tanya. All the GIs kept needling me. "Ask her what's for dinner, Sir! Go on ask her!" I said, "You ask her!" They kept pestering. "Go on, Sir, ask her what's for dinner?" Finally as she came by, I got her attention and said, "What's for dinner, Tanya?" She stopped, put her hands on her hips and with a great big smile said in good American, "Same old thing! Fucking "C" rations!" I'm sure my jaw dropped, but she kept on with that great big innocent smile and went about her duties. Those ornery GIs!

After dinner I took five guys and checked the airplanes. Everything seemed OK. They were all buttoned up with a Russian guard on every one. The American colonel and a Russian officer—I don't remember his rank—went with me; the American could talk to him in Russian. I didn't want any Russians fooling with our airplanes, 'cause I was told our crewchiefs would be down from Poltava the following day. We had sent a selected few along with the bombers as waist gunners, but they had gone to a different base. The American colonel assured me, through the Russian, that no one would touch our airplanes. I believed him!

After our inspection tour we went back to the tent line and there with all the guys we held a bull session critique. By that time we had word that Hofer had landed damaged in Kiev—what damage we didn't know—but the story was they were going to transport him over to us. There had been some Focke Wulfs seen south of Poznan but although a few of our boys had disengaged from the escort, no one had made any contact or claims at that time. It had been a good show—we had accomplished half our mission, now all we had to do was get back.

It wasn't real cold that night, slightly chilly but not real cold. The GI sleeping bags were something else. They were formfitting—wide at the shoulders, narrow at the waist, wider at the hips, then narrowed down for your legs, with a big hump for your feet to stick up in. They zipped up on the inside and then had a flap that buttoned over the zipper. Really quite complicated. Most of us just unbuttoned and unzipped them and used them sort of as pads to sleep on. 'Course we did pull the tops over our shoulders, but not Lum Blanding. Lum was from Carolina and I guess Russia was a lot colder even in June than where he came from. Lum zipped all the zippers and buttoned all the buttons. He looked like a mummy laying there on the cot. The comments from all the guys in our tent were many; we laughed and kidded Lum well into the night. All night long we heard airplanes going over, but to us that didn't mean anything. We were used to them in England. I think I finally went to sleep—I think—but in the middle of the night nature called so I had to get up. I sat on the edge of the cot, pulled on my boots. Everybody else was asleep. There were a lot of airplanes going over. I walked out between the tents to relieve myself and was standing there in my underwear with my vitals in hand when all of a sudden there was a pop and the night lit up like the brightest day. I don't know how long I stood there looking up at that flare—it was fascinating, you could see the parachute it was hanging from. Then pop, pop, pop and there were three more. About that time guns started going and I could see tracers flying past the flares. Then whumph, whumph, whumph, WHUMPH, a stick of bombs fell not too far away. Remember, we were up on a hill, the airfield was below us and all that ack-ack was coming from the airfield. As the flares got lower so did the tracers till finally they were going through the tops of the tents. Someone yelled, "J.C.! They're strafing!" I ran back in the tent to get my hat. That was all I could think of. It was confusion! I was almost bowled over by two guys coming out, and inside Lum was hopping about like a rabbit. He was locked in his sleeping bag. I yelled at Lum, "let's get the hell out of here!" He didn't answer but just took off—or I should say hopped off—like a Jackrabbit, only twice as fast.

I stood in the doorway for a moment there and watched everybody go by. I'll never forget seeing one kid by the name of Sharp, from McArthur, Ohio, go by like a whirlwind. I certify his nose wasn't two inches off the ground and his feet behind him were going like a steamboat paddle wheel—only at about 3000 rpm. I stood there in amazement wondering how in the hell he could do that. The flak kept getting worse, the noise was shattering, but I could see everything 'cause it was as light as day. I could see Lum hopping like mad for a big hole not too far from our tent on the downslope of the hill, so I took off at full speed after Lum. Never did catch him. I saw him go headfirst into the hole and I went in behind him and on top of him. The guys were four deep in that hole but nobody moved until the shooting stopped. All I heard was, "Christ, they're strafing! Anybody hit? Smells like shit in here!" It did! And there was! One thing we found out about the Russians was that whenever they found a hole in the ground, they'd you-know-what in it. The Cold War started right there as far as we were concerned.

The next day we found out what had happened. Seems like the wily Hun had followed us into Russia and knew where we were. It was obvious we had to get out.

The Germans had actually passed us over and gone on to Poltava where they had destroyed 77 B-17s on the ground that night. I knew our turn was next. From all reports we had lost only one man, a lieutenant from one of the bomb groups at Poltava, but it was reported that over 2000 Russians had been killed trying to put out fires while the bombing was going on. The Americans hit whatever hole they could find—slit trenches, latrines, no matter what was in them—but the Russians were throwing sand on the fires and never quit while the bombing was going on.

There had been assigned to us a full colonel by the name of Ben Kelsey of the 8AF technical service. Ben had had no ops but he could fly and he was a great—and I mean great—help the next day. We had to get out! and Ben and I spent from first light on trying to find some place to go out of bomber range. The airfield had no heavy guns—just light 40mm and 20mm cannons, with free swinging search lights. The light ack-ack and searchlights had been placed in a circle around the airbase with no radar control on the lights or any predicted flak. When the Germans came over, they turned on the lights, which made a perfect circle around the field—a lighted ring, a perfect target like a bullseye for them to shoot at. We had to get out! We argued, we pleaded, we begged, we cussed, we stormed, we called Stalin names, and everybody in the Russian Army by every word Ben and I had ever heard of in West Virginia and Oklahoma. There just wasn't any other base that could handle 64 P-51s and the pilots that went with them. Finally they came up with three bases that were over 400 miles farther away and we figured that would get us out of bomb range. One was Zaporozhe on the Dnieper river, Odessa on the Black Sea, and Chingueue east of Karkov. As I remember, Odessa was the farthest away but it was also easiest to find because it was south and on the Black Sea. Zaporozhe shouldn't be hard to find—all you had to do was follow the Dnieper river south and east and it was on the east side of the river. We had no maps! Chingueue was another problem—it was over 1100 miles due east on the other side of Karkov, but according to what we were able to understand, it was the biggest and had more facilities. I made a decision—I sent Lum to Zaporozhe with 336 squadron (16), Ben to Odessa with 335 and a flight of four from the 352nd group, and I took 334 squadron and three flights, or 12, from the 352nd group to Chingueue.

I don't know if Ben or Lum got any maps, but you should have seen the one I got. I swear it was made on meat wrapping paper, brown and slick. There were no colors, no contours, just black lines. It later proved that the towns were on the wrong side of rivers and the rivers were on the wrong side of the tracks, but we made it—fighter pilots' navigation and luck. It was late in the afternoon of that second day before we could get everything arranged. I had everybody eat a second lunch and carry with him all the leftovers, 'cause I didn't know when we would eat again. We checked watches and called a rendezvous back at Piryatin for the following day at 1000 hours and took off.

I was lost all the way to Chingueue. The weather was fine, but there wasn't one landmark all the way that I could identify with that silly map. When the time ran out for the distance traveled, I circled, having no idea what the town of Chingueue looked like let alone what the airport looked like. We seemed to be in the right area; there was a railroad track and a river, but they didn't add up as to direction or anything else with the map. All of a sudden one of the guys yelled, "Hey Deac! They're shooting a lot of flares over there at 3 o'clock!" Sure enough they were. The airfield was a perfectly round grass field. Not a building on it. There wasn't a wind sock or a "T," let alone a runway. I picked a direction, called for the guys to tuck it in, pulled a hairy peel off and landed.

I taxied straight ahead to the end of the field and turned left to clear anybody still landing, swung around and parked. I kept the radio on and told everybody to park around the edge of the field in order, keeping at least 100 ft. between airplanes. I told them to secure their own aircraft and after they were secure to meet me at my airplane. By the time I had finished filling out the Form One and One A and completing all the other paper I had neglected since I'd been in Russia, a few of the guys had collected around the airplane. I unhooked everything and got out on the wing and there stood three Russians with their fingers in their ears. The Americans salute one way, the British another, the French another, but when the Russians salute, it looks like they're sticking their fingers in their ears. I saluted, they saluted, we repeated it three times. You can never get ahead of the Russkies. They always want the last word. Finally I said, "Shit!" and got down off the wing.

Then the fun began! There were the three Russkies jabbering like monkeys and I couldn't understand them and they couldn't understand me! All I wanted to know was where were we supposed to go! Were we to spend the night under the aircraft? Did they have any fuel, or did they have a battery ack! But I couldn't get anything across—nothing. In the meantime with all the arm yanking, expletives, head shaking, and disgust, all the guys had assembled. One thing for sure! We had them outnumbered. Finally one of the guys said, "Hey Deac, why don't you use your language card?" We had all been issued a phonetic language card that had Russian, Turkish, German, French, Arabic, and I don't know what all language printed in phonetic conversion. It was useless! I couldn't find a thing on there that made any sense in our situation. There was for example, "How do I cross this river? What is the next town? How do I buy a third class ticket? How much do I owe you?" The Russkies took the card, they handed it back in disgust after searching their side. I yelled at Malmsten "Say something you bastard, that's what we brought you along for!" Malmsten had married a Russian girl and professed to be fluent in Russian, but all he could say was "I love you, do you want to sleep with me?" He was useless. I looked at the card again and found "To Golodein"——phonetic for, "I'm hungry." It was a success! I was greeted with a bunch of Da Da's and lots of belly patting. Hell, we weren't hungry—we had just eaten two lunches just in case—but that made such a big hit, I looked on down and found "Ka-cha-ta-pit," which translated to, "I'm thirsty." That really made a hit. The Russkies beamed and, with a big arm wave including all the guys, said, "Snahaps?" Now me being from West Virginia, snahaps always meant beer to me, so I said, "Da da snahaps, give em all snahaps, it'll do them all good."

A Studebaker 6x6 pulled up about this time and it was indicated that we should all get in. Twenty-seven guys filled the back end of that truck, but when I started to get in, there was a bunch of Nyets and head shaking. I was not allowed to get in. Instead, up pulled a brown, rattly looking 1933 Ford V-8 with the slanty radiator and all. A '33 Ford V-8 isn't very big. I was put in the middle in the back seat. Two of the biggest Russkies crawled in beside me. The other got in the front with the driver. It was damned uncomfortable, crowded, and I hit bottom on every bump on that corduroyed road. I would have much rather ridden with the guys in that truck—but there was no way. The Russkies stood high on protocol and that V-8 was evidently considered the best.

Fortunately it wasn't too far to where we were going. We pulled up to this long narrow two-story building with a sort of landscaped yard in front. I found out later it was a hospital training unit. There were quite a few Russian GIs standing out front, both men and women. We were greeted with beaucoup smiles, but no flowers this time, and were ushered upstairs to a small room—large enough to hold us all, but not all that big. In the center was a shallow metal trough about four feet wide and maybe 15 feet long. Hanging over the center of the trough was a row of cans about no. 10 size with a plunger sticking out of the bottom of each can. I had never seen anything like it before and I guess none of the guys had, for we just stood there looking at it and wondering what to do. One of the Russian broads reached over and pushed up on one of the plungers and water came out of the cans into the trough. We still didn't know what to do. Whether to wash in it or pee in it! Malmsten said, "Hell, let's find out," so he peed in it! That wasn't the right thing to do! 'Cause it caused a hell of a commotion among the Russkies. The broads rushed out of there with all kinds of exclamations! So heck, we washed in it. On with the Cold War!

After we finished washing up, there was no soap and no towels. We kinda stood around drying off and then were led into a long room at the end of the building with one bed—but you've never seen such a bed. It held 28 fighter pilots. The bed was built all along one long wall. It started about 3 feet up on the wall and sloped down to about one foot, a good 7 feet wide with a footboard at the low end to keep you from sliding off and a pillow at the top end for each and every guy. It appeared to be strawticking covered with rough canvas. It wasn't hard, but it wasn't soft either. Actually it seemed a hell of a good idea and was rather comfortable. I had my spot all picked out with Hedrick alongside. I could see by now that I was going to need him, since the protocol was getting kind of heavy already. We didn't last long there, however, but were led into a small private room down the hall with two bunks in it. The bunks actually had clean white sheets on them along with pillows, but—would you believe it!—there were no springs or even a semblance of a mattress. Those sheets covered just plain boards. There was no way we could get back in the room with the rest of the guys. Those boards were reserved for us and that's where we stayed. Man, it was getting evident I needed an interpreter.

We were no more than settled when the congenial Russki Polcolonel who seemed to be head cheese arrived with the V-8 and the Studebaker truck to carry us off to dinner. The ride this time was a little better. I shared the back seat with Hedrick only, and the head cheese sat up with the driver—still corduroy roads, however. We were taken into Chingueue and although it was dusk the town seemed rather small. Funny thing, as much as I insisted later on, I was never allowed to visit Chingueue in the daytime. I was escorted through Karkov—and that's another story—but never through Chingueue. I'll never know what they were hiding. We pulled up to a castle and I mean a castle. I had seen Warwick and many others in England, but this was a *castle*. We were led in through a very small door—it certainly wasn't the main entrance—and back through a bunch of dark passageways to a large low ceilinged, many pillared hall. There was a full orchestra playing at one end, and in the center was a long table with a small table set like a T across one end. I was placed in the center of the T with the Russian Polcolonel on my left and Hedrick on my right and all the guys were ranged around the long table.

The table was lavish with flowers, salads, and one of the most curious things were foot-long sausages about as big around as your ring finger. We weren't hungry—remember we had eaten heavily before we left Piryatin—but the salads and sausages were real good so everybody fell to. You should have seen that Russian Polcolonel slice those sausages. He could take one of those foot-long skinny things and lay a row of perfectly thin sliced pieces across your plate faster than the eye could follow. The music was real good. That orchestra stayed with us the entire time we were in Chingueue and was assigned to all the pilots. They played for breakfast, lunch, and dinner, in the middle of the afternoon, night, or whenever the guys were assembled. But me? Hell, the next day I was assigned my own combo, that followed me everywhere. If I went in my office (which I was later assigned) they followed. If I sat down, they played. If I stood up, they played. If somebody came in they played very softly; if I went out to the airplanes they followed. If the big orchestra was playing for the guys, they joined the orchestra. It consisted of two square-cut guitars and a full-size push button accordion. The music was real good—no "Volga Boatman" stuff, but Russian popular music that was current at that time. Later through the general's interpreter they asked if I had any requests. The only Russian song I could think of was *Orche Chonia*—"Dark Eyes." They didn't know it! And that caused a hell of a commotion. I was sorry I had asked!

We were really enjoying the dinner and the music when all of a sudden there appeared the biggest Russian I have ever seen. He had a huge tray a good four feet in diameter, held shoulder high in one hand, steadied by the other, loaded with what looked to be large water carafes. He sat one down at our table and proceeded to set another down at about every other guy completely around the table. This was all done with great flourish and, as I remember, the orchestra even stopped playing during what was evidently quite a ceremony. Somebody mentioned the word "Snahaps"—I think it was the Russian Polcolnic (Colonel)—but anyway, after the first part of the ceremony was over, he stood up, filled my glass (a regular GI water tumbler), then Hedrick's, then his own. He raised his glass in salute and said, "Roosevelt!" I was kinda suspicious—I had never seen any beer that looked like that! I knew it wasn't water, 'cause it was slightly milky, but I thought, maybe its "Choc beer"? Out in Oklahoma, where I went to college, the Choctau Indians made a concoction out of potatos called "Choc beer." I sniffed and kinda tasted it. It didn't smell and it didn't seem to have any taste. The Polcolnic evidently noticed my concern for he giggled and with that downed the whole glass, turned it upside down, and banged it on the table. There just wasn't anybody going to get ahead of any of us—Blakeslee taught us that—and besides all the guys were watching, so I said, "Stalin!"

Drank that whole cotton picking glass! The whole trouble was, it hit! Before I was able to turn it upside down on the table, I had to sit down! From a sitting position I said to the guys, "Fellas! That ain't beer! And I'll have the ears of any one of you that gets drunk! Eat all your potatos, and for Chrissake take it easy!" You know, believe it or not, that Polcolnic went around that table and with about every third guy drank another whole glass. Man, that was Vodka! And genuine Russian Vodka!

The sausages and salads were mere aperitifs but most of us were so stuffed by the time the real dinner came we couldn't eat. I could see the guys were getting a little tipsy— fact is, I could feel it myself and was about to give another dissertation on the evils of alcohol when a Russian officer appeared out of nowhere and said something to the Polcolnic which caused him to come to a brace. The only thing I could make of it was the word general, and that evidently he wanted to see me. I gave my dissertation and warned them all again that it would be difficult to fly without their ears, assured everybody I would be back, and followed the strange officer out of the hall. Hedrick trailed along behind, for it had been made clear that he was to come too. We proceeded down some more dark passageways, finally came to a small door somewhere along the way— we seemed to be in the basement or the dungeon for that matter—but when the door opened—Surprise!

There was the whole General Staff resplendent in full uniform—medals, and everything! What a dirty trick! Hedrick and I looked like bums! GI shirts and pants, old dirty A2 jackets. I had on an old parachute scarf that I had gone down in the Channel with. Hedrick didn't look much better, and these guys looked like movie stars. We were seated at a kidney shaped table, Hedrick on my right opposite the general who was on the inside of the kidney—and there we sat. The general said something! I didn't know what he said! It took a good 10 minutes for his staff to get across to Hedrick and me that all he said was welcome—more or less. So I said, "Russia reminds me very much of Oklahoma except the dirt is blacker!" That took 30 minutes to explain but finally, with a handdrawn map of the U.S. and Oklahoma spotted in the middle, I think we got that across. This went on and on, in the meantime more food, more toasts, more Vodka and Stodka. Stodka is red Vodka—tastes the same, but is prettier. Hedrick and I drank the Stodka—much to the Russians' disgust—but at least it looked different. Hedrick was getting tipsy—he would lean over to me and say, "Look at those silly SOBs!" I'd say, "For Chrissake shut up! Somebody here might understand English!" A sad looking skinny American GI was brought in to translate. He was no help, more of a hindrance, rather. About the only thing we made out from him was that he was American. This went on and on. We couldn't eat. We were already stuffed. Finally we got down to coffee and cigarettes. The general pulled out a package of the first kingsize filters I had ever seen. I pulled out a package of Camels. I offered him a Camel, he took it. He offered me one of his, I took it. I gave him my package of Camels; he gave me his package. I noticed he used a holder, so I gave him mine (his wouldn't fit American cigarettes); he gave me his. I took out a $5.00 bill (it was the smallest I had), signed it, and gave it to him. He took out a 500 Ruble note, signed it, gave it to me. This went on and on—you can't get ahead of these Russkies. Finally I couldn't think of anything else to give him, so I reached down, pulled off my Cowboy belt with a silver buckle, and gave it to him. Man, I don't know what that means in Russian, but it means something! The general, the whole Russian staff, hit their feet. The general then very ceremoniously took off his belt, rolled it up, kissed it, and handed it to me. I took it, kissed it, and put it on. Hell, it went around me one and a half times. He took my belt, kissed it, and, believe it or not, put it on. How, to this day I'll never know, but he did, and then sat down.

Needless to say, the party didn't last very long after that. Hell, the general couldn't breathe! Both Hedrick and I were feeling no pain by that time. Thank goodness for all the food we had been forced to consume, 'cause for the amount of Vodka and Stodka we had toasted, even a fighter pilot would have been swamped. Hedrick has always claimed that on leaving I went around kissing the whole general staff full on the mouth. I don't believe him. I must say, however, our private boards with sheets on them felt like feather beds that night.

The next day back to Piryatin. We refueled and checked all arms. Most of the day was spent in cussing and discussing with Lum Blanding, Ben Kelsey, and the American Colonel there about what to do, what not to do, how to get some maintenance, how to get some communications. Still no Blakeslee, therefore still no definite command. In the middle of one of the cussings, two Me109s made a pass over the south end of the field as big as life. I formed a readiness flight immediately. Ben Kelsey was the knowing guy. How in the hell he did it I don't know, but he rigged a mike and earphones through one of our 51s to the tower. We had about three Russians on telephones, supposedly in contact with field telephones somewhere. We had the American Colonel, a half-assed Russian interpreter, and one of those crazy maps. We put Lum in command of the readiness flights and kept four airplanes at the end of the runway with pilots strapped in, ready to go at the pop of a flare. This caused quite some conjecture among some of the Russians, but mainly with the Polcolnic who seemed to be in charge.

Overnight the Russians had moved in antiaircraft, and they kept it coming in all that day. It came in hauled by horses drawing wagons and even sleds. There were tractors hauling guns, and 1918 model Ford vans, some of them hauling sleds. It appeared to us that they were only reenforcing the circle of lights that we had noticed the previous night. All in all, we weren't happy. We had no communications, no radar, we were fast running out of maintenance and the air seemed to be loaded with Huns.

I spent all of the day in the tower. That was the most central spot. I had a pretty good view of the field and if anybody wanted me, they knew where I was. We had several flurries with reported aircraft and that was about all they turned out to be, flurries. The Russkies on the telephones would all of a sudden start flurrying about and jabbering—hell, I couldn't even understand the so-called translator, but with a lot of arm waving and pointing at different spots on that so-called map, I gathered there were E/A in the area. A flare out the window would put four P-51s in the air like—Now! Only once did I figure we got pretty close to getting one and that was one time when the points to the spots on the map made a damn good line and I had four guys all ready in the air. I had good communications with the readiness flights, thanks to Ben Kelsey, and I thought I had them, at least I had the guys at the spot all the Russkies were pointing to. Trouble was, I didn't know their altitude, didn't know how current the info was, didn't know what they were, didn't know how many, and, besides, all I had were my fingers to count on and a good instinct. We tried. I do believe if we'd had a good interpreter we could have made it. I kept yelling for one—we had to do something!

Late that afternoon (it didn't get dark till about 11 o'clock in the evening at those latitudes), Ben Kelsey, the American Colonel, and the Polcolnic in command appeared in the tower and made us stop. I mean we had to cease and desist. There seemed to be no rhyme or reason, but the Russian was adamant. We had to quit. I blew my stack. I wasn't going to stay there overnight and Chingueue wasn't the place to be without any communications with the rest of the guys, and if they wouldn't let me put up my own defense flights, I wasn't coming back to that miserable Hun-infested base.

Finally after a lot of Russian telephone calls, a lot of talk between the Polcolnic and the American Colonel, and a lot of talking between me, Lum, and Ben Kelsey, we got it figured. The American colonel assured me that he had been in touch with the mission in Moscow and that we each would be furnished, on the following day, a radio at our separate bases and that we would be able to communicate. If we could not defend ourselves, we didn't want to come back to Piryatin. We decided to go back to Chingueue, Zaporozhye, and Odessa, and wait one day for a radio. If it didn't show, we would meet back at Piryatin the day following and set course for Italy. I truly didn't believe we would ever get a radio even with all the assurances of Ben and the American Colonel. Still no Blakeslee; still no Hofer. We made a quick exodus, for I was sure I'd never find Chingueue in the dark.

Landing back at Chingueue was fairly routine except for one incident. I guess that area around Karkov had been the scene of many tank battles and many bombings. Anyway we found out too late that the airbase was pockmarked with shell and bomb craters. All the Russkies did was fill them in. No markers around the edges, no packing of the holes, no flags, no anything. One poor guy, I can't recall his name, trying to disperse his Mustang like I had ordered, taxied right into one—no fault of his—and sank slowly into the hole. Fortunately he felt himself going and had the good sense to kill the engine before the propeller hit. When I got there it was the saddest sight you ever saw! There was what looked like a beautiful Mustang sitting on the ground with only the wings supporting it. At first it looked like it had made a perfect belly landing, but you could see the wheel tracks going in. I took one look and said to myself, "Hell! That means jacks, shims, a crane . . . and," I wondered, "could we get two guys out in one airplane," 'cause at that time I just couldn't fathom how we would ever raise 14,000 lbs. without equipment. What a day! It had started out with a hangover and it sure looked like it was going to end with one.

The next morning started real decently. We had had a good dinner the night before—no schnapps—and had come back to the barracks. The orchestra had been set up out in front and played till there were no more guys to listen. The Russians put on a real show for us with all the dances they are famous for; some of the guys tried them too. I had been introduced to three young handsome Russian officers, one of whom spoke a fair amount of English. Real soon we were getting along real well—all four of us! With the little bit of French we all knew, the little bit of English they knew, and the little bit of Russian I was learning, we had no trouble finding words for just about everything. I was really impressed with those three. I got my dues back. I introduced them to the bottle of bourbon I had brought along and got a real kick at watching them try to drink that. You never saw so much snorting, coughing, or eye watering in your life. That bottle would have lasted a month in that crowd. I explained my problem with the buried airplane. We even went out to see it that night, and before I went to sleep on my board, I felt I was going to get some help the next day. I have said many times since that of all the officer corps I met during the war, the Russian corps was one of the most impressive. Those three guys sure helped in forming that impression. They all spoke German, most of them French, and some spoke English. Those three were big, good looking—according to our criteria handsome, intelligent young men—but that was the last I ever saw of them. They never appeared again.

We had all been awakened that morning, led into a small room upstairs and given a shave and a haircut. We thought that was something special, but found it was standard and routine with that army. Everybody had to furnish their own soap—mine was Palmolive—then the barber would shave a series of tissue thin slices into an empty sardine can, lather it up with a brush like I never saw Palmolive lather before, and proceed with the task. That made two items that were good bargaining bits—soap and toilet paper!

Breakfast caused a stir. There was cereal with milk—sort of an all-bran type cereal. The milk was served in the same type GI water tumblers that the schnapps had been served in that memorable evening, but the main course was the *pièce de résistance* and everybody resisted. It looked like a raw Blue Gill with one eye looking square up at you. I couldn't go it, nor could any of the others. I looked around the room, which consisted of blank stares. Nobody wanted to embarrass the Russians—question was what to do? I saw Malmsten slip his fish into his A2 jacket, so, when I thought no one was looking, in went mine. I bet those Russians thought we swallowed them whole, for all of a sudden every plate was clean—not a bone on one. All in all, we fed good throughout the stay—different for sure. There were many guesses as to what some things were, from mule to sow belly—but there was plenty of it. I particularly liked the bread!

After we came back from breakfast in the 6x6 and the 33 Ford V8 (we were always transported to meals—never again to the castle—but to somewhere else), I was shown into and given an office. There were two desks, one in the center which was for me, and one back in the corner which a Russian GI occupied. What he was there for or what he did I never found out. I sat down, and in came my two square-cut guitars and push button accordion, and started to play. So began the day!

Before you could say "Jack Robinson" there was some sort of fuss outside my door and in came a slightly built, middle-aged Russian captain. Most of the Russians I had met before were, if not huge, extremely large men. The women too were well endowed. This captain, however, was middle sized, very excitable, a nervous type, but he wore the proper medals—one of which I found out later to be "The Order of Lenin." There was still no interpreter but by this time I was becoming more adept at figuring what all the gestures meant, and it was soon obvious that he wanted to get my airplane out of the bomb crater. Outside was the 6x6, this time loaded with Russian GIs. I took my 33 V8—the captain had his own transport—and out to the airfield we went. One thing I noticed about the Russkies—they used the direct approach. No sooner had we arrived than those GIs had out shovels and picks, and the dirt was really flying. They were going to dig it out! The captain was a real foreman, running everywhere, showing people where to dig, encouraging them on, shouting, patting people on the back, cussing—he had at least 40 diggers going full tilt. In no time they had a hole completely around that airplane. The captain surveyed the hole, walked all around to make a few adjustments, and then at a single command they all piled into that hole and grabbed hold of that airplane wherever they could. They were going to lift it out! I stopped that! Heck, there are only a few lift points on any airplane. You just can't lift a Mustang at many other places. We had a conference! I was finally able to make him understand and showed him where he could lift. That didn't seem to deter him a bit. Back to work they went. They dug a bigger hole and a deeper one. To this day, I can't believe it—but I saw it. Anyway, down into the hole they went again. They had hands lifting on hands, lifting on hands that were lifting. I checked every lift point and the captain watched me all the way. Finally I threw up my hands and, with a shrug, nodded to the captain. He took that for an OK. With that they all started a little song, which kinda ended up with an "umph!" The song kept getting a little stronger and a little louder, but on about the fourth "umph!" they lifted up all 14,000 pounds, walked out of that hole and set it down. I certify! There was no damage. It only remained to wash the mud off the undercarriage, start it up, and go!

I believe it was that afternoon that the Commissar arrived. He arrived in his own Russian Packard, called a ZIV, I think, along with his own interpreter. It was real odd to hear a Russian talking American—no accent whatsoever, just plain American. He informed me he actually was Polish, had been born in America and moved back to Poland in 1938. It makes a great difference to have an interpreter, although to this day I can't trust them for I'm not sure they are saying exactly what I said to the other party. But it's a hell of a lot easier than drawing pictures in the dirt.

Aces of the 4th Fighter Group

Highest Rank, Name	Squadron	Enemy Aircraft Destroyed		
		Air	Ground	Total
Maj. John T. Godfrey	336th	18	12.60	30.60
Lt. Ralph K. Hofer	334th	16.50	14	30.50
Maj. James A. Goodson	336th	15	15	30 (1)
Maj. Don S. Gentile	336th	21.80	6	27.80
Lt. Col. Claiborne H. Kinnard	Hqts.	8	17	25 (2)
Maj. Duane W. Beeson	334th	19.33	4.75	24.08
Maj. Frederick W. Glover	336th	10.30	12.50	22.80
Maj. Pierce W. McKennon	335th	12	9.68	21.68
Col. Donald J. M. Blakeslee	Hqts.	15.50	2	17.50(3)
Maj. Gerald E. Montgomery	334th	3	14.50	17.50
Maj. George Carpenter	335th	13.33	4	17.33
Maj. Louis H. Norley	334th	11.33	5	16.33
Lt. Col. James A. Clark	Hqts.	11.50	4.50	16
Capt. Charles F. Anderson	335th	10.50	5.50	16
Capt. Nicholas Megura	334th	11.84	3.75	15.59
Capt. Willard W. Millikan	336th	13	2	15
Capt. Albert L. Schlegel	335th	10	5	15
Maj. Howard D. Hively	334th	12	2.50	14.50
Maj. Carroll W. McColpin	336th	12		12 (4)
Capt. Joseph L. Lang	334th	7.84	4	11.84
Lt. Hipolitus T. Biel	334th	5.33	6	11.33
Capt. Frank C. Jones	335th	5	5.50	10.50
Capt. Donald M. Malmsten	334th	3.50	7	10.50
Capt. Ted E. Lines	335th	10		10
Lt. Steve N. Pisanos	334th	10		10
Capt. Kendall E. Carlson	336th	6	4	10
Lt. Paul S. Riley	335th	6.50	3	9.50
Col. Everett W. Stewart	Hqts.	7.83	1.50	9.33(5)
Lt. Col. Sidney S. Woods	Hqts.	8	1	9 (6)
Lt. Van E. Chandler	336th	5	4	9
Lt. Col. Jack G. Oberhansly	Hqts.	5	4	9 (7)
Capt. Shelton W. Monroe	Hqts.	4.33	4.50	8.83
Maj. James R. Happel	335th	4	4.68	8.68
Capt. Victor J. France	334th	4.33	4.33	8.66
Capt. Bernard L. McGrattan	335th	8.50		8.50
Capt. David W. Howe	334th	6	2.50	8.50
Lt. Joe H. Joiner	336th	4.50	4	8.50
Maj. William J. Daley	335th	8		8 (8)
Lt. William E. Whalen	334th	6	2	8

Highest Rank, Name	Squadron	Enemy Aircraft Destroyed		
		Air	Ground	Total
Capt. Carl R. Alfred	336th	3	5	8
Lt. James W. Ayers	334th	1	7	8
Lt. Grover C. Siems, Jr.	334th	4.33	3.50	7.83
Lt. Vermont Garrison	336th	7.33	.25	7.58
Capt. William B. Smith	334th	2.50	4.75	7.25
Maj. Gregory A. Daymond	334th	7		7 (9)
Col. Chesley G. Peterson	Hqts.	7		7 (10)
Capt. Donald R. Emerson	336th	4	3	7
Lt. Brack Diamond, Jr.	335th	1	6	7
Lt. William O. Antonides	334th		7	7
Capt. Joseph H. Bennett	336th	6.50		6.50(11)
Capt. Raymond C. Care	334th	6	.50	6.50
Lt. Col. Roy W. Evans	335th	6		6
Maj. Henry L. Mills	334th	6		6
Maj. Michael G. H. McPharlin	334th	5	1	6 (12)
Maj. Winslow M. Sobanski	334th	5	1	6
Lt. Robert F. Nelson	336th	1	5	6
Lt. Frank E. Speer	334th	1	5	6
Lt. Arthur R. Bowers	334th		6	6
Lt. Loton D. Jennings	335th		6	6
Lt. Douglas P. Pederson	336th		6	6
F/O Charles E. Poage, Jr.	335th		6	6
Lt. Col. Oscar H. Coen	334th	5.50		5.50(13)
Capt. Archie W. Chatterley	334th	4.50	1	5.50
Capt. Carl G. Payne	334th	2	3.50	5.50
Capt. Thomas R. Bell	334th		5.50	5.50
Lt. Clemens A. Fiedler	335th	4.33	1	5.33
Maj. Gerald C. Brown	334th	5		5 (14)
Lt. Col. Selden R. Edner	Hqts.	5		5 (15)
Lt. Alex Rafalovich	334th	4	1	5
Capt. Kenneth B. Smith	335th	3	2	5
Capt. Vasseure H. Wynn	334th	3	2	5 (16)
Capt. Harry N. Hagan	336th	2	3	5
Capt. Robert D. Hobert	336th	2	3	5
Capt. William J. O'Donnell	336th	2	3	5
Lt. George W. Ceglarski	335th	1	4	5 (17)
F/O Donald P. Baugh	336th		5	5
Lt. Gordon A. Denson	334th		5	5
Capt. Nelson M. Dickey	336th		5	5
Lt. Kenneth G. Helfrecht	334th		5	5
Lt. Gilbert L. Kesler	336th		5	5
Lt. Jack D. McFaddan	334th		5	5

(1) 2 victories with 15th AF.
(2) Includes score with 355th FG.
(3) 3 victories with the RAF.
(4) Victories scored with RAF and 9th AF, none with the 4th FG.
(5) Includes score with 355th FG.
(6) Includes score with the Pacific 5th AF and 479th FG.
(7) Includes score with 78th FG.

(8) Victories scored with RAF and 9th AF, none with the 4th FG.
(9) Victories scored with the RAF, none with the 4th FG.
(10) 6 victories with the RAF.
(11) Includes score with 56th FG.
(12) Includes score with the RAF and 339th FG.

(13) 1.50 victories with the RAF.
(14) Victories scored with 55th FG.
(15) Victories scored with the RAF, none
    with the 4th FG.

(16) 2.50 victories with the RAF.
(17) Includes score with 355th FG.

4TH FIGHTER GROUP VICTORIES BY SQUADRON

Squadron	Air	Ground	Total
334th Fighter Squadron	210.17	185.25	395.42
335th Fighter Squadron	165.17	97.33	262.50
336th Fighter Squadron	174.66	183.42	358.08

NOTE: At the end of the war in Europe, the 4th Fighter Group's confirmed victories totalled 1,016 enemy aircraft destroyed in the air and on the ground. Subsequently, VIII Fighter Command reappraised all claims and then credited the 4th with a total of 1,-058½ enemy planes destroyed. The earlier figure, however, is considered truer and is more representative of the actual times when the Debden Eagles led all other groups in scoring.

4th Fighter Group Squadron Commanders

334th Fighter Squadron

Maj. Gregory A. Daymond; Sept. 29, 1942 to Mar. 3, 1943.
LtCol. Oscar H. Coen; Mar. 3, 1943 to Apr. 13, 1943.
Maj. Thomas J. Andrews; (Acting CO) Apr. 13, 1943 to May 19, 1943.
LtCol. John F. Malone; (Acting CO) May 19, 1943 to Aug. 4, 1943.
LtCol. Oscar H. Coen; Aug. 4, 1943 to Oct. 26, 1943.
LtCol. James A. Clark; Oct. 26, 1943 to Mar. 15, 1944.
Maj. Duane W. Beeson; Mar. 15, 1944 to Apr. 5, 1944.
Capt. Raymond C. Care; Apr. 6, 1944 to Apr. 15, 1944.
Maj. Winslow M. Sobanski; Apr. 15, 1944 to Jun. 6, 1944.
Maj. Howard D. Hively; Jun. 6, 1944 to Jul. 29, 1944.
Maj. Gerald Brown; (Acting CO) Jul. 29, 1944 to Nov. 1, 1944.
Maj. Howard D. Hively; Nov. 1, 1944 to Jan. 25, 1945.
Maj. Louis H. Norley; Jan. 25, 1945 to Sept. 21, 1945.
Capt. Carl F. Brown; Sept. 21, 1945 to Nov., 1945.

335th Fighter Squadron

Maj. William J. Daley; Sept. 29, 1942 to Nov. 22, 1942.
Col. Donald J. Blakeslee; Nov. 22, 1942 to May 19, 1943.
Maj. Gilbert O. Halsey; May 19, 1943 to Aug. 13, 1943.
Maj. Roy W. Evans; Aug. 13, 1943 to Feb. 5, 1944.
Maj. George Carpenter; Feb. 5, 1944 to Apr. 18, 1944.
Maj. James A. Happel; Apr. 18, 1944 to Jun. 21, 1944.
Maj. Leon M. Blanding; Jun. 21, 1944 to July 29, 1944.
Capt. Robert C. Church; July 29, 1944 to Aug. 18, 1944.
Maj. Pierce W. McKennon; Aug. 18, 1944 to Aug. 28, 1944.
Maj. Louis H. Norley; Aug. 30, 1944 to Sept. 22, 1944.
Maj. Pierce W. McKennon; Sept. 22, 1944 to Sept. 21, 1945.
? ; Sept. 21, 1945 to Nov., 1945.

336th Fighter Squadron

Maj. Carroll W. McColpin; Sept. 29, 1942 to Nov. 28, 1942.
Maj. Oscar H. Coen; Nov. 28, 1942 to Mar. 3, 1943.
Maj. John G. DuFour; Mar. 4, 1943 to Sept. 1, 1943.
Maj. Carl H. Miley; Sept. 1, 1943 to Oct. 10, 1943.
Maj. Leroy Gover; Oct. 10, 1943 to Nov. 29, 1943.
LtCol. Selden R. Edner; Nov. 29, 1943 to Jan. 1, 1944.
Maj. Gilbert O. Halsey; Jan. 1, 1944 to Mar. 8, 1944.
Maj. James A. Goodson; Mar. 8, 1944 to Apr. 13, 1944.
Maj. Willard W. Millikan; (Acting CO) Apr. 13, 1944 to May 10, 1944.

Maj. James A. Goodson; May 10, 1944 to Jun. 20, 1944.
Maj. Wilson V. Edwards; Jun. 21, 1944 to Jul. 5, 1944.
Col. Benjamin S. Kelsey; (Acting CO) Jun. 21, 1944 to Jul. 5, 1944.
Maj. John D. McFarlane; Jul. 5, 1944 to Aug. 24, 1944.
Maj. Frederick W. Glover; Aug. 24, 1944 to Jun. 2, 1945.
Maj. William J. O'Donnell; Jun. 2, 1945 to Sept. 22, 1945.
Capt. Francis M. Grove; Sept. 22, 1945 to Nov., 1945.

Note: These dates should be considered as approximate only. In actual practice the assignment and relief of command often preceded the dates given on unit general orders by some days. An officer may have finished his tour and been commander in name only while his successor in fact led the unit. Actual circumstances of command often differed from orders.

Group Personnel Structure on January 15, 1945

Pilot Officers

Lt. Colonels: 4
Majors: 6
Captains: 20
1st. Lieutenants: 54
2nd. Lieutenants: 30
Flight Officers: 3

Administrative Officers

Lt. Colonels: 1
Majors: 11
Captains: 35
1st. Lieutenants: 39
2nd. Lieutenants: 8
Chief Warrant Officers: 1
Warrant Officers (JG): 2
Attached Officers: 1

Enlisted Men	*Hq. Sqd.*	*334FS*	*335FS*	*336FS*
1st./Sgt.	0	1	1	1
Master/Sgts.	7	6	6	5
Tech/Sgts.	8	18	16	20
Staff/Sgts.	7	68	69	71
Sgts.	16	60	67	65
Cpls.	18	63	62	56
Pfcs.	9	11	17	11
Pvts.	4	9	10	13

Victories of the 4th Fighter Group in WWII

9-26-42	336FS.	*Capt. Marion E. Jackson,* FW-190, Air, 1730 hrs., Brest, Fr.
10-2-42	334FS.	*Capt. Oscar Coen,* FW-190, Air, 1435 hrs., Calais–Dunkirk, Fr.
		Lt. Stanley M. Anderson, FW-190, Air, 1435 hrs., Calais–Dunkirk, Fr.
		Lt. James A. Clark, ½ FW-190 (shared W/C Wooley RAF), Air, 1435 hrs., Calais–Dunkirk, Fr.
		W/C. R.M.B. Duke-Woolley (RAF), ½ FW-190 (shared Lt. Clark), Air, 1435 hrs., Calais–Dunkirk, Fr.
	335FS.	*F/O. Gene B. Fetrow,* FW-190, Air, 1435 hrs., Calais–Dunkirk, Fr.
11-19-42	335FS.	*Lt. Frank J. Smolinsky,* FW-190, Air, 1500 hrs., 10 mi. s/w of Flushing, Neth.
11-20-42	335FS.	*Lt. Roy W. Evans,* FS-156, Air, 1135 hrs., 3 mi. s/e of Furnes, Belg.
12-6-42	335FS.	*Lt. Gene B. Fetrow,* U/I/A/C, Air, unk, unk.
1-14-43	334FS.	*Lt. Stanley M. Anderson,* FW-190, Air, 1155 hrs., 3 mi. west of Ostend, Belg.
		Lt. Robert A. Boock, FW-190, Air, 1155 hrs., 3 mi. west of Ostend, Belg.
1-22-43	335FS.	*Lt. Stanley M. Anderson,* FW-190, Air, 1515 hrs., St. Omer, Fr.
		Lt. Robert A. Boock, FW-190, Air, 1515 hrs., St. Omer, Fr.
	335FS.	*Maj. Oscar Coen,* FW-190, Air, 1515 hrs., Dunkirk–Mardyk, Fr.
		Lt. Joseph G. Matthews, ME-109, Air, 1515 hrs., Dunkirk–Mardyk, Fr.
4-15-43	334FS.	*L/Col. Chesley G. Peterson,* FW-190, Air, 1750 hrs., North Sea 5 mi. off Ostend–Blankenberghe, Belg.
		Lt. Robert A. Boock, FW-190, Air, 1750 hrs., North Sea 5 mi. off Ostend–Blankenberghe, Belg.
	335FS.	*Maj. Donald J. Blakeslee,* FW-190, Air, 1701 hrs., Knocke–Bruges Belg.
	335FS.	*Maj. Donald J. Blakeskee,* FW-190, Air, 1307–1325 hrs., KnockeSt. Nicholas, Belg.
	336FS.	*Capt. Lee Gover,* FW-190, Air, 1307–1325 hrs., Knocke–St. Nicholas, Belg.
5-15-43	334FS.	*L/Col. Chesley G. Peterson,* FW-190, Air, unk., North Sea off Ostend, Belg.
5-18-43	334FS.	*Capt. Thomas J. Andrews,* ME-109G, Air, 1702 hrs., Blankenberghe–Knocke, Belg.
		Lt. Duane W. Beeson, ME-109, Air, 1702 hrs., Ostend–Blankenberghe, Belg.
5-21-43	334FS.	*Lt. Brewster W. Morgan,* ME-109, Air, approx. 1350 hrs., near Ghent, Belg.
6-22-43	335FS.	*Lt. Fonzo D. Smith,* FW-190, Air, 0920 hrs., Noord Beveland–Walcheren, Neth.

Lt. Ernest D. Beatie, FW-190, ME-109, Air, 0920 hrs., Noord Beveland–Walcheren, Neth.

336FS.   *Lt. James A. Goodson*, FW-190, Air, 0915 hrs., 10 mi. n/w of Hulst, Neth.

6-26-43   334FS.   *Lt. Raymond C. Care*, ME-109, Air, 1859 hrs., English Channel 10 mi. off Dieppe, Fr.

Lt. Duane W. Beeson, ME-109, Air, 1859 hrs., English Channel 10 mi. off Dieppe, Fr.

7-28-43   334FS.   *Lt. Duane W. Beeson*, ME-109, Air, 1210–1220 hrs., Westhooft–Emmerich, Ger.

Lt. Raymond C. Care, FW-190, Air, 1220 hrs., Westhooft–Emmerich, Ger.

335FS.   *Capt. Roy Evans*, ME-109, Air, 1155 hrs., 15 mi. west of Arnheim, Neth.

Lt. Frank Boyles, FW-190, Air, 1155 hrs., 10 mi. s/e of Utrecht, Neth.

Lt. Leon Blanding, FW-190, Air, 1155 hrs., 10 mi. s/e of Utrecht, Neth.

336FS.   *Capt. Lee Gover*, FW-190, Air, 1204 hrs., 25 mi. east of Rotterdam, Neth.

Col. Edward W. Anderson, 2 FW-190, Air, 1200 hrs., east of Rotterdam, Neth.

Capt. Carl H. Miley, ME-109, Air, 1200 hrs., east of Rotterdam, Neth.

7-30-43   335FS.   *Capt. Donald A. Young*, FW-190, Air, 1130 hrs., 15 mi. s/e of Rotterdam, Neth.

Lt. Pierce W. McKennon, FW-190, Air, 1135 hrs., Zalt Boomel, Neth.

Lt. Frank Boyles, FW-190, Air, 1135 hrs., Zalt Boomel, Neth.

Lt. Aubrey C. Stanhope, FW-190, Air, 1135 hrs., south of Arnhem, Neth.

Lt. Kenneth G. Smith, FW-190, Air, 1140 hrs., over Schouwen Island, Neth.

8-12-43   334FS.   *Capt. William T. O'Regan*, ME-109, Air, 0930 hrs., 15 mi. east of Sittard, Neth.

Capt. James A. Clark, FW-190, Air, unk, unk. (probably in Sittard area about the same time).

Lt. Steve N. Pisanos, ME-109, Air, unk., unk. (probably in Sittard area about the same time).

335FS.   *Lt. Cadman V. Padgett*, ME-109G, Air, 0927 hrs., west of Duren, Ger.

8-16-43   334FS.   *Capt. James A. Clark*, 2 FW-190, Air, 0950–0955 hrs., 10 mi. north of Paris, Fr.

F/O. Clyde D. Smith, 2 FW-190, Air, 1000 hrs., s/e of Paris, Fr.

Lt. Henry Mills, 2 FW-190, Air, 0950 hrs., n/w of Paris, Fr.

Lt. Howard D. Hively, FW-190, Air, 0950 hrs., n/w of Paris, Fr.

Lt. Raymond C. Care, FW-190, Air, 0950 hrs., north section of Paris, Fr.

335FS.   *Lt. James A. Happel*, FW-190, Air, 0945 hrs., north section of Paris, Fr.

Capt. Roy W. Evans, ME-109, Air, 0940 hrs., 8 mi. south of Paris, Fr.

Lt. Aubrey C. Stanhope, ME-109, Air, 1000 hrs., Melun–Paris area, Fr.

		Lt. Fonzo D. Smith, FW-190, Air, 0950 hrs., s/e section of Paris, Fr.
		Capt. Donald A. Young, FW-190, Air, 0940 hrs., 5 mi. n/w of Paris, Fr.
		Capt. Donald A. Young, ½ FW-190 (shared, Lt. Fink), Air, 0940 hrs., 5 mi. n/w of Paris, Fr.
		Lt. Frank M. Fink, ½ FW-190 (shared, Capt. Young), Air, 0940 hrs., 5 mi. n/w of Paris, Fr.
	336FS.	*Lt. Joseph G. Matthews*, FW-190, Air, 0920 hrs., St. Denis–L'Isle Adam, Fr.
		Lt. James A. Goodson, 2 FW-190, Air, 1000 hrs., Paris area, Fr.
		Maj. John G. DuFour, ME-109, Air, 0930 hrs., 1 mi. north of Paris, Fr.
9-6-43	335FS.	*Maj. Roy W. Evans*, FW-190, Air, unk., north of Chateau-Thierry, Fr.
9-27-43	336FS.	*Lt. Willard W. Millikan*, FW-190, Air, 1010 hrs., Norderney Island, Ger.
10-2-43	334FS.	*Lt. Duane W. Beeson*, FW-190, Air, unk., east of Wilhelmshaven, Ger.
10-8-43	334FS.	*Capt. James A. Clark*, ME-109, Air, unk., Meppel–Zwolle area, Neth.
		Lt. Duane W. Beeson, 2 ME-109, Air, unk., Meppel–Zwolle area, Neth.
		F/O. Ralph K. Hofer, ME-109, Air, unk., Meppel–Zwolle area, Neth.
	335FS.	*Lt. Donald H. Ross*, ME-210, Air, unk., unk.
		Maj. Roy W. Evans, FW-190, Air, unk., unk.
11-3-43	334FS.	*Lt. Alexander Rafalovich*, ME-109, Air, unk., n/e of the Zuider Zee, Neth.
11-5-43	335FS.	*Capt. Fonzo D. Smith*, FW-190, Air, unk., unk.
11-26-43	335FS.	*Lt. Cadman V. Padgett*, ME-109, Air, unk., Hude, ?.
11-29-43	335FS.	*Capt. Fonzo D. Smith*, ME-109, Air, unk., unk.
12-1-43	336FS.	*Lt. John T. Godfrey*, ME-109, Air, unk., unk.
12-11-43	334FS.	*Lt. Victor J. France*, ME-109, Air, unk., Leeuwarden area, Neth.
12-16-43	336FS.	*Capt. Don S. Gentile*, ⅓ JU-88 (shared Norley & Garrison), Air, unk., unk.
		Lt. Louis H. Norley, ⅓ JU-88 (shared Gentile & Garrison), Air, unk., unk.
		Lt. Vermont Garrison, ⅓ JU-88 (shared Gentile & Norley), Air, unk., unk.
12-20-43	336FS.	*Lt. Willard W. Millikan*, ME-109G, Air, 1159 hrs., n/w of Bremen, Ger.
12-22-43	334FS.	*Lt. Vasseure H. Wynn*, ME-109, ½ ME-109 (shared Godfrey), Air, unk., (1) Enschede, Neth., (½) Munster, Ger.
	336FS.	*Lt. John T. Godfrey*, ME-109, ½ ME-109 (shared Wynn), Air, unk., (1½) Munster Ger.
1-5-44	336FS.	*Capt. Don S. Gentile*, FW-190, Air, unk., 15 mi. west of Tours, Fr.
		Lt. Robert J. Messenger, FW-190, Air, unk., 15 mi. west of Tours, Fr.
1-7-44	336FS.	*Lt. Col. Donald Blakeslee*, FW-190, Air, unk., Hesdin area, Fr.
		Capt. James A Goodson, 2 FW-190, Air, unk., Hesdin area, Fr.
1-14-44	334FS.	*Lt. Duane W. Beeson*, FW-190, Air, 1515–1520 hrs., Soissons–Cambrai area, Fr.
		Lt. Edmund D. Whalen, FW-190, ½ FW-190 (shared Rafalovich), Air, 1515–1520 hrs., Soissons, Fr.

                  Lt. Alexander Rafalovich, ½ FW-190 (shared Whalen), Air, 1515–1520 hrs., Soissons, Fr.

                  Lt. Gerald Montgomery, FW-190, Air, 1520 hrs., Soissons, Fr.

                  Lt. H. Thomas Biel, FW-190, Air, 1515–1520 hrs., Cambrai, Fr.

    336FS. *Capt. Don S. Gentile, 2 FW-190, Air, unk., unk. (all).*

                  F/O Robert H. Richards, FW-190, Air, unk., unk.

                  Lt. Vermont Garrison, FW-190, ½ FW-190 (shared Norley), Air, unk., unk.

                  Lt. Louis H. Norley, ½ FW-190 (shared Garrison), Air, unk., unk.

1-21-44   336FS. *Lt. Robert H. Richards, FW-190, Air, unk., unk.*

1-29-44   334FS. *Capt. Henry L. Mills, 2 ME-109, Air, 1100 hrs., Aachen, Ger.*

                  Lt. Duane W. Beeson, ME-109, FW-190, Air, 1100 hrs., Aachen, Ger.

                  Lt. Archie W. Chatterly, ME-109, Air, 1100 hrs., Aachen, Ger.

                  Lt. Edmund D. Whalen, ME-109, Air, 1100 hrs., Aachen, Ger.

                  Lt. Victor J. France, FW-190, Air, 1100 hrs., Hasselt, Belg.

                  Lt. Steve N. Pisanos, 2 ME-109, Air, 1100 hrs., Hasselt, Belg.

1-30-44   335FS. *Lt. Charles F. Anderson, U/I E/A, Air, 1125 hrs., 10 mi. n/w of Lingen, Ger.*

1-31-44   334FS. *Capt. Winslow M. Sobanski, ME-109, Air, 1456 hrs., Gilze-Rijen, Neth.*

                  Lt. Duane W. Beeson, ME-109, Air, 1455 hrs., Gilze-Rijen, Neth.

    335FS. *Lt. Raymond P. Clotfelter, ME-109, Air, 1500 hrs., Gilze-Rijen, Neth.*

                  Lt. Paul M. Ellington, ME-109, Air, 1500 hrs., Gilze-Rijen, Neth.

    336FS. *Lt. Vermont Garrison, ME-109, Air, unk., unk..*

                  Lt. Kendall E. Carlson, ME-109, Air, unk., unk.

2-6-44   334FS. *F/O Ralph K. Hofer, ME-109, Air, 1125 hrs., west of Paris, Fr.*

    336FS. *Lt. Vermont Garrison, FW-190, Air, 1120 hrs., Beauvais–Margny area, Fr.*

                  Lt. Robert D. Hobert, FW-190, Air, 1130 hrs., Beauvais–Margny area, Fr.

2-10-44   334FS. *Lt. Victor J. France, FW-190, Air, 1110 hrs., Lingen, Ger.*

                  Lt. Gerald Montgomery, ME-109G, Air, 1055 hrs., Emmerich, Ger.

                  Lt. H. Thomas Biel, ME-109G, Air, 1105 hrs., Hengelo, Neth.

    335FS. *Lt. Charles F. Anderson, ½ ME-109 (shared Schlegel), Air, 1115 hrs., 2 mi. s/e of Hannover, Ger.*

                  Lt. Albert L. Schlegel, ½ ME-109 (shared Anderson), Air, 1115 hrs., 2 mi. s/e of Hannover, Ger.

                  Lt. Cecil E. Manning, FW-190, Air, 1115 hrs., 10–20 mi. s/w of Hannover, Ger.

    336FS. *Lt. Willard W. Millikan, FW-190, Air, unk., north of Dummer Lake, Ger.*

                  Lt. Vermont Garrison, ME-109, Air, unk., unk.

                  Lt. Louis H. Norley, ME-109, Air, unk., unk.

2-20-44   334FS. *Capt. Henry L. Mills, FW-190, Air, 1500 hrs., Aachen, Ger.*

                  Capt. Duane W. Beeson, FW-190, Air, 1500 hrs., Aachen, Ger.

    335FS. *Lt. Pierce W. McKennon, FW-190, Air, unk., unk. Marienbourg, Belg.*

                  Lt. Paul S. Riley, ½ ME-110 (shared Reed), Air, 1455 hrs., near Koblenz, Ger.

                  Lt. Richard I. Reed, ½ ME-110 (shared Riley), Air, 1455 hrs., near Koblenz, Ger.

2-21-44   334FS. *Lt. David W. Howe, FW-190, Air, 1340 hrs., Dummer Lake, Ger.*

Capt. Raymond C. Care, FW-190, Air, 1340 hrs., Dummer Lake, Ger.

335FS. *Lt. Raymond P. Clotfelter,* ME-210, Air, 1347 hrs., Mavern area, Ger.

2-22-44 335FS. *Maj. George Carpenter,* FW-190, Air, 1517 hrs., Erkelenz, Ger.

Lt. Bernard J. McGrattan, FW-190, Air, 1517 hrs., Erkelenz, Ger.

Lt. Pierce W. McKennon, ME-109, Air, 1517 hrs., Koblenz, Ger.

Lt. Albert L. Schlegel, FW-190, Air, unk., unk.

2-25-44 334FS. *Capt. Duane W. Beeson,* FW-190, Air, 1245 hrs., Beckingen, Ger.

335FS. *Lt. Pierce W. McKennon,* FW-190, Air, 1245 hrs., south of Luxembourg, Luxbg.

336FS. *Capt. Don S. Gentile,* FW-190, Air, 1240 hrs., 20 mi. s/e of Luxembourg, Luxbg.

Lt. Vermont Garrison, FW-190, Air, 1230 hrs., Luxembourg area, Luxbg.

Lt. Glenn A. Herter, FW-190, Air, 1240 hrs., 20 mi. s/e of Luxembourg, Luxbg.

2-28-44 334FS. *Lt. William B. Smith,* ¼ JU-88 (shared 4 pilots), Ground, 1500 hrs., Soissons area (A/D), Fr.

Lt. Nicholas Megura, ¼ JU-88 (shared 4 pilots), as above.

Capt. Duane W. Beeson, ¼ JU-88 (shared 4 pilots), as above.

336FS. *Lt. Vermont Garrison,* ¼ JU-88 (shared 4 pilots), as above.

3-2-44 334FS. *Lt. Vasseure H. Wynn,* ME-109, Air, 1155 hrs., 15 mi. south of Koblenz, Ger.

336FS. *Lt. Glenn A. Herter,* FW-190, Air, 1147 hrs., 30 mi. s/w of Koblenz, Ger.

3-3-44 336FS. *Capt. Don S. Gentile,* 2 FW-190, Air, 1130–1150 hrs., Wittenburg area, Ger.

Lt. Kendall E. Carlson, ME-110, Air, 1130 hrs., east of Hannover, Ger.

Lt. Willard W. Millikan, ME-110, Air, 1130–1150 hrs., Wittenburg area, Ger.

Capt. Phillip H. Dunn, ME-210, HE-111, Air, 1130–1150 & 1545 hrs., Wittenburg area, Ger. & St. Peel, Fr.

Lt. Vermont Garrison, ME-110, FW-190, Air, 1200–1230 hrs., n/w of Berlin, Ger.

3-4-44 334FS. *Lt. Nicholas Megura,* ME-109, Air, 1330 hrs., n/w of Leipzig, Ger.

Lt. Nicholas Megura, JU-52, Ground, 1330 hrs., n/w of Leipzig, Ger.

335FS. *Lt. Hugh A. Ward,* U/I S/E E/A, Air. Unk., unk.

336FS. *Lt. Woodrow F. Sooman,* JU-52, Air, unk., unk.

3-5-44 334FS. *Lt. Steve N. Pisanos,* 2 ME-109, Air, 1150–1200 hrs., Bordeaux area, Fr.

Lt. Howard D. Hively, 2 ME-109, Air, 1150–1155 hrs., Mont De Marsan area, Fr.

Capt. Duane W. Beeson, ME-109, Air, 1155 hrs., south of Bordeaux, Fr.

335FS. *Lt. James F. Steele,* FW-200, Air, 1130 hrs., Bergerac A/D, Fr.

Lt. Edward P. Freeburger, ½ FW-200 (shared Smith), Air, 1230 hrs., Bergerac A/D, Fr.

Capt. Fonzo D. Smith, ½ FW-200 (shared Freeburger), Air, 1230 hrs., Bergerac A/D, Fr.

Lt. James D. Dye, FW-190, Air, 1305 hrs., Reden, Fr.

| | 336FS. | *Capt. Kenneth D. Peterson,* FW-200, Air, 1215–1220 hrs., Bordeaux area, Fr. |

3-6-44 334FS. *Capt. David A. Van Epps,* ½ ME-110 (shared Moulton), Air, 1250–1350 hrs., Nienburg area, Ger.

Lt. Howard N. Moulton, ½ ME-110 (shared Van Epps), Air, 1250–1350 hrs., Nienburg area, Ger.

Lt. Edmund D. Whalen, ME-110, Air, 1250–1350 hrs., Nienburg area, Ger.

Capt. Henry L. Mills, FW-190, Air, 1315–1330 hrs., west of Brandenburg, Ger.

Lt. Archie W. Chatterley, ME-110, Air, 1315–1330 hrs., west of Brandenburg, Ger.

Lt. Alexander Rafalovich, ME-109, Air, 1250–1300 hrs., Brandenburg area, Ger.

Lt. Nicholas Megura, 2 ME-110, Air, unk., s/w of Berlin, Ger.

335FS. *Lt. Pierce W. McKennon,* ME-109, Air, 1245 hrs., south of Berlin, Ger.

Lt. Lloyd W. Waterman, ME-110, Air, 1225 hrs., s/w of Berlin, Ger.

Lt. Bernard J. McGrattan, JU-88, Air, 1225 hrs., n/e of Magdeburg, Ger.

Lt. Charles F. Anderson, DO-217, Air, 1235 hrs., Lehnin area, Ger.

Lt. James D. Dye, DO-217, Air, 1225 hrs., 20 mi. s/w of Berlin, Ger.

336FS. *Lt. John T. Godfrey,* ME-109, Air, 1450 hrs., 20 mi. north of Hannover, Ger.

3-8-44 334FS. *Maj. James A. Clark,* ME-109, Air, 1350 hrs., south of Berlin, Ger.

Lt. Allan F. Bunte, FS-156, Air, 1350–1405 hrs., s/w of Berlin–Brunswick, Ger.

Lt. Victor J. France, ME-109, Air, 1400 hrs., Stendal area, Ger.

Lt. David W. Howe, ME-109, Air, 1320–1330 hrs., 30 mi. south of Berlin, Ger.

Lt. Nicholas Megura, ME-109, FW-190, Air, 1350 hrs., west of Berlin, Ger.

335FS. *Lt. Raymond P. Clotfelter,* FW-190D, Air, 1337 hrs., Magdeburg, Ger.

Capt. Fonzo D. Smith, ME-110, Air, 1334 hrs., Magdeburg, Ger.

Lt. James D. Dye, FW-190, Air, 1359 hrs., Luckenwalde–Dahme area, Ger.

336FS. *Capt. Don S. Gentile,* 3 ME-109, ½ ME-109 (shared Godfrey), Air, 1350–1420 hrs., Berlin suburbs, Ger.

Lt. John T. Godfrey, 2 ME-109, ½ ME-109 (shared Gentile), Air, 1350 hrs., Berlin suburbs, Ger. (ace).

Lt. Robert S. Tussey, JU-88, Air, 1400 hrs., Magdeburg area, Ger.

3-16-44 334FS. *F/O. Ralph K. Hofer,* ME-110, Air, 1200 hrs., Munich area, Ger.

Lt. Archie W. Chatterley, ME-110, Air, 1150 hrs., Munich area, Ger.

335FS. *Maj. George Carpenter,* 2 ME-110, Air, 1150 hrs., 40 mi. n/w of Munich, Ger.

Capt. Fonzo D. Smith, ME-110, Air, 1150 hrs., 40 mi. n/w of Munich, Ger.

Lt. Paul S. Riley, ME-110, Air, 1150 hrs., n/w of Munich, Ger.

336FS. *Maj. James A. Goodson,* 2 ME-110, Air, 1200 hrs., s/w of Munich, Ger.

Lt. Kendall E. Carlson, 2 ME-110, Air, 1200 hrs., Kaufburen area, Ger.

F/O Frederick W. Glover, 2 ME-110, Air, 1200 hrs., Kaufburen area, Ger.

Lt. John T. Godfrey, ME-110, Air, 1200 hrs., Kaufburen area, Ger.

3-18-44 334FS. *Capt. Duane W. Beeson*, ME-109, Air, 1335 hrs., east of Mannheim, Ger.

F/O Ralph K. Hofer, 2 ME-109, Air, 1335 hrs., s/e of Mannheim, Ger.

Lt. Archie W. Chatterley, ME-109, Air, 1335 hrs., s/e of Mannheim, Ger.

Lt. Nicholas Megura, ME-109, Air, 1335 hrs., s/e of Mannheim, Ger.

335FS. *Maj. George Carpenter*, ME-109, Air, 1435 hrs., 20 mi. s/w of Saarbrucken, Ger.

Lt. Bernard J. McGrattan, HE-111, Air, 1350 hrs., Augsburg, Ger.

Capt. Kenneth G. Smith, FW-190, Air, 1445 hrs., Gunzburg, Ger.

336FS. *Maj. James A. Goodson*, 2 HE-111, Ground, 1400 hrs., Mannheim–Ludwigshafen area, Ger.

Col. Donald Blakeslee, FW-190, Air, unk., unk.

Capt. Don S. Gentile, FW-190, Air, 1425–1445 hrs., Augsberg, Ger.

3-21-44 334FS. *Lt. Archie W. Chatterley*, ½ FW-190 (shared Megura), Air, 1345 hrs., n/e of Bordeaux, Fr.

Lt. Nicholas Megura, HE-177, ½ FW-190 (shared Chatterley), Ground & Air, 1345 hrs., 30 mi. north of Bordeaux & n/e of Bordeaux, Fr.

Lt. Howard D. Hively, ½ JU-88 (shared Goodwyn), Ground, 1350 hrs., Bordeaux–Langen area, Fr.

F/O Ralph K. Hofer, HE-177, Ground, 1350 hrs., Langen A/D, Fr.

Lt. Victor J. France, 2 FW-190, Ground, 1345–1415 hrs., Bordeaux area, Fr.

Lt. Alexander Rafalovich, ½ DO-217 (shared Van Epps), Ground, 1350 hrs., east of Bordeaux, Fr.

Capt. David A. Van Epps, ½ DO-217 (shared Rafalovich), Ground, as above.

Maj. James A. Clark, FW-190, FW-190, Air & Ground, 1345 & 1345 hrs., Bordeaux & Landes De Bassac A/D, Fr.

335FS. *Lt. Clemens A. Fiedler*, FW-190, Ground, 1340 hrs., Landes De Bassac A/D, Fr.

Lt. John W. Goodwyn, ½ JU-88 (shared Hively), Ground, as above.

Maj. George Carpenter, FW-190, ½ FW-190, ½ FW-190, ⅓ JU-52, Air, Ground, Air, Ground, 1415 & 1340 & 1415 & 1340 hrs., 100 mi. north of Bordeaux, north of Bordeaux, 100 mi. north of Bordeaux, north of Bordeaux, Fr. (shared Anderson, Anderson, Anderson, Anderson & Church).

Lt. Charles F. Anderson, FW-190, ½ FW-190, ½ FW-190, ⅓ JU-52, Air, Ground, Air, Ground, 1415 & 1340 & 1415 & 1340 hrs., 100 mi. north of Bordeaux, north of Bordeaux, 100 mi. north of Bordeaux, north of Bordeaux, Fr. (shared Carpenter, Carpenter, Carpenter, Carpenter & Church).

Lt. Pierce W. McKennon, FW-190, Air, 1400 hrs., 2 mi. west of Landes De Bassac A/D, Fr.

Lt. Albert L. Schlegel, HE-111, Air, 1350 hrs., south of Nantes, Fr.

Lt. Robert C. Church, ⅓ JU-52 (shared Carpenter, Anderson), Ground, 1340 hrs., 20 mi. n/e of Bordeaux, Fr.

Lt. William C. Hawkins, ME-110, Air, 1530 hrs., 20 mi. n/e of Bordeaux, Fr.

336FS.   *Capt. Robert D. Hobert,* FW-190D, Air, 1440 hrs., s/w of Evreux A/D, Fr.

Maj. James A. Goodson, ME-410, Ground, 1430 hrs., Evreux A/D, Fr.

3-23-44   334FS.   *Capt. Duane W. Beeson,* 2 ME-109, Air, 1115 hrs., Munster area, Ger.

Lt. Leonard R. Pierce, ME-109, Air, 1110 hrs., Munster–Hamm area, Ger.

Lt. Allan F. Bunte, ME-109, Air, 1200 hrs., Osnabruck–Herford area, Ger.

Maj. James A. Clark, FW-190, Air, unk., s/e of Steinhuder Lake, Ger.

F/O. Ralph K. Hofer, FW-190, Air, 1120 hrs., east of Hamm–Munster, Ger.

Lt. Nicholas Megura, FW-190, Air, 1110–1115 hrs., Munster area, Ger.

336FS.   *Maj. James A. Goodson,* 2 ME-109, Air, 1115 hrs., Munster area, Ger.

Capt. Don S. Gentile, 2 ME-109, Air, 1115 hrs., Munster area, Ger.

Lt. John T. Godfrey, ME-109, Air, 1115 hrs., Munster area, Ger.

3-27-44   334FS.   *Capt. Duane W. Beeson,* JU-88, HE-126, ½ JU-88 (shared Biel), (2½) Ground, 1500, 1500, & 1445 hrs., (2½) Cazaux A/D, Fr.

Lt. H. Thomas Biel, JU-88, ME-410, ½ JU-88, (shared Beeson), (2½) Ground, (2½) 1445 hrs., (2½) Cazaux A/D, Fr.

Lt. Shelton W. Monroe, ME-410, Ground, 1445 hrs., Cazaux A/D, Fr.

Lt. Archie Chatterley, ME-109, Ground, 1445–1500 hrs., Angouleme area, Fr.

Lt. William B. Smith, ME-109, Air, 1445–1500 hrs., Lake Biscarosse, Fr.

Lt. William B. Smith, ME-109, Ground, 1445–1500 hrs., Angouleme area, Fr.

Lt. Howard D. Hively, JU-88, Ground, 1450 hrs., Cazaux A/D, Fr.

Lt. Alfred H. Markel, ½ JU-88 (shared Megura), Ground, 1415 hrs., Cazaux A/D, Fr.

Capt. Nicholas Megura, ½ JU-88 (shared Markel), Ground, as above.

Lt. Victor J. France, JU-52, JU-88, 2 Ground, 1445 hrs., Cazaux A/D, Fr.

Lt. Gerald Montgomery, JU-52, FW-190, JU-88, 3 Ground, 1445 hrs., Cazaux A/D, Fr.

Lt. Vasseure H. Wynn, DO-217, JU-88, 2 Ground, 1445 hrs., Cazaux A/D, Fr.

335FS.   *Maj. George Carpenter,* FW-190, Air, 1520 hrs., 15 mi. s/w of Bordeaux, Fr.

Lt. Charles F. Anderson, FW-190, Air, 1520 hrs., 10 mi. east of Bordeaux area, Fr.

336FS.   *Capt. Don S. Gentile,* 2 ME-110, 2 Ground, 1500 hrs., Cazaux A/D, Fr.

Lt. Willard W. Millikan, HE-177, Ground, 1500 hrs., Cazaux A/D, Fr.

Lt. Louis H. Norley, JU-88, Ground, 1500 hrs., Cazaux A/D, Fr.
Maj. James A. Clark, JU-88, ½ JU-88 (shared Emerson), Ground, 1500 hrs., Cazaux A/D, Fr.
Lt. Donald R. Emerson, ½ JU-88 (shared Clark), Ground, 1500 hrs., Cazaux A/D, Fr.

3-28-44   335FS.   *Lt. Charles F. Anderson,* U/I T/E E/A, Ground, unk., unk.
3-29-44   334FS.   *Lt/Col. James A. Clark,* FW-190, Air, 1450 hrs., Magdeburg area, Ger.*

Lt. Allan F. Bunte, FW-190, Air, 1450 hrs., Magdeburg area, Ger.
Capt. Winslow M. Sobanski, JU-52, Ground, 1330–1350 hrs., near Hannover and Steinhuder Lake, Ger.
Lt. David W. Howe, FW-190, Air, 1329 hrs., 10 mi. n/w of Brunswick, Ger.
Lt. H. Thomas Biel, FW-190, Air, 1330 hrs., Gifhorn area west of Brunswick, Ger.

335FS.   *Maj. George Carpenter,* ⅓ HE-111 (shared Glover & Godfrey), Air, 1330 hrs., Brunswick area, Ger.
Lt. Pierce W. McKennon, FW-190, Air, unk., Brunswick area, Ger.
Lt. Clemens A. Fiedler, ME-109, Air, unk., unk.
Lt. Charles F. Anderson, 2 FW-190, Air, unk., unk.
Lt. Ralph W. Saunders, ME-109, Air, unk., unk.
Lt. Robert C. Church, ME-109, Air, unk., unk.
Lt. Paul S. Riley, ME-109, Air, unk., unk.

336FS.   *Capt. Don S. Gentile,* 2 FW-190, ME-109, 3 Air, 1330 hrs., Brunswick area, Ger.
1400 hrs., n/e of Brunswick, Ger.
Lt. Oscar F. Lejeunesse, JU-88, Air, 1330 hrs., east of Hannover, Ger.
Lt. John T. Godfrey, 2 FW-190, ⅓ HE-111 (shared Carpenter & Glover), 2⅓ Air, 1330 hrs., Brunswick area, Ger.
F/O. Frederick W. Glover, FW-190, ⅓ HE-111 (shared Godfrey & Carpenter), 1⅓ Air, 1330 hrs., Brunswick area, Ger.
Capt. Kenneth D. Peterson, 2 FW-190, Air, 1315 hrs., s/w of Brunswick, Ger.

4-1-44   334FS.   *Capt. Duane W. Beeson,* ME-109, Air, 1044 hrs., north of Lake Constance, Ger.
Lt. Nicholas Megura, ME-109, Air, unk., unk.
335FS.   *F/O. Ralph K. Hofer,* ME-109, Air, unk., unk.
336FS.   *Capt. Don S. Gentile,* ME-109, Air, unk., unk.

4-5-44   334FS.   *Capt. Duane W. Beeson,* ⅓ JU-88 (shared Biel & Fiedler), JU-88, ⅓ Air, 1 Ground, 1515 hrs. & 1520 hrs., Brandenburg–Briest A/D & Weissewarte/Bush A/D, Ger.
Lt. H. Thomas Biel, ⅓ JU-88 (shared Beeson & Fiedler), HE-111, ⅓ Air, 1 Ground, 1515 hrs. & 1515 hrs., (1⅓) at Brandenburg–Briest A/D, Ger.
Lt. Charles D. Carr, JU-88, Ground, 1520 hrs., Weissewarte/Bush A/D, Ger.
Lt. Victor J. France, ⅓ He-111 (shared Pierce & Blanchfield), Ground, 1515 hrs., Brandenburg–Briest A/D, Ger.
Lt. Leonard R. Pierce, ⅓ HE-111 (shared France & Blanchfield), JU-88, 1⅓ Ground, both at 1515 hrs., all at Brandenburg–Briest A/D, Ger.
Lt. Herbert J. Blanchfield, ⅓ HE-111 (shared France & Pierce),

DO-217, 1⅓ Ground, both at 1515 hrs., all at Brandenburg–Briest A/D, Ger.

Lt. Gerald Montgomery, 2 JU-88, Ground, 1510 hrs., Brandenburg–Briest A/D, Ger.

335FS.   *Lt. Paul S. Riley,* ½ HE-111 (shared Goodwyn), HE-111, ½ Air, 1 Ground, ½ 1450 hrs., 1 1500 hrs., (½) near Brandenburg, (1) near Brandenburg and Plaus A/D, Ger.

Lt. Ralph W. Saunders, JU-52, Ground, unk., unk.

Maj. George Carpenter, U/I E/A, unk., unk.

Lt. Charles F. Anderson, 2 U/I E/A, Ground, unk., unk.

Lt. Clemens A. Fiedler, ⅓ JU-88 (shared Beeson & Biel), Air, 1515 hrs., Brandenburg–Briest A/D, Ger.

Lt. Frank C. Jones, 2 U/I T/E E/A, Ground, 1445 hrs., 20–30 mi. s/e of Berlin, Ger.

Lt. John W. Goodwyn, ½ HE-111 (shared Riley), Air, 1450 hrs., near Brandenburg, Ger.

Lt. Albert L. Schlegel, HE-111, JU-88, unk., unk., unk.

336FS.   *Maj. James A. Goodson,* JU-52, FW-190, JU-88, ½ JU-88 (shared Gentile), ½ JU-88 (shared Emerson), ½ JU-88 (shared 336FS), All on Ground, All at 1515 hrs., All at Stendal A/D, Ger.

Capt. Don S. Gentile, 3 JU-88, ½ JU-88 (shared Goodson), ½ JU-88 (shared Godfrey), All on Ground, All at 1515 hrs., All at Stendal A/D, Ger.

Lt. Kendall E. Carlson, JU-88, 2 JU-52 (shared unk.), Ground, 1515 hrs., Stendal A/D, Ger.

Lt. Robert S. Tussey, ME-110, Ground, 1515 hrs., Stendal A/D, Ger.

Lt. Frederick W. Glover, JU-52, 1515 hrs., Ground, Stendal A/D, Ger.

Lt. Warren E. Johnson, JU-88, ½ U/I T/E E/A, (shared 336FS), Ground, 1515 hrs., Stendal A/D, Ger.

Lt. John T. Godfrey, JU-88, ME-110, ½ JU-88 (shared Gentile), 2½ Ground, 1515 hrs., Stendal A/D, Ger.

Lt. Reuben Simon, 2 U/I T/E E/A, 2 Ground, 1515 hrs., unk. A/D 20 mi. west of Brandenburg, Ger.

Lt. Robert F. Nelson, JU-88, Ground, 1450 hrs., Brandenburg area, Ger.

Lt. Donald R. Emerson, ½ JU-88 (shared Goodson & unk.), ½ JU-88 (shared 336FS), ½ & ½ Ground, 1515 hrs., Stendal A/D, Ger.

Lt. Donald J. Patchen, 2 JU-88 (shared 336FS), Ground, 1515 hrs., Stendal A/D, Ger.

Capt. Robert D. Hobert, 3 JU-88, Ground, 1515 hrs., Stendal A/D, Ger.

4-8-44   334FS.   *Lt. Alfred H. Markel,* FW-190, Air, 1320 hrs., near Celle, Ger.

Capt. Raymond C. Care, ME-109, Air, 1350 hrs., Ulzen, Ger.

F/O. Ralph K. Hofer, ME-109, Air, 1315 hrs., near Celle, Ger.

Lt. Howard N. Moulton, ME-109, Air, 1315 hrs., near Celle, Ger.

Lt. William B. Smith, FW-190, Air, 1315 hrs., near Celle, Ger.

Lt. H. Thomas Biel, JU-52, Ground, 1310 hrs., s/w of Celle, Ger.

Lt. Shelton W. Monroe, FW-190, ½ FW-190 (shared Schlegel), ½ ME-109 (shared Schlegel), All in air, All at 1315 hrs., near Celle, Ger.

335FS.   *Lt. Pierce W. McKennon,* FW-190, Air, 1430 hrs., Celle area, Ger.

Lt. Bernard J. McGrattan, ME-109, unk., 1400 hrs., Wolfenbuttel area, Ger.

Lt. George I. Stanford, ME-109, unk., unk., unk.

Maj. George Carpenter, 2 FW-190, unk., unk., unk.

Lt. Charles F. Anderson, FW-190, Air, 1420 hrs., Gifhorn, Ger.

Capt. James A. Happel, HE-111, Air, 1335 hrs., 20 mi. south of Ulzen, Ger.

Lt. Clemens A. Fiedler, 2 FW-190, unk., unk., unk.

Lt. Paul S. Riley, FW-190, unk., unk., unk.

Lt. Albert L. Schlegel, FW-190, ½ FW-190 (shared Monroe), ½ ME-109 (shared Monroe), 1 Ground, ½ & ½ Air., 1415–1500 hrs., All in Brunswick area, Ger.

336FS. *Capt. Don S. Gentile,* 3 FW-190, Air, 1350 hrs., near Ruhrburg, Ger.

Lt. Louis H. Norley, 3 FW-190, Air, 1350 hrs., Ulzen, Ger.

Lt. Willard W. Millikan, 3 ME-109, Air, 1350 hrs., Ulzen, Ger.

Lt. Reuben Simon, FW-190, Air, 1400 hrs., near Brunswick, Ger.

Capt. Joseph H. Bennett, ME-109, Air, 1359 hrs., Moden, Ger.

F/O Frederick W. Glover, FW-190, Air, 1350 hrs., Ulzen, Ger.

Lt. Robert E. Hughes, FW-190, Air, 1400 hrs., Ulzen, Ger.

4-9-44 335FS. *Capt. James A. Happel,* ⅕ 2 JU-88 (shared McKennon, Godfrey, & 2 other 4FG pilots), Ground, 1335 hrs., Lingen Plartlune A/D, Ger.

Lt. Pierce W. McKennon, ⅕ 2 JU-88 (shared Happel, Godfrey, & 2 other 4FG pilots), as above.

336FS. *Lt. John I. Godfrey,* ME-410, ⅕ 2 JU-88 (shared Happel, McKennon, & 2 other 4FG pilots), as above.

4-10-44 334FS. *Lt. Gerald Montgomery,* BU-131, ½ BU-131 (shared Siems), Ground, 0955 hrs., Romorantin A/D, s/w of Orleans, Fr.

Lt. Grover C. Siems, ½ BU-131 (shared Montgomery), Ground, as above.

Lt. Robert L. Hills, S/E Biplane, Ground, as above.

Lt. H. Thomas Biel, U/I S/E E/A, Ground, as above.

Lt. David W. Howe, U/I S/E E/A, Ground, as above.

Lt. Herbert Blanchfield, HS-126, Ground, as above.

335FS. *Capt. James A. Happel,* 2 BU-131, Ground, 1000 hrs., Romorantin A/D, Fr.

Lt. George I. Stanford, BU-131, Ground, as above.

Lt. Paul S. Riley, BU-131, U/I E/A, Ground, as above.

Lt. Albert L. Schlegel, 2 U/I Trng. E/A, Ground, 0945 hrs., as above.

Lt. James W. Russell, U/I Trng. E/A, Ground, 1000 hrs., as above.

Lt. Charles F. Anderson, BU-131, Ground, as above.

336FS. *Maj. James A. Goodson,* 4 U/I Trng. E/A, HS-126, U/I Trng. E/A (shared Shilke), 5½ Ground, 0955–1005 hrs., Romorantin A/D, Fr.

Lt. Charles H. Shilke, U/I Trng. E/A, ½ U/I Trng. E/A (shared Goodson), 1½ Ground, as above.

Lt. Robert F. Nelson, 2 U/I Trng. E/A, Ground, as above.

4-11-44 334FS. *Capt. Raymond C. Care,* ME-110, Air, 1230 hrs., 20 mi. s/e of Stettin, Ger.

F/O. Ralph K. Hofer, ME-110, Air, as above.

Lt. (?) Smith, DO-217, Air, 2 FW-190, Ground, as above.

Lt. H. Thomas Biel, ME-410, ME-110, 2 Air, 1225 hrs., as above.

Lt. Robert L. Hills, FW-190, JU-88, 1 Ground, 1 Air, 1230 & 1230 hrs., Stargard A/D & 20 mi. s/e of Stettin, Ger.

4-12-44 335FS. *Lt. Charles F. Anderson*, 2 ME-109, Air, 1410 hrs., 10 mi. n/w of Brunswick, Ger.

Maj. George Carpenter, ME-109, 1410 hrs., as above.

Lt. Frank C. Jones, ME-109, Air, 1410 hrs., Volkenrode A/D, Ger.

4-13-44 334FS. *Lt. Nicholas Megura*, FW-190, Air, 1400 hrs., s/e of Mannheim, Ger.

Capt. Woodrow M. Sobanski, FW-190, Air, 1350–1400 hrs., Ludwigshafen, Ger.

335FS. *Maj. George Carpenter*, FW-190, Air, 1350 hrs., 20 mi. s/w of Schweinfurt, Ger.

Lt. Pierce W. McKennon, FW-190, Air, 1350 hrs., 20 mi. s/w of Schweinfurt, Ger.

336FS. *Lt. Louis H. Norley*, FW-190, Air, 1400 hrs., Schweinfurt, Ger.

4-15-44 334FS. *Lt. Herbert J. Blanchfield*, JU-88, Ground, 1330 hrs., Hagenow A/D, Ger.

Lt. Gerald E. Montgomery, HE-177, JU-88, 2 Ground, 1330 hrs., Hagenow A/D, Ger.

Capt. Raymond C. Care, ½ JU-52 (shared Biel), ½ Ground, 1345 hrs., Magdeburg–Hannover area, Ger.

Lt. H. Thomas Biel, ½ JU-52 (shared Care), ½ Ground, as above.

335FS. *Lt. Charles F. Anderson*, HE-177, Ground, 1400 hrs., Hagenow A/D, Ger.

Lt. Albert L. Schlegel, HE-177, Ground, as above.

Lt. Frank C. Jones, HE-177, Ground, as above.

336FS. *Lt. Robert F. Nelson*, FS-156, Air, 2 HE-177, Ground, 1400 hrs., Fassberg A/D, Ger.

Lt. Willard W. Millikan, HE-177, Ground, 1400 hrs., Hagenow A/D, Ger.

Lt. Robert S. Tussey, HE-177, Ground, as above.

F/O Frederick W. Glover, ME-110, Ground, as above.

4-18-44 334FS. *Col. Donald Blakeslee*, HE-177, Ground, 1500 hrs., Fassberg A/D, Ger.

Lt. Joseph L. Lang, 3 JU-52, 3 Ground, 1510–1525 hrs., Juterbog A/D, Ger.

Lt. Nicholas Megura, ⅓ ME-109 (shared France, Siems), Air, 1445–1500 hrs., Brandenburg–Stendal area, Ger.

Lt. Victor J. France, ⅓ ME-109 (shared Megura, Siems), Air, as above.

Lt. Grover C. Siems, ⅓ ME-109 (shared France, Megura), Air, as above.

Lt. Shelton W. Monroe, 2 JU-52, Ground, 1510–1525 hrs., Juterbog A/D, Ger.

Lt. David W. Howe, 2 JU-52, Ground, as above.

Lt. Donald M. Malmsten, JU-52, Ground, 1445–1500 hrs., as above.

Lt. Robert P. Kenyon, HE-111, Ground, 1500 hrs., Fassberg A/D, Ger.

F/O Ralph K. Hofer, 2 HE-177, Ground, 1520 hrs., as above.

335FS. *Lt. Pierce W. McKennon*, FW-190D, Air, 1435 hrs., Rhin Canal–Rathenow area, Ger.

Maj. George Carpenter, ME-109, Air, 1425 hrs., 2 mi. n/w of Nauen–Rhin Canal area, Ger.

Maj. George Carpenter, FW-190, Air, 1425 hrs., Rathenow area, Ger.

336FS. *Lt. Donald R. Emerson,* ME-109, Ground, 1530 hrs., Wazendorf A/D, Ger.

Lt. Robert F. Nelson, ME-109, Ground, 1550 hrs., Genthin A/D, Ger.

Lt. Neil Van Wyk, ½ FW-190 (shared Logan), 1530 hrs., Wenzendorf A/D, Ger.

Lt. George H. Logan, ½ FW-190 (shared Van Wyk), as above.

4-19-44 334FS. *Lt. Robert P. Kenyon,* ME-109, Air, 1025 hrs., Eschwege, Ger.

Capt. Woodrow M. Sobanski, ME-109, Air, 1025 hrs., Kassel–Eschwege area, Ger.

335FS. *Lt. Pierce W. McKennon,* ME-109, Air, 1045 hrs., Eschwege area, Ger.

Lt. Bernard J. McGrattan, ME-109, ½ FW-190 (shared Megura), 1½ FW-? 20 mi. s/w of Eschwege area, Ger., Air, 1030 & 1025 hrs., Me-? Eschwege area, Ger.

334FS. *Lt. Nicholas Megura,* ½ FW-190 (shared McGrattan), Air, 1025 hrs., 20 mi. s/w of Eschwege area, Ger.

336FS. *Lt. Willard M. Millikan,* ME-109, Air, 1045 hrs., n/e of Eschwege, Ger.

4-22-44 334FS. *Lt. William B. Smith,* ½ ME-109G (shared Riley), Air, 1800 hrs., Eder Lake s/w of Kassel, Ger.

335FS. *Lt. Albert L. Schlegel,* 2 ME-109G, Air, 1750 hrs., south of Kassel, Ger.

Lt. Frank C. Jones, ME-109G, Air, 1756 hrs., Kassel, Ger.

Lt. Paul S. Riley, ½ ME-109G (shared W. B. Smith), Air, 1800 hrs., south of Kassel, Ger.

336FS. *Col. Donald Blakeslee,* 2 ME-109, Air, 1800–1820 hrs., s/w of Kassel, Ger.

Lt. John Godfrey, 3 ME-109, Air, 1800–1820 hrs., s/w of Kassel, Ger.

Lt. Willard W. Millikan, 4 ME-109, Air, 1800–1825 hrs., Lake near Sachenhausen, s/w of Kassel, Ger.

Lt. Louis Norley, 2 ME-109, Air, 1800–1825 hrs., s/w of Kassel, Ger.

Lt. Reuben Simon, ME-109, Air, 1800 hrs., s/w of Kassel, Ger.

Lt. Kendall Carlson, ME-109, ½ ME-109 (shared Emerson), 1½ Air, 1800 hrs., s/w of Kassel, Ger.

Lt. Donald Emerson, ½ ME-109 (shared Carlson), Air, 1800 hrs., s/w of Kassel, Ger.

4-24-44 334FS. *Lt. Nicholas Megura,* 2 FW-190, Air, 1245 hrs., 20 mi. south of Frankfurt, Ger.

Lt. Joseph Lang, ME-109, Air, 1245 hrs., Darmstadt, Ger.

Lt. David Howe, ME-109, Air, 1300 hrs., Darmstadt area, Ger.

335FS. *Lt. Albert Schlegel,* 2 FW-190, ½ FW-190 (shared Blakeslee), 2½ Air, 1250 hrs., north of Worms, Ger.

Col. Donald Blakeslee, FW-190, ½ FW-190 (shared Schlegel), 1½ Air, 1250 hrs., north of Worms, Ger.

Lt. James Happel, FW-190, Air, 1250 hrs., n/e of Worms, Ger.

Lt. Bernard McGrattan, FW-190, Air, 1415 hrs., Knocke area, Belg.

Lt. Leighton M. Read, FW-190, Air, 1250 hrs., north of Worms, Ger.

Lt. George Stanford, FW-190, Air, 1250 hrs., n/e of Worms, Ger.

Lt. Paul Riley, 2 FW-190, Air, unk., unk.

	336FS.	*Lt. John Godfrey,* FW-190, Air, 1245 hrs., n/w of Ludwigshafen, Ger.
		Maj. James Goodson, 2 ME-109, Air, unk., Wiener Neustadt, Ger. (scored flying with 31FG in MTO.).
4-27-44	335FS.	*Lt. Leighton Read,* U/I S/E E/A, Ground, 1915 hrs., Toul, Fr.
4-29-44	334FS.	*Lt. Nicholas Megura,* JU-52, Ground, 1150 hrs., Nordhausen, Ger.
		Lt. Nicholas Megura, ½ JU-52 (shared Barden), ½ JU-52 (shared Monroe), ½ & ½ Ground, as above.
		Lt. John L. Barden, ½ JU-52 (shared Megura), Ground, as above.
		Lt. Shelton Monroe, JU-52, ½ JU-52 (shared Megura), 1½ Ground, as above.
	336FS.	*Lt. John Godfrey,* DO-217, 2 JU-52 (shared Grounds), All Ground, unk., unk.
		Lt. Ira E. Grounds, ½ JU-52 (shared Godfrey), Ground, unk., unk.
		Lt. Joseph A. Patteeuw, ½ JU-52 (shared Godfrey), unk., unk.
4-30-44	334FS.	*Lt. Joseph Lang,* ME-110, ⅓ ME-110 (shared Sobanski & Monroe), Air, Ground, unk., Lyon–Bron area, Fr.
		Capt. Woodrow Sobanski, ⅓ ME-110 (shared Lang & Monroe), Air, unk., 20 mi. north of Lyon, Fr.
		Lt. Shelton Monroe, ⅓ ME-110 (shared Sobanski & Lang), Air, unk., as above.
	336FS.	*Col. Donald Blakeslee,* ¼ 3 Seaplanes (shared Godfrey, Harris, Patteeuw, McDill), Ground, unk., French lake returning from St. Dizier–Lyon area, Fr.
		Lt. John Godfrey, Lt. Ferris S. Harris, Lt. Joseph Patteeuw, Lt. Thomas K. McDill, ¼ 3 Seaplanes (all shared with Blakeslee), Ground, unk., as above.
		Capt. FrederickW. Glover, ½ French U/I T/E A/C (shared Frederick), Ground, 1125 hrs., Valence A/D, Fr.
		Lt. Harold H. Frederick, ½ French U/I T/E A/C (shared Glover), Ground, as above.
5-1-44	334FS.	*Lt. Ralph Hofer,* ME-109, Air, unk., near Cologne, Ger.
	335FS.	*Lt. Frank Jones,* ME-109, Air, 1830 hrs., Zweibrucken, Ger.
		Lt. Bernard McGrattan, ME-109, Air, 1830 hrs., Losheim area, Ger.
	336FS.	*Lt. John Godfrey,* ME-109, Air, 1850 hrs., n/w of Saarbruken, Ger.
5-9-44	334FS.	*Lt. Grover Siems,* JU-88, Ground, 1000 hrs., Reims–Champagne area, Fr.
5-12-44	334FS.	*Lt. Ralph Hofer,* ½ ME-109 (shared Pierce), Air, unk., 20 mi. north of Coburg, Ger.
		Lt. Leonard Pierce, ½ ME-109 (shared Hofer), Air, as above.
		Capt. Howard Hively, ME-109, Air, unk., Plaven, Ger.
		Lt. Grover Siems, ME-109, Air, unk., near Coburg, Ger. (flew mission with 336FS.).
	335FS.	*Maj. James Goodson,* ME-109, Air, 1240 hrs., Kassel area, Ger.
		Capt. James Happel, ME-109, Air, 1300 hrs., east of Giessen–Marburg, Ger.
		Lt. Robert Homuth, ME-109, Air, 1300 hrs., as above.
		Lt. Ted Lines, ME-109, Air, 1245 hrs., east of Frankfurt, Ger.
		Lt. Elliot Shapleigh, 1½ ME-109 (shared Stanford), Air, 1245 hrs., east of Giessen–Marburg, Ger.
		Lt. George Stanford, 1½ ME-109 (shared Shapleigh), Air, as above.
	336FS.	*Lt. Thomas McDill,* ME-109, Air, 1245 hrs., Kassel area, Ger.
5-19-44	334FS.	*Capt. Howard Hively,* 3 ME-109, Air, unk., Lubeck–Schwerin, Ger.

Maj. Michael McPharlin, ½ ME-109 (shared Scott), Air, unk., Lubeck–Schwerin, Ger.

Lt. James F. Scott, ½ ME-109 (shared McPharlin), Air, as above.

Lt. David Howe, ME-109, Air, unk., Neustadt Bay, Ger.

Lt. Joseph Lang, ME-109, U/I E/A, 2 Air, unk., Wismar area, Ger.

5-21-44 334FS. *Lt. Aubrey E. Hewatt,* ½ BU-131 (shared Hofer), Air, unk., Rathenow A/D, Ger.

Lt. Ralph Hofer, ½ BU-131 (shared Hewatt), Air, as above.

Lt. Grover Siems, 2 ME-210, Ground, unk., Rathenow A/D, Ger.

Lt. Frank Speer, JU-52, JU-88, 2 Ground, unk., Rathenow A/D, Ger.

5-22-44 334FS. *Capt. Nicholas Megura,* ½ ME-109 (shared unknown P-38 pilot), Air, unk., s/w of Kiel, Ger.

Lt. Ralph Hofer, ME-109, Air, unk., near Hamburg, Ger.

336FS. *Capt. Willard Millikan,* ME-109, Air, 1255 hrs., n/w of Kiel, Ger.

5-24-44 334FS. *Capt. Howard Hively,* ME-109, Air, unk., Hamburg area, Ger.

Lt. Willard G. Gillette, ME-109, Air, unk., n/e of Hamburg, Ger.

Lt. Joseph Lang, ME-109, Air, unk., north of Hamburg, Ger.

Lt. Ralph Hofer, 2 FW-190, Air, unk., east of Hamburg, Ger.

Lt. Thomas E. Fraser, FW-190, Air, unk., as above.

Lt. Frank Speer, ME-109, Air, unk., as above.

335FS. *Lt. Frank Jones,* U/I E/A, Air, unk., unk.

Lt. James W. Russell, ME-109, Air, 1025 hrs., Hamburg–Lubeck area, Ger.

336FS. *Capt. Willard Millikan,* FW-190, Air, unk., F.O. 349show.

5-25-44 336FS. *Maj. James Goodson,* FW-190, Air, 1000 hrs., Strasbourg area, Fr.

Capt. Joseph H. Bennett, 2 ME-109, Air, unk., Strasbourg area, Fr.

Lt. Thomas McDill, 2 ME-109, Air, unk., Strasbourg area, Fr.

5-28-44 334FS. *Capt. Woodrow Sobanski,* ME-109, Air, unk., Magdeburg area, Ger.

Lt. Ralph Hofer, ME-109, Air, as above.

Maj. Michael McPharlin, ME-109, Air, as above.

Lt. Grover Siems, FW-190, Air, as above.

Lt. Mark H. Kolter, ME-109, Air, as above.

Lt. Joseph Lang, ME-109, ½ ME-109 (shared unk. P-38 pilot), 1½ Air, unk., Magdeburg area, Ger.

Lt. Robert P. Kenyon, ME-109, Air, unk., as above.

5-29-44 334FS. *Lt. Orrin Snell,* ME-109, Air, unk., Cammin, ?.

Lt. Ralph Hofer, 3 HE-177, ½ 2 HE-177 (shared Speer), All on Ground, 1400 hrs., Mackfitz A/D, Ger.

Lt. Frank Speer, 2 HE-177, ½ 2 HE-177 (shared Hofer), All on Ground, as above.

Maj. Michael McPharlin, DO-18, on water, unk., Dieuenew Seaplane base, Ger.

Lt. Mark Kolter, AR-196, on water, unk., as above.

335FS. *Capt. Bernard McGrattan,* FW-190, Air, 1500 hrs., Laaland Is., ?.

Lt. Robert C. Church, ME-109E, Air, 1500 hrs., Laaland Is., ?.

336FS. *Col. Donald Blakeslee,* ME-410, Air, 1350 hrs., north of Falkenburg, ?.

Lt. Donald Emerson, ½ ME-410 (shared Netting), Air, as above.

Lt. Conrad J. Netting, ½ ME-410 (shared Emerson), Air, as above.

5-30-44 334FS. *Lt. Ralph Hofer,* 2 FW-190, ½ FW-190 (shared Jones), 2½ Ground, 1120 hrs., Oscherleben A/D, Ger.

Lt. James Scott, ME-109, Air, unk., Dessau area, Ger.

Lt. Thomas S. Sharpe, 2 FW-190, Ground, unk., Oscherleben, Ger.

335FS.   *Lt. Frank Jones,* FW-190, ½ FW-190 (shared Hofer), 1½ Ground, 1120 hrs., Oscherleben A/D, Ger.

336FS.   *Lt. Oscar F. Lejeunesse,* ME-109, Air, 1115 hrs., Magdeburg, Ger.

5-31-44 334FS.   *Lt. Ralph Hofer,* 3 BU-181, Ground, 1220 hrs., Luxeuil A/D, Fr.

6-6-44   334FS.   *Lt. Jack T. Simon,* ½ FW-190 (shared Fernandez), Air, 1230–1245 hrs., Evereux A/D, Fr.

Lt. Joseph P. Fernandez, ¼ FW-190 (shared Simon), Air, as above.

Lt. James Scott, FW-190, Air, 1230–1245 hrs., Evereux A/D, Fr.

Lt. Shelton Monroe, FW-190, Air, as above.

Lt. Grover Siems, FW-190, Air, as above.

6-20-44 334FS.   *Lt. Willard Gillette,* ½ JU-88 (shared Shilke), Ground, DO-217, Ground, JU-88, Air, 1010 hrs., Neubrandenburg A/D, Ger., 0930 hrs., Neubrandenburg A/D, Ger., 0930 hrs., east of Pasewalk, Ger.

Lt. Shelton Monroe, ME-109, Air, 0930–0945 hrs., east of Pasewalk, Ger.

Lt. Robert A. Dickmeyer, ME-109, Air, 0915 hrs., east of Pasewalk, Ger.

Capt. Thomas E. Joyce, ½ ME-109 (shared Cwiklinski), Air, 0930–0945 hrs., east of Pasewalk, Ger.

Lt. Arthur C. Cwiklinski, ½ ME-109 (shared Joyce), Air, as above.

Lt. Donald Malmsten, JU-88, Air, 0930 hrs., east of Pasewalk, Ger.

335FS.   *Capt. George Stanford,* ½ ME-210 (shared Godwin), Air, 0925 hrs., Ratzeburger Lake area, Ger.

Lt. Lester B. Godwin, ½ ME-210 (shared Stanford), Air, as above.

Capt. Frank Jones, ME-109, Air, 0920 hrs., Stettin Area, Ger.

L/Col. James Clark, ME-410, Air, as above.

Lt. George W. Cooley, ME-109, Air, 0920 hrs., Politz area, Ger.

336FS.   *Lt. Otey M. Glass,* ME-109, Air, 0930 hrs., south of Anklan, Ger.

Lt. Charles H. Shilke, DO-217, ½ JU-88 (shared Gillette), 1½ Ground, 1010 hrs., Neubrandenburg A/D, Ger.

Lt. Donald Emerson, FW-190, Air, 0930 hrs., south of Anklan, Ger.

Lt. Ferris S. Harris, DO-217, Ground, 0955–1010 hrs., Neubrandenburg A/D, Ger.

6-21-44 334FS.   *Lt. Joseph Lang,* ME-109, Air, 1145 hrs., 50 mi. s/w of Warsaw, Pol.

335FS.   *Capt. Frank Jones,* ME-109, Air, as above.

7-2-44   334FS.   *Capt. Howard Hively,* 2 ME-109, Air, 1045 hrs., over Budapest, Hungary.

Lt. Grover Siems, ME-109, Air, 1045 hrs., near Budapest, Hung.

Capt. William F. Hedrick, ME-109, Air, 1015 hrs., near Budapest, Hung.

335FS.   *Capt. Frank Jones,* ME-109, Air, unk., near Budapest, Hung.

336FS.   *Col. Donald Blakeslee,* ME-109, Air, unk., near Budapest, Hung.

Lt. Donald Emerson, ½ ME-109 (shared Higgins), Air, 1045 hrs., 10 mi. west of Budapest, Hung.

Capt. Joseph W. Higgins, ½ ME-109 (shared Emerson), Air, as above.

7-7-44   334FS.   *Capt. Thomas Joyce,* 2 ME-109, Air, 0915–0945 hrs., Aschersleben, Ger.

Lt. Preston B. Hardy, ME-109, Air, 0945 hrs., Blankenberg, ?.

Lt. Willard Gillette, ME-109, Air, 0925–0950 hrs., Blankenberg, ?.

Lt. John J. Scally, ME-410, Air, 0910 hrs., Sangerhausen, Ger.

335FS.   *Lt. John W. Goodwyn,* ME-109, Air, 0915 hrs., Bad Frankhausen, Ger.

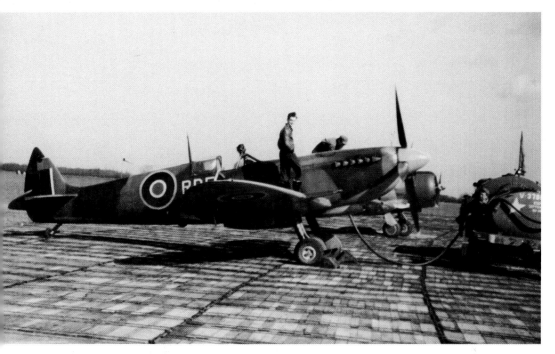

March, 1945: Visiting RAF Spitfire LF IX gets petrol at the transient hardstand by the Debden tower. Three-letter code group ahead of fuselage roundel denotes personal initials of a Wing Commander. (*Edward Richie*)

June, 1945: Red/White/Blue-cowled P-47 5F-R is one of eight 5th Emergency Rescue Squadron a/c attached to 4thFG for use as trainers to convert pilots to the type. The Malcolm-hooded bird retains the life raft containers under the wings for rescuing downed airmen in the sea. (*Edward Richie*)

May, 1945: Maj. Pierce W. McKennon runs up his WD-A 44–72308 RIDGE-RUN-NER III. A/C bears 20 white/red/black kill crosses of his victories at war's end. Note twin mirrors, red navigation light by emblem, red tape over gun camera orifice in wing root. (*Joseph Sills*)

Spring, 1945: VF-S 44-72181 SUNNY VIII is the mount of the group CO at this time, Col. Everett W. Stewart. Blue antiglare panel was applied to only two a/c, Stewart's and Maj. Glover's. (*Don Allen*)

April 5, 1944: Duane Beeson and his P-51B BOISE BEE just before he was shot down. Note the aircraft carries a splotchy two-toned olive drab finish. The propeller blades have seen some weather as well. (*Popperfoto*)

Circa April 1, 1944: Capt. Don S. Gentile and his VF-T 43-6913 SHANGRI-LA at the time he was close to tying Rickenbacker's WW1 score. (*USAF*)

Spitfire VB AV-D (D for Daley) was assigned to 335th's first commander, Maj. William J. Daley, ex-122 ES. He used it for about a month and a half on 4FG ops before returning to the U.S. in November 1942.

P-47D VF-G (G for Gover) was flown by the 336th's CO, Maj. Lee Gover, ex 133-ES. The a/c appears in its final markings prior to Gover's return to the U.S. after 257 combat sorties. A/C art by Sgt. Hutton.

P-47D QP-B (B for Beeson) in its markings after Maj. Duane W. Beeson's seventh victory in late January 1944. A/C art by S/Sgt. Don Allen.

P-51B QP-J in the livery of Maj. Howard D. Hively on June 6, 1944 (D-Day). That afternoon it was shot down with Maj. W. M. Sobanski (KIA) in the cockpit. The red rudder band seems to be pilot art rather than official marking. A/C art by S/Sgt. Don Allen.

Above, top to bottom:
P-51B WD-A of Maj. Pierce W. McKennon. "Mac" flew an A-coded a/c during all of his tours. He was an American Western history buff, hence the "cowboy on a mustang" motif. "Joe" was his CC, S/Sgt. Joe Sills. The a/c was lost on 5/9/44 with Lt. Waterman. A/C artist unknown.

P-51D QP-X was assigned to 4FG CO LtCol. Jack J. Oberhansly in early January 1945. Oberhansly was an ace and former squadron CO in the 78FG at Duxford. A/C art by S/Sgt. Don Allen.

P51-D VF-1 is believed to have been assigned to Lt. Douglas N. Groshong in the Spring of 1945. The a/c had post-VE underwing codes later. Note two red formation lights on fusilage side, and the red edge to unusual A.G. (antiglare) panel shaping. A/C art copied from a 334FS a/c painted by S/Sgt. Don Allen.

Sideview art © copyright Mike Bailey 1980

April 11, 1944: Two newly decorated heroes, Capt. Don S. Gentile and Col. Donald Blakeslee, after the Supreme Allied Commander, Gen. Eisenhower, had pinned the DSC on their tunics. (*USAF*)

April 11, 1944: The "Top Brass" of the AAF ETO gather on the Debden Officers' Club steps for their picture during Ike's visit. *Left to right*: B/Gen. Jesse Auton (65FW), Gen. Eisenhower (SACE), Lt/Gen. Carl Spaatz (USSAFE), Lt/Gen. James Doolittle (8AF), M/Gen. William Kepner (8FC), and Col. Don Blakeslee (4FG). (*USAF*)

Late August, 1944: 4th Group Commander, Col. Don Blakeslee, poses for the photographers in the cockpit of his P-51D WD-C 44-13779. Note the newly mounted K-14 computing gyro gunsight under the windscreen. (*USAF*)

ate June, 1944: Lt. James ane confers with the crew f his VF-J 44-13307 UTCH. Lack of fin fillet enotes early D-model. ote 500-lb. bombs by a/c. *dward Richie*)

March 23, 1945: A/C of the various fighter group commanders who met this date at Debden to discuss plans for Rhine River crossing operation. *Right to left*: WR-A 44-15625 MAN O WAR (Col. Kinnard), unknown, 5Q-Z (Col. John Henry), 5E-O (LtCol. Eugene Roberts), CL-P 44-72296 (LtCol. Elwyn Righetti), PI-Z 44-15069 JUDY (Col. Philip Tukey). (*Edward Richie*)

November, 1944: QP-B 44-13984 MEG belonged to Lt. Clarence Boretsky. Also parked on the mat south of the 334th shack is Lt. James Ayers's QP-*K* 43-6518.

	336FS.	*Lt. Gerald C. Chapman*, FW-190, Air, 0935 hrs., Bernberg area, Ger.

7-19-44 335FS. *Lt. Curtis Simpson*, ME-109, Air, unk., unk.

336FS. *Lt. Ira Grounds*, 2 ME-109, Air, 1000–1020 hrs., east of Munchen, Ger.

Lt. Francis M. Grove, ME-109, Air, 1000–1015 hrs., 30 mi. east of Munchen, Ger.

8-5-44 336FS. *Lt. Frederick Glover*, ME-109, Air, 1330 hrs., Gandeligen, Ger.

Capt. John Godfrey, 3 JU-52, Ground, ME-109, Air, 1345 hrs., s/e of Munden A/P, Ger., 1420 hrs., 20 mi. east of Osnabruck, Ger.

8-6-44 336FS. *Lt. Fred Glover*, ME-109, unk., unk., 20 mi. s/e of Berlin, Ger.

Capt. John Godfrey, ME-410, Air, 1350 hrs., 20 mi. s/e of Berlin, Ger.

Capt. Otey Glass, 2 JU-52, Ground, 1350 hrs., as above.

Lt. Joseph Patteeuw, ME-410, Ground, as above.

8-8-44 335FS. *Capt. Frank Jones*, JU-88, Ground, 1505 hrs., Stravanger/Sola A/D, Norway.

8-16-44 336FS. *Lt. Ira Grounds*, ME-109, Air, unk., unk.

8-18-44 334FS. *Lt. Preston Hardy*, ME-109, Air, 2nd mission, s/w of Beauvais, Fr.

Lt. Arthur Cwiklinski, 2 ME-109, Air, 2nd mission, as above.

Lt. William E. Whalen, ME-109, Air, 2nd mission, s/w of Beauvais, Fr.

335FS. *Lt. Brack Diamond*, ME-109, Air, as above.

Lt. Donald D. Perkins, ME-109, Air, as above.

Lt. Paul S. Iden, ME-109, Air, as above.

8-24-44 335FS. *Lt. Ted Lines*, 2 ME-109, Air, 1255 hrs., near Leer, s/e of Emden, Ger.

336FS. *Capt. John Godfrey*, 4 JU-52, Ground, unk., 8 mi. n/e of Nordhausen, Ger.

Lt. Melvin N. Dickey, 3 JU-52, Ground, as above.

Capt. Pierce Wiggin, JU-52, Ground, as above.

8-25-44 336FS. *Lt. Ira Grounds*, ME-109, Air, 1220 hrs., 10 mi. s/w of Rostock, Ger.

Lt. George H. Logan, ME-109, Air, as above.

Lt. Harry N. Hagan, ME-109, Air, as above.

9-1-44 334FS. *L/Col. Claiborne H. Kinnard*, ME-109, Air, unk., Halle, Ger.

L/Col. Claiborne H. Kinnard, ME-410, Ground, unk., Limburg A/D, Ger.

Lt. Leonard R. Werner, ME-109, Air, unk., Eisenach–Gotha area, Ger.

Capt. Gerald Montgomery, ME-109, Air, unk., Aschersleben area, Ger.

9-10-44 335FS. *Lt. Ted Lines*, 3 ME-109, JU-88, (4) Air, 1115 hrs., Strasbourg area, Fr.

9-11-44 335FS. *L/Col. Claiborne Kinnard*, ME-109, Air, ME-410, Ground, 1140 hrs., Halle area, Ger.

Lt. Richard J. Rinebolt, ME-109, Air, 1145 hrs., n/w of Naumburg, Ger.

Lt. George Cooley, 2 FW-190, Air, as above.

336FS. *Lt. Harry E. Dugan*, ME-109, Air, 1120 hrs., Korbach, Ger.

Lt. Joseph A. Joiner, ME-109, Air, as above.

Lt. Charles W. DuPree, 2 FW-190, Ground, 1120 hrs., Langensalza A/D, Ger.

F/O. Donald J. Pierini, 2 FW-190, Ground, as above.

Lt. *Francis Grove*, FW-190, Ground, as above.
Lt. *Henry A. Ingalls*, FW-190, Ground, as above.
Lt. *C. H. Patterson*, FW-190, Ground, as above.

9-12-44 334FS. Lt. *Robert Dickmeyer*, FW-190, ½ FW-190 (shared Hustwit), (1½) Air, 1230 hrs., Weisbaden, Ger.

335FS. Lt. *Albert J. Davis*, ½ ME-109 (shared Evans), Air, 1235 hrs., n/e of Frankfurt, Ger.
Lt. *Charles H. Evans*, ½ ME-109 (shared Davis), Air, as above.

336FS. Lt. *Van E. Chandler*, FW-190, Air, 1230 hrs., Weisbaden, Ger.
Lt. *James C. Lane*, 2 ME-109, Air, 1230 hrs., n/w of Frankfurt, Ger.
Lt. *Earl A. Quist*, ME-109, Air, as above.
Lt. *Gilbert Hunt*, ME-109, Air, as above.
Lt. *Earl F. Hustwit*, FW-190, ½ FW-190 (shared Dickmeyer), (1½) Air, 1230 hrs., Weisbaden, Ger.

9-13-44 334FS. Capt. *William B. Smith*, U/I T/E E/A, Ground, 1140 hrs., Schwabisch Hall A/D, south of Frankfurt, Ger.

335FS. Lt. *Brack Diamond*, 3 HS-123, (3) Ground, 1145 hrs., Gelcheim A/D, Ger.
F/O. *Charles E. Poage*, 3 HS-123, 3 Ground, as above.
Lt. *Wilbur Eaton*, HS-123, Ground, as above.
Lt. *George Ceglarski*, 2 U/I S/E Biplanes, Ground, as above.
L/Col. *Claiborne Kinnard*, 2 HS-123, (2) Ground, as above.

9-17-44 335FS. Capt. *Louis Norley*, FW-190, Air, 1345 hrs., Bocholt, Ger.
Lt. *Ted Lines*, 3 FW-190, Air, as above.
Lt. *Albert J. Davis*, 2 FW-190, Air, as above.

9-25-44 336FS. Lt. *Warren Williams*, JU-88, Ground, 1330 hrs., Bad Lippspringe, Ger.

9-27-44 334FS. Lt. *Arthur J. Senecal*, ME-109, Air, unk., Giessen area, Ger.

336FS. Capt. *John D. McFarlane*, FW-190, Air, 1030 hrs., 20 mi. s/w of Kassel, Ger.
Lt. *George C. Smith*, FW-190, ME-109, (2) Air, as above.
Lt. *Charles DuPree*, FW-190, Air, as above.

9-28-44 334FS. Lt. *David Howe*, FW-190, Air, unk., n/e of Kassel, Ger.

10-6-44 334FS. Lt. *Leonard Werner*, ME-109, Air, unk., Nauen, Ger.

335FS. Lt. *Elmer N. McCall*, ½ ME-410 (shared Lewis), Air, 1100 hrs., 10–20 mi. n/w of Heligoland Is., Ger.
Lt. *Ralph E. Lewis*, ½ ME-410 (shared McCall), Air, as above.

336FS. Lt. *Joseph Joiner*, ME-109, Air, 1200 hrs., 15 mi. east of Berlin, Ger.

10-9-44 335FS. Capt. *Ted Lines*, ME-109, Air, ME-109, Ground, (2) 1515 hrs., s/w of Gedern, Ger.

10-14-44 334FS. Capt. *Joseph L. Lang*, 2 ME-109, Air, 1310 hrs., Nancy–St. Dizier area, Fr.

10-26-44 335FS. Capt. *Ted Lines*, 2 FW-190, Air, 1425 hrs., Osnabruck, Ger.

11-2-44 335FS. Capt. *Louis Norley*, ME-163, Air, 1215 hrs., s/e of Leipzig, Ger.
Lt. *Charles L. Brock*, ME-109, Air, 1215 hrs., Merseburg, Ger.
Lt. *John E. Kolbe*, ME-109, Air, 1220 hrs., Leipzig, Ger.

336FS. Capt. *Fred Glover*, ME-163, Air, 1415 hrs., east of Leipzig, Ger.

11-6-44 334FS. Lt. *Jack D. McFadden*, ME-109, Air, 1110–1125 hrs., Rheine, Ger.

336FS. Lt. *Van Chandler*, FW-190, Air, 1130 hrs., Minden area, Ger.

11-18-44 334FS. Maj. *Howard Hively*, ME-262, Ground, unk., Leipheim A/D, Ger.
Maj. *Robert A. Ackerly*, ME-262, Ground, as above.
F/O. *Charles W. Harre*, 2 ME-262, (2) Ground, as above.
Lt. *Carl F. Brown*, 2 ME-262, (2) Ground, as above.
Lt. *Carl G. Payne*, ME-262, Ground, as above.

5FS. *Lt. Wilbur Eaton*, ME-262, Ground, 1300 hrs., Leipheim A/D, Ger.
Lt. John Kolbe, ME-262, Ground, as above.
Capt. William C. Anderson, ME-262, Ground, as above.
Capt. John C. Fitch, ½ ME-262 (shared Creamer), Air, 1245 hrs., 1 mi. south of Leipheim A/D, Ger.
Lt. John N. Creamer, ½ ME-262 (shared Fitch), Air, as above.

336FS. *Lt. Francis Grove*, ME-262, Ground, unk., Leipheim A/D, Ger.
Lt. Donald Pierini, ME-262, Ground, as above.
Capt. Donald Emerson, ME-109, Ground, as above.

11-21-44 335FS. *Lt. John Kolbe*, ME-109, Air, 1230 hrs., n/w of Merseburg, Ger.
336FS. *Capt. Fred Glover*, 3 ME-109, Air, 1140 hrs., 15 mi. west of Merseburg, Ger.
Lt. Douglas N. Groshong, 2 ME-109, Air, as above.

12-2-44 334FS. *Lt. Jack McFadden*, FW-190, Air, 1245 hrs., Hottenback area, Ger.
12-5-44 334FS. *Maj. Howard Hively*, FW-190, Air, 1115 hrs., n/w of Nordhorn, Ger.

12-18-44 334FS. *Lt. Henry E. Clifton*, ME-109, Air, 1435 hrs., 30 mi. east of Dortmund, Ger.
335FS. *Capt. William O'Donnell*, ½ FW-190 (shared Stallings), ME-109, (1½) Air, 1415 & 1445 hrs., both n/e of Frankfurt, Ger.
Lt. Robert L. Stallings, ½ FW-190 (shared O'Donnell), Air, 1415hrs., n/e of Frankfurt, Ger.

12-24-44 335FS. *Lt. Calvin W. Willruth*, ME-109, Air, 1430 hrs., 20 mi. west of Giessen, Ger.

12-25-44 334FS. *Lt. Timothy J. Cronin*, ½ FW-190 (shared McKennon), Air, 1200–1215 hrs., 10–15 mi. south of Bonn, Ger.
Lt. Timothy Cronin, FW-190, Air, 1200 hrs., 15 mi. south of Bonn, Ger.
Lt. Victor R. Rentschler, FW-190, ½ ME-109 (shared Hoelscher), (1½) Air, both 1200–1230 hrs., both n/e of Trier, Ger.
Lt. William B. Hoelscher, ½ ME-109 (shared Rentschler), FW-190, (1½) Air, both 1200–1230 hrs., both in Trier area, Ger.
335FS. *Capt. Pierce W. McKennon*, ½ FW-190 (shared Cronin), Air, 1200–1215 hrs., 10–15 mi. south of Bonn, Ger.
Lt. Charles Poage, 2 FW-190, Air, unk., unk.
336FS. *Maj. Fred Glover*, FW-190D, Air, 1230 hrs., s/w of Koblenz, Ger.
Lt. Van Chandler, FW-190, ME-109, (2) Air, 1230 hrs., s/w of Koblenz, Ger., 40 mi. from Leacher See.
Capt. Donald Emerson, 2 FW-190, (2) Air, 1230 hrs., s/w of Koblenz, Ger.

1-1-45 336FS. *Lt. Donald Pierini*, ME-109, Air, 1230 hrs., Ulzen area, Ger.
Lt. Franklin W. Young, ME-109, ME-262, Air, Air, as above.
Lt. Van Chandler, ME-109, Air, as above.
Lt. Gilbert L. Kesler, ½ ME-109 (shared Wallace), Air, as above.
Lt. Alvin O. Wallace, ½ ME-109 (shared Kesler), Air, as above.

1-2-45 334FS. *Lt. Carl Payne*, ½ ME-109 (shared Rentschler), ½ ME-109 (shared Senecal), (½ & ½) Air, 1400 hrs., n/e of Koblenz–Westerburg, Ger.
Lt. Victor Rentschler, ½ ME-109 (shared Payne), Air, as above.
Lt. Arthur Senecal, ½ ME-109 (shared Payne), Air, as above.

1-16-45 334FS. *Lt. James W. Ayers*, ½ HE-177 (shared Kennedy), Ground, 1400 hrs., Neuburg A/D, Ger. ?
Lt. Michael Kennedy, ½ HE-177 (shared Ayers), Ground, as above.
Lt. Carl F. Brown, ½ ME-262 (shared Jahnke), Ground, as above.
Lt. Jerome E. Jahnke, ½ ME-262 (shared Brown), Ground, as above.

336FS.   *Maj. Fred Glover,* 2 FW-190, ME-109, (3) Ground, unk., Neuhausen A/D, near Cottbus A/D, Ger.
Lt. Henry A. Kaul, FW-109, Ground, as above.
Lt. Van Chandler, 3 FW-190, JU-87, (4) Ground, as above.
Capt. Leroy A. Carpenter, ME-109, Ground, as above.
Lt. Douglas Groshong, FW-190, Ground, as above.
Lt. William D. Riedel, FW-190, Ground, as above.
Capt. Carl R. Alfred, FW-190, Ground, as above.
Lt. Richard J. Corbett, 3 FW-190, Ground, as above.
Lt. Alvin Wallace, FW-190, Ground, as above.
Capt. Kendall Carlson, FW-190, JU-88, (2) Ground, as above.
Lt. Gilbert Kesler, FW-190, Ground, as above.
Lt. Thomas A. McCord, HE-177, FW-190, (2) Ground, as above.
Capt. Joseph Joiner, 4 FW-190, (4) Ground, as above.
Lt. Harry Hagan, JU-87, Ground, as above.

2-20-45   336FS.   *Capt. Joseph Joiner,* FW-190, ½ FW-190 (shared Carlson), (1½) Air, 1318 hrs., 15 mi. north of Ingolstadt, Ger.
Capt. Kendall Carlson, ½ FW-190 (shared Joiner), Air, as above.

2-22-45   336FS.   *Maj. Fred Glover,* ME-109, DO-217, (2) Ground, unk., Halberstadt A/D, Ger.
Maj. John McFarlane, DO-217, Ground, as above.
Lt. Harold R. Crawford, 3 FW-190, Ground, as above.
Capt. Carl Alfred, ME-410, DO-217, (2) Ground, as above.

2-25-45   334FS.   *Lt. Donald Malmsten,* ½ FW-190 (shared O'Bryan), Air, 1030 hrs., Dessau area, Ger.
Lt. William C. O'Bryan, ½ FW-190 (shared Malmsten), Air, as above.
Lt. Arthur R. Bowers, ME-110, FW-190, ME-410, (3) Ground, 1100 hrs., Rohrensee A/D, Ger.
Lt. Carl Payne, ME-262, Air, ½ ME-410 (shared Bell), Ground 1040–1100 hrs., 4 mi. s/e of Naunburg, Ger., 1100 hrs., Rohrensee A/D, Ger.
Capt. Thomas R. Bell, FW-190, Ground, 2 ME-110 (shared Denson), Ground, ½ ME-410 (shared Payne), Ground, (3½) 1100 hrs., Rohrensee A/D, Ger.
Lt. Gordon A. Denson, 2 ME-110 (shared Bell), Ground, 1100 hrs., Rohrensee A/D, Ger.

336FS.   *Lt. Richard Corbett,* HE-111, Ground, unk., Kothen A/D near Dessau, Ger.
Capt. Kendall Carlson, U/I 4/E E/A, Ground, as above.
Lt. James E. Hileman, U/I 4/E E/A, Ground, as above.
Lt. Paul M. Morgan, ½ FW-190 (shared Brooker), Air, 1030 hrs., Kothen A/D near Dessau, Ger.
Lt. Beachem O. Brooker, ½ FW-190 (shared Morgan), Air, as above.

2-27-45   334FS.   *Lt. James Ayers,* 3 U/I T/E E/A, ½ JU-52 (shared Voyles), (3½) Ground, 1315 hrs., Weimar A/D, Ger.
Lt. Robert S. Voyles, ½ JU-52 (shared Ayers), Ground, as above.
Lt. Carl Payne, 2 ME-108, Ground, as above.
Lt. Jack McFadden, ME-108, JU-87, (2) Ground, as above.
Lt. Donald Malmsten, 3 U/I S/E E/A, ME-109, 2 JU-88, (6) Ground, as above.
Lt. Leo C. Garvin, ME-108, Ground, as above.
Lt. Charles Harre, ME-108, Ground, as above.
Capt. Henry Clifton, 3 ME-108, Ground, as above.

Lt. William O. Antonides, 2 JU-88, Ground, as above.

Capt. Tom Bell, 3 ME-109, Ground, as above.

Maj. Gerald Montgomery, DO-217, ME-108, JU-87, (3) Ground, as above.

Lt. Lewis F. Wells, ME-109, Ground, as above.

336FS. *Maj. Fred Glover*, 2 ME-109, FW-190, (3) Ground, 1315 hrs., Weimar A/D, Ger.

Maj. John McFarlane, 2 ME-108, unk., as above.

Lt. Gilbert Kesler, 2 JU-52, ME-109, (3) Ground, as above.

Lt. Robert O. Davis, JU-88, Ground, as above.

Lt. Melvin N. Dickey, JU-87, C-47, (2) Ground, as above.

Lt. Earl Hustwit, ME-410, Ground, as above.

Lt. Harry L. Davis, ME-108, Ground, as above.

Lt. Douglas P. Pedersen, U/I T/E E/A, Ground, as above.

Lt. Harold Crawford, U/I T/E E/A, Ground, as above.

3-19-45   334FS. *Maj. Louis Norley*, ME-109, Air, 1615 hrs., 10 mi. s/e of Frankfurt, Ger.

3-21-45   334FS. *Lt. Donald Malmsten*, 2 ME-109, Ground, 1000 hrs., Achmer A/D, Ger.

Lt. Philio M. Burney, ME-109, Ground, as above.

Lt. William Hoelscher, FW-190, Ground, as above.

335FS. *Capt. William O'Donnell*, ME-262, Ground, as above.

336FS. *Capt. Carl Alfred*, 3 DO-217, (3) Ground, as above.

Lt. Wilmer W. Collins, ME-410, Ground, as above.

3-22-45   334FS. *Lt. Jerome Jahnke*, FW-190, Air, 1300 hrs., Eggersdorf A/D, Ger.

Lt. Fred E. Farington, FW-190, Air, 1300–1310 hrs., Furstenwalde A/D, Ger.

336FS. *L/Col. Sidney S. Woods*, 5 FW-190, (5) Air, 1300–1320 hrs., Furstenwalde A/D area, Ger.

Lt. William Riedel, 2 FW-190, Air, 1300 hrs., n/e of Ruhland, Ger.

Lt. Harry Hagan, FW-190, Air, 1320 hrs., s/e of Berlin, Ger.

Lt. Robert O. Davis, FW-190, Air, 1320 hrs., Furstenwalde A/D, Ger.

4-4-45   334FS. *Lt. Michael Kennedy*, ¼ ME-262 (shared Baugh, Ayer, Frederick), Air, 1000 hrs., 5 mi. south of Ludwigslust, Ger.

Capt. Robert H. Kanaga, ME-262, Air, 0945 hrs., Schwerin, Ger.

Lt. Raymond A. Dyer, ME-262, Air, 0950 hrs., 10 mi. s/e of Parchim, Ger.

336FS. *Lt. Harold H. Fredericks*, ¼ ME-262 (shared Ayer, Baugh, Kennedy), 1000 hrs., 5 mi. south of Ludwigslust, Ger.

Lt. William H. Ayer, ¼ ME-262 (shared Fredericks, Baugh, Kennedy), as above.

Lt. Donald P. Baugh, ¼ ME-262 (shared Fredericks, Ayer, Kennedy), as above.

4-7-45   334FS. *Maj. Louis Norley*, FW-190, Air, 1215 hrs., Dannerburg area, Ger. (FW-190 collided with B-17 avoiding Norley's attack).

Lt. Ralph H. Buchanan, ME-109, Air, 1230 hrs., s/e of Krummel, Ger.

Lt. William Hoelscher, ME-109, Air, as above.

Lt. James Ayers, ME-109, Air, 1215 hrs., n/e of Duneberg, Ger.

336FS. *Lt. William Riedel*, ME-109, Air, 1315 hrs., s/e of Neumunster, Ger. (Possibly shared victory).

Lt. Marvin L. Davis, ME-109, Air, 1330 hrs., s/w of Bremen, Ger. (Possibly shared victory).

4-9-45   335FS.   *Maj. Pierce McKennon,* 2 JU-52, ME-410, (3) Ground, 1645–1715 hrs., Munich–Brunnthal A/D, Ger.
Lt. Henry A. Lee, ME-410, Ground, as above.
Lt. Loton D. Jennings, JU-88, Ground, as above.
Lt. Leslie I. Burgess, JU-88, Ground, as above.
Lt. Thomas H. Elffner, 2 ME-410, Ground, as above.
Lt. Mack D. Heaton, U/I S/E E/A, Fi-156, (2) Ground, as above.
Lt. Robert C. Hunter, U/I T/E E/A, Ground, 1645–1715 hrs., Munich–Brunnthal A/D, Ger.
Lt. Robert C. Bucholz, 3 U/I E/A, (3) Ground, as above.

4-10-45 334FS.   *Maj. Gerald Montgomery,* ME-410, Ground, 1600 hrs., Wittstock A/D, Ger.
Lt. Jack McFadden, JU-88, Ground, as above.
Lt. Donald G. Lowther, JU-52, Ground, as above.
Lt. Robert J. Miller, U/I T/E E/A, Ground, as above.

           336FS.   *Lt. Wilmer W. Collins,* ME-262, Air, 1445 hrs., Lubeck, Ger.

4-13-45 335FS.   *Capt. William O'Donnell,* AR-196, on water, 1615 hrs., Ratzeburger Lake, Ger.
Lt. Loton Jennings, HE-115, on water, as above.

4-16-45 334FS.   *Maj. Louis Norley,* 2 FW-190, JU-52, U/I T/E E/A, (4) Ground, 1705–1745 hrs., Gablingen A/D, Ger.
Lt. Gordon Denson, 2 FW-190, ME-410, HE-177, (4) Ground, as above.
Lt. Raymond Dyer, FW-190, ME-109, U/I T/E E/A, (3) Ground, as above.
Lt. Charles Harre, ME-109, U/I T/E E/A, (2) Ground, as above.
Lt. William J. Dvorak, 2 U/I T/E E/A, (2) Ground, as above.
Lt. William Antonides, 2 ME-109, FW-190, ME-410, U/I S/E E/A, (5) Ground, as above.
Lt. James Ayers, ME-109, U/I T/E E/A, FW-190, (3) Ground, as above.
Lt. Arthur Bowers, 2 ME-109, JU-88, (3) Ground, as above.
Lt. Kenneth G. Helfrecht, 2 ME-410, 2 FW-190, HE-177, (5) Ground, as above.
Lt. Ralph Buchanan, FW-190, ME-410, (2) Ground, as above.
Lt. Marvin W. Arthur, ½ FW-190 (shared Spencer), ME-109, Ground, as above.
Lt. Milton L. Spencer, ½ FW-190 (shared Arthur), Ground, as above.
Lt. William G. Spencer, ME-109, FW-190, U/I T/E E/A, (3) Ground, as above.
Lt. Donald Lowther, U/I T/E E/A, Ground, 1705–1745 hrs., Gablingen A/D, Ger.
Lt. William O'Bryan, 3 U/I T/E E/A, (3) Ground, as above.
Lt. Paul E. Burnett, U/I T/E E/A, Ground, as above.
Lt. Michael Kennedy, U/I S/E E/A, Ground, as above.

           335FS.   *Maj. Pierce McKennon,* 2 DO-217, U/I T/E E/A, (3) Ground, 1500 hrs., Three A/Ds (Kbely, Cakovice, Letnany), Prague, Czech.
Lt. Robert L. Couse, 2 DO-217, Ground, as above.
Lt. Robert Hunter, 2 DO-217, JU-88, (3) Ground, as above.
Capt. William O'Donnell, 2 U/I T/E E/A, (2) Ground, as above.
Lt. Loton Jennings, 2 DO-217, 2 ME-110, (4) Ground, as above.
Lt. George D. Green, U/I T/E E/A, 2 JU-88, DO-217, (4) Ground, as above.

Lt. Howard B. Miller, JU-52, DO-217, (2) Ground, as above.

Lt. Oliver B. Bucher, 2 JU-52, ME-410, (3) Ground, as above.

F/O. Lucien W. Freeman, HE-177, Ground, as above.

Lt. James E. Halligan, FW-190, JU-52, U/I T/E E/A, JU-88, (4) Ground, as above.

Lt. William D. Henderson, U/I T/E E/A, Ground, as above.

Lt. Wade F. Underwood, U/I S/E E/A, FW-190, ME-410, (3) Ground, as above.

Lt. Charles B. Greenlese, U/I T/E E/A, Ground, as above.

336FS.   *Lt. Douglas Pedersen,* 4 JU-52, 3 ME-110, U/I T/E E/A, (8) Ground, as above.

Capt. Leroy Carpenter, ME-410, Ground, as above.

Lt. William H. Hastings, ME-110, Ground, as above.

Lt. Melvin C. Franklin, 2 JU-52, Ground, as above.

Lt. John P. Murchake, 2 JU-88, Ground, as above.

Lt. Beachem Brooker, 2 ME-410, Ground, as above.

Lt. Marvin Davis, ME-110, Ground, 1500 hrs., Three A/Ds, Prague, Czech.

Lt. Harold Fredericks, ME-110, 2 JU-88, (3) Ground, as above.

Lt. Wilmer Collins, ME-109, DO-217, (2) Ground, as above.

F/O. Donald Baugh, 5 JU-88, Ground, as above.

Lt. William B. Meredith, ½ ME-109 (shared Hagan), Ground, unk., U/I A/D 10 mi. s/w of Pilzen, Ger.

Capt. Harry Hagan, ½ ME-109 (shared Meredith), Ground, unk., as above.

4-17-45   336FS.   *Maj. Fred Glover,* JU-87, Ground, unk., Pilzen A/D, Ger.

Lt. Wilmer Collins, ME-110, Ground, unk., as above.

Lt. William Meredith, U/I T/E E/A, Ground, unk., as above.

Lt. Douglas Groshong, ME-110, Ground, unk., as above.

4-25-45   334FS.   *Lt. William Hoelscher,* probably destroyed a ME-262 in the air at 0945 hrs., at Prague/Ruzyne A/D, Czech., before he was hit by AA. and bailed out.

Finie la guerre!

4th Fighter Group Personnel Losses

LEGEND

1. The date of the personnel loss. All dates in the appendices are in the U.S. civil date style—month/day/year. The losses are listed chronologically.
2. The casualty's name, with the last name first.
3. The rank of the casualty at the time of the loss.
4. The unit the casualty was assigned to at the time of loss.
5. The casualty's fate: KIA (killed in action), KIFA (killed in flying accident), WIA (wounded in action), POW (prisoner of war, returned after VE-Day), Evader (downed in enemy territory and eluded capture to return; usually the pilot did not go back into combat until the occupied peoples who aided him were liberated). Internees did not go back into combat after exchange to the Allied powers. Wounded pilots resumed combat when they were declared fit.
6. The location and time of the loss.
7. Brief details of the loss.
8. The type, serial number, and code letters of the a/c lost with the casualty, where this is known.

9-21-42   *Slater, John T.*—2Lt., 335FS—KIA—Overflakee Island, Neth.

9-26-42   *Brettell, Edward G.*—Flt. Lt., 133 Sq. RAF—POW/KIA—Executed by Germans on 3-24-44 for part in Great Escape of 76 POWs from Stalag Luft III. He was Stalag camp escape-map maker—Morlaix, Fr.—Spitfire IX BS313.

9-26-42   *Baker, William H.*—P/O, 133 Sq. RAF—KIA—Morlaix, Fr.—Spitfire IX BS446.

9-26-42   *Cook, Charles A.*—Capt. 133 Sq. RAF—POW—Morlaix, Fr.—Spitfire IX BR640.

9-26-42   *Jackson, Marion E.*—Capt. 133 Sq. RAF—POW—Morlaix, Fr.—Spitfire IX BS279.

9-26-42   *Middleton, George H.*—Lt. 133 Sq. RAF—POW—Morlaix, Fr.—Spitfire IX BS301.

9-26-42   *Neville, Gene P.*—Lt. 133 Sq. RAF—KIA—Morlaix, Fr.—Spitfire IX BS140.

9-26-42   *Ryerson, Leonard T.*—Lt. 133 Sq. RAF—KIA—Morlaix, Fr.—Spitfire IX BS275.

9-26-42   *Smith, Dennis D.*—Lt. 133 Sq. RAF—KIA—Morlaix, Fr.—Spitfire IX BS137.

9-26-42   *Smith, Robert E.*—2Lt. 133 Sq. RAF—Evader—Morlaix, Fr.—Escaped, back to visit Debden on 2-9-43—Spitfire IX BS447.

9-26-42   *Sperry, George B.*—Lt. 133 Sq. RAF—POW—Morlaix, Fr.—Spitfire IX BR638.

9-26-42   *Wright, Gil P.*—Lt. 133 Sq. RAF—POW—Morlaix, Fr.—Spitfire IX BS138.

10-20-42 *Seaman, Anthony J.*—Lt. 334FS—KIA—10 mi. east of Harwich, UK. at 1430 hrs., on convoy patrol with Hopson, had engine trouble, exploded in mid-air, and crashed into the sea.—Spitfire VB.

11-26-42 *Sprague, Robert S.*—Capt. 334FS—KIFA—Local area in UK—Crashed and killed on non-operational flight—Spitfire VB.

1-22-43 *Grimm, Chester P.*—2Lt. 335FS—KIA—Dunkirk/St. Omer area, Fr. at approx. 1500 hrs.—Hit by Flak—Spitfire VB.

2-1-43 *Mitchellweis, John, Jr.*—2Lt. 336 FS—KIFA—8 mi. n/w of Debden near Duxford, Essex, UK. at 1410 hrs.—Caught fire at 5000 ft., bailed out, chute pulled off, fell to his death.—P-47C 41-6200 "OO."

2-5-43 *Kelly, William P.*—Capt. 335FS—KIA—Walcheren Island, Neth. at 1200 hrs.—Hit by ship Flak, went into sea from 1200 ft. with his A/C.—Spitfire VB.

2-13-43 *Powell, Jap A.*—2Lt. 336 FS—KIA—North Sea off East Coast, UK. at 1525 hrs.—On convoy patrol, had engine trouble, bailed out too low, drowned before rescue.—Spitfire VB AR341.

3-12-43 *Anderson, Hazen S.*—Lt. 336FS—POW—10 mi. n/w of St. Omer, Fr. at approx. 1630 hrs.—Bailed out—Spitfire VB BL240.

4-3-43 *Smolinsky, Frank J.*—Lt. 335FS—KIA—Sawbridgeworth A/D, Hertford, UK.—Returning from forward base, crashed in flames off take-off.—P-47C 41-6181 WD-D.

4-15-43 *Anderson, Stanley M.*—Capt. 334FS—KIA—In North Sea off coast between Ostend and Blankenberghe, Belg. at approx. 1700 hrs.—In combat with FW-190s at time.—P-47C 41-6407 QP-E.

4-15-43 *McMinn, Richard D.*—Capt. 334FS—KIA—In North Sea 5 mi. off coast near Ostend, Belg. at approx. 1700 hrs.—Hit by FW-190 fire, a P-47 was reported in flames.—P-47C 41-6204 QP-M.

4-27-43 *Wilkinson, James W.*—Lt. 334FS—WIFA—Castle Camps, Essex, UK. at 1020 hrs.—Tail of A/C cut off by Lt. Chatterly in mock dogfight at 8000 ft., bailed out, 3-chute panels tore, wrenched or broke back, off operations for months, later joined 78FG.—P-47C 41-6405 QP-S?.

5-4-43 *Lutz, John F.*—1 Lt. 334FS—KIA—2 mi. south of Flushing, Neth. at approx. 1845 hrs.—Engine smoked and lost speed, went into North Sea 55 mi. east of Clacton, UK., bailed out too late, chute not seen to open, seen in water with face awash, not rescued, no trace.—P-47C 41-6196 QP-P.

5-18-43 *Boock, Robert A.—2Lt. 334FS—KIA—In North Sea off coast between Knocke & Blankenberghe, Belg. at 1702 hrs.—Shot down into sea.—P-47C QP-S.*

5-21-43 *MacFarlane, Leland L.*—2 Lt. 334FS—KIA—Near Ghent, Belg. at approx. 1350 hrs.—Last seen following E/A inland after fight near Ghent.—P-47D 42-7920 QP-N.

5-21-43 *Morgan, William Brewster*—Lt. 334FS—POW—North Sea off Ostend, Belg. at approx. 1350 hrs.—Shot up by E/A, ditched in sea, wounded in face and foot.—P-47D 42-8644? QP-U.

5-21-43 *Whitlow, Gordon H.*—Lt. 334FS—KIA—Near Ghent, Belg. at approx. 1350 hrs.—Last seen following E/A inland after fight near Ghent, buried in France.—P-47C 41-6406 QP-H.

6-14-43 *King, Garrett C.*—Lt. 334FS—KIFA—Near Swaffham, UK. at 1435 hrs.—Practicing homing with MOR, flew into thunderhead and struck by lightning, crashed in flames.—P-47 QP-T.

6-19-43 *Castle, Vincent R.*—Lt. 334FS—KIFA—Debden base, Essex, UK. at 1625 hrs.—In landing pattern, flew past A Flt. line low and climbing, reached top of bank over E-W runway road near E. end of runway, stalled, dove straight in and exploded.—P-47D 42-7881 QP-E.

7-14-43 *Wortman, Ward K.*—Lt. 335FS—KIA—In France, LeTreport to Sangette area at approx. 0750 hrs.—Not seen after E/A attack.—P-47D 42-7939 WD-Z.

7-28-43   *Ayres, Henry L. Jr.*—Lt. 336FS—POW—In Belgium at approx. 1220 hrs.— heard to call May-Day over Belg., thought to have bailed out.—P-47C 41-6238 VF-?.

7-30-43   *Merritt, Frederick D.*—Lt. 335FS—KIA—?—Either hit by B-17 fire or followed ME-109 down which his leader, Don Young, had shot at. Not seen after attack on ME-109.—P-47C 41-6248 WD-?.

8-16-43   *Matthews, Joseph G.*—1Lt. 336FS—Evader—Last seen near St. Denis/L'Isle Adam, Fr. at 0920 hrs.—Not seen to go down, later returned to England in late 43.—P-47D 42-7949.

9-2-43   *Leaf, Dale B.*—1Lt. 334FS—KIA—Near Formerie, Fr. at approx. 1750 hrs.—Sqd. bounced by 22 E/A, 1 P-47 seen to dive vertical followed by 4 FW-190s.—P-47 (?) QP-I.

9-7-43   *Stanhope, Aubrey C.*—1 Lt. 335FS—POW—On show to Hulst, Belg. at approx. 0840 hrs.—A P-47 was seen diving chased by an FW-190, both A/C were hit by Flak as they dived.—P-47C 41-6207 WD-X.

9-9-43   *Fink, Frank M.*—1Lt. 335FS—POW—Near Paris, Fr. at approx. 0900 hrs.— Bailed out due to engine failure.—P-47C 41-6328.

10-8-43   *Smith, Clyde D.*—F/O. 334FS—POW—Near Meppel, Neth. at approx. 1430 hrs.—Bailed out, P-47 seen to dive vertical from 24000 ft., 2 chutes seen to open.—P-47D 42-7915 QP-U.

10-8-43   *Patterson, Robert G.*—Lt. 335FS—POW—Downed at 1440 hrs.—Not seen to go down, got by as evader for 2 months in Belg. & Neth.—P-47D 42-7911.

11-3-43   *Gallion, Frank D.*—F/O. 334FS—KIA—Near Hypolitushoef, Neth. at approx. 1230 hrs.—Downed on coast of Zuider Zee, not seen to go down.—P-47D 42-7924 QP-F.

11-3-43   *Moon, Ivan R.*—1Lt. 334FS—KIA—Near Opmeer, Neth. in Zuider Zee at approx. 1230 hrs.—Went down in flames into the Zee.—P-47C 41-6587 QP-M.

12-2-43   *McNabb, John P.*—F/O. 334FS—KIFA—Near Kenton, UK. at 1322 hrs.— On X-country flt., burst into flames in air, dove in at 40 deg. angle, scattered over 4 acres.—P-47C 41-6484 QP-L.

1-29-44   *Wyman, Burton C.*—Lt. 335FS—KIA—Not seen to go down—P-47D 42-75119 WD-N.

1-30-44   *Mead, Edwin R.*—Lt. 335FS—POW—In Lingen, Ger. area at approx. 1125 hrs.—Not seen to go down during fights in this area.—P-47D 42-8506 WD-B.

2-3-44   *Cox, William A.*—F/O. 334FS—KIA—Near Emden, Ger. at 1056 hrs.—Separated from Ldr. Sobanski due to clouds and icing. Not seen to go down.— P-47D 42-75254 QP-X.

2-6-44   *Ballew, Hubert N.*—2Lt. 335FS—POW—Over Paris, Fr. at approx. 1130 hrs.—Shot down by FW-190 and bailed out.—P-47D 42-8495 WD-W.

2-20-44   *Reed, Richard I.*—Lt. 335FS—KIA—n/e of Koblentz, Ger. at approx. 1500 hrs.—Shot down by E/A. Not seen to go down—P-47D 42-75051 WD-R.

2-24-44   *Sullivan, Joseph W.*—Lt. 335FS—KIA—n/w of Koblentz, Ger. at 1420 hrs.—Last seen in this area.—P-47C 41-6369 WD-Y.

2-28-44   *Frazer, Robert B.*—1Lt. 334FS—KIFA—Debden airfield at 1545 hrs.— Turning into field from west, stalled, flicked over, went straight in and exploded and burned.—P-51B 43-6656 QP-N.

3-2-44   *Villinger, George K.*—1Lt. 336FS—KIA—On show to Frankfurt, Ger.—data unk.—P-51B 43-6985.

3-3-44   *Herter, Glenn A.*—Lt. 336FS—KIA—Near Wittenberg, Ger. at approx. 1130 hrs.—Lured after low decoy at start of fight with 60-plus E/A, not seen after.—P-51B 43-6740 VF-R?.

3-3-44   *Garrison, Vermont*—Lt. 336FS—POW—Near Boulogne, Fr. at approx. 1410 hrs.—Hit by Flak crossing enemy coast on way home, bailed out okay.—P-51B 43-6871 VF-H?.

3-3-44   *Dunn, Phillip H.*—Capt. 336FS—POW—Near St. Peel, Fr. at approx. 1550 hrs.—Got lost on way home, no radio to cross Channel so he made for Spain, finished gas downing HE-111, bailed out 8 mi. from Spain. P-51B 43-6903 VF-Y?.

3-3-44   *Barnes, George W.*—Lt. 335FS—KIA—Last seen off Dutch coast on way home with motor cutting out badly at approx. 1215 hrs.—P-51B 43-6643 WD-L.

3-4-44   *Ellington, Paul M.*—Lt. 335FS—POW—Off Dutch coast at unk. time—heard to say over R/T that he had motor trouble, believed to be off Dutch coast at time.—P-51B 43-7004 WD-U.

3-4-44   *Ward, Hugh A.*—1Lt. 335FS—POW—Near Berlin, Ger. at 1300 hrs.—bounced by 20-plus E/A, the wing, tail, and canopy came off his P-51 in a dive on E/A.—P-51B 43-6810 WD-R.

3-4-44   *Richards, Robert H.*—Lt. 336FS—KIA—Near Framlingham, UK. at approx. 1545 hrs.—crashed and killed due to unk. causes while returning from a mission.—P-51B 43-6786 VF-?.

3-5-44   *Pisanos, Steve N.*—Capt. 334FS—Evader—10 mi. south of Le Havre near Angouleme/Limoges, Fr. at 1339 hrs.—tried to bail out and rode his A/C into a crash while half out of cockpit, survived okay and became an evader. Returned to Debden on 9-2-44.—P-51B 43-6798 QP-D.

3-6-44   *Messenger, Robert J.*—Lt. 336FS—POW—Not seen to go down—P-51B 43-6630.

3-6-44   *Manning, Cecil E.*—Capt. 335FS—POW—Near Sogal, Ger. at approx. 1350 hrs.—Bailed out after a slug from a DO-217 he was attacking drained his engine oil or coolant and his A/C started to burn at 3,000 ft.—P-51B 43-6887 WD-H.

3-6-44   *Whalen, Edmund D.*—1Lt. 334FS—KIA—In Nienburg, Ger. area at approx. 1350 hrs.—His A/C hit by debris of his exploding ME-110 kill. A back-pack chute seen to open in vicinity.—P-51B 43-6899 QP-O.

3-6-44   *Mills, Henry L.*—Maj. 334FS—POW—West of Brandenburg, Ger. near Berlin at approx. 1330 hrs.—reported over R/T that he had engine trouble and he was going to bail out. Chute not seen.—P-51B 43-6690 QP-Q.

3-8-44   *Edner, Selden R.*—Maj. 4HQ.—POW—In Berlin, Ger. area at approx. 1400 hrs.—not seen to go down, was leading Grp.—P-51B 43-6442 VF-?.

3-16-44   *Skilton, Ernest R.*—1Lt. 336FS—KIA—Details unknown. Large fight took place between Kaufburen and Hurn Lake west of Munich. Possibly lost then at approx. 1200 hrs.—P-51B 43-6652 VF-?.

3-18-44   *Sooman, Woodrow F.*—1Lt. 336FS.—POW—He aborted with a glycol coolant leak near Frankfurt, Ger. about 1400 hrs.—P-51B 43-6936 VF-D.

3-18-44   *Freeburger, Edward P.*—Lt. 335FS.—KIA—Near Nancy, Fr. at approx. 1435 hrs.—He reported 4 Huns on his and his leader, Capt. Smith's, tails, and was not heard from again.—P-51B 43-6460 WD-F.

3-21-44   *Brandenburg, James H.*—Lt. 335FS.—KIA—North of Bordeaux, Fr. at approx. 1400 hrs.—Bailed out. Chute reported to have opened at tree-top level.—P-51B 43-6641 WD-E.

3-21-44   *Carlow, Earle W.*—Capt. 335FS—POW—North of Bordeaux, Fr. at approx. 1400 hrs.—Hit by Flak, bailed out. Later escaped and made it to Spain, returning to UK 6-10-44.—P-51B 43-6639 WD-P.

3-21-44   *Goetz, Joseph*—F/O 335FS—KIA—North of Bordeaux, Fr. at approx. 1400 hrs.—Was seen to crash into ground and explode.—P-51B 43-12469 WD-L.

3-21-44   *Hawkins, William C.*—1Lt. 335FS.—Evader—North of Bordeaux, Fr. at approx. 1400 hrs.—Thought to have bailed out okay.—Returned on 7-16-44 and sent home.—P-51B 43-6316 WD-H.

3-21-44   *Rafalovich, Alexander*—1Lt. 334FS.—POW—North of Bordeaux, Fr. at 1445 hrs.—Bailed out okay—P-51B 43-6839 QP-N.

3-21-44   *Dye, James D.*—1Lt., 335FS.—WIA—Hit in leg by Flak, he returned to base. Into hospital, did not resume combat.

3-21-44   *Smith, Kenneth G.*—1Lt. 335FS.—POW—Somewhere in eastern central France at approx. 1500 hrs.—Not seen to go down—Returned to Debden on 4-20-45.—P-51B 43-6803 WD-K.

3-21-44   *Williams, Robert G.*—1Lt. 334FS.—POW—North of Angers, Fr. at 1505 hrs.—Bailed out okay.—P-51B 43-6869 QP-U.

3-27-44   *Chatterley, Archie W.*—Capt. 334FS.—POW—10 miles south of Tours, Fr. at 1515 hrs.—Hit by Flak on towers & barges on the shore of Lake Biscarosse and bailed out okay.—P-51B 43-6860 QP-G.

3-28-44   *Clotfelter, Raymond P.*—1Lt. 335FS.—POW—Near Dreaux–Vernoullet A/D, Fr. at approx. 1415 hrs.—His A/C was streaming glycol and he bailed out okay.—P-51B 43-6843 WD-B.

3-29-44   *Peterson, Kenneth D.*—Capt. 336FS.—POW—Between Brunswick and Hannover, Ger. at approx. 1315 hrs.—He attacked 12 E/A alone, who were shooting up crippled B-17. After destroying 2 FW-190s, his rudder was shot away. In inverted spin with no control, he bailed out okay at 10,000 ft.—P-51B 43-6696 VF-F?.

3-29-44   *Newell, William E.*—Lt. 335FS.—POW—Near Dummer Lake, Ger. at approx. 1400 hrs.—Got a 20mm hit in left side of A/C below the canopy and lost his coolant. He bailed out okay.—P-51B 43-6759 WD-P.

3-21-44   *Lehman, Peter G.*—1Lt. 336FS.—KIFA—Near Duxford, Cambs., U.K. in the afternoon. He was doing low-level mock dog-fighting and flicked over and spun into the ground, probably due to vices of torque and change of C/G in early 51Bs. P-51B VF-S.

4-5-44   *Hobert, Robert D.*—Capt. 336FS.—KIFA—Downed in the North Sea on show return. He was rescued, but died from exposure at midnight in a coastal hospital. Had a coolant leak on way back. P-51B 43-6836 VF-?.

4-5-44   *Carr, Charles, D.*—1Lt. 334FS.—POW—West of Brandenburg, Ger. at 1600 hrs.—Hit by Flak at Gardelegen A/D.—P-51B 43-6837 QP-I.

4-5-44   *Bunte, Allan F.*—1Lt. 334FS.—POW—Crashed with his A/C into a lake near Potsdam, Ger. at 1515 hrs.—Hit a high-tension wire near Gardelegen A/D.—P-51B 43-6946 QP-L.

4-5-44   *Beeson, Duane W.*—Maj. 334FS.—POW—West of Gardelegen A/D, Ger. at 1600 hrs.—Hit by Flak at the A/D and bailed out okay near Stendal after losing coolant.—P-51B 43-6819 QP-B.

4-8-44   *Hughes, Robert E.*—1Lt. 336FS.—POW—Near Celle, Ger. at approx. 1400 hrs.—Shot down and bailed out okay.—P-51B 43-6866 VF-?.

4-8-44   *Moulton, Howard N., Jr.*—Capt. 334FS.—POW—West of Wittengen, Ger. at 1315 hrs.—Shot down by an FW-190D in a big airfight near Celle, Ger.— Seen to bail out okay.—P-51B 43-6967 QP-D.

4-8-44   *Boyles, Frank R.*—Cap. 335FS.—KIA—Near Celle, Ger. at approx. 1415 hrs.—He was last seen at the start of a big airfight in the same area.—P-51B 43-7098 WD-F.

4-8-44   *Claus, Robert P.*—2Lt. 334FS.—KIA—Near Brunswick, Ger. at approx. 1315 hrs.—He was in the big airfight near Celle.—Not seen to go down.—P-51B 43-7029 QP-U.

4-9-44   *Van Epps, David A.*—Capt. 334FS.—POW—Near Tutrow A/D, Ger. at 1325 hrs.—While returning on deck, he made 2 passes at the A/D and got a

Flak hit.—Pulled up to 1,000 ft. and bailed okay, with the chute just opening before he landed between 2 houses.—P-51B 43-6941 QP-T.

4-10-44   *Fiedler, Clemens A.*—1Lt. 335FS.—KIA—At Romorantin A/D, Fr. at 0950 hrs.—Hit by Flak at the A/D, streaming glycol, said he was bailing out, pulled up to altitude, rolled over and went into ground.—No chute seen.—P-51B 43-7190 WD-W.

4-13-44   *Saunders, Ralph W.*—Lt. 335FS.—KIA—Lost somewhere in Holland. Time and place unknown. Not seen to go down.—P-51B 43-6325 WD-Z.

4-13-44   *Wynn, Vasseure H.*—Capt. 334FS.—POW—South of Aschaffenburg, Ger. at 1345 hrs.—Shot down by FW-190 in big airfight and bailed out okay. Capt. Megura shot down his victor right after Wynn was downed.—P-51B 43-7035 QP-X.

4-15-44   *Seifert, Robert H.*—2Lt. 336FS.—KIA—In North Sea at approx. 1230 hrs.—Bailed out after a hasty May-Day Call during climb thru bad clouds to 31,-500 ft. off enemy coast on way in.—P-51B 43-6818 VF-?.

4-15-44   *Care, Raymond C.*—Capt. 334FS.—POW—Near Celle, Ger. at 1445 hrs.—Bailed out due to unknown cause.—P-51B 43-7183 QP-R.

4-18-44   *Henry, Lloyd F.*—Lt. 335FS.—KIA—Near Rhin Canal area, Berlin, Ger. at approx. 1435 hrs.—Not seen to go down.—P-51B 43-6579 WD-S.

4-18-44   *Carpenter, George*—Maj. 335FS.—POW—In Rathenow, Ger. area at 1430 hrs.—Not seen to go down.—Scored 2 victories in an airfight prior.—P-51B 42-106675 WD-I.

4-18-44   *France, Victor J.*—Capt. 334FS.—KIA—Near Stendal, Ger. at 1450 hrs.—He was chasing an ME-109 at low-level when his A/C struck the ground and exploded into flames.—P-51B 43-6832 QP-K.

4-19-44   *Anderson, Charles F.*—Capt. 335FS.—KIA—Downed in Belgium, time and place unknown.—P-51B 43-7181 WD-L.

4-22-44   *Nelson, Robert F.*—1Lt. 336FS.—POW—South/east of Kassel, Ger. at approx. 1800 hrs.—His engine failed completely in midfight and he bailed out okay at 3000 ft. and landed in a tree. He successfully eluded the enemy for over four days.—P-51B 43-6802 VF-Y.

4-24-44   *Scarbrough, Milton G.*—Lt. 335FS.—POW—Near Worms, Ger. at approx. 1250 hrs.—His A/C was hit in the engine by an E/A and his engine caught fire. His right arm was burned by a fire in his fuselage gas tank and his face burned by hot coolant. He bailed out successfully.—P-51B 43-6767 WD-F.

4-24-44   *Riley, Paul S.*—1Lt. 335FS.—POW—Near Worms, Ger. at approx. 1250 hrs.—He collided with an FW-190 and lost ¼ of his left wing, but climbed for home when AA blew his left wing tank off. He bailed out okay.—P-51B 43-6922 WD-Y.

4-24-44   *Biel, Hipolitus Thomas*—1Lt. 334FS.—KIA—South of Darmstadt, Ger. at 1245 hrs.—He was shot down in aerial combat.—P-51B 42-106636 QP-X.

4-29-44   *Barden, John L.*—2Lt. 334FS.—POW—Near Nordhausen, Ger. at 1150 hrs.—His A/C was crippled by stray gunfire from a fellow 4TH F.G. pilot while strafing after escort and he bailed out okay.—P-51B 42-106682 QP-B.

4-29-44   *Kennedy, Pete R.*—2Lt. 334FS.—POW—Near Dummer Lake, Ger. at 1255 hrs.—His engine quit at 8,000 ft. from Flak hit and he bailed out okay.—P-51B 43-6646 QP-L.

4-30-44   *Glover, Frederick W.*—2Lt. 336FS.—Evader—Six miles north of Tain, France at approx. 1125 hrs.—His A/C was hit by Flak at Valences A/D, lost the coolant, bailed out okay, picked up by the French Resistance Forces and evaded back to England.—P-51B 42-106856 VF-?.

5-6-44   *Boyce, Ralph G.*—2Lt. 335FS.—KIFA—While on a local training flight, he crashed and was killed upon landing at Ridgewell 8AF Base, Essex, U.K.—P-51B (?).

5-9-44   *Waterman, Lloyd W.*—1Lt. 335FS.—POW—Near Reims, Fr.—He was not seen to go down after last contact near Reims, Fr.—P-51B 42-106911 WD-A.

5-9-44   *Sherman, Robert S.*—Lt. 334FS.—POW—In a field northwest of St. Dizier A/D, Fr. at approx. 1000 hrs.—He belly-landed his A/C after the propeller hit the ground when he was strafing the enemy A/D.—P-51B 43-7002 QP-D.

5-9-44   *Burroughs, Vernon A.*—1Lt. 334FS.—POW—40 miles southwest of St. Dizier, Fr. at 1005 hrs.—He bailed out okay.—P-51B 43-6636 QP-N.

5-9-44   *Blanchfield, Herbert J.*—Capt. 334FS.—POW—20 miles southwest of St. Dizier A/D, Fr. at 1000 hrs.—His A/C was hit by Flak at St. Dizier A/D and he bailed out okay.—P-51B 42-106767 QP-E.

5-11-44   *Tussey, Robert S.*—1Lt. 336FS.—KIA—Bailed into the North Sea during a mission.—He was picked up and died in hospital of head injuries.—P-51B 43-24771 VF-?.

5-13-44   *Pierce, Leonard R.*—1Lt. 334FS.—KIA—In the North Sea 30 miles east of Southwold, U.K. at 1335 hrs.—He bailed out into the sea and was seen struggling with his chute 150 yds. from his dinghy. The chute drowned him before rescue.—P-51B 42-106441 QP-G.

5-19-44   *Patchen, Donald J.*—1Lt. 336FS.—POW—Near Hannover, Ger. at approx. ?   —His A/C was hit by rocket Flak at 28,000 ft. and he bailed out okay at 9,000 ft.—P-51B 43-6584 VF-A.

5-21-44   *Hunt, William W.*—Lt. 335FS.—KIA—Near Zossen, Ger.—His A/C was hit by Flak while strafing trains in a marshalling yard.—He was not seen to go down.—P-51B 43-6901 WD-F.

5-22-44   *Megura, Nicholas*—Capt. 334FS.—Internee—He bellied-in his badly damaged A/C at Kalmar A/D, Sweden. Time unk.—He was attacking 3 ME-109s southwest of Kiel, Ger. when a AAF P-38 hit him with gunfire. Losing coolant, his section escorted him to Laaland, Denmark. At 12,000 ft. at 1330 hrs. he set course for Sweden.—P-51B 43-7158 QP-F.

5-24-44   *Jennings, Harry E.*—Lt. 335FS.—KIA—Last seen chasing an E/A in the Hamburg–Lubeck area, Ger. at approx. 1025 hrs.—P-51B 42-106429 WD-W.

5-25-44   *McDill, Thomas K.*—2Lt. 336FS.—POW—Near Strasbourg, Fr. at approx. 1000 hrs.—He was shot down in an engagement with a greatly outnumbering enemy force.—P-51B 43-6633 VF-Q.

5-25-44   *Bennett, Joseph H.*—Capt. 336FS.—POW—Near Strasbourg, Fr. at approx. 1000 hrs.—Outnumbered and shot down in an airfight along with Lt. McDill.—P-51B 43-6572 VF-N.

5-27-44   *Shapleigh, Elliot H.*—Lt. 335FS.—Evader—Aborted and turned back early on show due to A/C trouble. He rejected an escort home and was not seen to go down.—P-51B 42-106464 WD-O.

5-28-44   *Bopp, Richard L.*—2Lt. 334FS.—POW—Near Ruhland, Ger. at 1415 hrs.—Cause of downing unknown.—P-51B 42-106846 QP-H.

5-28-44   *Hewatt, Aubrey E.*—2Lt. 334FS.—POW—5 miles east of Magdeburg, Ger. at 1405 hrs.—He was hit by an ME-109 and bailed out okay. His A/C blew up after his bail-out.—P-51B 43-6933 QP-Y.

5-29-44   *Speer, Frank E.*—2Lt. 334FS.—POW—Northeast of Stargard, Ger. at 1400 hrs.—He was hit by Flak at Mackfitz A/D and bellied in near the A/D. He said over R/T that he was okay.—P-51B 43-6560 QP-W.

5-30-44   *Millikan, Willard W.*—Capt. 336FS.—POW—Near Wittenburg, Ger. at approx. 1030 hrs.—He bailed out after Lt. Young collided in mid-air with him. Lt. Young was dodging Flak at the time.—P-51B 43-24769 VF-U.

5-30-44   *Young, Sam H., Jr.*—2Lt. 336FS.—POW—Near Wittenburg, Ger. at approx. 1030 hrs.—While dodging Flak, he collided in mid-air with his leader, Capt. Millikan. Both bailed out okay.—P-51B 43-24787 VF-?.

5-30-44   *Kolter, Mark H.*—2Lt. 334FS.—KIA—Last seen southwest of Brandenburg, Ger. at 1115 hrs.—He called for a homing over the R/T at 1355 hrs. Not seen to go down.—P-51B 43-7178 QP-Q.

5-31-44   *Homuth, Robert H.*—Lt. 335FS.—KIA—Near Walcheren Is., Neth. at approx. 1000 hrs.—He aborted with Capt. McElroy and both were not seen again. It is thought they may have been hit by AAF bomber gunners.—P-51B 43-7032 WD-S.

5-31-44   *McElroy, Carroll B.*—Capt. 335FS.—POW—Near Walcheren Is., Neth. at approx. 1000 hrs.—He aborted with Lt. Homuth and one or both of them may have been hit by AAF bomber gunners.—P-51C 42-103609 WD-G.

6-4-44   *Kackerback, Robert L.*—2Lt. 336FS.—KIFA—Near Steeple Bumpstead, Essex, U.K. at 2000 hrs.—He crashed to his death while on a local training flight.—P-51B 43-7059 VF-?.

6-6-44   *Fraser, Thomas E.*—2Lt. 334FS.—POW—Seen entering cloud at 0430 hrs. while patroling East of Rouen, Fr. He was given a vector at 0642 hrs. and was not reported thereafter.—P-51B 43-24825 QP-G.

6-6-44   *Garbey, Cecil E.*—Lt. 335FS.—KIA—Near Rouen, Fr. at 1840 hrs.—The entire 335FS.— Blue Section was shot down when E/A bounced them out of low cloud when they were on the deck.—P-51B 43-6575 WD-E.

6-6-44   *Lejeunesse, Oscar F.*—1Lt. 336FS.—POW—In No-Mans-Land behind the Normandy beaches, Fr. at approx. 1445 hrs.—He was hit by Flak and bailed out okay.—P-51C 42-103332 VF-?.

6-6-44   *McGrattan, Bernard J.*—Capt. 335FS.—KIA—Near Rouen, Fr. at 1840 hrs.—His Blue Section (he was leader) was bounced by E/A out of low cloud and all shot down.—P-51B 42-106576 WD-D.

6-6-44   *McPharlin, Michael G. H.*—Maj. 339th Ftr. Grp.—KIA—Last heard from in the Dreux, Fr. area at 2100 hrs.—He said over the R/T that his left magneto was out and the motor was rough, and that he was aborting the mission. He was not seen or heard from again.—He was flying with 334FS. and the 4th F.G.—P-51B 42-106909 6N-Z.

6-6-44   *Ross, Harold L., Jr.*—Lt. 335FS.—KIA—Near Rouen, Fr. at 1840 hrs.—He was part of 335's Blue Section which was bounced out of low cloud by E/A and all shot down.—P-51B 42-106786 WD-K.

6-6-44   *Smith, Walter (nmi)*—F/O 335FS.—KIA—Near Rouen, Fr. at 1840 hrs.—He was part of 335's Blue Section which was bounced out of low cloud by E/A and all shot down.—P-51B 43-7172 WD-H.

6-6-44   *Sobanski, Winslow Michael*—Maj. 334FS. CO—KIA—Near Dreux, Fr. at approx. 2035 hrs.—He asked Lt. Steppe over the R/T to check his A/C after hitting some wires while strafing a train. Last heard R/T report was Lt. Steppe saying "watch those behind you White Leader." No further contact was made.—P-51B 43-6898 QP-J.

6-6-44   *Steppe, Edward J.*—Lt. 334FS.—KIA—Near Dreux, Fr. at 2035 hrs.—He said to Maj. Sobanski on his last heard R/T report, "watch those behind you White Leader." No further contact was made with him.—P-51B 43-6957 QP-M.

6-6-44   *Fredericks, Harold H.*—1Lt. 336FS.—Evader—Near Evreux, Fr. at approx. 1445 hrs.—His A/C was hit by Flak and he crash-landed. He ran from the wreck and successfully evaded back to England.—P-51C 42-103287 VF-?.

6-7-44   *Smith, Kenneth D.*—Lt. 336FS.—KIA—Approx. a mile south of Debden A/D, Essex, U.K. at 1430 hrs.—After take-off on a mission, he had a mid-air collision with Lt. Pierini, 336FS., and crashed to his death.—P-51B 43-6673 VF-?.

6-7-44   *Jones, Osce R.*—Lt. 335FS.—POW—Near Dol-Deb/Medard, Fr.—He crashlanded after being hit by Flak, got out okay and ran into the woods.—P-51B 43-7042 WD-J.

6-8-44   *Allen, Eacott G.*—2Lt. 334FS.—Evader—LeMans, Fr. area.—While fighter-bombing he collided with Lt. Scott, cutting off Scott's tail. He bailed onto the roof of a house and was back at DB on 8-23-44.—P-51B 42-106823 QP-K.

6-8-44   *Scott, James F.*—2Lt. 334FS.—KIA—LeMans, Fr. area.—Lt. Allan collided with him and cut the tail off his A/C. The A/C dove into the ground instantly killing him.—P-51B 43-7150 QP-P.

6-8-44   *Byrd, James T., Jr.*—2Lt. 334FS.—KIFA—In the vicinity of Leiston A/D, UK. at 1810 hrs.—While flying formation with Capt. Hively, his A/C dived into the ground and exploded.—P-51B 43-6433 QP-D.

6-10-44   *Netting, Conrad J.*—1Lt. 336FS.—KIA—In the area of Evreux, Fr.—The manner of loss is unk.—P-51B 42-106669 VF-?.

6-10-44   *Caple, Frank D.*—2Lt. 336FS.—POW—He is believed to have landed due to unknown causes on the French coast during the day's 2nd show.—P-51B 43-6889 VF-?.

6-11-44   *Noon, Harry B.*—2Lt. 334FS.—KIA—Near Villedieu-les-poeles, Fr. at 1400 hrs.—On a low bomb run, his A/C hit the trees, flicked a couple times, turned over, hit the ground, skidded a ways, and exploded with 2 250# bombs in it.—P-51B 43-6586 QP-U.

6-11-44   *Cole, Leon J., Jr.*—2Lt. 334FS.—KIA—At 1330 hrs. near Villedieu-les-poeles, Fr.—His A/C hit the ground while strafing, pulled up pouring black smoke and exploded in the air.—P-51C 42-103292 QP-B.

6-17-44   *Caswell, Robert B.*—Pvt. 335FS.—Judged a suicide—He shot himself with a carbine during the night.

6-18-44   *Arnold, Harvie J.*—2Lt. 336FS.—KIA—Not seen to go down.—P-51D 44-13307 VF-?.

6-18-44   *Little, Robert W.*—Lt. 335FS.—POW—Dol-Deb, Fr. area.—While strafing a convoy, his A/C was hit by rifle fire and crashlanded into a haystack and on into a house's side.—P-51B 43-6770 WD-G.

6-18-44   *Glynn, James H.*—Lt. 335FS.—Evader—Avranches area, Fr.—His A/C was hit by rifle fire while strafing a horse convoy and he bailed out okay.—P-51B 43-7187 WD-B.

6-19-44   *Hill, Dean J.*—Lt. 335FS.—KIA—He was not seen to go down in bad cloud and overcast. Show was recalled at Cholet, Fr. with 6-8/10th cloud over the English Channel.—P-51B 43-6896 WD-F.

6-20-44   *Harris, Vol. R., Jr.*—Lt. 335FS.—POW—Near Lubeck, Ger.—Manner of loss is unk.—P-51B 42-106706 WD-R.

6-20-44   *Goodson, James A.*—Maj. 336FS.—POW—Neubranden A/D, Ger. at approx. 0900 hrs.—During his 2nd pass at the A/D, a cannon shell hit his coolant and he was forced to belly land in a field. The sqd. then destroyed his A/C by strafing it.—P-51D 44-13303 VF-B.

6-21-44   *Sibbett, Frank T.*—Lt. 335FS.—KIA—At approx. 1240 hrs. near Sieddice, Pol.—Not seen to be lost during fight with 20-25 109s at this point on Russia Shuttle.—P-51B 43-6784 WD-X.

6-21-44   *Gilbert, Robert L.*—S/Sgt. 336FS.—Evader—He bailed out of the B-17 he was gunner in during the Shuttle trip when it got shot down and he fought with Russian Guerrillas for several weeks before returning to DB on 8-17-44.—B-17 unit unk.

6-27-44   *Perez, Estanislado M.*—Cpl. 336FS.—Died due to unknown cause on duty at Debden.

7-2-44   *Norris, J. C.*—2Lt. 336FS.—POW—Manner of loss at approx. 1045 hrs. in Budapest, Hung. area is unknown.—P-51B 43-6650 VF-?.

7-2-44   *Stanford, George I., Jr.*—1Lt. 335FS.—POW—At approx. 1045 hrs. in the Budapest, Hung. area he was shot down.—P-51D 44-13402 WD-K.

7-2-44   *Siems, Grover C., Jr.*—1Lt. 334FS.—WIA—At approx. 1045 hrs. in the Budapest, Hung. area.—He was shot severely in the shoulder, neck, and chin, and paralysed on his left side. However he managed to return to a Foggia, Italy base, trip the landing gear lever with his foot, land, and fire his guns to attract help. Returned to the U.S. in serious condition.—P-51D 44-13322 QP-O.

7-2-44   *Sharp, Thomas S.*—Lt. 334FS.—KIA—Near Budapest, Hung. at approx. 1045 hrs.—He was last seen having trouble releasing his wing tanks.—P-51B 42-106650 QP-D.

7-2-44   *Hofer, Ralph Kidd*—Lt. 334FS.—KIA—Near Budapest, Hung. at approx. 1045 hrs.—He was last seen climbing to engage 20-plus 109's. He and his plane's wreckage were found at Mostar, Yugoslavia.—P-51B 43-6746 QP-X.

7-7-44   *Scally, John J.*—2Lt. 334FS.—POW—In the vicinity of Nordhausen, Ger.— He had a mid-air collision with an ME-410. His A/C lost a wing and spun in.—P-51B 43-6567 QP-E.

7-11-44 *Hanrahan, James. S.*—Lt. 335FS.—POW (escaper)—Time and area unk.— Not seen to go down. He said over the R/T that he was aborting. It is believed he got lost.—P-51B 43-6562 WD-N.

7-13-44 *Edwards, Wilson V.*—Maj. 336FS.—POW—His A/C was hit by Flak near Metz, Fr.—He bailed out and landed okay.—P-51D 44-13608 VF-?.

7-19-44 *Simpson, Curtis* (nmi)—Lt. 335FS.—Evader/Internee—At approx. 1045 hrs. he was heard to say on the R/T that he was over Switzerland with a glycol leak.—He returned to DB on 10-15-44.—P-51B 42-106438 WD-?.

7-19-44 *Dahlen, Kermit O.*—Lt. 335FS.—KIA—At approx. 1015 hrs. near Munich, Ger., his A/C exploded in mid-air during a fight with 10–15 ME-109s.—P-51B 43-6463 WD-?.

7-20-44 *Godwin, Lester B.*—Lt. 335FS.—Evader—Near Aachen, Ger. at 26,000 ft., his A/C was hit by Flak. He flew back to Antwerp, Belg. and bailed out okay.—P-51C 42-103561 WD-H.

7-22-44 *Kingham, Lloyd G.*—Lt. 335FS.—KIA—At approx. 1620 hrs. near Audley End, Essex, UK.—He crashed a couple minutes after takeoff on a mission in bad cloud conditions.—He spun in with the A/C.—P-51D 44-13641 WD-R.

8-2-44   *Chapman, Gerald C.*—2Lt. 336FS.—KIA—He was not seen after leaving Beauvais A/D, Fr.—P-51B 43-6846 VF-?.

8-3-44   *Smith, Fonzo D.*—Maj. 4HQ. SQ.—POW—While on an escort to the Paris, Fr. area, he was not seen to go down and failed to return.—P-51D 44-13934 VF-?.

8-7-44   *Wadsworth, Sidney V.*—Lt. 335FS.—POW—Flak hit his A/C in the coolant, which streamed out. He crashlanded violently and was at first thought killed in the crash, but was later reported POW.—P-51B 43-6437 WD-V.

8-7-44   *Malmsten, Donald M.*—Capt. 334FS.—Evader—Dijon, Fr. at 1700 hrs.—Hit by Flak over the town, he crashlanded, suffering burns and wounds. After evading a month, he returned to DB on 9-12-44.—P-51C 43-24979 QP-U.

8-8-44   *Fischer, Robert G.*—Lt. 335FS.—KIA—At 1550 hrs. he was hit by Flak over Norway and said over the R/T that he was heading for Sweden. Nothing further was heard from him.—P-51B 42-106940 WD-N.

8-8-44   *Jones, Frank C., Jr.*—Capt. 335FS.—KIA—Soon after leaving Norway at 1550 hrs., he ditched his canopy and the A/C hit the water. As it did so his parachute could be seen floating on the surface. Apparently he didn't get out of it. It was his last mission and he was to be wed in 10 days.—P-51D 44-14027 WD-P.

8-8-44   *Underwood, Thomas A.*—2Lt. 334FS.—POW—Varnaug, Norway at 1455 hrs.—Just after the Beaufighter attack, he reported via a bad R/T that his engine was on fire and he was bailing out. The trouble was not thought to be due to enemy action.—P-51B 43-24793 QP-C.

8-8-44   *Blanding, Leon M.*—Maj. 335FS.—WIA—While leading 335 home from Norway at about 1550 hrs., his A/C was hit in the canopy by Flak. Glass badly injured his head on one side. Blood on the fuselage to the tail. He tore his trousers to bandage himself and led by Kolbe & Berry, he guided his wobbling A/C to Acklington, Northern England. He later recovered from the wound.—P-51D WD-G.

8-13-44 *Boren, Stephen R.*—Lt. 335FS.—KIA—Near Troesnes, Fr. at 1925 hrs.— While strafing, his A/C hit a tree tearing a wing off and then crashed into the ground killing him.—P-51D 44-13997 WD-W.

8-15-44 *Achen, Norman W.*—2Lt. 334FS.—POW—He was downed near Bad Zwischenahner Lake A/D, Ger.—Manner of his loss is unk.—P-51B 43-6882 QP-A.

8-18-44 *Dailey, Leo (nmi)*—2Lt. 335FS.—KIA—At Merard-per-bury (Oise), Fr. at 2000 hrs.—Bounced by 50-plus 109's after strafing in Les Andelys, Fr. area. Not seen to go down.—P-51B 42-106555 WD-M.

8-18-44 *Cooper, Robert J.*—Lt. 335FS.—KIA—In the Les Andelys area, Fr. at approx. 2000 hrs.—Jumped by 50-plus 109's after strafing. Not seen to go down.—P-51B 42-106855 WD-Z.

8-18-44 *Conley, John T.*—Lt. 335FS.—KIA—Near Les Andelys, Fr. at 2000 hrs.— Bounced by 50-plus 109's. Not seen to go down.—P-51B 43-24813 WD-N.

8-18-44 *Glass, Otey M., Jr.*—Capt. 336FS.—Evader—In the Gisors, Fr. area.—He was shot down by E/A while strafing ammunition trucks. After evading, he returned to DB on 9-2-44.—P-51B 42-106797 VF-G?.

8-18-44 *Rosenson, Bernard J.*—Lt. 335FS.—KIA—At 2000 hrs. near Les Andelys, Fr.—He was not seen to go down after the group was bounced by 50-plus E/A.—P-51D 44-13567 WD-O.

8-18-44 *Smith, Donald E.*—2Lt. 335FS.—KIA—At 2000 hrs. in the area of Les Andelys, Fr.—Not seen to go down.—P-51D 44-13563 WD-R.

8-18-44 *Cwiklinski, Arthur. C.*—2Lt. 334FS.—At approx. 1930 hrs. south of Beauvais, Fr.—While strafing, a 109 shot him down, and he bailed out okay. He was back to DB on 9-9-44.—P-51D 44-13314 QP-X.

8-18-44 *Howard, C. G.*—2Lt. 334FS.—KIA—Near Beauvais, Fr. at 1930 hrs.—He was shot down by 15 109's in a bounce.—P-51B 43-24841 QP-D.

8-18-44 *Lange, Dean E.*—2Lt. 334FS.—POW—5–10 mi. s/w of Beauvais, Fr. at 1935 hrs.—His A/C was hit by bouncing 109's and he bailed out.—P-51C 42-103791 QP-N.

8-24-44 *Godfrey, John T.*—Capt. 336FS.—POW—8 mi. n/e of Nordhausen, Ger.— His A/C was hit by his wingman's fire and he bellied it in.—P-51D 44-13412 VF-F.

8-25-44 *Rudkin, Kenneth J.*—2Lt. 334FS.—POW—At 1230 hrs. near Lubeck, Ger.—Not seen to go down, but he was believed hit by Flak.—P-51D 44-13732 QP-R.

8-28-44 *Harris, Ferris S.*—1Lt. 336FS.—KIA—He was downed during strafing south of Strasbourg, Fr.—Manner of loss is unk.—P-51C 42-103796 VF-?.

8-28-44 *Vandervate, Herbert, Jr.*—1Lt. 334FS.—KIA—At approx. 0845 hrs. in the vicinity of Strasbourg, Fr.—He was not seen to go down after strafing a truck convoy in the area.—P-51D 44-14310 QP-K.

8-28-44 *McKennon, Pierce W.*—Maj. 335FS.—Evader—At approx. 0845 hrs. near Niederbronn, Fr.—His A/C was hit by Flak and he bailed out okay, landing in some trees. The French Maquis hid him for a month and he returned to DB on 9-24-44.—P-51D 44-13883 WD-A.

8-28-44   *Schlegel, Albert L.*—Capt. 335FS.—KIA—In the Strasbourg, Fr. area.—Not seen to go down—P-51D 44-14066 WD-O.

8-28-44   *Thomson, Archibald M.*—Maj. 335FS.—Evader—In the Strasbourg, Fr. area.—Not seen to go down—P-51D 44-13534 WD-F.

9-10-44   *White, Robert W.*—Lt. 336FS.—KIA—At approx. 1345 hrs. at Boxted, Essex, UK.—He crashed and was killed on his return from the mission.—P-51B 43-6891 VF-?.

9-11-44   *Patterson, Roy L.*—2Lt. 336FS.—KIA—In the Lutsendorf, Ger. area at an unk. time.—He bailed out, but he was too near the ground and the chute streamed, but did not open before he hit the ground.—P-51D 44-14266 VF-?.

9-11-44   *Ingalls, Henry. A.*—Lt. 336FS.—POW—Near Langensalsa, Ger. he crash-landed and ran from his A/C.—P-51B 43-6573 VF-?.

9-11-44   *Russell, James W., Jr.*—Capt. 335FS.—POW—Between Fulda and Giessen, Ger.—A 20mm round exploded in his cockpit wounding him twice in the head and cutting some coolant lines. He crashlanded the airplane, because one of his chute straps was cut.—P-51D 44-14158 WD-R.

9-11-44   *Iden, Paul S.*—Lt. 335FS.—KIA—Near Naumburg, Ger. at approx. 1145 hrs.—He was lost when 30-plus 109's bounced the sqdn. and he was not seen to go down.—P-51B 43-6959 WD-Z.

9-11-44   *Groseclose, William R.*—Lt. 335FS.—POW—At approx. 1145 hrs. n/w of Naumburg, Ger.—He was not seen to go down when 30-plus 109's jumped the sqdn.—P-51D 44-14431 WD-Q.

9-12-44   *Lane, James C.*—1Lt. 336FS.—POW—20-30 mi. n/e of Trier, Ger.—He bailed out due to loss of his engine coolant. A bomber crew saw him land okay.—P-51D 44-13260 VF-?.

9-12-44   *Joyce, Thomas E.*—Capt. 334FS.—POW—At 1245 hrs. near Darmstadt, Ger.—He was probably hit by Flak and he bellylanded his A/C.—P-51D 44-14271 QP-K.

9-13-44   *Smith, William B.*—Capt. 334FS.—KIA—At 1115 hrs. near Ulm, Ger.—His A/C was hit by Flak in the engine and cockpit while strafing an airdrome. He went a mile, pulled up to 400 ft., rolled over, and exploded on impact with the ground.—P-51D 44-14281 QP-Y.

9-17-44   *Holske, Clifford F.*—1Lt. 335FS.—POW—In the Bocholt, Ger. area at 1345 hrs.—A red-nosed P-51 was seen to go down in flames during a fight. He burned both hands badly when he bailed out and received no treatment until two days after his capture.—P-51D 44-14054 WD-I.

9-17-44   *Vozzy, Nicholas W.*—Lt. 335FS.—KIA—At 1345 hrs. in the Bocholt area, Ger.—He was not seen to go down.—P-51B 43-6841 WD-J.

10-2-44   *Logan, George H., Jr.*—1Lt. 336FS.—KIA—2 mi. n/e of Apelsdoorn, Neth.—His A/C was seen to leave the formation and spin into the cloud. Possibly due to oxygen loss or G-Suit trouble?—P-51D 44-14172 VF-?.

10-14-44 *Lang, Joseph L.*—Capt. 334FS.—KIA—At 1520 hrs. 4 mi. s/e of Eurville-sur-Marne, Fr.—His last R/T message was, "This is Lang, I am down below clouds with 10 109's, I got two, I don't know where I am and I need help." This was near Kaiserslautern, Ger. Visibility at the time he was seen (by ground troops) to crash was 3 mi.—P-51D 44-14123 QP-Z.

11-5-44   *Anderson, Russell J.*—Lt. 335FS.—POW—He was heard to say on the R/T that he was bailing out. He was not observed at all at this time.—P-51D 44-14339 WD-U.

11-6-44   *Mead, Charles Y.*—2Lt. 336FS.—KIFA—Near Little Walden, Essex, UK.—While on a local flt. he bailed out too low, it is thought, as his chute streamed but did not open.—P-51C 42-103794 VF-?.

11-6-44   *Walsh, Earl C.*—1Lt. 334FS.—POW—At 1110 hrs. near Rheine, Ger.—He was shot down by 109's.—P-51D 44-14229 QP-N.

11-6-44   *Childs, John L.*—2Lt. 334FS.—KIA—In the vicinity of Rheine, Ger. at 1110 hrs.—Last heard to say on the R/T, "What will I do, I have an FW-190 on my tail." His A/C was seen to take no evasive action, roll on its side and go straight in smoking. He did not bail out.—P-51D 44-14772 QP-Z.

11-8-44   *Quist, Earl A.*—2Lt. 336FS.—POW—He was last heard from near the German border. He was not observed to go down.—P-51D 44-13961 VF-L.

11-18-44 *Lewis, Ralph E.*—2Lt. 335FS.—KIA—He was not seen to go down.—P-51D 44-14529 WD-X.

11-20-44 *Bennett, Donald L.*—1Lt. 334FS.—POW—At 1245 hrs. s/e of the Zuider Zee, Neth.—The manner of his loss is unk.—P-51D 44-13615 QP-R.

11-20-44 *Werner, Leonard R.*—1Lt. 334FS.—KIA—At 1245 hrs. s/e of the Zuider Zee, Neth.—He was lost while flying thru thick cloud. His compass and gyro froze doing this on a previous mission. Perhaps it occurred again?—P-51D 44-13411 QP-Q.

11-21-44 *Klaus, George L.*—2Lt. 336FS.—POW—4 mi. n/e of Halle, Ger. at 1245 hrs.—His A/C was hit by Flak at 18,000 ft., started to burn at 6,000 ft., and he bailed out okay.—P-51B 43-6942 VF-D.

11-21-44 *Delnero, Carmen J.*—Lt. 334FS.—KIA—At Meerane, Ger. at 1300 hrs.—A 109 got hits on his A/C. It blew up before he got out and it crashed from 500 ft. in rain and snow.—P-51D 44-14119 QP-H.

12-11-44 *Kennedy, Michael J.*—2Lt. 334FS.—Evader?—This loss is either a case of evasion or a very late return from a stopover abort on the continent. The various records consulted differ and they are quite vague on this matter. They state: Last seen at 1330 hrs. near the Saarbrucken area aborting the show. The pilot is listed as flying operations with 334th on 1-16-45?—A/C flown on 12-11-44 was QP-W.

12-18-44 *Hewes, Charles D.*—Capt. 335FS.—KIA—Near Giessen, Ger. at 1430 hrs.—He was last seen at this position/time at 4,000 ft. just as enemy A/C engaged the squadron. Not seen to go down.—P-51D 44-15455 WD-?.

12-25-44 *Poage, Charles E., Jr.*—2Lt. 335FS.—POW—n/w of Laacher Lake, Ger.—He was bounced by a 190 which set his A/C on fire and he bailed out okay.—P-51D 44-14540 WD-?.

12-25-44 *Emerson, Donald R.*—Capt. 336FS.—KIA—He was found in the wreckage of his A/C by the British in Belgium within Allied lines. The British state that he was killed by ground fire crossing the lines and was dead before crashing. His last R/T message said he was starting home on the deck after downing 2 190's in a lone fight with 6 190's.—P-51D 44-15054 VF-D.

1-2-45   *Senecal, Arthur J.*—2Lt. 334FS.—KIA—At 1414 hrs. near Konigsfeld, Ger.—His A/C was hit by Flak in the coolant. He tried to reach Allied lines and got too low. His chute did not open in time after he bailed out.—P-51B 43-6587 QP-Z.

1-16-45   *Rentschler, Victor R.*—2Lt. 334FS.—POW—In the Reutlingen–Ulm area, Ger. at 1400 hrs.—His A/C was hit in the coolant by Flak at Neuburg A/D. He bailed out in Jack-in-the-box style after the coolant resumed leaking, having once stopped.—P-51D 44-15324 QP-M.

1-16-45   *Hall, Frederick D.*—Lt. 336FS.—KIA—At Folkstone, UK. at 1515 hrs.—He was trying to land his A/C at a forward base when it dove into the ground upon returning from the show.—P-51D 44-14533 VF-?.

1-17-45   *Stallings, Robert L.*—Lt. 335FS.—KIA—1125 hrs. 20 mi. east of Lowestoft, UK. in the North Sea.—He reported on the R/T having some trouble west of Den Helder, Neth. at 1050 hrs., and said he was turning back. He was not found after bailing out.—P-51D 44-11339 WD-?.

2-4-45   *Wallace, Alvin O.*—2Lt. 336FS.—KIFA—Near Great Sampford, Essex, UK.—While on a local flight, his A/C spun into the ground.—P-51D 44-15531 VF-?.

2-6-45   *Santos, Paul G.*—Lt. 335FS.—KIA—He was last seen strafing M/T in the Torgau, Ger. area at approx. 1325 hrs.—Not seen to go down.—P-51D 44-15615 WD-?.

2-6-45   *Bates, William D.*—F/O. 334FS.—KIA—1017 hrs. 40 mi. east of Leiston, UK. in the North Sea.—His body was recovered at 1245 hrs. from the sea.—P-51D 44-13884 QP-V.

2-11-45   *Kaul, Henry A.*—Lt. 336FS.—KIA—At 0940 hrs. north of Lemgo, Ger.—His A/C crashed from hitting a tree while he was trying to drop his wing tanks on a truck.—P-51D 44-63233 VF-D.

2-11-45   *Savage, Morton R.*—2Lt. 334FS.—KIFA—At Nuthampton, U.K. at 1550 hrs.—His A/C struck a radio tower while he was trying to return to the forward base at Wattisham where he had landed on the show return. He had reached DB, but bad fog prevented his landing.—P-51D ? QP-W.

2-20-45   *Fitch, John C.*—Capt. 335FS.—POW—He bailed out okay at 1335 hrs. 4 mi. s/w of Neumarkt, Ger.—While strafing trains, his A/C was hit by Flak. P-51D 44-15351 WD-?.

2-21-45   *Rabe, August W.*—Lt. 335FS.—POW—5 mi. s/w of Coburg, Ger.—His A/C hit a tree while strafing. He made a good bellylanding and asked on the R/T for someone to destroy his downed A/C. McKennon dropped his tanks on it and Cammer ignited it with a couple of bursts.—P-51D 44-14435 WD-O.

2-21-45   *Lacy, Andrew C.*—2Lt. 334FS.—POW—1 mi. west of Neresheim, Ger. at 1225 hrs.—He bailed out after being hit by Flak and losing gas and oil pressure of his A/C.—P-51K 44-11677 QP-P.

2-24-45   *Hand, Alvin L.*—F/O. 334FS.—POW—At 1345 hrs. near Emmen, Neth.—While strafing a barge he was hit by Flak and bellylanded the A/C.—P-51K 44-11661 QP-X.

2-25-45   *Carlson, Kendall E.*—Capt. 336FS.—POW—Kothen A/D near Dessau, Ger. at 1030 hrs.—While strafing he mushed in and hit the ground. After the bellylanding he called in targets around the airfield on the R/T of his crashed A/C.—P-51D 45-11356 VF-Y?.

2-27-45   *Crawford, Harold R., Jr.*—2Lt. 336FS.—POW—Weimar, Ger. at 1515 hrs.—He crashlanded okay after his A/C was hit by either Flak, exploding ammo of German A/C on ground, or the fire of a 4FG A/C on his tail.—P-51D 44-11665 VF-?.

2-27-45   *Voyles, Robert S.*—1Lt. 334FS.—POW—Weimar A/D, Ger. at 1415 hrs.—His A/C got a 20mm hit in the windscreen and began losing coolant.—A few minutes later he had to bail out.—P-51D 44-14537 QP-A.

3-3-45   *Green, Kenneth*—1Lt. 335FS.—POW—Over the Rhine river 5 mi. south of Rotterdam, Neth.—He seemed to be hit and kept circling. Cammer couldn't get him on the R/T and lost sight of him avoiding Flak. Not actually seen to go down.—P-51D 44-14923 WD-?.

3-3-45   *Davis, George H.*—Capt. 335FS.—POW—Near Celle-Ulzen, Ger.—His A/C was hit by locomotive Flak while strafing and he bailed out at 700 ft. He landed in a forest and broke his ankle on a stump when he hit ground.—P-51D 44-63599 WD-?.

3-12-45   *McFarlane, John D.*—Maj. 336FS.—Evader—Mon Island, Denmark at 1147 hrs.—He bailed out due to coolant trouble and was seen to run from the area okay. He evaded thru Copenhagen to Sweden successfully.—P-51D 44-14350 VF-L?.

3-18-45   *McKennon, Pierce W.*—Maj. 335FS.—Evader—Near Neubrandenburg A/D,

Ger.—His A/C was hit by Flak and he bailed out okay. His wingman, George Green, landed in the field with him, picked him up, and they successfully took off sitting on top of each other. They then flew home to DB amidst R/T cheers by the escorting sqdn.—P-51D 44-63166 WD-A.

3-21-45   *Cammer, Robert A.*—1Lt. 335FS.—POW—1005 hrs. west of Achmer A/D, Ger.—He reported on R/T that he was hit and losing coolant and oil pressure. He was last seen steering 220 deg. for Allied Lines.—P-51D 44-14361 WD-K.

3-21-45   *Davis, Albert J.*—Capt. 335FS.—KIA—At approx. 1000 hrs. 2 mi. north of Hesepe A/D, Ger.—His A/C was hit by Flak on the first pass at the A/D. He said on the R/T, "I'm bailing out," but he was only at 50 ft. and the chute was not seen to open in time.—P-51D 44-63670 WD-?.

3-26-45   *Davis, Harry L.*—Lt. 336FS.—KIA—At Woodbridge, Suffolk, UK. at 1503 hrs.—His port wing was seen on fire when he came out of low cloud. The A/C dove vertical from 700 ft. to the ground. Possibly involved in a mid-air collision?—P-51D 44-13317 VF-B?.

3-26-45   *Hustwit, Earl F.*—2Lt. 336FS.—KIA—2 mi. west of Valkenbury, Ger. at 1415 hrs.—His A/C developed coolant trouble and he was thrown clear trying to bail out.—P-51?   ? VF-?.

3-31-45   *Foster, Kenneth E.*—F/O. 334FS.—POW—Downed in Germany. Details of his loss are unk.—P-51D 44-11336 QP-Z.

4-8-45   *Smith, Homer C.*—2Lt. 336FS.—KIFA—Northwest of Cambridge, Cambs., UK. at unk. time.—He was killed instantly in the crash while on a local 4TH OTU flight.—P-51C 42-103603 VF-T.

4-9-45   *Rasmussen, Herman S.*—2Lt. 335FS.—KIA—His A/C was hit by Flak at Munich-Brunnthal A/D, Ger. at 1708 hrs.—He bailed out at 400 ft. but his chute was not seen to open. The A/C crashed and exploded 2 mi. south of Neubiburg A/D, Ger. P-51D 44-13788 WD-?.

4-9-45   *Bucholz, Robert C.*—Lt. 335FS.—KIA—At 1720 hrs. at Munich–Brunnthal A/D, Ger.—His A/C was hit by Flak while strafing the A/D and he was not seen to bail out before it crashed.—P-51D 44-14389 WD-T.

4-10-45   *Miller, Robert T.*—Lt. 334FS.—WIA—He was hit by MG fire at Wittstock A/D, Ger. at 1600 hrs.—MEW directed him to B-78 AF at Eindhoven, Neth. He asked on the R/T for hospitalization. Not known to have returned to 4FG duty.—P-51D QP-F.

4-15-45   *Wozniak, Edward J.*—Lt. 334FS.—WIA—His A/C developed engine trouble while he was on R/T Relay. He crashlanded 10 mi. north of B-53 AF Wattau, Belg. and he received a slight concussion and severe forehead lacerations. It is not known whether he returned to 4FG duty.—P-51D 44-63583 QP-T.

4-16-45   *Carpenter, Leroy A., Jr.*—Capt. 336FS.—KIA—His A/C was hit by Flak at Praha A/D, Czech. at 1500 hrs. He was not seen to go down.—P-51D 44-63831 VF-?.

4-16-45   *Ayer, William H.*—Lt. 336FS.—POW—His A/C was hit by Flak at Praha A/D, Czech. at 1500 hrs.—He was not seen to go down.—P-51D 44-13375 VF-?.

4-16-45   *Alfred, Carl R.*—Capt. 336FS.—KIA—His A/C was hit by Flak at Praha A/D, Czech. and he was not seen to go down.—P-51D 44-72523 VF-?.

4-16-45   *Griffin, Benjamin L.*—2Lt. 336FS.—POW—He was hit by Flak at 1520 hrs. at Praha A/D, Czech., but he was not seen to go down.—P-51D 44-14277 VF-H.

4-16-45   *Miller, Maurice W., Jr.*—2Lt. 336FS.—POW—He was downed by Flak at Praha A/D, Czech. at 1510 hrs.—P-51D 44-14527 VF-?.

4-16-45   *Gimbel, Edward L.*—Capt. 336FS.—POW—His A/C was hit by Flak at Praha A/D, Czech. at 1520 hrs.—P-51D 44-72769 VF-?.

4-16-45   *McLoughlin, Edward J.*—2Lt. 335FS.—POW—His A/C was hit by Flak while strafing Praha A/D, Czech. He was last seen over the target airdromes at Praha.—P-51D 44-13389 WD-?.

4-16-45   *Woods, Sidney S.*—LtCol. 4TH HQ. SQDN.—POW—He was shot down by Flak at Praha A/D, Czech. at approx. 1500 hrs.—P-51D 44-72251 QP-A.

4-17-45   *Davis, Robert O.*—1Lt. 336FS.—KIA—He bailed out at 1545 hrs. 10 mi. east of the enemy lines near Eger–Marienbad, Ger. He was seen to hit ground okay after his A/C was hit in the coolant by Flak at Pilzen A/D, Ger.—P-51D 44-14387 VF-?.

4-25-45   *Hoelscher, William. B.*—2Lt. 334FS.—Evader—He was hit by Flak while chasing an ME-262 over Praha–Ruzyne A/D, Czech. and lost his engine coolant. He bailed out at 1000 hrs. near Rakovnik/Jechnitz, Czech., and walked away. His A/C had a 40mm hit in the wing root and the left elevator torn off.—P-51D 44-15347 QP-V.

5-17-45   *Tannehill, Richard L.*—Capt. 335FS.—KIFA—Near Llanbedr, North Wales, UK. at 1045 hrs.—While on a practice flight at 30,000 ft., it is assumed he passed out from lack of oxygen and spun in and crashed to his death.—P-51D 44-72340 WD-?.

5-29-45   *Wilhoit, Barnaby M.*—1Lt. 336FS.—KIFA—He left DB at 1000 hrs. as part of a ferry flight taking surplus P-51Ds to Speke Air Depot near Liverpool. The cloud went right to the ground and he crashed into the mountains near Burtonwood, UK. while letting down thru the weather.—P-51D ? VF-?.

5-29-45   *Fredericks, Harold H.*—1Lt. 336FS.—KIFA—He led a ferry flt. of surplus A/C to Speke Air Depot near Liverpool at 1000 hrs. While letting down thru bad cloud from 7,000 ft. near Manchester, UK., he crashed and exploded; killed him instantly. He hit the ground near Crewe, UK.—P-51D 44-72181 VF-S.

Combat Pilots of the 4th Fighter Group

LEGEND

1. Pilot's rank. The highest known rank attained in 4FG service.
2. The pilot's name. All are in alphabetical order. Many pilots served in several squadrons and each squadron will list his service in that particular squadron.
3. The pilot's nickname where it is known and was frequently used.
4. The WW2 home address of the pilot.
5. The date he joined the squadron, the date he left the squadron, his post-4FG duty assignment where it is known, the reason for his relief from squadron duty (wound, capture, death). If no reason is given, it is assumed his combat tour was completed. A posting to a replacement depot means return to the U.S. If he was a combat loss, the a/c type, serial number, and Missing Aircrew Report Number (MARN) is given. The MARN can be traced through government sources for more detail of the loss than it is possible to include herein.
6. The pilot's WW2 decorations and/or career decorations where these are known. This item is not 100 per cent complete for every man. Those that are complete were supplied by the pilots directly. Not all surviving 4FG pilots would supply service data when contacted. Many pilots also held equivalent foreign service decorations not listed here, *i.e.*, RAF, RCAF, etc.
7. Command positions held at various times and the date of assignment to same.
8. The type and serial number and/or code letters of a/c regularly assigned to the pilot and, if known, the period of assignment.
9. Unit served in prior to 4FG duty and date of joining it, if known.
10. The highest known career rank attained and remarks, etc.
11. Pilots assigned after VE-Day and rotation transferees are not included in this combat period history and pilot listing. After VE-Day the personnel were in a constant flux that has no bearing on the actual wartime combat period.
12. Dates are given in month/day/year; "nmi" means "no middle initial"; @ stands for "approximately."

RANKS AND DUTIES OF COMBAT OFFICERS AT THE SQUADRON AND GROUP LEVEL

1. *Flight Officer* (F/O)—Equivalent to a Warrant Officer j.g. The lowest rank of fighter pilot in the 4FG. His combat duty was as a subordinate wingman to other ranks. Until he built up a little combat time and squadron seniority he had no assigned a/c. Upon acquiring the preceding he would share an a/c with another pilot until he moved up in rank.
2. *First and Second Lieutenants*—In combat these ranks would command: an element (2 a/c); a section (4 a/c, which were color-coded red, white, blue, and green); a

170

flight (8 a/c); and on infrequent occasions a squadron (16 a/c). In the air only, a squadron had a major in top command. Late in 1943 a fifth purple section was added sometimes to make a 20 a/c squadron. From late 1944 on the squadrons often put up 20–24 a/c to fly two 8–12 a/c squadrons in both A & B 4th Groups. A lieutenant might hold such squadron non-flying duties as Gunnery Officer, Oxygen Officer, Historian, etc. He usually had a regularly assigned a/c which he shared with another officer, when not scheduled to fly a mission. The pilot assigned to the a/c with senior rank and/or command had the right to paint his personal artwork emblem on the a/c. A lieutenant might command a squadron flight. Each squadron had an A-B-C-D flight of 6 a/c and 6–8 pilots, with 4 flying and 2–4 pilots off duty on leave, pass, sick call, or DS, etc.

3. *Captain*—He led a section or a flight, and often a squadron in the air, sharing mission leads with the major in squadron command. On the ground he served as Squadron Operations Officer or Asst. Ops. Officer, or on minor Group Staff duties. If he was Ops. Officer he could veto the use of his a/c by others and he had first crack at new replacement a/c for his own use.

4. *Major*—He always commanded a squadron or held Group Staff posts as Group Operations Officer, Tactical Inspector, etc. A major had his own a/c and could veto its use if he wished, or let a friend take it. The Squadron CO naturally had first call on a new a/c arrival.

5. *Lieutenant Colonel*—He only commanded a Group or served on Group Staff in such posts as Group Operations Officer, Group Executive Officer, or Deputy Group Commander and Station Commander. LtCol's. had their personally assigned a/c and a vehicle as well.

6. *Colonel*—A full colonel either commanded a Group and the station or served in a higher echelon above Group. He had his own a/c and vehicle assigned to him and got the best of each on the base. And the best of everything else on the base, including quarters, liquor stocks, etc. Ranks higher than colonel are not pertinent to a Group structure. Group level combat pilots usually rotated the Group Lead at the head of different squadrons from show to show. Therefore no one squadron got first attack on the enemy constantly.

334TH FIGHTER SQUADRON PILOTS:

2Lt. Norman W. Achen "Doc"; Los Angeles, Cal.; To sq. 6/11/44–8/15/44—POW, P-51B 43-6882, MARN-8147; asgnd. a/c P-51B 43-6882.

Maj. Robert A. Ackerly; Middletown, N.Y.; To sq. 10/6/44–11/7/44—335FS.; asgnd. Sq. Ops. Off.—10/18/44; Sq. a/c P-51D MAN-I-ACK.

1Lt. George W. Adams; To sq. 10/30/43–11/3/43—336FS.; Asst. Sq. Ops. Off.

2Lt. Eacott G. Allen; Robstown, Tex.; To sq. 4/17/44–6/8/44—Evader, P-51B 42-106823, MARN-5613.

Capt. Stanley M. Anderson; Indianapolis, Ind.; To sq. 9/15/42–4/15/43—KIA, P-47C 41-6407; AM-OLC; asgnd. a/c Spit VB BL376 11-42, P-47 41-6538 4/4/43; 71ES 3/3/42.

F/O Andre J. Andreu; To sq. 5/24/43–5/25/43—336FS.

Maj. Thomas J. Andrews; Costa Mesa, Cal.; To sq. 9/16/42–9/11/43—12th RCD; DFC, AM-2OLC; A Flt. CO-4/16/43, Sq. Ops. Off.-6/2/43, Acting Sq. CO-4/13/43; asgnd. a/c Spit VB AB929 11-42; P-47C 41-6413 4/4/43; 71ES 9/7/41.; Lt. Col. USAF.

Lt. William O. Antonides; Glenwood Springs, Colo.; To sq. Spring, 45—9/15/45—10th Air Depot Grp.; AM-OLC.

2Lt. Marvin W. Arthur; Indianapolis, Ind.; To sq. 11/16/44–EOW; AM-2OLC; asgnd. a/c P-51D 44-13984 3-45.

1Lt. James W. Ayers; Tulsa, Okla.; To sq. 6/11/44–EOW; AM-7OLC; *C* Flt. CO-3/27/45; asgnd. a/c P-51B 43-6518 1-45.

2Lt. John L. Barden; Ithaca, Mich.; To sq. 4/17/44–4/29/44—POW, P-51B 42-106682; MARN-4671; 9 missions; Major USAF ret.

F/O William D. Bates; Cullman, Ala.; To sq. 11/16/44–2/6/45—KIA, P-51D 44-13884.

2Lt. Calvin H. Beason; Anderson, Ind.; To sq. 11/16/44–EOW; AM-3OLC; asgnd. a/c P-51D NAD Spring, 45.

Maj. Duane W. Beeson "Bee"; Boise, Id.; To sq. 10/13/42–4/5/44—POW, P-51B 43-6819; MARN-3606; DSC, DFC-6OLC, Silver Star, AM-5OLC, Purple Heart, Belgian Croix de Guerre; Sq. Gunnery Off.—9/25/43, Grp. Gunnery Off.-11/15/43, *C* Flt. CO-12/28/43, Sq. Ops. Off.-3/7/44, Sq. CO-3/15/44; Asgnd. a/c Spit VB BL422, Spit VB AD464, Spit VB AB975, P-47D 42-7890, P-51B 43-6819; 71ES 9/1/42; LtCol. USAF, deceased 2/13/47.

Capt. Thomas R. Bell; Shawboro, N.C.; To sq. 9/28/44–EOW; AM-6OLC; *C* Flt. CO-12/21/44, asst. Ops. & Gunnery Off.-3/27/45.

1Lt. Donald L. Bennett; Bellflower, Cal.; To sq. 9/22/44–11/20/44—POW, P-51D 44-13615; MARN-10536; asgnd. a/c P-51D 44-13615.

1Lt. Hipolitus Thomas Biel; St. Paul, Mn.; To sq. 9/7/43–4/24/44—KIA, P-51B 42-106636; MARN-4311; DFC, AM-OLC; Asgnd. a/c P-51B QP-I.

Capt. Herbert J. Blanchfield; Paterson, N.J.; To sq. 8/18/43–5/9/44—POW, P-51B 42-106767; MARN-4685; DFC-OLC, AM-OLC; asgnd. a/c P-47C 41-6187, P-51B 43-6746, P-51B 42-106767.

Capt. Vernon A. Boehle; Indianapolis, Ind.; To sq. 10/13/42–11/23/43—9AF FC; DFC, AM-OLC; asgnd. a/c Spit VB EN783, P-47C 41-6400; 71ES 8/28/42.

2Lt. Robert A. Boock; Springfield, Ill.; To sq. 10/13/42–5/18/43—KIA, P-47C; DFC, AM-OLC; asgnd. a/c Spit VB AB941, P-47C 41-6405; 71ES 9/8/42.

1Lt. Douglas E. Booth "Tiger"; N.Y.C., N.Y.; To sq. 5/25/43–9/12/43—12th RCD; DFC, AM-2OLC; 121ES.

2Lt. Richard L. Bopp; Revere, Mass.; To sq. 5/16/44–5/28/44—POW, P-51B 42-106846; MARN-5726; Asgnd. a/c P-51B QP-H.

1Lt. Clarence L. Boretsky; Milwaukee, Wis.; To sq. 6/2/44–3/4/45—70th Repl. Depot.; AM-5OLC; *D* Flt. CO-12/21/44; asgnd. a/c P-51B QP-M MEG, P-51D 44-13984.

2Lt. Arthur Reed Bowers; Tiskilwa, Ill.; To sq. 11/16/44–EOW; AM-OLC, Purple Heart-3/26/45. Wounded in neck by Flak hit on canopy of P-51D 44-53223 QP-S n/e of Erlangen, Ger.; asgnd. a/c P-51D QP-S SWEET ARLENE.

Lt. W. C. Brite; Evansville, Ind.; No data on service located.

Capt. Carl F. Brown; Huntington, Pa.; To sq. 6/2/44–EOW; AM-8OLC; *D* Flt. CO-12/31/44, asst. Sq. Ops. & Gun. Off.-7/10/45, Sq. CO-11-45.

Maj. Gerald Brown; Phoenix, Ariz.; To sq. 6/30/44–10/9/44—70th Repl. Dep.; Sq. Ops. Off.-7/14/44, acting Sq. CO-7/29/44 to approx. 9/25/44.; Col. USAF.

1Lt. Ralph H. Buchanan "Buck"; Los Angeles, Cal.; To sq. 7/27/44–EOW; AM-6OLC; asgnd. a/c P-51D 44-72155.

1Lt. Allan F. Bunte; Eustis, Fla.; To sq. 5/25/43–4/5/44—POW, P-51B 43-6946; MARN-3609; DFC, AM-OLC; RCAF 3/30/41.

1Lt. Paul E. Burnett; Chelsea, Okla.; To sq. 11/16/44–9/21/45—64FW; AM-2OLC, Purple Heart?; P-51D 44-72377, crashed with a/c and got minor wounds on 4/16/45 near Otterburg, Ger. Evac to Paris by 12TAC.

2Lt. Philo M. Burney; Dallas, Tex.; To sq. 1/23/45–9/15/45—10th Air Depot, Kassel, Ger.; AM-OLC.

1Lt. Vernon A. Burroughs "Cub"; Los Angeles, Cal.; To sq. 5/3/44–5/9/44—POW, P-51B 43-6636; MARN-4682; AM-2OLC.

2Lt. James T. Byrd, Jr.; Atlanta, Ga.; To sq. 6/5/44–6/8/44—KIFA, P-51B 43-6433.

2Lt. James F. Callahan; Wilkes-Barre, Pa.; To sq. 5/1/44–9/14/44—70th Repl. Dep.

Capt. Raymond C. Care "Bud"; Angola, Ind.; To sq. 10/13/42–2/29/44—to HQ.

65FW., to sq. 4/6/44–4/15/44—POW, P-51B 43-7183; MARN-4061; DFC-2OLC, AM-2OLC; *B* Flt. CO-10/29/43, Sq. CO-4/6/44; asgnd. a/c P-47C 41-6404, P-47D 42-7981, P-51B 43-7183; 71ES. 9/8/42; Col. USAF ret.

Maj. Donald R. Carlson; Rockford, Ill.; To sq. 6/11/44–8/10/44—HQ. Sq. 4FG; Sq. Ops. Off.-6/11/44.

1Lt. Charles D. Carr "Chuck"; Lincoln, Neb.; To sq. 10/10/43–4/5/44—POW, P-51B 43-6837; MARN-3607; DFC, AM-OLC.

1Lt. Vincent R. Castle "Bud"; Bluffs, Ill.; To sq. 2/19/43–6/19/43—KIFA, P-47D 42-7881; AM.; 17 sq. sorties; asgnd. a/c P-47C 41-6407, P-47D 42-7881.

Capt. Archie W. Chatterley; San Diego, Cal.; To sq. 1/20/43–3/27/44—POW, P-51B 43-6860; MARN-3439; DFC-OLC, AM-2OLC; *C* Flt. CO-3/1/44, asst. Sq. Ops. & Gun. Off.-3/21/44; asgnd. a/c P-47C 41-6407, P-47C 41-6358, P-51B 43-6860.

2Lt. John L. Childs; Floral Park, N.Y.; To sq. 10/27/44–11/6/44—KIA, P-51D 44-14772; MARN-10444; asgnd. a/c P-51D 44-14772.

Maj. Shannon Christian; To sq. 8/8/43–8/11/43—353FG; Commander of 351FS. on DS to 4TH for operational training; Did not fly combat with 4TH.

LtCol. James A. Clark, Jr. "Jim"; Westbury, N.Y.; To sq. 9/15/42–3/15/44—HQ. Sq. 4FG.; Silver Star, DFC-?OLC, AM-?OLC; Sq. Ops. Off.-5/22/43, *C* Flt. CO-6/2/43, *B* Flt. CO-7/11/43, *A* Flt. CO-9/10/43, Sq. CO-3/1/44; asgnd. a/c Spit VB BM293, P-47C 41-6195, P-47C 41-6413, P-51B 43-6560, P-51B 42-106650, P-51D 44-13372; 71ES. 6/9/42.

2Lt. Robert P. Claus; Bronx, N.Y.; To sq. 2/8/44–4/8/44—KIA, P-51B 43-7029; MARN-3611.

Capt. Henry E. Clifton, Jr.; Little Rock, Ark.; To sq. 7/12/44–3/20/45—70th Repl. Dep.; AM-7OLC; *A* Flt. CO-12/31/44.

LtCol. Oscar H. Coen; Marion, Ill.; To sq. 3/3/43–10/26/43—356FG (8FC); DFC-OLC; Sq. CO-3/3/43; asgnd. a/c P-47C 41-6413; on U.S. leave 6/6/43–8/4/43; 104 sorties, 295 ops. hrs.; 71ES. 4/19/41; Col. USAF ret.

2Lt. Leon J. Cole, Jr.; Nashville, Tn.; To sq. 6/2/44–6/11/44—KIA, P-51B 42-103292; MARN-5572.

1Lt. Lynd J. Cox; Troy, N.Y.; To sq. 6/11/44–1/25/45—70th Repl. Dep.; AM-?OLC; No data available.

F/O William A. Cox; Dallas, Tex.; To sq. 12/28/43–2/3/44—KIA, P-47D 42-75254; MARN-2143; AM-5OLC; asgnd. a/c P-47 QP-S.

2Lt. Timothy J. Cronin "Tim"; Oconomowoc, Wis.; To sq. 5/25/44–3/4/45—70th Repl. Dep.; AM-5OLC.

2Lt. Arthur C. Cwiklinski; Milwaukee, Wis.; To sq. 6/5/44–8/18/44—Evader, P-51D 44-13314; MARN-7940; asgnd. a/c P-51D QP-X 44-13314.

Maj. Gregory A. Daymond "Gus"; Burbank, Cal.; To sq. 9/29/42–3/3/43—Trfd. to U.S.; Sq. Cmmdr.-9/29/42; asgnd. a/c P-47C 41-6204; LtCol. USAFRES.

Lt. Carmen J. Delnero; Springfield, Mass.; To sq. 9/22/44–11/21/44—KIA, P-51D 44-14119; MARN-10537.

1Lt. Gordon A Denson; Rockville, Conn.; To sq. 1/23/45–9/21/45—64FW; DFC recommended, but VE intervened, AM-3OLC, AF Commendation Medal, AF Meritorious Service Medal, Freedom Foundation Honor Medal; asgnd. P-51D QP-E PRISCILLA; 24 missions, 126 combat hrs.; Col. USAF ret.

1Lt. Robert A. Dickmeyer; Ada, Ohio; To sq. 6/2/44–12/26/44—70th Repl. Dep.; AM-7OLC; *D* Flt. CO-11/20/44; asgnd. a/c P-51D 44-13956.

1Lt. Richard V. Douglas "Dick"; Dallas, Tex.; To sq. 1/20/43–9/29/43—2906th Obs. Trng. Grp.; AM.; asgnd. a/c P-47C 41-6410.

Capt. William J. Dvorak; Western Springs, Ill.; To sq. 8/20/44–EOW.; AM-6OLC; *B* Flt. CO-3/8/45.

2Lt. Raymond A. Dyer; Glassport, Pa.; To sq. 9/2/44–9/21/45—4th Mobile Sq. R&R.; AM-6OLC; asgnd. a/c P-51D 44-14323.

1Lt. Fred E. Farington, Jr.; Falls City, Neb.; To sq. 9/28/44–EOW; AM-3OLC; asgnd. a/c P-51D QP-N SKIPPY.

2Lt. Joseph P. Fernandez; Fayetteville, Ark.; To sq. 5/16/44–?—trfd. to 65FW; AM-8OLC.

Capt. Gervais W. Ford; Lake Charles, La.; To sq. 1/31/45–?; AM-3OLC; bomber pilot on 30-day TDY.

F/O Kenneth E. Foster; Oil City, Pa.; To sq. 9/7/44–3/31/45—POW, P-51D, 44-11336; MARN-13945; AM-5OLC.

Capt. Victor J. France "Vic"; Dallas, Tex.; To sq. 10/13/42–4/18/44—KIA, P-51B 43-6832; MARN-5012; DFC-2OLC, AM-OLC; *C* Flt. CO.-3/21/44; asgnd. a/c Spit VB AD196, P-47C 41-6414, P-47D 42-7876, P-51B 43-6832; 71ES 8/7/42.

2Lt. Thomas E. Fraser; Atlanta, Ga.; To sq. 5/1/44–6/6/44—POW, P-51B 43-24835; MARN-5608.

1Lt. Robert B. Frazer; Fullerton, Cal.; To sq. 8/17/43–2/28/44—KIFA, P-51B 43-6656; AM-OLC; asgnd. a/c P-51B 43-6656.

Lt. Joseph E. Gallant; Chelsea, Mass.; No data is available.

F/O Frank D. Gallion; Millersburg, Ohio; To sq. 10/10/43–11/3/43—KIA, P-47 42-7924; MARN-1048.

Lt. Vermont Garrison; Mt. Victory, Ky.; To sq. 8/22/45–9/21/45—4th MR&R Sq.; former 336FS POW returned.

Lt. Leo C. Garvin; Bay City, Mich.; To sq. ?–9/15/45—10th Air Depot Grp.

Lt. Willard G. Gillette; Homewood, Tex.; To sq. 5/1/44–10/25/44—70th Repl. Dep.

F/O Lawrence O. Grey; Park Ridge, Ill.; To sq. 8/26/43–11/29/43—311th Ferry Sqd.

2Lt. Benjamin L. Griffin; Jacksonville, Fla.; To sq. 10/27/44–12/19/44—336FS.

Lt. ? ? Gross;?; Guest pilot; Flew ops. on 2/21/44, 2/22/44, 2/24/44.

2Lt. James E. Halligan; Boston, Mass.; To sq. 9/29/45–?; AM.

F/O Alvin L. Hand; West Newton, Pa.; To sq. 1/23/45–2/24/45—POW, P-51D 44-11661; MARN-12625.

1Lt. Preston B. Hardy; Dillon, S.C.; To sq. 4/17/44–Oct., 44—to U.S. after end of tour; DFC-OLC, AM-15OLC, Bronze Star, Purple Heart, Legion of Merit, PUC-3OLC, DUC-2OLC; Col. USAF ret.

1Lt. Charles W. Harre; Brownstown, Ill.; To sq. 9/7/44–4/27/45—70th Repl. Dep.; AM-5OLC.

Lt. James C. Harrington; Buffalo, N.Y.; To sq. 9/29/42–?; asgnd. a/c Spit VB BL370; 71ES.

Capt. William F. Hedrick; Denver, Colo.; To sq. 5/25/44–2/5/45—HQ. USSAFE.; DFC, AM-5OLC; *A* Flt. CO prior to 12/31/44.

1Lt. Kenneth G. Helfrecht; Madison, Wis.; To sq. 10/27/44–9/21/45—4th Mobile R&R. Sq.; AM-5OLC; asgnd. a/c P-51D 44-14110, P-51D 44-63223.

Capt. Roy A. Henwick "Dutch"; South Africa; To sq. 7/20/44–10/25/44—SAAF; asgnd. a/c QP-M; SAAF officer on exchange tour of duty to 4FG.

2Lt. Aubrey E. Hewatt; ? ; To sq. 4/17/44–5/28/44—POW, P-51B 43-6933, MARN-5397; asgnd. a/c P-51B 43-6933.

Lt. ? ? Hill; ? ; Guest pilot on ops. of 2/15/44, 2/20/44, 2/22/44.

Capt. Robert L. Hills; New Milford, Conn.; To sq. 10/10/43–9/14/44—70th Repl. Dep.; DFC-OLC, AM-OLC; *D* Flt. CO.-7/14/44; asgnd. a/c QP-S; ex-RAF pilot.

Maj. Howard D. Hively "Deacon"; Norman, Okla.; To sq. 9/17/42–1/29/45—4FG HQ Sq.; DSC, DFC-6OLC, AM-7OLC, Purple Heart; Sq. CO-6/6/44, acting 4TH Dep. Grp. & Station CO-8/9/44; On U.S. leave 8/14/44–11/1/44; asgnd. a/c P-47C 41-6576, P-51B 43-6898, P-51D 44-15347; 71ES. 7/2/42; USAF ret.

Capt. William B. Hoelscher "Brad"; Indianapolis, Ind.; To sq. 8/12/44–4/25/45—Evader, P-51D 44-15347; MARN-14047; AM-6OLC; *D* Flt. CO.-3/27/45; USAF career off.

Lt. Ralph Kidd Hofer "Kidd"; Salem, Mo.; To sq. 9/22/43–7/2/44—KIA, P-51B 43-

6746; MARN-6801; DFC-3OLC, AM-OLC; *A* Flt. CO.-6/2/44; asgnd. a/c P-51B 42-106924.

Capt. Walter J. Hollander "Lulu"; Honolulu, Hi.; To sq. 9/15/42–5/18/43—6FW; Sq. Ops. Off.-12/6/42; asgnd. a/c P-47C 41-6538; 71ES. 11/17/41; KIFA post-war.

Capt. Alfred H. Hopson "Hoppy"; Dallas, Tx.; To sq. 9/16/42–12/14/43—2nd. Gen. Hospital, injured in accident; DFC, AM-3OLC; *C* Flt. CO.-9/10/43; asgnd. a/c Spit VB EN915, P-47C 41-6212; 71ES. 6/10/42.

2Lt. C. G. Howard (name only initials); Tulsa, Okla.; To sq. 6/11/44–8/18/44—KIA, P-51B 43-24841; MARN-7943; asgnd. a/c P-51B 43-24841.

Capt. David W. Howe; East Hickory, Pa.; To sq. 9/22/43–3/30/45—70th Repl. Dep.; DFC-OLC, AM-12OLC; asst. Sq. Ops. & Gun. Off. vice *B* Flt. CO.-1/31/45; asgnd. a/c P-51D 44-13884; 500 combat hrs. (2 tours) without an abort.; ex-RCAF pilot; Bell A/C test pilot 1974.

2Lt. Walter R. Hughes; Memphis, Tn.; To sq. 10/27/44–1/6/45—355FG.; AM; back in 4FG on ?; asgnd. to 4th Mobile R&R Sq.-9/21/45.

1Lt. Jerome E. Jahnke "Bruiser"; Los Angeles, Cal.; To sq. 7/27/44–EOW; AM-7OLC; asgnd. a/c QP-Q.

2Lt. Daniel L. James; Waynesboro, Va.; To sq. 1/23/45–EOW; Maj. USAF.

Lt. J. E. Jones; Victor, N.Y.; To sq. ?; no data available.

Capt. Thomas E. Joyce; Ulysses, Kan.; To sq. 5/1/44–9/22/44—POW, P-51D 44-14271; MARN-8988.

Capt. Robert H. Kanaga; Detroit, Mich.; To sq. 8/16/44–4/25/45—70th Repl. Dep.; AM-5OLC; deceased.

2Lt. Michael J. Kennedy "Mike"; Philadelphia, Pa.; To sq. 10/27/44–9/21/45—4TH Mobile R&R. Sq.; AM-4OLC.

2Lt. Pete R. Kennedy; ? ; To sq. 4/17/44–4/29/44—POW, P-51B 43-6646; MARN-4541.

Capt. Robert P. Kenyon; Detroit, Mich.; To sq. 3/9/44–10/25/44—70th Repl. Dep.; DFC; *C* Flt. CO-7/14/44.

1Lt. Garrett C. King; Morland, Wy.; To sq. 1/20/43–6/14/43—KIFA, P-47 QP-T; AM; 13 sorties total; asgnd. a/c P-47C 41-6196.

2Lt. Mark H. Kolter; Lima, Ohio; To sq. 4/4/44–5/30/44—KIA, P-51B 43-7178; MARN-5607.

2Lt. Andrew C. Lacy; Sullivan, Ohio; To sq. 9/18/44–2/21/45—POW, P-51D 44-11677; MARN-12595; AM-3OLC; asgnd. a/c P-51K 44-11677.

Capt. Joseph L. Lang; Boston, Mass.; To sq. 12/28/43–10/14/44—KIA, P-51D 44-14123; MARN-9495; DFC-OLC; *B* Flt. CO.-6/2/44; ex-RAF pilot; asgnd. a/c P-51D 44-14123.

2Lt. Dean E. Lange; St. Paul, Minn.; To sq. 6/15/44–8/18/44—POW, P-51B 42-103791; MARN-7944.

1Lt. Dale B. Leaf; Marshalltown, Iowa; To sq. 5/25/43–9/2/43—KIA, P-47 QP-I; AM-OLC.

2Lt. Donald G. Lowther; Columbus, Ohio; To sq. 1/23/45–EOW; AM-OLC.

1Lt. John F. Lutz "Pappy"; Fulton, Mo.; To sq. 9/16/42–5/4/43—KIA, P-47 41-6196; asgnd. a/c P-47C 41-6196; 71ES. 7/1/42.

2Lt. Leland L. MacFarlane; Portland, Ore.; To sq. 1/20/43–5/21/43—KIA, P-47 42-7920; MARN-2663; asgnd. a/c P-47 41-6406.

Capt. Donald M. Malmsten; Burwell, Neb.; To sq. 4/4/44–EOW; DFC, AM-10-OLC, Purple Heart; *B* Flt. CO-1/31/45; asgnd. a/c P-51B 43-6957; killed post-war.

LtCol. John F. Malone; ? ; To sq. 5/19/43–7/10/43—4TH HQ. SQ.; Sq. CO.-5/19/43 (probably acting CO for Coen on U.S. leave).

Capt. Alfred H. Markel; Claymont, Dela.; To sq. 5/17/43–8/18/44—4TH Hq. Sq.; To sq. 11/8/44–?; DFC, AM-OLC; Off ops. in May, 44 after tour done and asgnd. Sq. Eng. Off. Asgnd. Sq. OTU CO.-11/8/44.

Capt. Jack D. McFadden; Brookville, Pa.; To sq. 6/11/44–EOW; AM-10-OLC; A Flt. CO-3/8/45.

Capt. Richard D. McMinn; Salt Lake City, Utah; To sq. 9/16/42–4/15/43—KIA, P-47 41-6204; AM; B Flt. CO-11/28/42; asgnd. a/c Spit VB AD464, P-47C 41-6204; 71ES. 12/23/41.

F/O John P. McNabb; Joplin, Mo.; To sq. 9/26/43–12/2/43—KIFA, P-47 41-6484.

Maj. Michael G. H. McPharlin "Wee Mac"; Hastings, Mich.; Member of 339FG who liked to fly with his old 71 E.S. chums in 334FS.; KIA with 334FS–6/6/44, P-51B 42-106909 6N-Z.; Ex-RCAF pilot.

Capt. Nicholas Megura "Cowboy"; Ansonia, Conn.; To sq. 7/3/43–Internee–5/22/44, P-51B 43-7158; 7/16/45–to U.S.. Off ops. after return from Swedish internment 6/28/44. DSC, DFC-4OLC, AM-?OLC, Purple Heart; C Flt. CO-5/44; asgnd. a/c P-51B 43-6636; Wounded 4/29/44 in left arm; Ex-RCAF pilot; LtCol. USAFRES. ret.

Lt. Robert J. Miller; Chicago, Ill.; To sq. ?–4/10/45—WIA, P-51D QP-F; Landed at B-78 Eindhoven, Neth., for hospitalizing. Not known to return to 334FS.

Maj. Henry L. Mills "Hank"; New York City, N.Y.; To sq. 10/23/42–3/6/44—POW, P-51B 43-6690; MARN-3044; DFC, AM-2OLC; B Flt. CO-9/10/43, Sq. Ops. Off.-10/29/43; asgnd. a/c Spit VB AD564, P-47D 42-74751, P-51B 43-6690; 71ES. 8/29/42.

Maj. Shelton W. Monroe "Shel"; Waycross, Ga.; To sq. 1/23/44–1/26/45—335FS.; Silver Star, DFC-3OLC, AM-?; A Flt. CO-7/2/44, Asst. Sq. Ops. & Gun. Off.-11/9/44; asgnd. a/c P-51D 44-13411; On U.S. leave after 1st tour 8/19/44–11/1/44; KIA in Korean War.

Maj. Gerald E. Montgomery "Monty"; Dallas, Tx.; To sq. 5/15/43–EOW; DFC-3OLC, AM-11OLC; A Flt. CO. prior to 6/2/44, Sq. Ops. Off.-11/9/44; U.S. leave after 1st tour approx. 6/2/44–?; asgnd. a/c P-47D 42-7980, P-51D 44-14119, P-51D 44-15326 (had many new 51Ds); Believed KIA in Korean War.

1Lt. Ivan R. Moon; Palm Beach, Fla.; To sq. 9/7/43–11/3/43—KIA, P-47 41-6587; MARN-4139; AM.

1Lt. William Brewster Morgan "Brew"; Honolulu, Hi.; To sq. 9/15/42–5/21/43—POW, P-47 42-8644; AM-?; asgnd. a/c Spit VB BL550, Spit VB BL353, P-47 41-6191; On D.S. to 336FS 1/14/43–3/22/43; 71ES. 4/24/42.

Capt. Howard N. Moulton, Jr.; Sheffield, Mass.; To sq. 1/23/44–4/8/44—POW, P-51B 43-6967; MARN-3610; DFC. AM-?; Ex-RCAF pilot.

1Lt. David K. Needham; New Albany, Ind.; To sq. 5/25/44–9/14/44—70th Repl. Dep.; AM-?; asgnd. a/c QP-V.

2Lt. Harry B. Noon; Indianapolis, Ind.; To sq. 6/2/44–6/11/44—KIA, P-51B 43-6586; MARN-5571; asgnd. a/c P-51B 43-6591.

Maj. Louis H. Norley, Jr. "Red Dog"; Conrad, Mont.; To sq. 1/25/45–9/21/45—4TH Mobile R&R Sq.; DFC-?, AM-13OLC; Sq. CO-1/25/45–9/21/45; asgnd. a/c P-51D 44-15350, P-51D 44-72196; Started 3rd tour with 554 combat hrs. on 3/31/45; Korean War vet. Retired from USAF as LtCol. Deceased on 8/1/67 Oakland, Cal.

1Lt. William C. O'Bryan; ? ; To sq. 1/23/45–?; No data available.

Capt. William T. O'Regan; Los Angeles, Cal.; To sq. 9/16/42–9/27/43—12th RCD.; DFC, AM-2OLC; B Flt. CO-4/16/43, Sq. Ops. Off.–9/10/43; asgnd. a/c Spit VB AD564, P-47C 41-6392; 71ES. 12/23/41.

Capt. Carl G. Payne; San Antonio, Tx.; To sq. 9/22/44–9/21/45—4TH Mobile R&R. Sq.; AM-5OLC.; Sq. Ops. Off.-7/10/45; asgnd. a/c P-51D 44-72381.

1Lt. Leonard R. Pierce; Canandaigua, N.Y.; To sq. 3/9/44–5/13/44—KIA, P-51B 42-106441; DFC; asgnd. a/c P-51B 42-106441.

Capt. Steve N. Pisanos "The Greek"; Plainfield, N.J.; To sq. 10/24/42–3/5/44—Evader; 9/9/44 to 67FW Hq. MARN-3046; Legion of Merit, DFC-3OLC, AM-3OLC, Purple Heart, AFC medal, PUC-2OLC, Fr. Croix De Guerre with Silver Star, RAF Medallion; 106 WW2 sorties; 71ES. 10/13/42; Col. USAF active.

? *E. M. Potter "Gene";* Chicago, Ill.; Known to have flown with 334th in Nov. 42 with Spit VB EN783. Not known as reg. sq. pilot assigned; 71 & 121 ES.; Deceased ?.

Capt. Robert L. Priser "Junior"; Tucson, Ariz.; To sq. 9/15/42–11/23/43—9FC Sta. 476; DFC, AM-3OLC; *A* Flt. CO.-9/13/43; asgnd. a/c P-47C 41-6187; 71ES. 6/23/42.

Capt. Alexander Rafalovich; San Pedro, Cal.; To sq. 2/19/43–3/21/44—POW, P-51B 43-6839; MARN-3372; DFC-OLC, AM-OLC; *B* Flt. CO.-3/21/44; asgnd. a/c P-47C 41-6195; Retired in Cal.

Capt. Victor R. Rentschler "Neffie"; Cicero, Ill.; To sq. 6/11/44–1/16/45—POW, P-51D 44-15324; MARN-11852; AM-6OLC.

Maj. Benjamin Rimerman; 353FG officer attached for training. Flew ops. on 7/25/43–7/28/43 in P-47 LH-K.

Lt. Gilbert G. Ross; Albuquerque, N.M.; To sq. 9/15/42–8/10/43—87th AT Sq.; AM-OLC; asgnd. a/c P-47C 41-6410; 31 sorties; 71ES. 6/12/42; Deceased.

2Lt. Kenneth J. Rudkin; Sparta, Wis; To sq. 6/15/44–8/25/44—POW, P-51D 44-13732; MARN-7942.

Lt. Morton R. Savage "Doc"; Yeador, Pa.; To sq. 9/2/44–2/11/45—KIFA, P-51D QP-W; AM-4OLC.

2Lt. John J. Scally; Swampscott, Mass.; To sq. 6/11/44–7/7/44—POW, P-51B 43-6567; MARN-6803; Deceased.

Lt. John M. Schnell, Jr.; Mobile, Ala.; To sq. 3/24/45–?; Maj. USAF ret.

2Lt. James F. Scott; Brownwood, Tx.; To sq. 4/4/44–6/8/44—KIA, P-51B 43-7150; MARN-5605.

Lt. Anthony J. Seaman; Greenville, N.C.; To sq. 9/12/42–10/20/42—KIA, Spit VB.

Lt. Arthur J. Senecal; Worcester, Mass.; To sq. 8/12/44–1/2/45—KIA, P-51B 43-6587; MARN-11521; AM-4OLC.

Lt. Thomas S. Sharp; McArthur, Ohio; To sq. 5/1/44–7/2/44—KIA, P-51B 42-106650; MARN-6798.

Lt. Robert S. Sherman; Talcotville, Conn.; To sq. 4/4/44–5/9/44—POW, P-51B 43-7002; MARN-4684.

Lt. Thomas J. Siehl; Cincinnati, Ohio; To sq. 3/24/45–9/15/45—10th Air Depot Grp.; Now an M.D. in Ohio.

Lt. Grover C. Siems, Jr.; Wantagh, L.I., N.Y.; To sq. 4/4/44–9/14/44—70th Repl. Dep. (returned home from Italy after serious wounding 7/2/44 on Shuttle show to Hungary. 9/14/44 is date taken off 334th status.); P-51D 44-13322; Silver Star; asgnd. a/c P-51D 44-13322.

1Lt. Jack T. Simon "Red"; Long Beach, Cal.; To sq. 5/1/44–9/14/44—70th Repl. Dep.

1Lt. Billy F. Skinner; Evansville, Ind.; To sq. 3/24/45–9/18/45—10th Air Depot Grp., Y-96, Kassel, Germany.

Lt. Alan Skirball "Screwball"; Columbus, Ohio; To sq. 1/23/45–EOW; AM-OLC.

2Lt. Orville W. Slone; Ashland, Ky.; To sq. 3/24/45–9/15/45—10th Air Depot Grp.

Lt. Clyde D. Smith; Centerville, Utah; To sq. 5/15/43–10/8/43—POW, P-47 42-7915; MARN-937; DFC, AM-?.

Capt. William B. Smith; Bluefield, Va.; To sq. 5/23/43–9/13/44—KIA, P-51D 44-14281; MARN-8989; DFC-OLC, AM-?; *B* Flt. CO-prior to 6/2/44; asgnd. a/c P-47C 41-6410, P-51D 44-14281; On U.S. leave 6/2/44–8/17/44 to 2nd tour.

1Lt. Orrin C. Snell "Ossie"; Winnipeg, Can.; To sq. 5/13/44–8/10/44—AAF Sta. 370; Grounded on 5/15/44 until Central Medical Board takes action; Ex-RAF pilot.

Maj. Winslow M. Sobanski "Mike"; New York City, N.Y.; To sq. 5/25/43–6/6/44—KIA, P-51B 42-6898; MARN-5603; DFC-OLC, AM-2OLC; *A* Flt. CO-11/29/43, Sq. CO-prior to 4/15/44; asgnd. a/c P-47D 42-75126, P-51D QP-F (on 6/6/44).

Lt. Frank E. Speer; Allentown, Pa.; To sq. 4/17/44–5/29/44—POW/Escaper, P-51B

43-6560; MARN-5396; DFC, AM-3OLC, Bronze Star, PUC; asgnd. a/c P-51B 43-6957; Successful escape on 3rd try, walked 100-plus miles to freedom.

2Lt. Milton L. Spencer; Springville, N.Y.; To sq. 3/24/45–?.

2Lt. William G. Spencer; Boone, N.C.; To sq. 1/23/45–9/18/45—354FG R-29, Germany; AM-OLC; Sq. I.O.-7/25/45.

Capt. Robert S. Sprague; San Diego, Cal.; To sq. Sept., 42–11/26/42—KIFA, Spit VB, on local non-ops. flight and crashed fatally; 71ES.

1Lt. C. L. Stafford; To sq. 7/21/43–7/28/43 (353FG pilot attached for ops. training. Flew 3 shows with sq. in P-47 LH-J & X and returned to 353FG.)

Lt. Edward J. Steppe; L.I., N.Y.; To sq. 5/1/44–6/6/44—KIA, P-51B 43-6957; MARN-5604; Wingman to Sq. CO Sobanski when killed.

Lt. H. L. Stewart "Burt"; Raleigh, N.C.; To sq. Sept., 42–1/3/43—OTU 109th Observ. Sq., Atcham, Shrops.; 71 & 121ES.

2Lt. Raymond L. Sylvester; ? ; To sq. 3/24/45–9/15/45—10th Air Depot Grp.

LtCol. ? Taylor; Visitor who flew QP-X on 3/3/45 show, aborting after 2 hrs.

2Lt. Thomas A. Underwood; Wilmington, N.C.; To sq. 7/12/44–8/8/44—POW, P-51B 43-24793; MARN-7758.

1Lt. Herbert VanderVate, Jr.; Buffalo, N.Y.; To sq. 6/6/44–8/28/44—KIA, P-51D 44-14310; MARN-8300.

Capt. David A. Van Epps; Williams Bay, Wis.; To sq. 9/26/43–4/9/44—POW, Bronze Star awarded for POW heroism; P-51B 43-6941; MARN-3749; DFC, AM-2OLC, *D* Flt. CO-3/22/44; asgnd. a/c P-47D 42-8641, P-51B 43-6941; Col. USAF ret. Deceased 9/75. Was a RN FAA commander prior to AAF duty.

1Lt. Robert S. Voyles; Delmont, S.D.; To sq. 9/18/44–2/27/45—POW, P-51D 44-14537; MARN-12783; AM-3OLC; asgnd. a/c P-51D 44-14292.

1Lt. Earl C. Walsh; Jackson, Miss.; To sq. 6/6/44–11/6/44—POW, P-51D 44-14229; MARN-10446.

1Lt. Lewis F. Wells; Quitman, Ga.; To sq. 7/12/44–4/30/45—70th Repl. Dep.; AM-5OLC.

1Lt. Leonard R. Werner; Mt. Vernon, N.Y.; To sq. 6/11/44–11/20/44—KIA, P-51D 44-13411; MARN-10535.

1Lt. Edmund D. Whalen; Gouverneur, N.Y.; To sq. 11/18/43–3/6/44—KIA, P-51B 43-6899; MARN-2839; AM-OLC.

2Lt. William E. Whalen; ? ; To sq. 7/12/44–9/15/44—355FG (acting CO of the Grp., LtCol. Kinnard, exchanged pilots with his old Grp. to instill some 355FG experience in the 4TH).

1Lt. Gordon H. Whitlow; Denver, Colo.; To sq. 9/15/42–5/21/43—KIA, P-47 41-6406; asgnd. a/c Spit VB AB929, P-47C 41-6406; 71ES. 6/20/42.

Capt. James W. Wilkinson; Swarthmore, Pa.; To sq. 1/20/43–4/27/43—WIFA, P-47 41-6405; fractured his spine and was trfd. out of 4TH.; Later war record: Silver Star, DSC, DFC-4OLC, 78FG Sq. CO, KIFA on 6/4/44.; 4TH asgnd. a/c P-47C 41-6405.

Capt. Robert G. Williams "Digger"; St. Petersburg, Fla.; To sq. 5/25/43–3/21/44—POW, P-51B 43-6869; MARN-3373; DFC, AM-?; *D* Flt. CO-3/21/44.

Lt. ? Wink; Guest pilot on ops. of 2/20, 21, 24/44.

Lt. Edward J. Wozniak "Flak"; Girard, Ohio; To sq. 7/12/44–4/15/45—WIA, P-51D 44-63583; AM-5OLC; asgnd. a/c P-51D 44-63583; Not known if he returned to 4TH from hospital on Continent.

Capt. Vasseure H. Wynn "Georgia"; Dalton, Ga.; To sq. 9/17/43–4/13/44—POW, P-51B 43-7035; DFC, AM-OLC; *B* Flt. CO-3/22/44.

335TH FIGHTER SQUADRON PILOTS:

Maj. Robert A. Ackerly; Middletown, N.Y.; To sq. 1/28/45–6/1/45—4TH Hq. Sq.; AM-2OLC: C Flt. CO-3/23/45, Sq. Ops. Off.-4/8/45; asgnd. a/c P-51D 44-17415; Col. USAF ret.

Capt. David R. Allen; Saddle River, N.J.; To sq. 11/16/44–3/8/45—355FG; To sq. 5/13/45–9/18/45—354FG, R-29, Germany; A Flt. CO.-7/20/45.

Capt. Charles F. Anderson; Gary, Ind.; To sq. 8/11/43–4/19/44—KIA, P-51B 43-7181; MARN-4129; In 2nd. Gen. Hospital-10/14/43.

Lt. Russell J. Anderson; ? ; To sq. 8/18/44–11/5/44—POW, P-51D 44-14339; MARN-10445.

Capt. William C. Anderson; ? ; To sq. 9/29/44–2/21/45—479FG; No data available.

2Lt. Hubert N. Ballew; ? ; To sq. 9/2/43–2/6/44—POW, P-51B 42-8495; MARN-2142.

1Lt. William H. Bancroft; ? ; To sq. 9/4/44–1/8/45—355FG; To sq. 5/13/45–9/21/45—4TH Mobile R&R Sq.; On DS to Ferry Command-Nov.-12/28/45.

Lt. George W. Barnes; Canton, N.C.; To sq. 10/12/43–3/3/44—KIA, P-51B 43-6643; MARN-3043.

Lt. Ernest D. Beatie; Albany, Ga.; To sq. 10/14/42–11/29/43—5TH Gen. Hospital; DFC; 121ES.

1Lt. Darwin L. Berry; ? ; To sq. 6/5/44–12/17/44—After tour to U.S.; C Flt. CO-9/16/44, A Flt. CO-11/9/44; asgnd. a/c P-51D 44-14361; 270 combat hrs. completed-12/5/44.; Deceased.

Col. Donald J. M. Blakeslee "Col. Don" "Horseback"; Fairport Harbor, Ohio; To sq. 11/22/42–5/19/43—4TH Hq. Sq.; Full service data given in 4TH HQ. SQ. Pilots List.

Maj. Leon M. Blanding; Sumter, S.C.; To sq. 10/14/42–3/24/44—495FTG, Atcham, Shrops.; To sq. 6/21/44–7/29/44—4TH Hq. Sq.; Sq Ops. Off.-2/3/44, Sq. CO.-6/21/44; Led 335th on Russia Shuttle; 121ES.; LtCol. USAF ret.

Lt. Stephen R. Boren; Marinetta, Wis.; To sq. 7/27/44–8/13/44—KIA, P-51D 44-13997; MARN-8218.

Lt. George M. Bowyer; ? ; To sq. 6/6/44–?—Wounded in action. The records are inconclusive as to correct date of wounding. Possibly 6/13-18-25/44. Hit by slug in upper rt. arm. Bone taken from leg to strengthen damaged arm in operation. He did not return to 4FG.

2Lt. Ralph G. Boyce; ? ; To sq. 5/2/44–5/6/44—KIFA, P-51B; Crashed while landing at Ridgewell, Essex, UK.

Capt. Frank R. Boyles; Mt. Vernon. N.Y.; To sq. 9/16/42–10/16/43—65FW Hq.—KIA, P-51B 43-7098; MARN-3612; On DS to 335th from his assgnmt. at 65FW MOR when KIA.; 121ES.

Lt. James H. Brandenburg; Cincinnati, Ohio; To sq. 9/29/43–3/21/44—KIA, P-51B 43-6641; MARN-3379.

1Lt. Charles L. Brock; Lockhart, Tx.; To sq. 5/2/44–3/2/45—To U.S. after tour.; Maj. USAF active.

Lt. Robert C. Bucholz; Oklahoma City, Okla.; To sq. 11/16/44–4/9/45—KIA, P-51D 44-14389; MARN-13898.

Capt. Oliver B. Bucher, Jr.; Allentown, Pa.; To sq. 11/16/44–9/21/45—4th Mobile R&R. Sq.; AM-3OLC; A Flt. CO-4/8/45; Col. USAF ret., Deceased.

2Lt. Leslie I. Burgess; Norwich, Conn.; To sq. 1/24/45–9/18/45—354FG, R-29, Germany; AM.

1Lt. Robert A. Cammer; Houston, Tx.; To sq. 11/16/44–3/21/45—POW, P-51D 44-14361; MARN-13947.

Capt. Earle W. Carlow; ? ; To sq. 1/22/43–3/21/44—POW, P-51B 43-6639; MARN-3378; Escaped from POW camp on 5/7/44 and returned thru Spain to the UK on 6/10/44.

Maj. George Carpenter; Oil City, Pa.; To sq. 10/14/42–4/18/44—POW, P-51B 42-106675; MARN-4671; Sq. Ops. Off.-12/6/43, Sq. CO-2/5/44; asgnd. a/c Spit VB EN918, P-47C 41-6226, P-51B 43-6575, P-51B 42-106675; 143 AAF sorties, 257 combat hrs.; 121ES.

1Lt. George W. Ceglarski; Library, Pa.; To sq. 6/12/44–9/15/44—355FG. Transferred out to make room for 355FG pilots LtCol. Kinnard brought in.

Capt. Robert C. Church; Bedford, Mass.; To sq. 9/29/43–9/30/44—To U.S. after tour; AM-?, DFC; A Flt. CO-6/7/44, Sq. CO-8/9/44 (acting?); asgnd. a/c P-51B 43-24813, P-51D 44-13883.

Lt. Raymond P. Clotfelter; Hillsboro, Ill.; To sq. 10/12/43–3/28/44—POW, P-51B 43-6843; MARN-3525; AM-2OLC; Col. USAF active.

Lt. John T. Conley; St. Paul, Minn.; To sq. 7/27/44–8/18/44—KIA, P-51B 43-24813; MARN-8144.

Lt. Stanley W. Connors; Albany, Cal.; To sq. 9/29/44–5/4/45—To U.S. after tour.; AM-5OLC.

1Lt. George W. Cooley; Fairchance, Pa.; To sq. 6/12/44–11/20/44—To U.S. after tour.; asgnd. a/c P-51C 42-103291; Successful bail-out 15mi. S/E of Liege, Belg., on 9/11/44. Returned to 335th on 9/15/44.

Lt. Robert J. Cooper; Chicago, Ill.; To sq. 7/27/44–8/18/44—KIA, P-51B 42-106855; MARN-8141.

2Lt. Robert L. Couse; Asbury Park, N.J.; To sq. 1/24/45–9/21/45—64FW.; AM; asgnd. a/c P-51D 44-14570.

Capt. John N. Creamer; Rosedale, N.Y.; To sq. 8/18/44–3/27/45—To U.S. after tour; C Flt. CO-2/17/45; Tour of 300 hrs. done 3/1/45.

2Lt. James D. Crine; Englishtown, N.J.; To sq. 4/27/45–EOW.

2Lt. ? ? Curtis; ? ; To sq. 5/2/44–?; No data available.

Lt. Kermit O. Dahlen; Thompson, Iowa; To sq. 7/13/44–7/19/44—KIA, P-51B 43-6463; MARN-6828.

2Lt. Leo nmi Dailey; Hornell, N.Y.; To sq. 6/18/44–8/18/44—KIA, P-51B 42-106555; MARN-8143.

Maj. William J. Daley; Amarillo, Tx.; To sq. 9/24/42–11/22/42—To U.S.; Sq. CO.-11/18/42; asgnd. a/c Spit VB EN853; 121ES. CO 9/42.

Capt. Albert J. Davis; Ogden, Utah; To sq. 6/18/44–3/21/45—KIA, P-51D 44-63670; C Flt. CO-12/19/44, Asst. Sq. Ops. & Gun. Off.-1/20/45.

Capt. George H. Davis; Berlin, Md.; To sq. 1/27/45–3/3/45—POW, P-51D 44-63599; MARN-12899; AM-2OLC; B Flt. CO.-2/24/45; Deceased.

Capt. Brack nmi Diamond; ? ; To sq. 6/5/44–1/13/45—To U.S.; D Flt. CO.-9/16/44.

1Lt. Helmut R. Dimpfl; ? ; To sq. ?–9/21/45—4TH Mobile R&R. Sq.; D Flt. CO.-7/20/45.

2Lt. Carl S. Draughn; Mt. Olive, Miss.; To sq. 4/27/45–9/18/45—IX Air Serv. Commd.

Capt. James D. Dye; Dallas, Tx.; To sq. 2/22/43–3/21/44—WIA, P-51B WD-G; To 5th Gen. Hospital-4/25/44.; DFC.; Re-wounded by German air raid while in hospital.

1Lt. Wilbur B. Eaton; Portland, Ore.; To sq. 6/29/44–2/15/45—To U.S. after tour.; C Flt. CO.-1/16/45; asgnd. a/c P-51B 43-6897; Did tour as Spit & P-38 recon pilot prior to 4TH.

LtCol. Selden R. Edner; San Jose, Cal.; To sq. 9/16/42–1/8/43—Atcham, Shrops.; To sq. 8/20/43–10/9/43—336FS.; 121ES.

1Lt. Thomas H. Elffner; Fowler, Kan.; To sq. 9/4/44–5/4/45—To U.S. after tour.; AM-6OLC.; Crashed on takeoff on 2/9/45 demolishing a/c, but was okay.

Capt. Paul M. Ellington; Tulsa, Okla; To sq. 10/14/42–3/4/44—POW, P-51B 43-7004; MARN-3051; asgnd. a/c P-47C 41-6214, P-47 42-7965, P-51B 43-7004; 121ES.

Capt. Charles H. Evans; ? ; To sq. 5/26/44–1/8/45—BWAD; D Flt. CO.-12/19/44.

Maj. Roy W. Evans; San Bernardino, Cal.; To sq. 10/14/42–2/5/44—1AF (U.S.); On U.S. leave 3/2/43–4/21/43.; Silver Star, DFC, AM-3OLC.; Sq. CO-8/13/43; 359th

Ftr. Grp. commander-11/20/44—POW with 359FG.; asgnd. a/c P-47D 42-74686.; 121ES.

1Lt. Robert V. Farmer; Pratt, Kan.; To sq. 4/27/45–9/18/45—IX Air Serv. Cmmd.

Capt. Gene B. Fetrow; Upland, Cal.; To sq. 9/16/42–6/22/43—To U.S.; DFC; 121ES.

1Lt. Clemens A. Fiedler; Fredericksburg, Tx.; To sq. 8/18/43–4/10/44—KIA, P-51B 43-7190; MARN-4127; AM-OLC.

1Lt. Frank M. Fink; Philadelphia, Pa.; To sq. 10/14/42–9/9/43—POW, P-47; Talented artist of humorous caricature; 121ES.

Lt. Robert G. Fischer; Gotha, Fla.; To sq. 6/12/44–8/8/44—KIA, P-51B 42-106940; MARN-7760.

Capt. John C. Fitch; Riverdale, N.Y.; To sq. 9/10/44–2/20/45—POW, P-51D 44-15351; MARN-12546; *B* Flt. CO-12/19/44; In 8AF 5/42–11/43, to 12AF MTO, to Wright Fld., to ETO 3/44.

Capt. Bigelow nmi Fowler; ? ; To sq. 5/2/44–12/1/44—To U.S.; *B* Flt. CO.-9/16/44.

2Lt. Duane Fowler; Beach City, Ohio; To sq. 4/27/45–9/18/45—357FG, Munich, Ger.

Lt. Philip J. Fox; Larchmont, N.Y.; To sq. 10/14/42–12/8/42; 121ES.

Lt. Edward P. Freeburger; Edgewood, Md.; To sq. 2/9/44–3/18/44—KIA, P-51B 43-6460; MARN-3377.

F/O Lucian W. Freeman; Norwich, Conn.; To sq. 1/24/45–EOW?

Lt. Cecil E. Garbey; Tulsa, Okla.; To sq. 5/2/44–6/6/44—KIA, P-51B 43-6575; MARN-5602.

Capt. William H. George; Orlando, Fla.; To sq. 9/30/44–4/25/45—To U.S.; AM-5OLC; Sq. Flt. CO-?.

Lt. James H. Glynn; ? ; To sq. 6/6/44–6/18/44—Evader, P-51B 43-7187; MARN-6253; Returned 8/8/44.

Lt. Lester B. Godwin; ? ; To sq. 5/2/44–7/20/44—Evader, P-51B 42-103561; MARN-6849; Back in London on 9/24/44.

F/O Joseph Goetz; Buffalo, N.Y.; To sq. 2/5/44–3/21/44—KIA, P-51B 43-12469; MARN-3383; Trfd. from 62FS of 56FG on 2/5/44.

Capt. John W. Goodwyn; Saginaw, Mich.; To sq. 2/20/44–9/30/44—To 70th Repl. Dep.; DFC-OLC, AM-3OLC; *C* Flt. CO-5/26/44, Sq. Ops. Off. prior to 9/16/44; One of the 1st. U.S. trained pilots to join the 4FG.

Capt. George D. Green; Whittier, Cal.; To sq. 7/13/44–7/9/45—Trfd.; acting *B* Flt. CO-3/3/45 (asgnd. CO.-3/23/45); asgnd. a/c P-51D 44-63736 (famous McKennon "piggyback" rescue a/c), P-51D 44-14137; Bailed out of WD-H on 8/1/44 just after takeoff, barely got chute open due to catching on seat belt and not finding the D-ring.

1Lt. Kenneth Green; Trafford, Pa.; To sq. 2/6/45–3/3/45—POW, P-51D 44-14923; MARN-12900.

2Lt. Benson K. Green; ? ; To sq. 10/9/42–12/31/42—8AF Serv. Cmmd.; 133ES.

2Lt. Charles B. Greenlease; Memphis, Tn.; To sq. 1/24/45–EOW? AM-4/28/45.

2Lt. Chester P. Grimm; Farmington, Ill.; To sq. 10/17/42–1/22/43—KIA, Spit VB.

Lt. William R. Groseclose; ? ; To sq. 7/13/44–9/11/44—POW, P-51D 44-14431; MARN-8990.

Lt. Frank D. Guernsey; ? ; To sq. 8/26/44–8/31/44—356FG.

2Lt. James E. Halligan, Jr.; Boston, Mass.; To sq. 1/24/45–EOW?; AM-4/28/45.

Maj. Gilbert O. Halsey; Chickasha, Okla.; To sq. 9/24/42–8/13/43—4FG Hq. Sq.; Sq. CO.-5/19/43; 121ES.

Lt. James S. Hanrahan; ? ; To sq. 6/18/44–7/11/44—POW/Escaper, P-51B 43-6562; MARN-6712.

Maj. James A. Happel; Paulsboro, N.J.; To sq. 10/14/42–9/30/44 (finished tour on 6/23/44 & returned to U.S., dropped from rolls on 9/30); DFC; Sq. Ops. Off.-3/24/44, Sq. CO-4/18/44; asgnd. a/c P-47C 41-6182; 121ES.

2Lt. Charles A. Hardin; ? ; To sq. 10/14/42–2/2/43—8AF Serv. Cmmd.; 121 & 133ES.

Lt. Vol. R. Harris, Jr.; ? ; To sq. 6/5/44–6/20/44—POW, P-51B 42-106706; MARN-6249.

1Lt. William C. Hawkins; Langdale, Ala.; To sq. 3/10/44–3/21/44—Evader, P-51B 43-6316; MARN-3438; Returned from evading on 7/16/44; Wrote letter from U.S. in 12/44 imploring to come back to 4FG and get away from U.S. duty.

2Lt. Robert C. Hawley; Portville, N.Y.; To sq. 1/24/45–9/18/45—354FG, R-29, Ger.; AM.

1Lt. Mack D. Heaton; Piedmont, S.C.; To sq. 1/24/45–EOW? AM-4/28/45.

Capt. William D. Henderson; San Francisco, Cal.; To sq. 9/29/44–EOW; Asst. Sq. Ops. & Gun. Off.-5/5/45; AM-4OLC.

Lt. Lloyd F. Henry; Indianapolis, Ind.; To sq. 3/10/44–4/18/44—KIA, P-51B 43-6579; MARN-4138.

Capt. Charles D. Hewes; Biloxi, Miss.; To sq. 10/28/44–12/18/44—KIA, P-51D 44-15455; MARN-11312.

Lt. Dean J. Hill; Los Angeles, Cal.; To sq. 4/18/44–6/19/44—KIA, P-51B 43-6896; MARN-6261.

1Lt. Clifford F. Holske; ? ; To sq. 6/12/44–9/17/44—POW, P-51D 44-14054; MARN-8986.

Lt. Robert H. Homuth; Chicago, Ill.; To sq. 4/18/44–5/31/44—KIA, P-51B 43-7032; MARN-5669.

Lt. William W. Hunt; Pinos Altos, N.M.; To sq. 4/4/44–5/21/44—KIA, P-51B 43-6901; MARN-5289.

2Lt. Robert C. Hunter, Jr.; Johnstown, Pa.; To sq. 2/6/45–?; AM-OLC; *B* Flt. CO-7/9/45; In 335th to at least 8/7/45, later killed in Germany in 1945 on a flight from England.

1Lt. Franklin E. Hupe; Versailles, Ohio; To sq. 5/25/43–6/22/44—Trfd.; DFC, AM-OLC.

Lt. Paul S. Iden; Minerva, Ohio; To sq. 6/18/44–9/11/44—KIA, P-51B 43-6959; MARN-8985.

Lt. Harry E. Jennings; Buffalo, N.Y.; To sq. 5/2/44–5/24/44—KIA, P-51B 42-106429; MARN-5287.

1Lt. Loton D. Jennings, Jr.; Wayne, Maine; To sq. 10/29/44–7/45?; AM-4OLC; *A* Flt. CO.-7/45.

Capt. Frank C. Jones, Jr.; Montclair, N.J.; To sq. 3/25/44–8/8/44—KIA, 44-14027; *D* Flt. CO.-5/8/44, *B* Flt. CO.-5/26/44.

1Lt. Osce R. Jones; Baton Rouge, La.; To sq. 4/4/44–6/7/44—POW, P-51B 43-7042; MARN-5723; AM.

1Lt. Enoch Jungling; Carlton, Ore.; To sq. 9/29/44–EOW?; *C* Flt. CO.-4/8/45.

Capt. William P. Kelly "Bill"; Saratoga, N.Y.; To sq. 10/14/42–2/5/43—KIA, Spit VB; 121ES.

Lt. Lloyd G. Kingham; Grass Valley, Cal.; To sq. 6/29/44–7/22/44—KIA, P-51D 44-13641, just after mission takeoff in Essex, UK.

Lt. Olin A. Kiser; New Philadelphia, Ohio; To sq. 9/8/44–5/14/45—To U.S.; AM-6OLC; On DS 4/13/45–4/17/45 ferrying P-51s to Sweden; Deceased.

Lt. John E. Kolbe; Brooklyn, N.Y.; To sq. 6/5/44–12/18/44—Returned to U.S. after tour.

1Lt. Charles E. Konsler; Utica, Ky.; To sq. 9/8/44–5/14/45—To U.S. after tour; asgnd. a/c P-51D 44-14570; On DS 4/13/45–4/17/45 ferrying P-51s to Sweden; Col. USAF ret.

2Lt. Henry A. Lee; Hampton, Va.; To sq. 1/24/45–9/18/45—354FG, R-29, Ger.; AM.

2Lt. Ralph E. Lewis; Benton, Ill.; To sq. 9/4/44–11/18/44—KIA, P-51D 44-14529; MARN-10328.

2Lt. Hugh W. Lindsay; Paoli, Pa.; To sq. 7/13/44–3/27/45—To U.S.; *C* Flt. CO-3/3/45.

Capt. Ted E. Lines; Mesa, Ariz.; To sq. 4/4/44–11/30/44—To 70th Repl. Dep.; A Flt. CO.-9/16/44; asgnd. a/c P-51B 43-7172, P-51D 44-13555.

Lt. Robert W. Little; ? ; To sq. 6/5/44–6/18/44—POW, P-51B 43-6770; MARN-6262.

2Lt. James H. Looney; Maringouin, La.; To sq. 4/27/45–EOW?

1Lt. Paul J. Lucas, Jr.; Shamoki, Pa.; To sq. 1/24/45–9/18/45—354FG, R-29, Ger.; AM-OLC; Maj. USAF ret.

Capt. Robert J. Mabie; Marshalltown, Ia.; To sq. 7/13/44–5/4/45—To U.S.; AM-7OLC; D Flt. CO-1/16/45; asgnd. a/c P-51D 44-13564, P-51D 44-14221.

Lt. James. S. Macdonald; ? ; To sq. 10/9/42–11/27/42—12TH AF.; 133ES.

Capt. Cecil E. Manning; Lake Providence, La.; To sq. 7/10/43–3/6/44—POW, P-51B 43-6887; MARN-3049.

Lt. Elmer N. McCall; Mt. Lebanon, Pa.; To sq. 6/5/44–12/18/44—To U.S.; asgnd. a/c P-51D 44-14361.

Capt. Carroll B. McElroy; ? ; To sq. 5/2/44–5/31/44—POW, P-51B 42-103609; MARN-5670.

Capt. Bernard J. McGrattan; Utica, N.Y.; To sq. 9/18/43–6/6/44—KIA, P-51B 42-106576; MARN-5611; A Flt. CO.-4/18/44.

Maj. Pierce W. McKennon "Mac"; Ft. Smith, Ark.; To sq. 2/22/43–9/21/45—368FG, Ger.; DFC-4OLC, AM-16OLC, Purple Heart, Fr, Croix de Guerre, 560 combat hrs.; A Flt. CO-3/22/44, Sq. Ops. Off.-4/18/44, Sq. CO.-8/18/44; On U.S. leave 5/26/44–8/18/44; Evader in France 8/28/44–9/22/44; Evader in Germany on 3/18/45 for a few minutes (G. Green landed in enemy country and picked him up and flew them back to DB); wounded in rt. face by 20mm in his canopy on 4/16/45 and regained Allied lines.; asgnd. a/c P-47C 41-6582, P-51B 43-6896 & 42-106911, P-51Ds 44-13883 44-14570 44-63166 44-14221; Maj. USAF, KIFA 6/18/47.

2Lt. Edward J. McLoughlin; Brooklyn, N.Y.; To sq. 2/23/45–4/16/45—POW, P-51D 44-13389; MARN-13923.

Lt. Edwin R. Mead. "Sailer"; Ray, Minn.; To sq. 5/25/43–1/30/44—POW, P-47 42-8506; MARN-2115.

Lt. Frederick D. Merritt; Rockland, Maine; To sq. 1/22/43–7/30/43—KIA, P-47 41-6248.

Lt. Orval C. Miles; Cloverdale, Ore.; To sq. 5/26/44–3/10/45—To U.S.; A Flt. CO-12/19/44, Sq. OTU instructor-2/8/45.

2Lt. Howard B. Miller; Keyport, N.Y.; To sq. 2/23/45–9/15/45—10th Air Depot, Kassel, Ger.; AM.

2Lt. Robert A. Moe; Chippewa Falls, Wis.; To sq. 2/23/45–9/15/45—10th Air Depot, Kassel, Ger.

Maj. Shelton W. Monroe "Shel"; Waycross, Ga.; To sq. 1/25/45–4/8/45—4TH Hq. Sq.; Sq. Ops. Off.-1/25/45; refer to 334th & Hq. Sq.

Lt. William E. Newell; ? ; To sq. 3/10/44–3/29/44—POW, P-51B 43-6759; MARN-3524.

Maj. Louis H. Norley "Red Dog"; Conrad, Mont.; To sq. 8/30/44–1/25/45—334FS.; Sq. CO-8/30/44, Sq. Ops. Off.-10/1/44; asgnd. a/c 44-15028 P-51D; refer to 334th & 336th.

Maj. William J. O'Donnell "Bill"; Philadelphia, Pa.; To sq. 10/8/44–4/8/45—4FG Hq. Sq.; A Flt. CO-1/20/45; asgnd. a/c P-51D 44-14557; Col. USAF ret.

2Lt. Julian M. Osborne; Wash, D.C.; To sq. 9/24/42–11/11/42—8AFSC; 121ES.

2Lt. Leonard F. Otto; Camden, N.J.; To sq. 1/24/45–EOW?; AM.

Capt. Cadman V. Padgett; Bethesda, Md.; To sq. 9/24/42–1/20/44—1st. AF (U.S.); DFC, AM-3OLC; 121ES; LtCol. USAF ret.

1Lt. Richard W. Palmer; E. St. Louis, Ill.; To sq. 4/27/45–9/18/45—IX Air Serv. Commd., Ger.

Lt. Robert G. Patterson "Red"; Los Angeles, Cal.; To sq. 10/14/42–10/8/43—POW, P-47 42-7911; MARN-938; 121ES.

Capt. Donald D. Perkins; Palos Park, Ill.; To sq. 4/4/44–11/4/44—70th Repl. Dep.; DFC; *D* Flt. CO-5/26/44; asgna. a/c P-51D 44-13564.

1Lt. John N. Peters; Washington, Pa.; To sq. 6/12/44–1/8/45—BWAD.

1Lt. Donald J. Peterson; ? ; To sq. 7/27/44–4/24/45—To U.S.; *D* Flt. CO.-2/24/45, Sq. OTU instructor; asgnd. a/c P-51D 44-13977.

Lt. Charles E. Poage, Jr.; ? ; To sq. 7/13/44–12/25/44—POW, P-51D 44-14540.

Lt. August W. Rabe; Yonkers, N.Y.; To sq. 8/15/44–2/21/45—POW, P-51D 44-14435; MARN-12596; Ex-RAF pilot.

2Lt. Herman S. Rasmussen; Oakland, Cal.; To sq. 12/19/44–4/9/45—KIA, P-51D 44-13788; MARN-13946.

Capt. Leighton M. Read; Hillsboro, Tx.; To sq. 5/25/43–2/16/45—To U.S.; DFC-OLC; *B* Flt. CO.-4/18/44, Sq. Ops. Off.-5/26/44, Asst. Ops. & Gun. Off.-10/1/44; On U.S. leave after 1st tour on 6/23/44–?.

Lt. Richard I. Reed; St. Petersburg, Fla.; To sq. 10/14/43–2/20/44—KIA, P-47 42-75051; MARN-2664.

Lt. Paul S. Riley; York, Pa.; To sq. 9/23/43–4/24/44—POW, P-51B 43-6922; MARN-4310; DFC, AM.

Lt. Richard J. Rinebolt; Cutbank, Mont.; To sq. 7/27/44–3/10/45—To U.S.; DFC-?, AM-?; asgnd. a/c P-51D 44-13903.

Lt. Bernard J. Rosenson; Monessen, Pa.; To sq. 7/13/44–8/18/44—KIA, P-51D 44-13567; MARN-8145.

Lt. Donald H. Ross; Carson City, Nv.; To sq. 10/9/42–11/27/43—9AF.; DFC; 133ES.; Maj. Gen. USAF ret.

Lt. Harold L. Ross, Jr.; Greensboro, N.C.; To sq. 4/4/44–6/6/44—KIA, P-51B 42-106786; MARN-5612; AM.

Lt. William P. Rowles; McKeesport, Pa.; To sq. 1/26/44–6/22/44—Trfd.; AM.; To sq. 5/13/45–6/1/45—To U.S.

Capt. James W. Russell, Jr.; Bonham, Tx.; To sq. 4/4/44–9/11/44—POW, P-51D 44-14158; MARN-8987; *B* Flt. CO.-8/14/44; Col. USAF act.

Lt. James. M. Sanders; S. Nashville, Tn.; To sq. 10/17/42–5/13/43—6FW.

Lt. Paul G. Santos; New York, N.Y.; To sq. 8/15/44–2/6/45—KIA, P-51D 44-15615; MARN-12159; Ex-RAF pilot.

Lt. Ralph W. Saunders; Pekin, Ill.; To sq. 3/10/44–4/13/44—KIA, P-51B 43-6325; MARN-4143.

1Lt. James J. Scanlon; Los Angeles, Cal.; To sq. 3/5/45–EOW?; Ex-bomber pilot on 2nd tour in fighters; LtCol. USAF act.

Lt. Milton G. Scarbrough; Lubbock, Tx.; To sq. 4/4/44–4/24/44—POW, P-51B 43-6767; MARN-4309.

Capt. Albert L. Schlegel; Cleveland, Ohio; To sq. 7/3/43–8/28/44—KIA, P-51D 44-14066; MARN-8299; AM; *B* Flt. CO-3/5/44, Sq. Ops. Off.-8/18/44; On U.S. leave ?-8/18/44; asgnd. a/c P-51B 42-106464, P-51D 44-14066.

1Lt. Zack S. Sensibaugh; Decatur, Tx.; To sq. 4/4/44–9/19/44—To U.S.; asgnd. a/c P-51D 44-13903.

2Lt. Almond W. Seymour; Monroe, Ga.; To sq. 3/24/45–9/18/45—354FG, Ger.

Lt. Eliot H. Shapleigh; El Paso, Tx.; To sq. 4/4/44–5/27/44—Evader, P-51B 42-106464; MARN-5724; AM.

Lt. Frank T. Sibbett; San Francisco, Cal.; To sq. 5/2/44–6/21/44—KIA, P-51B 43-6784; MARN-6800.

Lt. Curtis nmi Simpson; Kermit, Tx.; To sq. 5/2/44–7/19/44—Evader, Internee, P-51B 42-106438; MARN-6848.

2Lt. Richard A. Skerritt; Detroit, Mich.; To sq. 3/24/45–9/18/45—357FG, Ger.

2Lt. Paul H. Skogstad; Phoenix, Ariz.; To sq. 3/24/45–9/15/45—10th Air Depot Grp., Ger.

Lt. John T. Slater; Waverly, N.Y.; To sq. 9/21/42–9/24/42—KIA, Spit VB (KIA before his paperwork came through); 121ES.

1Lt. Glenn J. Smart; Sedan, Ka.; To sq. 2/8/44–5/28/44—335th Hq. grd. officer; Bailed into N. Sea on 3/29/44 when motor quit on show return; Sq. Pers. Eqmnt. Off. prior to 9/16/44.

2 Lt. Donald E. Smith; Bedford Hills, N.Y.; To sq. 6/18/44–8/18/44—KIA, P-51D 44-13563; MARN-8146.

Maj. Fonzo D. Smith; Molockoff, Tx.; To sq. 9/15/42–8/3/44—POW, P-51D 44-13934; MARN-7453; DFC, AM-3OLC; Sq. Ops. Off.-10/4/43; Possibly 4FG Hq. Sq. asgnd. when captured; To 12th Repl. Pool on 11/29/43 after 1st tour.; asgnd. a/c P-47D 42-7936; 121ES.

2Lt. John H. Smith; Herrin, Ill.; To sq. 3/24/45–9/18/45—357FG, Ger.

Capt. Kenneth G. Smith; Boise, Id.; To sq. 10/14/42–3/21/44—POW, P-51B 43-6803; MARN-3381; asgnd. a/c P-47C 41-6207, P-51B 43-6803; 121ES.

F/O Walter nmi Smith; Birmingham, Ala.; To sq. 5/2/44–6/6/44—KIA, P-51B 43-7172; MARN-5606.

Lt. Frank J. Smolinsky; ? ; To sq. 10/14/42–4/3/43—KIA, P-47C 41-6181.

2Lt. William S. Sparkman; Tampa, Fla; To sq. 3/24/45–9/15/45—10th Air Depot Grp., Ger.

2Lt. Alston W. Stafford; ? ; To sq. 3/24/45–9/18/45—IX Air Serv. Cmmd., Ger.

Lt. Robert L. Stallings; Andrews, Ind.; To sq. 9/29/44–1/17/45—KIA, P-51D 44-11339; MARN-11920.

1Lt. George I. Stanford, Jr.; Southport, Conn.; To sq. 3/25/44–7/2/44—POW, P-51D 44-13402; MARN-6799; Asst. Sq. Ops. Off.-5/26/44.

Lt. Aubrey C. Stanhope; Bristol, Me.; To sq. 10/14/42–9/7/43—POW, P-47C 41-6207; DFC, AM-3OLC; asgnd. a/c P-47C 41-6233; 121ES.; LtCol. USAF ret.

Lt. James F. Steele; Coatesville, Pa.; To sq. 5/25/43–6/18/44—Trfd.; DFC, AM.

Lt. Joseph W. Sullivan; New York, N.Y. To sq. 2/9/44–2/24/44—KIA, P-47 41-6369.

2Lt. William H. Talbott; ? ; Va.; To sq. 8/27/43–12/2/43—2nd. Gen. Hosp.; Ex-RAF pilot.

Capt. Richard L. Tannehill; Stockton, Cal.; To sq. 4/27/45–5/17/45—KIFA, P-51D 44-72340.

2Lt. Benjamin A. Taylor; Salem, Ore.; To sq. 9/24/42–11/11/42—8AF Serv. Cmmd.; 121ES.

2Lt. Charles A. Thacker; Weatherford, Okla.; To sq. 3/24/45–9/18/45—357FG, Ger.

Maj. Archibald M. Thomson; Walden, N.Y.; To sq. 7/1/44–8/28/44—Evader, P-51D 44-13534; MARN-8297; acting Sq. CO-6/21/44 (Maj. Blanding, CO, on Russia Shuttle), Sq. Ops. Off.-7/5/44.

1Lt. Montgomery H. Throop; ? ; To sq. 2/4/43–11/27/43—9AF; DFC.

2Lt. Ralph C. Trietsch; Tipton, Ind.; To sq. 3/24/45–EOW?

1Lt. Robert N. Tyler; Haymarket, Va.; To sq. 9/29/44–7/20/45—Trfd.; AM-3OLC; D Flt. CO-6/45.

1Lt. Wade F. Underwood; Albermarle, N.C.; To sq. 1/24/45–9/21/45—4th Mobile R&R. Sq.; AM-OLC.

Capt. Neil Van Wyk "Dutch"; Paterson, N.J.; To sq. 11/8/44–2/27/45—?; DFC, AM; C Flt. CO-11/29/44.

Lt. Nicholas W. Vozzy; Abingdon, Pa.; To sq. 7/27/44–9/17/44—KIA, P-51B 43-6841; MARN-8984.

Lt. Sidney V. Wadsworth; ? ; To sq. 6/6/44–8/7/44—POW, P-51B 43-6437; MARN-7757.

1Lt. Hugh A. Ward; Charleston, S.C.; To sq. 10/12/43–3/4/44—POW, P-51B 43-6810; MARN-3047.

1Lt. Lloyd W. Waterman; Grand Rapids, Mich.; To sq. 9/23/43–5/9/44—POW, P-51B 42-106911; MARN-4686; D Flt. CO.-4/18/44.

1Lt. Robert G. Williams; ? ; To sq. 1/22/43–5/25/43—334FS.; To sq. 8/1/45–9/21/45—4th Mobile R&R. Sq.

Lt. Donald K. Willis; Leavenworth, Ind.; To sq. 10/20/42–4/22/43—8FC; 121ES.

Capt. Calvin W. Willruth; Lancaster, Mass.; To sq. 9/4/44–?; AM-7OLC; *D* Flt. CO.-4/2/45, Asst. Ops. & Gun. Off.-8/4/45; asgnd. a/c P-51D 44-15028.

Lt. Ward K. Wortman; Spokane, Wash.; To sq. 2/22/43–7/14/43—KIA, P-47 42-7939; MARN-3149; asgnd. a/c P-47D 42-7939.

Lt. Burton C. Wyman; Englewood, N.J.; To sq. 8/18/43–1/29/44—KIA, P-47 42-75119; MARN-2116.

Maj. Donald A. Young; Chanute, Ka.; To sq. 9/16/42–10/9/43—CO of Hq. Sq., ASC, Patterson Fld., Ohio; DFC-OLC, AM-3OLC; Sq. Ops. Off.-4/25/43; asgnd. a/c Spit VB BL477, P-47C 41-6185; 121ES.; LtCol. USAF ret.; Delta ALs. Capt. on L-1011 a/c actively.

336TH FIGHTER SQUADRON PILOTS:

1Lt. George W. Adams; Cleveland, Oh.; To sq. 11/6/43–?

Capt. Richard L. Alexander "Dixie"; Aylmer, Ont., Canada; To sq. 10/9/42–1/3/43—109th Observ. Sq., Atcham, Shrops.; DFC, Purple Heart, AM-11OLC, 6 victories WW2 (aerial); asgnd. a/c Spit VB BL722, Spit VB BL773; 133ES; In Spring, 43, led Flt. of P-39s to MTO from UK. Weather & bad motors caused two months internment in Spain. To 52FG MTO. Led 1st. MTO show to Southern France. POW in P-51 over Austria to Stalag Luft 3.; Capt. USAF ret. after 1947 accident in Germany.

Capt. Carl R. Alfred; Atwater, Oh.; To sq. 7/12/44–4/16/45—KIA, P-51D 44-72523; MARN-13858; DFC.

1Lt. Hazen S. Anderson; ? ; To sq. 10/9/42–?–3/12/43—POW, Spit VB.

F/O Andre J. Andreu; ? ; To sq. 5/25/43–6/18/43—6FW.

2Lt. Harvie J. Arnold; Oklahoma City, Okla.; To sq. 6/6/44–6/18/44—KIA, P-51D 44-13307; MARN-6251.

F/O Robert W. Awalt; Azusa, Cal.; To sq. 4/18/45–9/18/45—357FG, Ger.

F/O Harold Axe, Jr.; Bicknell, Ind.; To sq. 4/18/45–9/18/45—IX ASC, Ger.

Lt. William H. Ayer; Egypt, Mass.; To sq. 11/17/44–4/16/45—POW, P-51D 44-13375; MARN-14126.

F/O Henry R. Ayon; Baltimore, Md.; To sq. 4/18/45–7/21/45—70th RCD.

1Lt. Henry L. Ayres, Jr.; Indianapolis, Ind.; To sq. 10/9/42–7/28/43—POW, P-47 41-6238; 133ES.; Deceased.

Lt. William H. Baker, Jr.; Temple, Tx.; To sq. nix (KIA on day of AAF enlistmt.)—KIA, 9/26/42, Spit IX BS446; 133ES.

F/O Donald P. Baugh; Sioux City, Ia.; To sq. 11/17/44–7/21/45—70th RCD.; Maj. USAF ret.

Lt. R. N. Beaty; Rye, N.Y.; To sq. ? (Ex-133ES. Survivor of 9/26/42 show in Spit IX BS148, crashed on return from Brest, Fr. Not known if he trfd. to 336FS); Deceased 1968.

1Lt. Joe L. Bennett; Tucumcari, N.M.; To sq. 10/9/42–2/29/44—8FC (AJAX); 133ES.

Capt. Joseph H. Bennett; Morton, Tx.; To sq. 4/4/44–5/25/44—POW, P-51B 43-6572; MARN-5720; Ex-56FG pilot; Broke shoulder when his P-51B 43-6838 was rammed in mid-air in cloud off Dutch coast and he bailed out into N. Sea. Picked up by Walrus on 4/15/44.

Capt. Leicester. B. Bishop; ? ; To sq. 10/9/42–1/20/44—12th Repl. Dep.; *C* Flt. CO-9/26/43.

Col. Donald J. M. Blakeslee "Col. Don"; Fairport Harbor, Oh.; To sq. 9/29/42–11/22/42—335FS. Refer to 4th Hq. Sq. for service record.

F/O Raymond D. Bogusevic; Chicago, Ill.; To sq. 4/18/45–9/18/45—IX ASC.

F/O Oscar L. Bond, Jr.; Wiggins, Miss.; To sq. 4/18/45–9/18/45—357FG, Ger.; LtCol. USAF.

1Lt. Frank C. Bonds; Fresno, Cal.; To sq. 10/10/43–11/22/44—70th RCD.; asgnd. a/c P-51B 43-6891.

1Lt. Douglas E. Booth "Tiger"; New York, N.Y.; To sq. 9/29/42–5/25/43—334FS; asgnd. a/c Spit VB AD451; 121ES.

F/O Clarence H. Bousefield; Centerville, S.D.; To sq. 4/18/45–9/18/45—IX ASC, Ger.; asgnd. a/c P-51D 44-15613.

2Lt. Robert T. Bradley; ? ; To sq. 5/1/44–5/21/44—355FG.

Capt. Richard G. Braley "Needle-nose" "Roger the Lodger"; Pasadena, Cal.; To sq. ?–9/12/44—To U.S.; asgnd. a/c Spit VB BM530.

Flt. Lt. Edward George Brettell; British subject; Attached to 336FS on 9/26/42 Brest show. Downed as POW. Wounded when downed in Spit IX BS313. Executed by Gestapo 3/24/44 for part in "Great Escape" of 76 prisoners from Stalag Luft 3. He was escape compass-maker.

1Lt. Beachem O. Brooker, Jr.; Columbia, S.C.; To sq. 11/17/44–9/21/45—4th Mobile R&R. Sq.

2Lt. Donald K. Cameron; ? ; To sq. 10/9/42–?; Thought to have been killed in a flying accident at an OTU after leaving 4FG.

2Lt. Frank D. Caple; ? ; To sq. 6/6/44–6/10/44—POW, P-51B 43-6889; MARN-5722.

Capt. Kendall E. Carlson "Swede"; Red Bluff, Cal.; To sq. 7/25/43–2/25/45—POW, P-51D 45-11356; MARN-12737; DFC-OLC, AM; asgnd. a/c P-47C 41-6575.

Capt. Leroy A. Carpenter, Jr.; Austin, Tx.; To sq. 9/20/44–4/16/45—KIA, P-51D 44-63831; MARN-14123.

2Lt. Robert J. Cavallo; Wilmington, Ill.; To sq. 11/17/44–9/21/45—64FW.

Lt. Van E. Chandler; Rices Landing, Pa.; To sq. 6/6/44–6/1/45—1010th ABU Sq.; asgnd. a/c P-51D VF-U WHEEZY; Forced to bail out once in Allied lines. Col. USAF.

2Lt. Gerald C. Chapman; Stoughton, Mass.; To sq. 6/12/44–8/2/44—KIA, P-51B 43-6846; MARN-7716.

Maj. Lewis W. Chick, Jr. "Bill"; Blanco, Tx.; To sq. 1/21/43–4/22/43—8FC Combat Ops. Sec.; DFC; AM-13OLC; asgnd. a/c Spit VB, MD-X; In 355FG 10/7/43–11/27/43. To 325FG MTO 12/9/43–3/22/44; Flew 1st. P-51 into DB on 8/12/43; MTO ace; LtCol. USAF ret.

Maj. Oscar H. Coen; Marion, Ill.; To sq. ?–3/3/43—334FS.; DFC; Sq. CO-11/28/42; asgnd. a/c Spit VB BL582; 71ES.-4/19/41.

1Lt. Wilmer W. Collins; Lyons, Ga.; To sq. 11/17/44–7/21/45—70th RCD.

Capt. Charles A. Cook, Jr.; Alhambra, Cal.; To sq. nix (lost as POW on 9/26/42 Brest, Fr. show before he was to join AAF the next day); asgnd. a/c Spit IX BR640; 133ES.

Lt. Richard J. Corbett; Madison, Wis.; To sq. 5/25/44–3/11/45—To U.S.; Barely returned after hitting a tree in P-51B 43-6686, but landed at Manston okay on 8/28/44.

2Lt. Harold R. Crawford, Jr.; Seattle, Wash.; To sq. 11/17/44–2/27/45—POW, P-51D 44-11665; MARN-12784.

Capt. George H. Davis; Berlin, Md.; To sq. 9/30/44–1/26/45—335FS.; To sq. 7/9/45–?; asgnd. a/c P-51D 44-63233.

Lt. Harry L. Davis; Cotulla, Tx.; To sq. 11/17/44–3/26/45—KIA, P-51D 44-13317.

2Lt. Marvin L. Davis; Austin, Tx.; To sq. 11/17/44–? (possibly Harry L. Davis?).

1Lt. Robert O. Davis; Tallahassee, Fla.; To sq. 1/24/45–4/17/45—KIA, P-51D 44-14387; MARN-13922.

2Lt. Frederick C. Dettling; Hillside, Pa.; To sq. 4/18/45–9/18/45—357FG, Ger.

Capt. Melvin N. Dickey; Tampa, Fla.; To sq. 7/12/44–6/6/45—To U.S.; asgnd. a/c P-51D 44-13630.

P B. G. Downs; ? ; To sq. ?; Trfd. to N. Africa–?; Pilot no. 32 in sq.

2Lt. Donald D. Drage; Salt Lake City, Ut.; To sq. 4/18/45–9/18/45—357FG, Ger.

Maj. John G. DuFour; Alameda, Cal.; To sq. 10/9/42 ?–9/2/43—8FC Hq.; Sq. CO-3/4/43; asgnd. a/c Spit VB AB271, P-47C 41-6575; LtCol. USAF ret.

1Lt. Harry E. Dugàn, Jr.; Denver, Colo.; To sq. 5/25/44–12/26/44—70th RCD.

Capt. Phillip H. Dunn "Pappy"; Vancouver, Wash.; To sq. ?–3/3/44—POW, P-51B 43-6903; MARN-3050; DFC; asgnd. a/c P-47D 42-7933.

Lt. Charles W. DuPree; Stillwater, Okla.; To sq. 6/3/44–1/2/45—70th RCD.

2Lt. Joseph M. Edge; Mitchell, S.D.; To sq. 4/18/45–9/18/45—IX ASC, R-96, Ger.

LtCol. Selden R. Edner; San Jose, Cal.; To sq. 10/9/43–1/1/44—4FG Hq. Sq.; Sq. CO-11/11/43; 121ES.; LtCol. USAF, KIA, 2/12/49 in Karpenesion, Greece.

Maj. Wilson V. Edwards; Colorado Springs, Colo.; To sq. 6/21/44–7/5/44—4FG Hq. Sq.; acting Sq. CO & Sq. OTU cmmdr. during absence of Russia Shuttle personnel 6/21/44–7/5/44; 133ES.; LtCol. USAF ret.

Capt. Donald R. Emerson; Pembina, N.D.; To sq. 3/9/44–12/25/44—KIA, P-51D 44-15054; Sq. Ops. Off.-7/8/44, A Flt. CO-prior to 8/24/44; asgnd. a/c P-51B 43-6889, P-51D 44-13317.

2Lt. Claude R. Fleming; St. Mary's, Va.; To sq. 4/18/45–8/18/45—357FG, Ger.

1Lt. Lucius F. Foster; Los Angeles, Cal; To sq. 10/9/42–8/1/43—4ADW; asgnd. a/c Spit VB EN793.

2Lt. Melvin C. Franklin; Middletown, Oh.; To sq. 2/5/45–9/15/45—10th Air Depot Grp., Ger.; asgnd. a/c P-51D VF-N THE RING.

1Lt. Harold H. Fredericks; Oakland City, Ind.; To sq. 2/20/44–5/29/45—KIFA, P-51D 44-72181; Evader & on return to DS to ETOUSA HQ. during 6/6/44–9/5/44 period; Evader-MARN-5609; asgnd. a/c P-51D 44-14277.

1Lt. Ray G. Fuchs; St. Louis, Mo.; To sq. 10/9/42–11/26/43—9FC; asgnd. a/c Spit VB BM537.

Lt. Vermont Garrison; Mt. Victory, Ky.; To sq. 9/26/43–3/3/44—POW, P-51B 43-6871; MARN-3048; A Flt. CO-@3/44; asgnd. a/c P-47D 42-74663, P-51B 43-6871; Gunnery Instr. prior to 4FG; Double Jet Ace in Korean War; Col. USAF ret.

Maj. ? Gates; ? ; Non-4FG pilot who did one show on 2/2/44 in P-47 42-8528.

Capt. Don S. Gentile; Piqua, Oh.; To sq. 9/28/42–late April, 44—To U.S. leave after tour, did not return.; DSC, DFC-?OLC, AM-?OLC; B Flt. CO-9/26/43; asgnd. a/c Spit VB BL776, P-47D 42-8659, P-51B 43-6913; KIFA on 1/28/51 at Forestville, Md., in a T-33 a/c; 350 combat hrs. in WW2.; Capt. USAF active when KIFA.

Capt. Robert W. Gibson; Dallas, Tx.; To sq. 4/23/45–7/9/45—357FG, Ger.

Capt. Edward L. Gimbel; Chicago, Ill.; To sq. 6/28/44–4/16/45—POW, P-51D 44-72769; MARN-14129; Asst. Sq. Ops. Off. prior to 4/16/45; Crashed near Brussels, Belg., in 51D 44-14029 on 3/1/45 & did short hosp. stint.

Capt. Otey M. Glass, Jr.; Lynchburg, Va.; To sq. 6/5/44–9/6/44—70th RCD.; Evader during 8/18/45–9/2/44; MARN-8142; asgnd. a/c VF-G.

Maj. Frederick W. Glover "Freddie"; Asheville, N.C.; To sq. 2/20/44–6/1/45—2AD Hq. 8AF.; Evader on 4/30/44–5/28/44, P-51B 42-106856; MARN-5286; Silver Star, DFC-?OLC, AM-?OLC; Sq. Ops. Off.-8/17/44, Sq. CO-8/24/44; asgnd. a/c P-51B 43-12214, P-51D 44-14787, P-51D 44-64153; KIFA at Hazlehurst, Ga., on 7/7/56.

Maj. John Trevor Godfrey "Johnny"; Woonsocket, R.I.; To sq. 9/22/43–8/24/44—POW, P-51D 44-13412; MARN-7941; On U.S. leave 4/30/44–7/24/44; Silver Star-OLC, DFC-8OLC, AM-4OLC, Purple Heart; asgnd. a/c P-47D 42-7884, P-51B 43-6765; Rhode Island State Senator; Died of AL Sclerosis on 6/12/58.

Maj. James A. Goodson "Goody"; NYC, N.Y.; To sq. 10/9/42–6/20/44—POW, P-51D 44-13303; MARN-6252; DSC, DFC-?OLC, AM-?OLC; On DS to 15AF MTO P-51 Grp. on 4/12/44–5/10/44 @; A Flt. CO-9/26/43, Sq. CO @ 3/8/44–6/20/44;

asgnd. a/c Spit VB BL722, P-47D 42-7959, P-51B 43-24848, P-51D 44-13303; 133ES.; ITT Int. V.P. Europe in 1973.

Maj. Leroy Gover; San Carlos, Cal.; To sq. 9/23/42–1/4/44—To 4FG Hq. Sq.; Silver Star (1st in 4FG), DFC-2OLC, AM-3OLC, 8AF Commendation Medal, Army Commendation Medal, PUC-OLC, Amer. Defense Medal, Amer. Campaign Medal, ETO Medal, WWII Medal, WWII Victory Medal, Humane Action Medal, National Defense Medal, Armed Forces Medal, French Croix de Guerre, Brit. DFC, Brit. 39–45 Victory Medal, RAF Medallion, Caterpillar Pin, 4 victories; Sq. Ops. Off.-9/26/43, Sq. CO-@10/10/43–11/10/43; asgnd. a/c Spit VB BL722, P-47 42-74688, P-47C 41-6256, P-47C 41-6574; 257 combat sorties in WW2; 17,500 hrs. in career; 133ES; Col. USAF ret. (all service in fighters).

2Lt. Benjamin L. Griffin; Jacksonville, Fla.; To sq. 12/19/44–4/16/45—POW, P-51D 44-14277; MARN-14125.

1Lt. Douglas N. Groshong; Selma, Cal.; To sq. 9/22/44–7/21/45—70th RCD.

Capt. Ira E. Grounds; Talpa, Tx.; To sq. 4/17/44–11/10/44—70th RCD; Deceased 1957.

Capt. Francis M. Grove "Lefty"; Glen Cove, N.Y.; To sq. 5/1/44–11/10/45—4FG deactivated in U.S.; DFC-?OLC, AM-?OLC; Sq. CO-9/22/45 (last 336FS CO in that era); Maj. USAF.

1Lt. Allen Guest ?; ?; This pilot flew shows with 336FS in the middle of Feb., 44. No data available.

Capt. Harry N. Hagan; Yorkville, Oh.; To sq. 6/1/44–5/10/45—70th RCD.; Purple Heart; Bailed into tree at Folkstone, UK, on 1/17/45 show return.; asgnd. a/c P-51D 44-14317, P-51D 44-72053.

Lt. Frederick D. Hall; Coopers Plains, N.Y.; To sq. 10/28/44–1/16/45—KIA, P-51D 44-14533.

Maj. Gilbert O. Halsey "Gunner"; Chickasha, Okla.; To sq. 1/1/44–@3/8/44—To U.S.; asgnd. a/c P-47D 42-7884; 121ES, Deceased after war.

1Lt. Ferris S. Harris; Houston, Tx.; To sq. 4/17/44–8/28/44—KIA, P-51B 42-103796; MARN-8301.

2Lt. William H. Hastings; Washington Courthouse, Oh.; To sq. 2/5/45–9/15/45—10th Air Depot Grp., Ger.; Crashed P-51D 44-14492 VF-G on base aborting show on 3/2/45.

1Lt. Edward Hernandez; Long Beach, Cal.; To sq. 6/3/44–3/8/45—70th RCD.

Lt. Glenn A. Herter; E. Windsor, Ont., Can.; To sq. 5/25/43–3/3/44—KIA, P-51B 43-6740; MARN-3045; asgnd. a/c P-47C 41-6354.

Capt. Francis D. Hessey; Jacksonville, Fla.; To sq. 4/23/45–9/21/45—64FW, Y-76 AB.

Capt. Joseph W. Higgins, Philadelphia, Pa.; To sq. 4/17/44–9/30/44—70th RCD; asgnd. a/c P-51B 43-6942.

Lt. James E. Hileman; New Kensington, Pa.; To sq. 10/28/44–4/23/45—70th RCD; asgnd. a/c P-51D 44-15191.

Capt. Robert D. Hobert; Woodland, Wash.; To sq. @ 5/28/43–4/5/44—KIA, P-51B 43-6836; DFC; P-47C 41-6256, P-47D 42-75274.

Capt. Alfred H. Hopson "Hoppy"; Dallas, Tx.; To sq. 9/12/44–12/12/44—4207th Plant. Patient.; 71ES 6/10/42.

2Lt. William E. Hornickel; ? ; To sq. 7/26/44–9/20/44—355FG trfd.

1Lt. Robert E. Hughes; ? ; To sq. 9/2/43–4/8/44—POW, P-51B 43-6866; MARN-3608.

1Lt. Gilbert W. Hunt "Mike"; Hayes, Ka.; To sq. 4/17/44–11/10/44—70th RCD; DFC, AM-6OLC, 2 AF Commdtns., PUC-OLC, ETO-5OLC; asgnd. a/c P-51B JUDY VF-F (before 7/1/44), P-51D JUDY VF-F (after 7/1/44); Col. USAF ret.

2Lt. Earl F. Hustwit; Pittsburgh, Pa.; To sq. 7/26/44–3/26/45—KIA,; NYR on 2/6/45 when his a/c had coolant trouble and he landed in France, returned next day. Second time his a/c had coolant trouble he was KIA.

Lt. Henry A. Ingalls; Los Angeles, Cal.; To sq. 6/3/44–9/11/44—POW, P-51B 43-6573; MARN-8680.

1Lt. Conrad C. Ingold "Connie"; NYC, N.Y.; To sq. 5/25/43–2/5/44—4FG Hq. Sq. (taken off flight status due to poor eyesight, became grd. off.); DFC, AM-3OLC; asgnd. a/c P-47D 42-74663; Crash-landed P-47 42-74663 off South runway on 9/22/43 due to poor eyes; KIFA post-war in U.S.

2Lt. John W. Izant; Cleveland Heights, Oh.; To sq. 2/5/45–9/15/45—10th Air Depot Grp., Ger.

Capt. Marion E. Jackson; Corpus Christi, Tx.; To sq. nix (was a POW on 9/26/42 Brest, Fr., show prior to 336FS trf.); asgnd. a/c Spit IX BS279; 133ES; WIA on 9/26/42.

1Lt. Warren E. Johnson; Cleveland, Oh.; To sq. 3/9/44–9/19/44—70th RCD.

Capt. Joseph H. Joiner; Corpus Christi, Tx.; To sq. 5/25/44–6/1/45—128th Hq. AAF Sta. #1.; Col. USAF ret.

2Lt. Robert L Kackerback; ? ; To sq. 6/3/44–6/4/44—KIFA, P-51B 43-7059.

1Lt. Richard F. Kallner; Frankfurt, Ind.; To sq. 9/7/44–5/10/45—70th RCD.

Lt. Henry A. Kaul; Oak Park, Ill.; To sq. 10/28/44–2/11/45—KIA, P-51D 44-63233; MARN-12322.

Col. Benjamin S. Kelsey; Waterbury, Conn.; To sq. 6/21/44–7/5/44—Returned to duty as commander of 8AF Maintenance & Technical Services after DS as 336th CO on Russia Shuttle mission.

1Lt. Gilbert L. Kesler; Wash., D.C.; To sq. 9/7/44–5/10/45—70th RCD; Landed P-51D 44-72285 7 mi. N/E of Aachen, Ger., at 1125 hrs. on 4/6/45 and returned to base via ASC.

2Lt. George L. Klaus; Villa Park, Ill.; To sq. 10/28/44–11/21/44—POW, P-51B 43-6942; MARN-10334; Returned from POW, now an officer of ITT Int.

1Lt. Jack A. Knight; Cleveland, Ohio; To sq. 4/20/45–7/21/45—70th RCD.

Lt. Donald E. Lambert "Micky"; Exeter, Cal.; To sq. 10/9/42–1/3/43—109th Observ. Sq., Atcham, Shrops., UK; asgnd. a/c Spit VB EN793; 133ES.

1Lt. James C. Lane; Medford, Mass.; To sq. 4/4/44–9/12/44—POW, P-51D 44-13260; MARN-9167.

1Lt. Dale B. Leaf; Marshalltown, Iowa; To sq. @ 11/9/42–5/25/43—334FS; asgnd. a/c Spit VB AR372.

1Lt. Peter G. Lehman; NYC., N.Y.; To sq. 8/25/43–3/31/44—KIFA, P-51B VF-S; AM-OLC; asgnd. a/c P-47C 41-6573; The son of the N.Y. governor.

1Lt. Oscar F. Lejeunesse; Worcester, Mass.; To sq. 3/9/44–9/30/44—Mitchell Fld., N.Y.; POW-Escaper on 6/6/44–9/5/44 in P-51B 42-103332; MARN-5610.

1Lt. George H. Logan, Jr.; Upper Montclair, N.J.; To sq. 4/4/44–10/2/44—KIA, P-51D 44-14172; MARN-9253.

2Lt. William P. Mable; Binghamton, N.Y.; To sq. 4/20/45–7/21/45—70th RCD.

? N. J. MacDonald; No further data available.

1Lt. Joseph G. Matthews; Wallington, N.J.; To sq. 10/9/42–8/16/43—Evader, P-47D 42-7949; asgnd. a/c Spit VB AB988; 133ES; Returned to UK in late 43.

Maj. Carroll W. McColpin; Buffalo, N.Y.; To sq. 10/9/42–11/28/42—To U.S., AAF GHQ; Legion of Merit-2OLC, DFC-U.S. & Brit.; AM-6OLC, PUC-OLC, AFOUA, Fr. & Belg. Croix de Guerre; Sq. CO-9/29/42 (AAF period start); asgnd. a/c Spit VB EN793; 607 Sq. RAF, Hurricane P3641 DX-R; 71ES, Spit VB AB908 XR-Y; Post-4FG 3 ETO tours; CO-407FG & 404FG, Dir. Combat Ops.-29TAC; M/Gen. USAF, ret., CG-4th AF, Hamilton AFB, Cal.

1Lt. Thomas A. McCord; Oracle, Ariz.; To sq. 9/28/44–5/10/45—70th RCD.

1Lt. Thomas K. McDill; Oxford, Oh.; To sq. 4/4/44–5/25/44—POW, P-51B 43-6633; MARN-5721; USAF res. ret.

Maj. John D. McFarlane; Calais, Ma.; To sq. 6/28/44–3/12/45—Evader, P-51D 14350; MARN-13394; Sq. CO-7/5/44; Sq. Flt. Co.-9/27/44, Sq. Ops. Off.-8/24/44.

1Lt. James R. McMahon; Camden, N.J.; To sq. 2/15/45–9/15/45—10th Air Depot Grp.,

Ger.; asgnd. a/c P-51D 44-14276; LtCol. USAF ret. 100 missions in Korean War.

2Lt. Charles Y. Mead; ? ; To sq. 9/2/44–11/6/44—KIFA, P-51B 42-103794.

2Lt. William B. Meredith II; Norfolk, Va.; To sq. 2/15/45–7/21/45—70th RCD.

1Lt. Robert J. Messenger; Erie, Pa.; To sq. 10/9/42–3/6/44—POW, P-51B 43-6630; MARN-3042; asgnd. a/c Spit VB BL582, P-47D 42-75392.

Lt. George H. Middleton; Visalia, Cal.; To sq. nix (was a POW on 9/26/42 Brest, Fr., show prior to 336th trf.); 121 & 133 ES.

Maj. Carl H. Miley; Toledo, Oh.; To sq. 10/9/42–11/10/43—12th Repl. Dep.; Silver Star (for 200 hrs. combat), DFC, AM; Sq. Flt. CO-2/11/43, Sq. CO-9/1/43; asgnd. a/c Spit VB BL240, P-47C 41-6579; 133 ES; Deceased 11/26/68.

Capt. Ervin L. Miller "Dusty"; Oakland, Cal.; To sq. 9/28/42–8/17/43—2906th FTG; asgnd. a/c P-47C 41-6529; 133 ES; RAF Wg. Cmmdr., LtCol. USAF ret.

2Lt. Maurice W. Miller, Jr.; Jackson Heights, N.Y.; To sq. 1/24/45–4/16/45—POW, P-51D 44-14527; MARN-14124.

Maj. Willard W. Millikan; Rockport, Mo.; To sq. @ Fall, 43–5/30/44—POW, P-51B 43-24769; MARN-5488; DFC; acting Sq. CO-4/13/44–5/10/44 while Goodson was on DS to MTO; asgnd. a/c P-47C 41-6180, P-51B 43-6997, P-51B 43-24769; B/Gen. USAF Res., CG-TFW Andrews AFB. Deceased 1979.

1Lt. George E. Mirsch; ? ; To sq. 10/9/42–4/24/44—495FTG, Atcham A/B, UK; asgnd. a/c P-47C 41-6533, P-47C 41-6571; 133 ES.

2Lt. John Mitchellweis; Rockford, Ill.; To sq. 10/9/42–2/1/43—KIFA, P-47 41-6200; asgnd. a/c Spit VB P8791; 133 ES.

2Lt. Richard E. Moore; Barstow, Ill.; To sq. 1/24/45–9/18/45—354FG, Ger.; Wingman of LtCol. Woods on 3/22/45 5-kill day.

Lt. Paul M. Morgan; Lexington, Ky.; To sq. 6/15/44–4/4/45—70th RCD; asgnd. a/c P-51D 44-14432; Bailed out of P-51D 44-15350 at 1430 hrs. in Allied France on 12/11/44 and returned to DB later in week.

1Lt. John P. Murchake, Jr.; Annapolis, Md.; To sq. 1/24/45–9/21/45—64FW.

1Lt. Donald D. Nee; Long Beach, Cal.; To sq. 10/9/42–11/26/43—9FC; asgnd. a/c Spit VB AR372, P-47C 41-6197; 133 ES.

1Lt. Robert F. Nelson "Buffalo-grass"; Long Beach, Cal.; To sq. 8/18/43–4/22/44—POW; P-51B 43-6802; MARN-4130; DFC-OLC, AM-3OLC; Evaded capture for @ 4-days and ate buffalo-grass, earning his Stalag nickname.

1Lt. Conrad J. Netting; San Antonio, Tx.; To sq. 4/4/44–6/10/44—KIA, P-51B 42-106669; MARN-5725.

Lt. Gene P. Neville; Oklahoma City, Okla.; To sq. nix (KIA on 9/26/42 Brest, Fr., show prior to trf.); 133 ES.

Maj. Louis H. Norley "Red Dog"; Conrad, Mt.; To sq. 7/10/43–8/29/44—335FS; A Flt. CO-8/24/44; On U.S. leave @ late May, 44–8/17/44; asgnd. a/c P-47 41-6183, P-51B 43-12416, P-51B 43-6802; Refer to 334th & 335th for more data. Deceased.

2Lt. J. C. Norris; ? ; To sq. 6/3/44–7/2/44—POW, P-51B 43-6650; MARN-6802.

Maj. William J. O'Donnell; Philadelphia, Pa.; To sq. 6/2/45–9/22/45—4th Mobile R&R. Sq.; Sq. CO-6/2/45; Refer to 335th & 4th Hq. Sq. for more data.

1Lt. Donald J. Patchen; Bainbridge, N.Y.; To sq. 3/9/44–5/19/44—POW, P-51B 43-6584; MARN-5290.

Capt. Joseph A. Patteeuw "Patt"; Detroit, Mich.; To sq. 4/4/44–11/10/44—70th RCD; DFC-?OLC, AM-?OLC; asgnd. a/c P-51B 43-6840, P-51D 44-13325.

Lt. C. H. Patterson; Ft. Worth, Tx.; No data available.

2Lt. Rufus L. Patterson "Roy"; Roanoke, Va.; To sq. 7/12/44–9/11/44—KIA, P-51D 44-14266; MARN-8677.

1Lt. Douglas P. Pederson, Long Beach, Cal.; To sq. 11/14/44–7/21/45—70th RCD.

Capt. Kenneth D. Peterson "Blacksnake"; Mesa, Ariz.; To sq. 10/9/42–3/29/44—POW, P-51B 43-6696; MARN-3459; DSC, DFC-?OLC, AM-?OLC; asgnd. a/c Spit VB

BL773, P-47C 41-6539, P-51B 43-6696; 133 ES; KIFA of F-80 at Nellis AFB, post-war.

Capt. Donald J. Pierce; Alliance, Oh.; To sq. 9/30/44–2/19/45—479FG.

Capt. Donald J. Pierini; Trenton, N.J.; To sq. 5/25/44–3/8/45—70th RCD.

F/Lt. ? Plisner; ? ; Flew ops. with sq. in Nov–Dec., 44. Possibly SAAF DS pilot.

2Lt. Jap A. Powell; Indianapolis, Ind.; To sq. 10/9/42–2/13/43—KIA, Spit VB AR341.

2Lt. Earl A. Quist; ? ; To sq. 7/12/44–11/8/44—POW, P-51D 44-13961; MARN-10447; asgnd. a/c P-51D 44-15054.

1Lt. Jack L. Raphael; Tacoma, Wash.; To sq. 8/18/43–6/28/44—Trfd.; DFC, AM-3OLC; asgnd. a/c P-47C 41-6529, P-51B 43-6972.

Lt. Robert H. Richards; Walden, N.Y.; To sq. 9/26/43–3/4/44—KIA, P-51B 43-6786.

1Lt. George E. Ridler; E. Orange, N.J.; To sq. 3/1/45–9/21/45—4th Mobile R&R. Sq.; asgnd. a/c P-51D 44-15191; Col. USAF.

Capt. William D. Riedel "Buzz"; Ault, Colo.; To sq. 9/22/44–9/21/45—4th Mobile R&R. Sq.; Sq. Ops. Off.-6/2/45; KIFA of C-64 Norseman in Ger. after the war.

2Lt. Chesley H. Robertson; ? ; To sq. 10/9/42–?—?FTG OTU, UK; 133 ES; Deceased 1976.

Lt. Leonard T. Ryerson; Whitinsville, Mass.; To sq. nix (KIA on 9/26/42 show to Brest, Fr., prior to trf.); Buried in France.; 133 ES.

Lt. Woodrow W. Schaefer; Yoakum, Tx.; To sq. 9/22/44–4/23/45—70th RCD.

2Lt. Robert H. Seifert; Oneida, N.Y.; To sq. 4/4/44–4/15/44—KIA, P-51B 43-6818; MARN-4060.

1Lt. Charles H. Shilke; Somerset, Pa.; To sq. 4/4/44–11/10/44—70th RCD.

Capt. Reuben nmi Simon "Red"; Los Angeles, Cal.; To sq. 7/30/43–5/25/44—496FTG, Atcham, UK; DFC-?OLC, AM-?OLC, Soldiers Medal.

1Lt. Ernest R. Skilton; Hollywood, Cal.; To sq. 1/26/44–3/16/44—KIA, P-51B 43-6652; MARN-3380.

1Lt. William C. Slade, Jr.; Brama, Okla.; To sq. 10/9/42–5/12/43—6FW; asgnd. a/c Spit VB BL488; 133 ES.

Lt. Glenn J. Smart; Sedan, Ka.; To sq. 10/9/42–11/10/43—310th FTS Sq.; asgnd. a/c Spit VB AA924, P-47D 42-7895; 133 ES. See 335th for more data.

Lt. Dennis D. Smith; Orlando, Fla.; To sq. nix (KIA on 9/26/42 show to Brest, Fr., prior to trf.); 133 ES.

1Lt. George C. Smith; Los Angeles, Cal.; To sq. 5/25/44–12/18/44—70th RCD; asgnd. a/c P-51B 42-103602.

2Lt. Homer C. Smith; ? ; To sq. 3/24/45–4/8/45—KIFA, P-51B 42-103603, while still in OTU, not a combat pilot yet.

Lt. Kenneth D. Smith; Watsontown, Pa.; To sq. 4/17/44–6/7/44—KIA, P-51B 43-6673; Killed on post-takeoff form-up.

2Lt. Robert E. Smith; Wash., D.C.; To sq. nix (Evader on 9/26/42 show to Brest, Fr., prior to trf.); Visited DB on 2/9/43; 133 ES; LtCol. USAF ret.

1Lt. David L. Sneed; Winston/Salem, N.C.; To sq. 3/24/45–9/15/45—10th ADG.

Maj. Winslow M. Sobanski "Mike"; NYC, N.Y.; To sq. 10/9/42–5/25/43—334FS.; asgnd. a/c Spit VB BL383.; Refer to 334th.

1Lt. Woodrow F. Sooman "Woody"; Republic, Wash.; To sq. @ Fall, 43–3/18/44—POW, P-51C 43-6936; MARN-3382; asgnd. a/c P-47C 41-6192, P-51B 43-6936.

Lt. George B. Sperry; Alhambra, Cal.; To sq. nix (POW on 9/26/42 show to Brest, Fr. prior to trf.); 133 ES; Maj. USAF ret.

1Lt. Andrew J. Stephenson; Los Angeles, Cal.; To sq. 10/9/42–12/26/43—Trfd.; asgnd. a/c P-47 41-6573; 133 ES; LtCol. USAF ret.

Capt. Malta L. Stepp, Jr.; Ketchikan, Alaska; To sq. 10/9/42–5/19/43—4th Hq. Sq.; Sq. Flt. CO-2/11/43; asgnd. a/c Spit VB AB192, P-47C 41-6541; 121 ES; KIFA on 10/1/43. See 4th Hq. Sq.

2Lt. John J. Stumpf; Brooklyn, N.Y.; To sq. 3/24/45–9/15/45—10th ADG, Ger.

2Lt. John B. Swan, Jr.; Tampa, Fla.; To sq. 3/24/45–9/15/45—10th ADG, Ger.
2Lt. William P. Thompson; ? ; To sq. 3/24/45–9/18/45—IX ASC, Ger.
1Lt. Robert S. Tussey; Altoona, Pa.; To sq. 2/20/44–5/11/44—KIA, P-51B 43-24771.
Lt. ? Vagts; ? ; To sq. ?; Flew on shows in Feb., 44 with 336th. No data available.
Capt. Neil Van Wyk "Dutch"; Paterson, N.J.; To sq. 10/10/43–11/8/44—335FS; DFC, AM; asgnd. a/c P-47C 41-6194, P-51B 43-6772.
2Lt. Torgeir F. Vigmonstad; Detroit, Mich.; To sq. 2/15/45–7/21/45—70th RCD.
1Lt. George K. Villinger; Palmyra, N.J.; To sq. 8/27/43–3/2/44—KIA, P-51B 43-6985; MARN-2790; AM.
2Lt. Alvin O. Wallace; Niagara Falls, N.Y.; To sq. 9/20/44–2/4/45—KIFA, P-51D 44-15531.
Capt. Robert H. Wehrman; Old Greenwich, Conn.; To sq. 9/1/43–10/30/44; DFC, AM-OLC, Purple Heart; Wounded in action in thigh on 2/10/44; asgnd. a/c P-51B VF-N.
Lt. Robert W. White; Ft. Worth, Tx.; To sq. 6/12/44–9/10/44—KIA, P-51B 43-6891.
Wg. Cdr. Peter Wickham; SAAF; On DS to 4FG. He flew with the sq. @ 8/1/44. He was the Wg. CO of Southend (Hornchurch) Station, RAF.
1Lt. Pierce L Wiggin; Charleston, S.C.; To sq. 5/25/43–9/19/44—70th RCD; DFC; To 12th Station Hosp. on 2/14/44; asgnd. a/c P-47C 41-6541.
F/O Barnaby M. Wilhoit; Versailles, Ky.; To sq. 3/24/45–5/29/45—KIFA, P-51D.
1Lt. Warren H. Williams; Chicago, Ill.; To sq. 6/12/44–11/10/44—70th RCD.
Lt. Gil G. Wright; Wilkes Barre, Pa.; To sq. nix (POW on 9/26/42 show prior to trf.); 133 ES; LtCol. USAF ret.
Capt. Franklin W. Young; Marmora, N.J.; To sq. 6/15/44–5/10/45—70th RCD; asgnd. a/c P-51D 44-14276.
2Lt. Sam. H. Young, Jr.; Dallas, Tx.; To sq. 4/17/44–5/30/44—POW, P-51B 43-24787; MARN-5489.

4FG HEADQUARTERS SQUADRON PILOTS
(And pertinent people in the 4FG's history):

Maj. Robert A. Ackerly; Middletown, N.Y.; To sq. 11/7/44–1/28/45—335FS. To sq. 6/1/45–9/21/45—4th Mobile R&R. Sq.; AM-2OLC; Asst. Grp. Ops. Off-11/7/44, Grp. Air Inspector-6/1/45; Col. USAF ret.
Col. Edward W. Anderson; St. Petersburg, Fla.; To sq. 9/12/42–8/20/43—B/Gen. OIC 67FW, Walcot Hall, UK; Silver Star; 4th Grp. & Sta. CO-9/12/42; asgnd. a/c P-47C 41-6575; Entered Air Serv. in 1928; M/Gen. USAF ret. in 1958.
B/Gen. Jesse Auton; Covington, Ky.; CO of the 65FW, the 4FG's ranking command echelon most of the period the 4FG flew combat. He did not personally fly with the 4FG.
LtCol. William F. Becker; ? ; To sq. 9/21/45–11/10/45—?; 4th Grp. & Sta. CO-9/21/45–11/10/45.
Col. Donald J. M. Blakeslee "Col. Don"; Fairport Harbor, Oh.; To sq. 5/19/43–11/19/44—Cmmdr. of Page Fld., Ft. Meyers, Fla.; On U.S. leave 9/7/44–10/20/44; DSC-OLC, Silver Star-Bar, DFC-7OLC (U.S.), DFC (Brit.), AM-3OLC, @500 missions, @1000 hrs. combat; Duty asgnmts: 335FS CO-11/22/42, 4th Grp. Exec. & Ops. Off.-5/19/43, Relvd. Grp. Exec. Off.-7/10/43, 4th Grp. & Sta. CO-1/1/44; Rank dates: Capt.-9/29/42, Major-1/12/43, LtCol.-@ 5/19/43, Col.-3/8/44; Asgnd. a/c: Spit VB BL776, Spit VB BL545, P-47D 42-7863, P-51B 43-6437, P-51B 42-106726, P-51D 44-13779; Prior 4FG service: RCAF pilot, came to UK on 5/15/41, to 401 RCAF Sq., ME-109 kill, to 411 RCAF Sq., to 121 ES, to 133 ES, Flt. CO, 2 FW190s at Dieppe, 120 missions & 240 hrs. with RAF.; Remarks: Last WW2 mission on 10/30/44, Married Leola Freyer-9/18/44, ME-

110 kill with 354FG Dec. 43, His a/c shot up badly on 8/16/43 & 1/7/44.; Col. USAF ret.

Maj. Leon M. Blanding; Sumter, S.C.; To sq. 7/29/44–9/20/44—4199th Hosp.; Badly wounded in head on 8/8/44.; acting 4th Dep. Grp. & Sta. CO-7/29/44 in absence of LtCol. Clark.; 121 ES; LtCol. USAF ret.

Maj. Donald R. Carlson; Rockford, Ill.; To sq. 1/15/44–3/22/45—?; In 334FS on 6/11/44–8/10/44.; Grp. Tact. Inspector-1/15/44, Grp. Ops. Off.-8/10/44, Grp. Tact. Insp.-11/8/44, Grp. Gun. Off.-prior to 3/22/45.

LtCol. James A. Clark, Jr.; Westbury, N.Y.; To sq. 3/15/44–9/15/44—Trfd. to Asst. Military Attache for Air, U.S. Embassy, London.; Grp. Ops. Off.-3/15/44, acting 4th Grp. & Sta. CO-9/7/44 in absence of Col. Blakeslee.

LtCol. Harry J. Dayhuff; Ogden, Utah; To sq. 12/7/44–2/21/45—To U.S.; Silver Star, DFC-OLC, AM-5OLC, French Croix de Guerre; 4th Grp. & Sta. CO-12/7/44.

Wg. Cmdr. Raymond Myles B. Duke-Wooley; To sq. 9/12/42–Dec., 42 @; DFC (U.S., 2/25/43); Attached to the 4FG as operational air cmmdr. while the unit was under RAF FC control.

LtCol. Selden R. Edner; San Jose, Cal.; To sq. 1/1/44–3/8/44—POW, P-51B 43-6442; MARN-2838; Grp. Ops. Off.-1/1/44, Grp. Exec. Off.-2/3/44.; LtCol. USAF deceased.

Maj. Wilson V. Edwards; Colorado Springs, Colo.; To sq. 7/5/44–7/13/44—POW, P-51D 44-13608; 133 ES; LtCol. USAF ret.

Maj. Leroy Gover; San Carlos, Cal.; To sq. 1/4/44–3/15/44—To U.S. after tour.; Grp. Oxygen Off.-1/6/44; Col. USAF ret.

Maj. Gilbert O. Halsey; Chickasha, Okla.; To sq. 8/12/43–1/1/44—336FS; Believed to have been Grp. Ops. Off. in this period.

Maj. Howard D. Hively "Deacon"; Norman, Okla.; To sq. 1/29/45–?—To U.S.; acting 4th Dep. Grp. & Sta. CO-8/9/44 in absence of Clark & Blanding.

1Lt. Conrad C. Ingold "Connie"; NYC., N.Y.; To sq. 2/5/44–1/9/45—334FS; 334FS Intelligence Off.-1/9/45–EOW (off flight status due to poor eyes); Grp. Personal Equipmt. Off.-3/20/44.

Col. Claiborne H. Kinnard, Jr.; Franklin, Tn.; To sq. 9/8/44–11/29/44—355FG; DSC, Silver Star, DFC-6OLC, AM-6OLC, Croix de Guerre/Palm, DUC, ETO-7 stars.; Act. Dep. Grp. & Sta. CO-9/8/44, Act. Grp. & Sta. CO-9/15/44, 4th Grp. & Sta. CO-11/3/44; asgnd, a/c P-51D 44-14292; Deceased 9/18/66 of brain tumor.

LtCol. John F. Malone; ? ; To sq. 9/28/42–5/19/43—334FS; To 7/10/43–2/3/44— Trfd. from 4FG.; 4TH Sta. Exec. Off.-10/30/42, Grp. Exec. Off.-7/10/43.

Capt. Alfred H. Markel; Claymont, Dela.; To sq. 8/18/44–11/8/44—334FS; DFC; Grp. Tact. Insp.-8/18/44.

Capt. Shelton W. Monroe "Shel"; Waycross, Ga.; To sq. 4/8/45–9/21/45—4th Mobile R&R. Sq.; On DS on 4/13/45–5/6/45 ferrying P-51Ds to Sweden as an advisor to SAF; Grp. Ops. Off.-4/8/45.

LtCol. Jack J. Oberhansly; Spanish Fork, Utah; To sq. 12/4/44–2/26/45—Trfd. from 4FG; Dep. Grp. CO-12/4/44, Act. Grp. CO-12/5/44, Dep. Grp. CO-12/8/44.; asgnd. a/c P-51D 44-11661. Awards: DFC-3OLC; Leaf Clusters; Air Medal-5OLC, French Croix de Guerre avec Palm. Victories: 5 aerial, 4 ground. Record: 150 combat missions in World War II. Group CO of 372nd FG in zone of interior upon leaving 4FG. Deputy CO of 78FG prior to coming to 4FG.

Maj. William J. O'Donnell; Philadelphia, Pa.; to sq. 4/8/45–6/2/45—336FS; Grp. Air Insp.-4/8/45; Col. USAF ret.

Col. Chesley G. Peterson "Col. Pete"; Santaquin, Utah; To sq. 9/16/42–5/19/43—Asst. A-3, Ops. & Trng., 8FC.; To sq. 8/20/43–1/1/44—Combat Ops. Off.-9AF Hq.; Brit. DSO, Brit. DFC, Fr. Legion of Honor, RAF Medallion, DSC, DSM, Legion of Merit-OLC, AM-2OLC, Purple Heart, Amer. Campgn. Medal, European-African-Middle Eastern Campgn. Medal, WW2 Victory Medal, National Defense Serv.

Medal-Star, AF Longevity Serv. Award-SOLC; Ranks: Maj.-9/16/42, LtCol.-10/21/42, Col.-10/22/43, B/Gen.-7/21/63, Maj. Gen.-4/29/65, USAF ret.; 4th Grp. Exec. & Ops. Off.-9/16/42, 4th Grp. & Sta. CO-8/20/43; asgnd. a/c unk.; Prior 4th serv.: To 71 ES-11/40, 71 Sq. CO-11/41, 6 RAF victories, 1st. RAF Spit II flown on ops. was P7430.; Remarks: Bailed into the sea twice, second time his chute didn't open, but he survived. Taken off ops. flying on 5/19/43 with 200 sorties total. He originally washed out of the pre-war USAAC. Led the 1st ETO P-47 mission.

Capt. Malta L. Stepp, Jr.; Ketchikan, Alaska; To sq. 5/19/43–7/4/43—6FW.; Grp. Gunnery & Armament Off.-5/19/43; KIFA on 10/1/43 with another pilot from the OTU Sq. at Atcham A/B, UK, when they flew into a mountainside on instruments in bad weather.

Col. Everett W. Stewart; Abilene, Ka.; To sq. 2/21/45–9/21/45—4th Mobile R&R. Sq.; Silver Star, DFC-3OLC, AM-6OLC; 4th Grp. & Sta. CO-2/21/45; asgnd. a/c P-47D 42-26059WW, P-51D 44-72181, P-51D 44-72210; Prior 4th serv.: Commissioned 5/25/39; Flew 1st WW2 mission at Pearl Harbor on 12/7/41; In P-40 unit on Wake & Midway Is.-2/41-9/42, 280 hrs. in Pacific; To 355FG on 12/43, 355FG CO-11/4/44–2/21/45; Remarks: 10½ victories total, 180 missions, 510 combat hrs. in WW2.

LtCol. William A. Trippet; Waco Tx.; To sq. 11/8/44–6/1/45—Trfd. from 4FG; 4th Grp. Ops. Off.-11/8/44, 4th Grp. & Sta. CO-11/29/44–12/5/44, Grp. Ops. Off.-1/15/45.

LtCol. Sidney S. Woods "Sid"; Somerton, Ariz.; To sq. 2/26/45–EOW?; POW on 4/16/45 in P-51D 44-72251 for 13 days; MARN-14130; Dep. Grp. CO-2/26/45; Prior serv.: Was ace in the Pacific in P-40s. Scored 5 victories in a day on 3/22/45. He was in 479FG on 11/14/44. Also in 355FG with Col. Stewart. He was made POW on his 180th mission.

4th Fighter Group Combat Aircraft

1. The use of hyphens means the connected data pertain to each other.
2. The headings give the a/c type.
3. A/C are listed by serial numbers which denote the model block of the type with its equipment. Serious historians can refer to USAAF a/c block numbers in various literature elsewhere for further data.
4. The a/c squadron code and letter follow the serial number. A/C letters, if known, are given in order of use on the a/c, some having had more than one letter during their service. A hyphen after or a bar below the letter denotes the second of two such lettered a/c in the squadron at once. A double a/c letter means the same thing.
5. Next follows the a/c history, where known.
   a. The squadron the a/c was assigned to and the approximate periods of service. The fate of the a/c, which is denoted by the abbreviations: Trfd (transferred), Salv (salvaged), MIA (missing in action). The name of the pilot flying the a/c when lost is given after the loss date.
   b. A pilot's name and date denotes that he was known to fly the a/c at the period given. The a/c letter at the time of the pilot's assignment may be given here. An italicized pilot's name means the a/c was regularly assigned to him.
6. Capital letters denote the name of the a/c artwork which is followed by a short description of the art emblem if it is not explained by the name. The pilot author and the a/c letter in use at the time may precede the art name and emblem. A simple code lettering follows the pilot art emblem and/or art name to tell its location on the a/c. The proper fuselage side is denoted by L (left side), or R (right side). This is followed by a hyphen and letters to show the exact position of the marking on the a/c. The position is denoted by: N (nose cowling), M (under exhaust manifold), FW (firewall area, between the manifold and the firewall), Co (cowling ahead and below the windscreen), and Ca (below the central canopy area). AG is anti-glare panel.
7. Miscellaneous a/c marking, coloring, and equipment modification remarks follow pilot/artwork/name data.
8. The a/c groundcrew names are given if known. Duties are denoted by: CC (crewchief), ACC (assistant crewchief), and Arm (armorer).
9. First name initials are used to conserve space. Consult rosters for full names.
10. The 335FS listing of P-47 and P-51 a/c is 100 per cent complete. The 334FS and the 336FS listings are as complete as years of research and much album collating can make them, but there are possibly a few missing. No 100 per cent complete listings for these two squadrons are known to exist. However, they are at least 95 per cent complete.
11. Russia shuttle trip a/c are given where known. Name of shuttle pilot follows.
12. All known RAF Eagle Squadron Spitfires are included that may have been on squadron duty when they transferred to the 4FG and were then flown by the Group.

13. End-of-the-war is abbreviated to EOW.
14. Olive Drab and Gray camouflage was deleted from new replacement P-51B & C
a/c in early 1944, and these a/c flew in a bare metal basic finish. P-51Bs were all
NMF after serial number 43-7083, and P-51Cs became NMF after serial number
42-103179.

SPITFIRE AIRCRAFT

AA299	MD-	J. Mitchellweis-11/8/42.
AA720	AV-G	D. W. Beeson-2/2/43.
AA841	AV-D	W. J. Daley-9/42.
AA877	XR-F	D. W. Beeson-12/1/42.
AA920	XR-	AV-G J. A. Clark-11/42, 335-Spring, 43.
AA924	MD-	G. Smart-11/8-9-10/42.
AB192	MD-	M. L. Stepp-10-11/42-3/30/43—trfd 4/1/43.
AB271	MD-E	J. G. DuFour-10/42, DOREEN I.
AB810	XR-	71ES C. G. Peterson-9/4/41.
AB896	XR-	71ES C. W. McColpin-9/13/41.
AB899	XR-J	D. W. Beeson-12/12/42.
AB908	XR-Y	C. W. McColpin-9/41.
AB909	XR-	71ES C. G. Peterson-9/4/41.
AB929	XR-	G. H. Whitlow-11/42.
AB941	XR-	R. A. Boock-11/42.
AB974	AV-J	D. W. Beeson-2/3/43.
AB975	AV-A	D. W. Beeson-2/11/43—trfd 4/1/43.
AB988	MD-	J. G. Matthews-1/22/43, badly damaged in dogfight—trfd 4/1/43.
AD127	XR-F	D. W. Beeson-11/8/42.
AD192	MD-	M. L. Stepp-9/10/42.
AD196	XR-Q	*V. J. France*, MISS NORTH DALLAS, L-M.
AD199	AV-	121ES In 9/42.
AD299	MD-	W. C. Slade-10/9/42.
AD324	AV-P	9/42-Spring, 43—trfd 4/1/43.
AD385	MD-	J. Mitchellweis-11/9-10/42—trfd 4/1/43.
AD388	AV-Z	Spring, 43—trfd 4/1/43.
AD451	MD-	D. E. Booth-3/30-31/43, Nosed over by G. E. Mirsch at 1245 hrs at Bradwell Bay, UK on 1/14/43, trfd 4/1/43.
AD464	XR-L	MD- 334-11-12/42—336-3-4/43—trfd 4/1/43.
AD511	AV-E	Trfd 4/1/43.
AD564	XR-	W. T. O'Regan-11/42.
AD573	AV-H	Md- 335-1/22/43—336-3/28/43—trfd 4/1/43.
AR336	MD-	R. G. Fuchs-11/9-10/42.
AR341	MD-	C. H. Miley-11/9-10/42—MIA 2/13/43-J. A. Powell.
AR372	MD-	D. B. Leaf-11/9-10/42.
BL240	MD-	C. H. Miley-10/9-15-23-25-/42, L. B. Bishop-crashlanded badly at 1530 hrs on 1/13/43 at Manston, UK—MIA 3/12/43-H. Anderson.
BL255	MD-T	*D. S. Gentile*-10/9-15/42. BUCKEYE-DON-L-M, Boxing eagle on light color circle, 2 blk/wht kill swastikas under name.
BL346	XR-B	D. W. Beeson-10/21/42.
BL353	MD-J	*W. B. Morgan*, CC-G. Weckbacher.
BL370	XR-	J. C. Harrington-11/42.
BL376	XR-B	AV-T S. M. Anderson-11/42—335-Spring, 43—trfd 4/1/43.
BL383	MD-	W. M. Sobanski-3/30-31/43—trfd 4/1/43.
BL422	XR-J	*D. W. Beeson*-9-11/42.

BL437   XR-M   AV-N   334-9/19/42, 335 trfd—4/1/43.
BL477   AV-S   *D. A. Young*-6/2/42-2/3/43, trfd 4/1/43. Never had artwork on it.
BL488   XR-E   MD-   D. W. Beeson-9/7/42, 336—trfd 4/1/43.
BL523   MD-   G. E. Mirsch-11/6-8/42.
BL530   XR-B   AV-C   MD-   334-12/42, 335-2/43, 336—trfd 4/1/43.
BL545   MD-   C. W. McColpin-10/9-15/42, D. J. Blakeslee-11/9-10/42—trfd-4/1/43.
BL550   XR-Q   AV-U   334-11/42, 335—trfd 4/1/43.
BL582   XR-   MD-   334-11/42, 336—trfd 4/1/43.
BL673   MD-   336-3/24/43—trfd 4/1/43.
BL722   MD-B   *L. Gover*-10-11/42—trfd 4/1/43, top hat, cane, gloves, in wht circle, light manifold-L-M.
BL773   MD-   336-10/42.
BL766   MD-C?   D. J. Blakeslee-10/9-15-25/42-11/6-8/42—trfd 4/1/43.
BL975   XR-H   AV-I   335-Spring, 43—trfd 4/1/43.
BL986   AV-   121 ES-9/42.
BM260   MD-C   133 ES   E. D. Taylor-Summer, 42, a mounted knight emblem-L-Co.
BM293   XR-W   AV-L   *J. A. Clark*-11/42, 335—trfd 4/1/43.
BM309   XR-S   AV-V   335—trfd 4/1/43.
BM461   AV-F   MD-   335-Spring, 43, 336—trfd 4/1/43.
BM510   XR-A   AV-F?   G. Daymond—damaged in landing 10/25/42, 335-1/18/43.
BM530   MD-   R. G. Braley-3-4/43—trfd 4/1/43.
BM537   MD-   R. G. Fuchs-10/15-20/42.
BM578   AV-Q   Trfd 4/1/43.
BM581   AV-K   335-9/42—trfd 4/1/43.
BM590   AV-R   335-9/42-Spring, 43, OLGA-L-Co.
BM630   AV-B   MD-   335-2/11/43—336-3/14/43—trfd 4/1/43.
BR638   MD-   133 ES Spit IX—MIA 9/26/42-G. Sperry.
BR640   MD-   133 ES Spit IX—MIA 9/26/42-C. A. cook.
BS133   MD-N   133 ES Spit IXb-9/42.
BS137   MD-   133 ES Spit IX—MIA 9/26/42-D. D. Smith.
BS138   MD-   133 ES Spit IX—MIA 9/26/42-G. P. Wright.
BS140   MD-   133 ES Spit IX—MIA 9/26/42-G. P. Neville.
BS148   MD-   133 ES Spit IX-9/26/42-R. N. Beaty-crashed on return at Kingsbridge, UK.
BS275   MD-   133 ES Spit IX—MIA 9/26/42-L. T. Ryerson.
BS279   MD-   133 ES Spit IX—MIA 9/26/42-M. E. Jackson.
BS301   MD-   133 ES Spit IX—MIA 9/26/42-G. H. Middleton.
BS313   MD-   133 ES Spit IX—MIA 9/26/42-G. Brettell.
BS445   MD-   133 ES Spit IX-D. S. Gentile-9/26/42-aborted show.
BS446   MD-   133 ES Spit IX—MIA 9/26/42-W. H. Baker.
BS447   MD-   133 ES Spit IX—MIA 9/26/42-R. E. Smith.
EN483   XR-   334-11/13/42.
EN737   XR-A   334-9/29/42.
EN768   AV-W   335-Spring, 43—trfd 4/1/43.
EN783   XR-K   AV-D   334-11/42, 335—trfd 4/1/43.
EN793   MD-L   *C. W. McColpin*-10/42—trfd 4/1/43.
EN834   MD-   D. Leaf—trfd 4/1/43.
EN853   AV-D   *W. J. Daley*-9-10/42, No artwork or kill crosses.
EN873   XR-K   334-10/23/42.
EN900   XR-I   MD-   334-1/11/43, 336—trfd 4/1/43.
EN915   XR-I   MD-   334-11/11/42, R. D. Hobert-3-4/43—trfd 4/1/43, 1/14/43-

crashlanded by J. Mitchellweis at 1250 hrs at Bradwell Bay, UK.

EN918	AV-X	*G. Carpenter*-1/14/43-nosed over at Debden—trfd 4/1/43.
P8791	MD-	J. Mitchellweis-10/15-25/42.
W3209	MD-	A. J. Stephenson-10/23-25/42.
W3627	XR-	71 ES C. G. Peterson-9/4/41.
W3636	XR-C	334-11/6/42.
W3899	AV-M	335-9/42—trfd 4/1/43.
??289	AV-J	121 ES W. L. Jones.
??373	AV-C	121 ES L. A. Skinner.
??463	AV-G	121 ES D. W. McCloud.
??470	AV-B	121 ES ? Brown.
??501	AV-A	121 ES M. L. Stepp.
??513	AV-F	121 ES R. Tilley.
??871	AV-D	121 ES *W. J. Daley*, CC-C. Koenig.
??922	AV-K	121 ES H. Kennard.

P-47 Thunderbolt Aircraft:

42-22787	WD-	335-2/13/44-2/28/44—trfd.
42-25804	VF-G	R. H. Richards-Fall, 43.
42-26059	VF-3	War-weary, *E. W. Stewart*-6/15/45, codes under left wing, NMF, red cowl, blue rudder.
41-6162	WD-B	K. G. Smith-2/10/44.
41-6178	78 WD-E	334-1/24/43—335-3/17/43-1/14/44.
41-6180	80 VF-U	334-1/22/43—336-3/18/43—trfd 2/25/44, *W. W. Millikan*-MISSOURI MAULER, kicking mule emblem-L-N. CC-N. Gallagher.
41-6181	81 WD-D?	334-1/24/43—335-3/17/43—salv, 4/3/43, F. Smolinksy-KIFA.
41-6182	WD-B-X	From 56FG—335-3/11/43—2/24/44, J. A. Happel-2/20/44-X.
41-6183	83 VF-S-O	334-1/22/43—336-3/14/43-2/3/44—trfd, *L. H. Norley*-O-2/44-crashed at FB at 1030 hrs. on 12/13/43, RED DOG, Pluto urinating on map of Germany-L-N.
41-6184	84 VF-	334-1/23/43—336-3/23/43—?
41-6185	85 WD-S	334-1/22/43—335-3/17/43-2/25/44—trfd, *D. A. Young*-3/17/43-10/5/43, blue circle-L-N, white star on blue wheel covers.
41-6186	86	334-1/23/43—salv 1/29/43, L. F. Foster-crashlanded near Chipping Warden, UK.
41-6187	87 QP-L-E	334-1/22/43—?, *R. L. Priser*-L-4/4/43—QUACK, flying duck-L-N. *H. J. Blanchfield*-E-2/44-UNCLE DEN, Dogpatch cartoon man-L-N. CC-R. Kellett.
41-6190	90 WD-	334-1/16/43—335-6/14/43-9/20/43—?, L. Gover-1/29/43-nosed up on takeoff.
41-6191	91 QP-Q	334-1/16/43—?, *H. Mills/W. B. Morgan*-4/4/43, H. Mills-6/19/43-bellylanded off runway.
41-6192	92 VF-D	334-1/22/43—336-3/14/43-2/25/44—trfd, *W. Sooman*-D-2/44-LOLLAPOLUZA/NAN II, diving eagle with tommy gun-L-N.
41-6194	94 VF-X	334-1/23/43—336-3/23/43—trfd 2/25/44, *N. Van Wyk*-2/44.
41-6195	95 QP-W	334-1/16/43, *J. Clark/A. Rafalovich*-4/4/43.
41-6196	96 QP-P	334-3/1/43—MIA 5/4/43-*J. Lutz*, J. Lutz-forcelanded at Gt. Ashfield on 3/8/43, R. Boock, deadsticked near Norwich on 4/6/43, *J. Lutz/G. King*-4/4/43.
41-6197	97 VF-N	334-1/16/43—336-3/14/43—trfd 2/25/44, *D. Nee*-CISCO-R-Co.

41-6200   00   334-1/16/43—salv 2/1/43-J. Mitchellweis.
41-6202   02   QP-   334-1/22/43—damaged by RAF Mosquito crashing 2/18/43, A. *Hopson*-3/13/43.
41-6204   04   QP-M   334-1/16/43—MIA-4/15/43-*R. McMinn, G. Daymond*-2/43.
41-6206   06   WD-H   334-1/16/43—335-3/17/43-9/20/43, R. Evans-5/29/43.
41-6207   07   WD-X   334-1/24/43—335-3/17/43—MIA-9/7/43-A.   Stanhope, *K. G. Smith*-5/16/43-7/20/43-MARK II, a spring-legged cartoon man-L-N.
41-6212   12   QP-I   334-2/25/43—?, A. *Hopson*-4/4/43.
41-6214   14   WD-F   56FG—334-3/10/43—335-3/12/43—trfd-2/29/44, P. *Ellington.*
41-6224   WD-C-X   Salv 8/22/43—crashed and exploded near Halesworth, UK.
41-6225   25   WD-   334-1/23/43—335-3/17/43-9/20/43.
41-6226   26   WD-I   334-1/16/43—335-3/17/43-1/24/44, G. *Carpenter*-7/28/43-2/44. CC-W. Behm.
41-6233   33   WD-O   334-1/16/43—335-3/17/43—12/20/43,   A.   *Stanhope*-7/30/43-panther on *fleur de lis* emblem-L-Co.
41-6238   38   VF-   334-1/16/43—336-?—MIA 7/28/43-H. Ayres, A. Stanhope-badly damaged in bellylanding, D. Gentile-4/17-21/43.
41-6244   44   QP-   334-2/4/43—?
41-6247   47   334-1/16/43—salv 2/18/43-involved in crashlanding of an RAF Mosquito.
41-6248   WD-   335-3/12/43—MIA 7/30/43-F. Merritt.
41-6256   56   VF-G-I-C   334-2/4/43—336-4/13/43—trfd 2/25/44, L. *Gover*-3/10/43, L. Gover-deadsticked into DB from 20,000 ft on 2/27/43, R. *Hobert*-I-9/6/43-BLUE GOOFIS-L-N, C-1/31/44.
41-6258   58   334-2/4/43—salv 3/8/43, C. Patterson-wrecked in landing overshoot on E-W runway.
41-6260   WD-   335-3/10/43—MIA 6/12/43-E. Beatie, ex-56FG a/c.
41-6328   WD-   335-3/23/43—MIA-9/9/43-F. Fink.
41-6354   VF-R   334-?—336-4/43—?, J. Raphael, takeoff crash on 1/5/44, G. *Herter*-prancing horse emblem-L-N.
41-6356   WD-   335-3/23/43—trfd 5/19/43.
41-6358   58   QP-G   334-2/25/43—?, A. *Chatterley*-CAL OR BUST-L-N, prospector riding Grizzly bear.
41-6359   WD-K   335-3/23/43—?, takeoff accident with 41-6354 on 1/15/44.
41-6360   WD-   335-3/23/43—salv 3/11/43-L. Waterman, spun in on takeoff from Halesworth, UK.
41-6368   WD-   335-3/23/43—trfd 2/28/44.
41-6369   WD-Y   335-3/23/43—MIA 2/24/44-J. Sullivan.
41-6392   QP-X   334-4/43—?, W. *O'Regan*-4/4/43.
41-6400   00   QP-O   334-?—?, V. *Boehle*-4/4/43-INDIANAPOLIS-L-N, diving eagle emblem, 0 on cowl lip, no wheel cover markings.
41-6403   03   Salv 4/3/43-O. Coen, bailed out 1 mi. N/N/E of Alconbury, UK, due to inflight fire at 1615 hrs.
41-6404   QP-R-P   R. *Care*-4/4/43, R. Douglas-bellylanding due to gear collapse on 4/9/43 at 1605 hrs.
41-6405   QP-S   R. *Boock/J. Wilkinson*-4/4/43, salv 4/27/43-J. Wilkinson.
41-6406   QP-H   G. *Whitlow/L. MacFarlane*-4/4/43—MIA 5/21/43-G. Whitlow?
41-6407   QP-E   V. *Castle/A. Chatterly*-4/4/43—MIA 4/15/43-S. Anderson.
41-6410   QP-Y   G. *Ross/R. Douglas*-4/4/43, W. B. Smith-LITTLE BUTCH-L-Co, girl on a skyrocket-L-N.

41-6413	QP-V-W *O. Coen/T. Andrews*-4/4/43, no markings besides a V on wheel covers. *J. Clark*-Fall, 43.
41-6414	QP-K *V. France/S. Pisanos*-4/4/43—MIA 4/15/43-C. G. Peterson.
41-6484	QP-L Salv 12/2/43-J. McNabb.
41-6529	VF-M *E. Miller*-4/17-29/43, *J. Raphael*-8/23/43—2/25/44—trfd, J. Raphael-EAGER BEAVER-MISS BETH-L-N & L-Co, beaver in flight.
41-6533	VF-B *G. Mirsch*-7/28/43, G. Mirsch-a/c badly shot up, but returned at 0950 hrs on 9/3/43—salv 9/3/43?
41-6536	VF-N *D. Nee*-4/29/43-CISCO-R-Co, *R. Wehrman*—salv 2/9/44-badly shot up, but returned at 1250 hrs to UK coast a/f, CC-J. Terrill.
41-6538	QP-B *W. Hollander/S. Anderson*-4/4/43-WELAKAHAO-L-N, Hawaiian man running with spear and jug—salv 4/15/43-S. Anderson, bellied in at Langham, UK, at 1132 hrs after fuel leak fire in air.
41-6539	VF-F *K. Peterson*-4/17/43-2/25/44—trfd, *K. Peterson*-ARIZONA PETE-L-N, jack-rabbit in western gear, CC-L. Engber.
41-6541	VF-A *M. Stepp*-4/17-18/43, *P. Wiggin*-9/6/43-eagle dropping watermelon emblem-L-N, RAF roundels on wheel covers, CC-D. Painter.
41-6553	VF- 336—trfd 2/25/44.
41-6571	VF-B *G. Mirsch*-9/25/43-THE EARL-L-N, top hat, cane, gloves, and cigar. CC-L. Jones, ACC-M. Farrel.
41-6573	VF-S *A. Stephenson*-4/17/43-12/43, cigarette smoking penguin in flight helmet-L-N, *P. Lehman*-1/44—trfd 2/25/44-BEVOAPABM-L-N, emblem depicts name initials: bird's eye view of a pig's ass by moonlight. CC-E. Briel.
41-6574	VF-G 336-4/17/43—trfd 2/25/44, *L. Gover*-7/28/43—?, girl in nighty and big hat-L-N, MISS SAN CARLOS-L-Co, 1 kill cross-L-Ca.
41-6575	VF-E 336-4/17/43—trfd 2/25/44, *J. DuFour*-4/17/43-DOREEN II-R-Co, boxing eagle emblem-R-N, *K. Carlson*-12/18/43-2/25/44-boxing eagle retained, name deleted, CC-W. Belcher, ACC-G. Anderson.
41-6576	QP-J *D. Beeson/H. Hively*-4/4/43—MIA 6/15/43-H. Hively, bailed into Channel halfway across from Tangmere, UK, no emblem on a/c.
41-6578	WD- 335-4/6/43-9/26/43.
41-6579	VF-L-H *C. Miley*-L-4/17/43-Donald Duck emblem-L-N, *C. Ingold*-H—salv 9/22/43-bellied in and burned out off south runway.
41-6582	WD-A 335-4/6/43—trfd 2/28/44, *P. McKennon*-2/44, no emblem.
41-6587	QP-M MIA 11/3/43-I. Moon.
41-6597	VF- 336-4/17/43.
41-6621	WD-R 335-4/6/43-3/19/44—trfd.
42-7328	QP-Z Bellylanded near 335 dispersal on E-W runway.
42-74621	WD-L 335-9/27/43-3/19/44—trfd.
42-74663	VF-H *C. Ingold*-1/21/44-crashlanded at Gravesend, UK, at 1535 hrs on show return, *V. Garrison*-2/44.
42-74686	WD-E-M 335-9/18/43—salv 2/29/44, *R. Evans*-Eagle Squadron emblem-L-N, 4 kill crosses-L-Co.
42-74688	VF-G-J *L. Gover*-9/6/43-girl in nighty and big hat-L-N, MISS SAN CARLOS-L-Co. CC-W. Mehn, ACC-R. Foudree.
42-74717	WD-T 335-9/21/43—salv 2/21/44-W. Rowles, crashlanded at Eastchurch, UK, on show return.
42-74718	WD-H 335-9/21/43—trfd 3/23/44.
42-74726	WD- 335-9/16/43—trfd 2/28/44.
42-74751	QP-Q *H. Mills,* CC-D. Hall.
42-75051	WD-R 335-11/16/43—MIA 2/20/44-R. Reed.
42-75112	WD-Z 335-11/24/43—trfd 2/24/44.
42-75119	WD-N 335-11/24/43—MIA 1/29/44-B. Wyman.

42-75126   QP-F   *W. Sobanski*-MIKE IV-L-Co.
42-75250   QP-P   334-1/44-bellylanded in snowstorm on Abbotts Farm by 334th line.
42-75252   QP-W   *J. Clark*-11-12/43?
42-75254   QP-S-X MIA 2/3/44-W. Cox.
42-75274   VF-   *R. Hobert*-2/44—trfd 2/25/44.
42-75392   VF-   *R. Messenger*-2/44—trfd 2/25/44.
42-75702   WD-   335-1/21/44—trfd 1/27/44.
42-7863   WD-E-C   335-4/17/43—trfd 2/28/44, *R. Evans*-E-7/28/43, *D. Blakes-lee*-C-1/1/44-shot up and made it to Manston, UK.
42-7873   VF-J   Salv 6/17/43-J. L. Bennett, crashlanded at 1015 hrs at Carpenters Arms Pub, North Weald, UK.
42-7874   QP-   Salv 12/4/43.
42-7876   QP-K   *V. France*-MISS DALLAS-L-N, girly on map of Texas. CC-D. Allen, ACC-P. Fox.
42-7879   WD-M-O   335-4/18/43—trfd 2/28/44.
42-7881   QP-E   Salv 6/19/43-V. *Castle*, V. Castle-gremlins on a circle-L-N, gremlins on fuselage star fore edge-L-fus. CC-R. Kellett.
42-7884   VF-P   *J. Godfrey*-2/44—trfd 2/25/44, LUCKY-L-N, dog in horseshoe, red bordered U.S. star insg. REGGIES REPLY-L-Co, 3 kill swastikas-L-Co. Spitfire mirror.
42-7890   QP-B   *D. Beeson*-6/26/43—trfd 2/28/44, D. Beeson-BOISE BEE-L-N, two-gun bumblebee in flight gear on cloud, CC-W. Wahl.
42-7892   VF-   336-2/44.
42-7895   VF-K   336-9/43—trfd 2/25/44, *G. Smart*-hitchhiking angel emblem-L-N, on 9/7/43, *R. Simon*-2/44. CC-E. Certic, ACC-T. Jennings.
42-7901   WD-G   335-5/12/43—trfd 3/17/44.
42-7910   WD-C   War-Weary, 335-post-VE, OTU a/c, O/D and Gray, red/wht/blue rudder, yellow serials, white codes, red gloss full nose cowl, reg. canopy NMF, dark O/D on D-Day band areas.
42-7911   WD-   335-6/2/43—MIA 10/8/43-R. Patterson.
42-7915   QP-U   MIA 10/8/43-C. D. Smith.
42-7920   QP-N   MIA 5/21/43-L. MacFarlane.
42-7924   QP-F   MIA 11/3/43-F. Gallion.
42-7928   QP-Z   Bellylanded on E-W runway on ? date.
42-7933   VF-Y   336-9/43—trfd 2/28/44, *P. Dunn*-9/7/43-MISS SKIPPY-PAPPY-L-N and L-Ca, ying-yan wheel cover. CC-E. Rowe, ACC-D. Ratcliff.
42-7936   WD-W-D   335-5/12/43—trfd 2/28/44, *F. Smith*-W-9/15/43-PISTOL PACKIN MAMMA-L-N, cowgirl on map of Texas and star, D-2/44.
42-7939   WD-Z   335-5/4/43—MIA 7/14/43-*W. Wortman*, no emblems. CC-E. Jensen.
42-7945   QP-D   *S. Pisanos*-MISS PLAINFIELD-L-N, angel with lightning bolts on circle. CC-P. Fox.
42-7949   VF-   MIA 8/16/43-J. Matthews.
42-7959   VF-W   336-6/22/43—trfd 2/25/44, *J. Goodson*-9/6/43-diving eagle on a star and circle. CC-R. Gilbert, ACC-W. Cassidy.
42-7968   WD-U   335-5/12/43—trfd 2/28/44, *P. Ellington*-2/44.
42-7980   QP-H   *G. Montgomery*. CC-G. Fite, ACC-E. Nelson.
42-7981   QP-R   *R. Care*-6/26/43.
42-8409   WD-   335-1/30/44—trfd 2/28/44.
42-8414   WD-   335-1/30/44—trfd 2/29/44.
42-8457   WD-   335-1/28/44—trfd 2/29/44.
42-8495   WD-W   335-10/18/43—MIA 2/6/44-H. Ballew.
42-8506   WD-B   335-9/15/43—MIA 1/30/44-E. Mead.
42-8619   QP-O   War-Weary, OTU a/c, O/D and Gray a/c, MAN-MADE MON-

STER-L-Co, name yellow with red outline, red/wht/blue rudder, full red cowl.

42-8641 QP-I *D. Van Epps*-1/29/44-GREAT DANE II-L-Co, shot up and returned to Lashenden, UK, dead-stick landing on 1/29/44.

42-8644 QP-N-U N-LILLIPUT-L-N, girly in lingerie—MIA 5/21/43-W. B. Morgan-as a/c U.

42-8659 VF-T 336—trfd 2/25/44, *D. Gentile*-2/44-DONNIE BOY-L-N, 4FG boxing eagle emblem on light circle with 2 kill crosses on white nose band. CC-L. Krantz, ACC-J. Lammering.

42-8675 WD-E 335-9/21/43—trfd 3/19/44.

P-51B/C MUSTANG AIRCRAFT:

42-102999 WD- 335-4/25/44—trfd 7/24/44.
42-103009 VF- 336-3/6/44.
42-103036 WD- 335-2/25/44—trfd 3/1/44.
42-103287 VF- MIA 6/6/44-H. Frederick.
42-103291 WD-X 335-5/1/44-9/11/44—MIA-G. Cooley-bailed out and returned, near Liege, Belg., NMF-Malcom-ETO-½ D-DAY.
42-103292 QP-B MIA 6/11/44-L. Cole.
42-103332 VF- MIA 6/6/44-O. Lejeunesse.
42-103561 WD-H 335-6/10/44—MIA 7/20/44-L. Godwin.
42-103582 VF-Q NMF.
42-103602 VF-C *G. Smith*-6/44-CONNIE, red name-L-M, NMF-Malcom, Russia Shuttle-G. Smith. Often used by F. Glover.
42-103603 VF-T Salv 4/8/45-H. Smith, *F. Grove*-8-9/44, NMF-ETO (nix fin)-½ D-Day-Malcolm hood (10/44)-fin fillet, Russia Shuttle-R. Corbett.
42-103609 WD-G 335-5/24/44—MIA 5/31/44-C. McElroy.
42-103781 QP-Y 334-7/44—battle damage.
42-103784 WD- 335-6/20/44—trfd 2/22/45.
42-103786 VF-O Salv ?—C. W. Harre—overshot landing at Andrews Fld., UK, and turned over a/c at 1305 hrs., Russia Shuttle-P. Wiggin-ABT.
42-103791 QP-N MIA 8/18/44-D. Lange.
42-103794 VF- Salv 11/6/44-C. Mead.
42-103796 VF- MIA 8/28/44-*F. Harris*. Russia Shuttle-F. Harris.
42-106429 WD-*W* 335-4/22/44—MIA 5/24/44-H. Jennings, O/D and Gray a/c-JUDY IV-L-M.
42-106438 WD-U 335-7/5/44—MIA 7/19/44-C. Simpson.
42-106441 QP-G MIA 5/13/44-L. Pierce.
42-106464 WD-U-O 335-3/25/44—MIA-5/27/44-E.Shapleigh,"U"-4/8/44,"O"-4/15/44.
42-106467 ? MIA 6/21/44-7/5/44—on Russia Shuttle trip.
42-106555 WD-M 335-7/6/44—MIA 8/18/44-L. Dailey.
42-106576 WD-D 335-4/20/44—MIA 6/6/44-*B. McGrattan*. CC-S. Koenig.
42-106636 QP-X MIA 4/24/44-H. T. Biel, OD/Grey a/c.
42-106650 QP-W-D MIA 7/2/44-T. Sharp, NMF a/c, *J. Clark*-W-6/7/44.
42-106660 ? Trfd 7/6/44, probably a 334FS a/c too badly shot up on 7/2/44 to return from Italy during Russia Shuttle trip.
42-106669 VF- MIA 6/10/44-C. Netting.
42-106673 VF-K Salv 6/8/44-D. Pierini, mid-air collision with K. B. Smith after show takeoff, NMF a/c, reg. canopy.
42-106675 WD-I 335-4/11/44—MIA 4/18/44-*G. Carpenter*, NMF a/c.
42-106682 QP-B MIA 4/29/44-*J. Barden*, 1st. NMF a/c in 334.
42-106686 VF-T Capt. J. H. Bennett-Spring, 44-ANN III-L-Co, 8 blk/wht kill

crosses-L-FW, NMF a/c, blk ETO bands, O/D, reg. canopy. R. Corbett-8/28/44-hit tree in target area and landed at Manston, UK.

42-106706   WD-R   335-4/24/44—MIA 6/20/44-V. Harris.

42-106726   WD-C-S-W   335-4/14/44—?, believed scrapped due to battle damage, *D. Blakeslee* a/c as C, W on 5/24/44, NMF a/c, Malcolm hood.

42-106767   QP-E   MIA 5/9/44-*H. Blanchfield*, NMF a/c, reg. canopy.

42-106786   WD-K   335-5/11/44—MIA 6/6/44-H. Ross.

42-106797   VF-G   MIA 8/18/44-O. Glass, NMF a/c, reg. canopy, W. Johnson-Russia Shuttle abort.

42-106823   QP-K   MIA 6/8/44-E. Allen.

42-106846   QP-H   334-5/7/44—MIA 5/28/44-R. Bopp, NMF a/c, reg. canopy, no emblems.

42-106855   WD-Z   335-4/20/44—MIA 8/18/44-R. Cooper, NMF a/c, Russia Shuttle-J. Goodwyn.

42-106856   VF-   MIA 4/30/44-F. Glover.

42-106857   ?   MIA 7/5/44-Russia Shuttle loss.

42-106909   6N-Z   339FG a/c, 4FG—MIA 6/6/44-*M. McPharlin*, serviced by 334FS-5/7/44, *M. McPharlin*-WEE GINNY-R-FW, light color with dark outline, NMF a/c, reg. canopy, red/wht banded spinner/checkered nose band.

42-106911   WD-A   335-4/26/44—MIA 5/9/44-L. Waterman, *P. McKennon*-YIPPEE JOE-L-FW, cowboy on a bent-bucking P-51B a/c, NMF a/c, reg. canopy.

42-106924   QP-L   334-4/44—post 7/5/44, *R. Hofer*-SALEM REPRESENTATIVE-L-Ca, boxing winged mule on circle emblem, 11½ kill crosses-L-Co, whitewall tires, name KIDD in light color on blk ETO band of left gear cover, red ETO band on vert. tail, NMF a/c with full topside OD color profiling, blk ETO bands on wings, Malcolm hood after late May, 44. CC-R. Kellett.

42-106935   ?   Salv 6/27/44—left in either Russia or Italy due to battle damage or mechanical failure.

42-106940   WD-N   335-4/28/44—MIA 8/8/44-R. Fischer.

42-106975   VF-N   Post-1/45, NMF a/c, Malcolm hood, fin fillet, 3 kill crosses-L-Ca, blue rudder.

43-12177   WD-   335-2/13/44—trfd 2/25/44, to 334th or 336th?

43-12193   WD-2   War-weary, 335-11/15/44-Summer, 45, 2-seater OTU a/c, NMF a/c until painted all red in Spring, 45, with light blue trim, red/wht/blue rudder, 2 reg. canopies linked, converted by T/Sgt. E. Jensen, Sq. Tech. Insp.

43-12194   WD-   335-2/24/44—trfd 3/1/44.

43-12214   VF-C   336-3/16/44—?, *F. Glover*-4/1/44-REBEL QUEEN-L-FW, seated swimsuited girl, 6 kill crosses-L-Co, OD/Grey a/c. CC-J. Wilson, ACC-N. Meyers.

43-12407   WD-   335-2/24/44—trfd 2/25/44.

43-12412   QP-   334-2/13/44, 1st. P-51B asgnd. to 4FG and 334th.

43-12416   VF-O   336-2/28/44, *L. Norley*-2/28/44, 14-plus kill crosses at coincided time-L-Co, O/D and Gray a/c. CC-V. Giovenco.

43-12427   WD-   335-2/24/44—trfd 3/1/44.

43-12428   —   334-9/25/43, Test a/c asgnd. temporarily for a few days, O/D and Gray a/c, no white ETO bands, red U.S. star border, no code letters, radio compartment canopy blanked over.

43-12469   WD-L   335-3/6/44—MIA 3/21/44-J. Goetz.

43-24762   QP-   334-1/45, NMF a/c, Malcolm hood, red rudder, no D-Day bands.

43-24769   VF-U   336-5/44—MIA 4/30/44-*W. Millikan*, W. Millikan-MISSOURI MAULER-L-FW, same as P-47 emblem, 14 kill crosses, blk/red-L-Co, NMF a/c, blk. ETO bands, Malcolm hood. CC-N. Gallagher.

43-24771   VF-   MIA 5/11/44-R. Tussey.

43-24787	VF- MIA 5/30/44-S. Young.
43-24793	QP-C MIA 8/8/44-T. Underwood.
43-24794	WD- 335-5/1/44—trfd 8/1/44.
43-24813	WD-A-N 335-5/12/44—MIA 8/18/44-J. Conley, *R. Church*-5/29/44-A code.
43-24825	QP-G MIA 6/6/44-T. Fraser, *T. Fraser*-JERRY-L-M, drk. color name, NMF a/c, reg. canopy.
43-24841	QP-D MIA 8/18/44-C. Howard, NMF a/c, OD top profile, Malcolm hood, ½ D-Day.
43-24848	VF-B-? *J. Goodson*-Spring, 44, 30 drk kill crosses-L-Ca, Maj. Goodson in white on AG panel-L-Co, NMF a/c, Malcolm hood, Russia Shuttle-N. Van Wyk.
43-24877	VF- Salv 11/14/44?
43-24979	QP-U MIA 8/7/44-D. Malmsten.
43-25061	WD- 335-7/21/44—trfd 8/24/44.
43-6316	WD-H 335-3/6/44—MIA 3/21/44-W. Hawkins.
43-6325	WD-Z 335-2/24/44—MIA 4/13/44-R. Saunders.
43-6358	? Salv as of 7/5/44, Russia Shuttle loss, probably left with 325FG in Italy when damaged a/c were exchanged to get 4FG home.
43-6362	VF-H 336-3/19/44—salv 4/30/44-*H. Fredericks*, bellylanded at Manston, UK, on show return at 1315 hrs.
43-6388	— No codes, evaluation tests by Grp., at 334th dispersal, date unk., OD/Grey a/c, no ETO bands.
43-6433	QP-D Salv 6/9/44-J. Byrd, dived into ground and exploded near Leiston, UK, at 1810 hrs.
43-6437	WD-C-V 335-2/28/44—MIA 8/7/44-S. Wadsworth, *D. Blakeslee*-C-3/4/44, V-8/7/44, O/D and Gray a/c, all white ETO on 3/4/44, Malcolm hood.
43-6441	QP-G 334th-5/7/44.
43-6442	VF- 336-3/4/44—MIA 3/8/44-S. Edner.
43-6460	WD-F 335-2/28/44—MIA 3/18/44-E. Freeburger.
43-6463	WD- 335-6/10/44—MIA 7/19/44-K. Dahlen.
43-6489	QP- WD- 334-pre-6/6/44—trfd 335-12/1/44-3/2/45—trfd, O/D and Gray a/c, Malcolm hood.
43-6507	VF- 336-2/28/44. Russia Shuttle pilot?
43-6512	VF- 336-4/9/44.
43-6518	QP-*K* 334-7/44, *J. Ayers*-1/45, NMF a/c, Malcolm hood, D-Day bands-fus. bottom, fin fillet, blk ETO bands.
43-6542	QP- VF- Battle damage-8/18/44.
43-6557	WD- 335-9/14/44-? Battle damage-9/44.
43-6560	QP-W 334-?—MIA 5/29/44-F. Speer. *J. Clark* a/c, O/D and Gray a/c, Malcolm hood, 14½ kill swastikas-L-Ca-blk/wht outlined rows of 7-7½ red outlined codes. CC-R. Lonier, Arm-L. Hendel.
43-6562	WD-N 335-2/28/44—MIA 7/11/44-J. Hanrahan.
43-6567	QP-E 334-?—MIA 7/7/44-J. Scally. O/D and Gray a/c, Malcolm hood, dark "E" on fus., D-Day band.
43-6570	WD-3 War-weary-? 335-11/15/44—EOW. OTU a/c, JOES JUNK-L-FW, Malcolm hood, 1945 nose style, red/wht/blue rudder, AG panel motor top only to manifolds. CC-J. Sills.
43-6572	VF-N 336-3/20/44—MIA 5/25/44-J. Bennett.
43-6573	VF- 336-4/44—MIA 9/11/44-H. Ingalls.
43-6575	WD-I-L-E 335-2/28/44—MIA 6/6/44-C. Garbey, O/D and Gray a/c. *G. Carpenter*-2/28/44-4/11/44.
43-6579	WD-S 335-2/25/44—MIA 4/18/44-L. Henry. *C. Fiedler* a/c. SNAFU-L-

FW, mule kicking Hitler from behind on light circle. O/D and Gray a/c.

43-6584	VF- 336-3/19/44—MIA 5/19/44-D. Patchen.
43-6586	QP-U 334-?—MIA 6/11/44-H. Noon.
43-6587	QP-O-Z 334-5/44—MIA 1/2/45-A. Senecal. Arm-W. Plunk.
43-6591	QP-V 334-3/23/44—c. 9/44. *H. Noon* a/c.
43-6630	VF- 336-3/2/44—MIA 3/6/44-R. Messenger.
43-6633	VF-Q 336-3/2/44—MIA 5/25/44-T. McDill. *R. Nelson* a/c. O/D and Gray a/c.
43-6636	QP-N 334-?—MIA 5/9/44-V. Burroughs. *N. Megura* a/c. ILL WIND-L-FW, girl on circle, 15 blk/wht kill crosses-L-Co-5-5-5, O/D and Gray a/c. CC-P. Fox, ACC-J. Byrge.
43-6639	WD-P 335-2/28/44—MIA 3/21/44-E. Carlow.
43-6641	WD-E 335-2/25/44—MIA 3/21/44-J. Brandenburg.
43-6643	WD-L 335-2/24/44—MIA 3/3/44-G. Barnes.
43-6646	QP-L MIA 4/29/44-P. Kennedy.
43-6650	VF- Russia Shuttle-*J. Norris*—MIA 7/2/44-J. Norris.
43-6652	VF- 336-3/6/44—MIA 3/16/44-E. Skilton.
43-6656	QP-N *R. Frazer*—salv 2/28/44-R. Frazer. O/D and Gray a/c, full wht ETO.
43-6666	VF-O 336-c.4/44. Russia Shuttle-6/21/44-I. Grounds. L. Norley-4/44.
43-6673	VF- 336-4/44—salv 6/7/44-K. D. Smith.
43-6686	VF- 336-4/44. R. Corbett-8/28/44—hit tree in target area and made it back to Manston, UK.
43-6690	QP-Q 334-2/28/44—MIA 3/6/44-*H. Mills.*
43-6696	VF-F 336-2/28/44—MIA 3/29/44-*K. Peterson.*
43-6705	VF-W 336-2/29/44. *W. Johnson*-4/44. O/D and Gray a/c, reg. canopy.
43-6714	VF- 336-3/8/44—salv 6/7/44-D. Pierini-in mid-air collision S. of DB.
43-6717	QP-S 334-5/44. Battle damage-8/44. *R. Hills* a/c. OD/Gray a/c, no name or emblem, reg. canopy, Spitfire mirror. Arm-R. Lewis.
43-6718	WD-R 335-3/6/44—trfd 4/22/44. *J. Goodwyn* a/c.
43-6719	QP-T 334-7/44—MIA 10/7/44-K. Foster. A/C blew up after he bailed into N. Sea unhurt.
43-6725	WD-U 335-3/6/44—trfd 7/6/44—probably left in Italy damaged. *A. Schlegel* a/c.
43-6730	VF- 336-4/13/44.
43-6740	VF-R? 336-2/28/44—MIA 3/3/44-G. Herter.
43-6746	QP-E-X MIA 7/2/44-R. Hofer. *H. Blanchfield*-3/44, as E. O/D and Gray a/c, full wht. ETO bands, reg. canopy.
43-6753	WD-M 335-2/25/44—trfd 7/5/44, probably damaged in Italy.
43-6759	WD-P 335-3/22/44—MIA 3/29/44-W. Newell.
43-6765	VF-P 336-3/2/44-*J. Godfrey.* OD/Gray a/c, reg. canopy, no name or emblem, 3 rows red/wht checkers below manifolds., 11 wht kill crosses-L-Co, in 5/5/1 order. CC-L. Krantz.
43-6767	WD-D-F 335-2/28/44—MIA 4/24/44-M. Scarbrough. *B. McGrattan*-D-3/44.
43-6768	VF- 336-2/28/44-*R. Hughes.* Russia Shuttle-6/21/44-H. Dugan.
43-6770	WD-O-*O-G* 335-2/28/44—MIA 6/18/44-R. Little.
43-6772	VF-X 336-2/29/44. *N. Van Wyk*-4/44.
43-6784	WD-X 335-2/28/44—MIA 6/21/44-F. Sibbett. *J. Happel*-3-4/44.
43-6786	VF- 336-2/28/44—salv 3/4/44-*R. Richards.*
43-6798	QP-D MIA 3/5/44-*S. Pisanos.*
43-6802	VF-Y 336-3/20/44—MIA 4/22/44-R. Nelson. *L. Norley*-4/44. A/C possibly coded O.
43-6803	WD-K 335-2/26/44—MIA 3/21/44-*K. G. Smith.*

43-6810	WD-R 335-2/24/44—MIA 3/4/44-H. Ward.
43-6818	VF- 336-2/29/44—MIA 4/15/44-R. Seifert.
43-6819	QP-B 334-2/26/44—MIA 4/5/44-*D. Beeson.* BOISE BEE-L-FW, bee in flight gear holding six-guns on cloud with shield background, 20 blk/wkt kill crosses-L-Co-5-5-5-5, O/D and Gray a/c with splotchy new dark O/D spot touchups. Wht ETO bands on mainplanes only. CC-W. Wahl.
43-6823	QP-K 334-5/7/44. Arm-B. Fennell.
43-6832	QP-K 334-2/26/44—MIA 4/18/44-*V. France.* MISS DALLAS-L-Ca (under front of canopy), cowgirl bare on Texas map on sky blue circle, 8 blk/wht crosses-L-Co-5-3, O/D and Gray a/c, reg. canopy, red outlined codes, wht ETO bands, 1 mirror (Spitfire). CC-Don Allen.
43-6836	VF- 336-3/19/44—MIA 4/5/44-*D.* Hobert.
43-6837	QP-I 334-?—MIA 4/5/44-C. Carr.
43-6838	VF- 336-2/28/44—MIA 4/15/44-J. Bennett, ditched in N. Sea, pilot picked up with broken shoulder. *R. Simon* a/c.
43-6839	QP-N MIA 3/21/44-A. Rafalovich.
43-6840	VF-Z 336-3/2/44—possible salv 5/10/44, gear broken by new pilot on landing and slid into a/c bay. *J. Patteeuw* a/c nick-named ZED, no name on a/c, O/D and Gray a/c. CC-O. Garrison, ACC-N. Meyer.
43-6841	WD-J 335-2/24/44—MIA 9/17/44-N. Vozzy. NMF a/c.
43-6843	WD-B 335-2/28/44—MIA 3/28/44-R. Clotfelter. NMF a/c.
43-6846	VF- 336-2/28/44—MIA 8/2/44-G. Chapman.
43-6856	VF- MIA 4/30/44-F. Glover.
43-6860	QP-G MIA 3/27/44-A. Chatterley.
43-6863	WD-V 335-2/28/44—trfd 5/6/44.
43-6866	VF- 336-3/8/44—MIA 4/8/44-*R. Hughes.*
43-6869	QP-U MIA 3/21/44-R. Williams.
43-6871	VF- 336-2/28/44—MIA 3/3/44-V. Garrison.
43-6876	VF- 336-2/28/44. Russia Shuttle-6/21/44-Col. B. Kelsey.
43-6882	QP-A Arm-R. Simpson-5/7/44. MIA 8/15/44-N. Achen.
43-6887	WD-H 335-2/24/44—MIA 3/6/44-C. Manning.
43-6889	VF- 336-3/16/44—MIA 6/10/44-F. Caple. *D. Emerson*-4/44.
43-6891	VF- *F. Bonds*-4/44—salv 9/10/44-R. White.
43-6895	VF- 336-2/28/44. *J. Goodson*-2/28/44. O/D and Gray a/c.
43-6896	WD-A-F 335-2/28/44—MIA 6/19/44-D. Hill. *P. McKennon*-A-4/44. F-5/12/44-G. Stanford.
43-6897	WD-P-U 335-3/24/44—trfd 11/18/44. *F. Jones*-P-4/44. *W. Eaton*-U-Fall, 44-SEE ME LATER-L-FW, skull/halo/crossed lightning bolts on dark circle/name background also dark, all outlined by rope-L-M to FW. NMF a/c, D-Day bands under wing.
43-6898	QP-J MIA 6/6/44-W. Sobanski. *H. Hively*-Spring, 44-DEACON-L-FCa, preacher with Bible on yellow circle, 9 blk/wht. kill crosses-L-Co., O/D and Gray a/c, full a/c D-Day bands, red outlined codes, red ETO band on tail fin/rudder, Malcolm hood. CC-V. Andra, Arm-G. Roen.
43-6899	QP-O MIA 3/6/44-E. Whalen.
43-6901	WD-G-F 335-2/24/44—MIA 5/21/44-W. Hunt. G-3/6/44.
43-6903	VF-Y 336-2/28/44—MIA 3/3/44-*P. Dunn.*
43-6913	VF-T 336-3/2/44—salv 4/13/44-*D. Gentile.* SHANGRI-LA-L-FW, boxing eagle on yellow circle, 4 × 14 row red/wht checkers-L and R-Ms, 30-blk/wht kill crosses-L-Co to Ca on wht scroll in 2 rows, reg. canopy, O/D and Gray a/c, wht ETO bands on mainplanes only. CC-J. Ferra.
43-6922	WD-Y 335-2/25/44—MIA 4/24/44-P. Riley.
43-6924	QP-L Arm-F. Hennig-5/7/44.
43-6933	QP-Y MIA 5/28/44-A. Hewatt. CC-H. Hoffman.

43-6936	VF-D 336-2/28/44—MIA 3/18/44-*W. Sooman*. O/D and Gray a/c.
43-6941	QP-T MIA 4/9/44-D. Van Epps.
43-6942	VF-D MIA 11/21/44-G. Klaus. *J. Higgins*-8/13/44-MEINER KLEINER-L-M. D-Day bands on lower a/c, no ETO bands, O/D and Gray a/c, Malcolm hood, 1 mirror. CC-G. Weckbacher, Russia Shuttle-J. Higgins.
43-6946	QP-L MIA 4/5/44-A. Bunte. O/D and Gray a/c.
43-6957	QP-M MIA 6/6/44-E. Steppe. *D. Malmsten*-TURNIP TERMITE-L-Co, winged bug holding blunderbuss on light circle, O/D and Gray a/c, *F. Speer*-5/44. Arm-F. Pelosi-5/7/44.
43-6959	WD-T-Z 335-2/24/44—MIA 9/11/44-P. Iden.
43-6963	VF-
43-6967	QP-D MIA 4/8/44-H. Moulton.
43-6972	VF-N ?-PAUL-L-Co, 14 kill crosses-L-Co, O/D and Gray a/c. Possibly a 335 a/c trfd to 336. C. Anderson or A. Schlegel a/c?
43-6973	WD-W 335-2/28/44—MIA 3/29/44-G. Smart, bailed into N. Sea on show return, pilot unhurt. Motor quit.
43-6975	VF-S 336-12/25/44. NMF a/c, Malcolm hood, fin fillet, 1945 nose style, blue rudder, no fus. D-Day bands.
43-6985	VF-C 336-2/29/44—MIA 3/2/44-*G. Villinger*. O/D and Gray a/c, wht. nose and full wht. ETO bands, no personal emblems.
43-6997	VF-U *W. Millikan*-4/44—salv 6/18/44-H. Ingalls, crashlanded at DB out of fuel. O/D and Gray a/c.
43-7002	QP-D MIA 5/9/44-R. Sherman, Arm-L. Schwarting-5/7/44, CC-G. Russel, O/D and Gray a/c.
43-7004	WD-U 335-2/28/44—MIA 3/4/44-P. Ellington.
43-7005	VF-N 336-2/28/44—salv 3/5/44-R. Wehrman, crashlanded at Heathfield, UK at 1420 hrs, plugs fused, long glide, bellylanded., *G. Herter*-2/28/44, O/D and Gray a/c, full wht ETO bands, nose.
43-7029	QP-U MIA 4/8/44-R. Claus.
43-7032	WD-K-S 335-3/22/44—MIA 5/31/44-R. Homuth. K-4/24/44, S-5/12/44.
43-7035	QP-X MIA 4/13/44-V. Wynn.
43-7042	WD-J 335-5/13/44—MIA 6/7/44-O. R. Jones.
43-7059	VF- Salv 6/5/44-R. Kackerback.
43-7098	WD-F 335-3/25/44—MIA 4/8/44-F. Boyles.
43-7149	WD- 335-2/28/44—trfd 3/3/44.
43-7150	QP-P MIA 6/8/44-J. Scott.
43-7158	QP-F Salv MIA 5/22/44-N. Megura. NMF a/c, Malcolm hood, blk ETO bands, no personal emblems on R. side. Arm-R. Easley-5/7/44.
43-7164	WD- 335-2/28/44—trfd 3/3/44.
43-7172	WD-H 335-3/22/44—MIA 6/6/44-W. Smith. *T. Lines* a/c, THREE JOKERS-L-M, 3 joker cards carried by Joker figure shooting pistol, NMF a/c.
43-7178	QP-Q MIA 5/30/44-M. Kolter.
43-7181	WD-L 335-3/25/44—MIA 4/19/44-C. Anderson.
43-7183	QP-R MIA 4/15/44-*R. Care*.
43-7187	WD-B 335-3/30/44—MIA 6/18/44-J. Glynn.
43-7190	WD-W 335-3/30/44—MIA 4/10/44-C. Fiedler.
52?	VF-4 P-51B/C, NMF a/c, Malcolm hood, 1945 nose style, 1 mirror, reg. VF code ltrs., fin fillet, no ETO bands. Sqd. OTU a/c.
——	VF-4 336-3/17/45. P-51B 2-seat conversion by Mobile Repair Unit #4 of 45th Serv. Sq. by CM/Sgt. David Nelson. Reg. canopy in front with Malcolm hood on rear. A/C RAF PRU blue overall, but Grp. nose red and red glare panel stripes.

Six-355FG P-51Bs flown on loan by 4FG on show of 3/6/44. A/C codes OS-L-M-O-H-K-U.

P-51D MUSTANG AIRCRAFT:

44-11200 WD-F 335-10/25/44—EOW.
44-11225 QP-D 334-?—EOW.
44-11336 QP-Z MIA 3/31/45-K. *Foster*. K. Foster-12/23/44-taxiing accident with 44-14110.
44-11339 WD- 335-11/15/44—MIA 1/17/45-R. Stallings.
44-11356 VF- MIA 2/25/45-K. Carlson.
44-11661 QP-X MIA 2/24/45-A. Hand, *Lt. Col. J. Oberhansly*-IRON ASS, armored jackass in circle, name in red and black. CC-R. Lonier, Arm.-R. Easley.
44-11665 VF- MIA 2/27/45-H. Crawford.
44-11677 QP-P MIA 2/21/45-A. Lacy.
44-13260 VF- MIA 9/12/44-*J. Lane*, Russia Shuttle-J. Lane.
44-13300 VF-B? Salv. 6/7/44-J. Goodson-hit by Flak and crashlanded at Merston, UK, on show return, demolishing the a/c.
44-13303 VF-B MIA 6/20/44-*J. Goodson*, MAJ. GOODSON-L-Co, 30 kill crosses-L-Ca, full D-Day and ETO.
44-13306 QP-F
44-13307 VF- MIA 6/18/44-H. Arnold.
44-13314 QP-X MIA 8/18/44-A. Cwiklinski.
44-13315 VF- 336-8/1/44—EOW, B. Wilhoit-4/21/45.
44-13317 VF-L-B MIA 3/26/45-H. Davis, *D. Emerson*-L-9/3/44-Donald Duck emblem-L-Fw, 6 kill crosses-L-Co, Russia Shuttle-D. Emerson.
44-13319 WD- 335-6/8/44—trfd 9/18/44.
44-13322 QP-O Trfd 7/6/44-in Italy, *G. Siems*-GLORIA III-L-M, 9 kill crosses, Russia Shuttle-G. Siems.
44-13325 VF-Z Russia Shuttle-6/21/44-*P. Patteeuw*, ½ D-Day (fus. only), ETO wing and tail, no tail fillet.
44-13352 QP-Z 334-7/44, *J. Lang* a/c, CC-E. Eisler, ACC-W. Rushing.
44-13372 QP-W-B Salv 8/11/44-W. Gillette, *Lt. Col. J. Clark*-B-8/11/44, 16 kills-L-Ca, CC-R. Lonier.
44-13375 VF- 336-8/1/44—MIA 4/16/45-W. Ayer.
44-13389 WD- 335-6/12/44—MIA 4/16/45-E. Loughlin.
44-13399 WD- 335-6/10/44—MIA 6/21/44—salv in Russia on Shuttle trip.
44-13402 WD-K 335-6/8/44—MIA 7/2/44-G. Stanford.
44-13411 QP-Q 334-8/10/44—MIA 11/20/44-L. Werner. *S. Monroe* a/c.
44-13412 VF-F Russia Shuttle-6/21/44-G. Logan—MIA 8/24/44-J. Godfrey.
44-13519 VF- Russia Shuttle-C. Shilke—salv 12/10/44-R. Voyles, crashed at 1645 hrs at Shadlows Farm, Burnt Oak, Essex, UK, pilot cut slightly on head.
44-13534 WD-F 335-6/20/44—MIA 8/28/44-A. Thomson.
44-13555 WD-O-D 335-6/19/44—EOW. *T. Lines* a/c-0-11/44, THUNDERBIRD-L-FW, southwest Indian thunderbird emblem-L-FW. *C. Konsler*-D-EOW. CC-S. Koenig.
44-13563 WD-R 335-6/30/44—MIA 8/18/44-D. Smith.
44-13564 WD-I 335-7/7/44—trfd 9/18/44. *R. Mabie* a/c. *D. Perkins* a/c. CC-W. Behm.
44-13567 WD-O 335-7/4/44—MIA 8/18/44-B. Rosenson.
44-13608 VF- MIA 7/13/44-W. Edwards.
44-13615 QP-R MIA 11/20/44-D. Bennett.
44-13630 VF-R *M. Dickey*-2/45-BETTY JANE II-L-M. 3 kill crosses on OD canopy frame, blk ETO bands overall.

44-13641 WD-R 335-7/6/44—MIA 7/22/44-L. Kingham.

44-13649 VF-F 336-7/44-M. Miller, crashlanded at DB at 1345 hrs on show return, date unk. Blk ETO bands overall, fus. D-Day bands.

44-13691 VF- 336-4/21/45.

44-13727 WD- 335-8/24/44—EOW.

44-13732 QP-R MIA 8/25/44-K. Rudkin.

44-13777 WD- 335-2/22/45—trfd 4/18/45-left in France.

44-13779 WD-C 335-7/8/44—EOW-*D. Blakeslee*-7/44-11/44. Blk ETO bands on all but tail fin, wht rudder, red canopy frame, fus. D-Day bands, O/D right rear wing fillet.

44-13788 WD- 335-7/20/44—MIA 4/9/45-H. Rassmussen.

44-13799 ? Battle damage repaired by 45th Serv. Sq. in 9/44.

44-13883 WD-A 335-7/22/44—MIA 8/28/44-*P. McKennon.*

44-13884 QP-B-G-V 334-9/44—MIA 2/6/45-W. Bates. *D. Howe*-G-1/45.

44-13893 VF- 336-4/21/45.

44-13903 WD-L 335-?—salv 1/18/45-*R. Rinebolt. Z. Sensibaugh*-1/45-two dice in wht circle-L-Co.

44-13934 VF- MIA 8/3/44-F. D. Smith, 4FG Hq. Sq. pilot.

44-13956 QP-D *R. Dickmeyer*-JAN-L-M, girl in swimsuit, CC-G. Russel.

44-13961 VF-L 336-8/1/44—MIA 11/8/44-E. Quist. Fus. D-Day bands.

44-13977 WD-H- 335-7/25/44—EOW. *D. Peterson*-COOKIE-L-M, red canopy frame, 1 mirror, CC-J. Gibson.

44-13982 WD-V 335-8/24/44—trfd 9/10/44-C. Poage, a/c left at Amiens, Fr., and pilot came back by Dakota transp.

44-13984 QP-B-U *C. Boretsky*-B-Fall, 44, MEG-L-M, red name with blk outline. Fus. D-Day bands, red outlined codes, blk ETO on horizontal flt. surfaces only. *M. Arthur*-U-3/45, DAVY LEE-L-M, name in red with blk outline.

44-13997 WD-W 335-7/24/44—MIA 8/13/44-S. Boren.

44-14027 WD-P 335-7/31/44—MIA 8/8/44-F. Jones.

44-14029 VF- Salv 3/1/45-E. Gimbel, crashed at Brussels, Belg., and had a short hospital stay there. A/C named HARD LUCK.

44-14047 ? MIA 8/9/44?

44-14051 WD-W 335-8/16/44—EOW. A/C named WAVA. Red canopy and tail border.

44-14054 WD-I 335-8/27/44—MIA 9/17/44-C. Holske.

44-14056 ? MIA 9/5/44?

44-14066 WD-O 335-8/24/44—MIA 8/28/44-*A. Schlegel.*

44-14098 WD-P-R 335-8/24/44—? *J. Russell* a/c CC-E. Cool.

44-14102 WD- 335-8/16/44—trfd 9/27/44.

44-14110 QP-R *K. Helfrecht*-GEORGIE-L-M, boy's face-L-FW. CC-R. Lewis. A/C in taxi collision with 44-11336 on 12/23/44, piloted by T. Cronin.

44-14119 QP-H MIA 11/21/44-C. Delnero. *G. Montgomery*-SIZZLIN LIZ-L-M, red name with blk outline. CC-E. Nelson, ACC-R. Hadden.

44-14123 QP-Z MIA 10/14/44-*J. Lang.*

44-14125 WD- 335-8/24/44—trfd 12/19/44.

44-14137 WD-KK 335-8/24/44—EOW. *G. Green* a/c-post VE-Day. Red canopy frame, blk ETO bands. CC-B. Schultz, ACC-"Cess" Poole, crew names on panel forward of canopy-L side.

44-14142 QP-O-Q Salv 4/7/45-*J. Jahnke,* crashed off E. runway at 1650 hrs. from 100 ft. J. Jahnke-O, collided with D. Malmsten in QP-Y while taxiing on 1/6/45.

44-14158 WD-R 335-8/24/44—MIA 9/11/44-J. Russell.

44-14172 VF- MIA 10/2/44-G. Logan.

44-14202 QP-Q *J. McFadden*-2/45.

44-14221   WD-A-I 335-9/19/44—? 4/17/45-bellylanded or gear failure on French a/d. *P. McKennon*-RIDGE RUNNER III-L-FW, wild boar under name, 20 kill crosses in red/blk on wht square-L-M-10-10, 1 mirror, red canopy frame, glide-bomb marks on leading edge of wing. *R. Mabie*-I.

44-14229   QP-N MIA 11/6/44-E. Walsh.

44-14266   VF- MIA 9/11/44-R. Patterson.

44-14271   QP-K MIA 9/12/44-T. Joyce.

44-14276   VF-A 336-11/44—EOW. *F. Young*-MARTHA JANE-L-M, OD canopy frame, no D-Day bands, no ETO bands, blue rudder, codes shadow edged. *J. McMahon*-4/20/45-MARCY-L-M, shamrock in green-L-M, crew names-L-Co. CC-G. Anderson, ACC-M. Weddle, Arm-J. Terrill.

44-14277   VF-H MIA 4/16/45-B. Griffin. *H. Frederick*-JERSEY BOUNCE III-L-M, red name with blk outline, O/D canopy frame with red lower edge, red edge to AG panel, blue rudder, no ETO bands, 1 mirror.

44-14281   QP-Y MIA 9/13/44-W. B. Smith.

44-14292   QP-A 334-10/44—EOW. *C. Kinnard*-10/44-MAN O WAR-L-M, red oblique band on AG panel, 18 kill flags-L-canopy frame, 2 mirrors, fus. D-Day bands, blk ETO bands except tail fin, red outlined codes, wavy O/D stripes over top profile. CC-R. Lonier, ACC-B. Anderson, Arm-R. Easley. *R. Voyles*-1/45-OLD WITCH-L-M/FW, girl on broom on dark circle, no fus. D-Day bands, no topside stripes, no kill marks. CC-E. Pfankuche.

44-14310   QP-K MIA 8/28/44-H. Vandervate.

44-14317   VF-Y MIA 1/16/45-*H. Hagan*. H. Hagan-DUKE-L-FW, O/D canopy frame and AG panel edged in red, 1 mirror, red shadow-edged codes, blk ETO bands, except tail fin. CC-E. Rowe.

44-14323   QP-VV *R. Dyer*-1/45-DYER RIA-THE POINTER-L-M, roughly painted cat emblem-L-M, 1 mirror, no ETO bands, no D-Day bands. A/C had name LAZY DAZY-L-M at unk. date.

44-14339   WD-U 335-9/14/44—MIA 11/5/44-R. Anderson.

44-14350   VF- MIA 3/12/45-J. McFarlane.

44-14361   WD-K 335-9/29/44—MIA 3/21/45-R. Cammer. *E. McCall* a/c.

44-14387   VF- MIA 4/17/45-R. Davis.

44-14389   WD-T 335-8/31/44—MIA 4/9/45-R. Bucholz. No D-Day bands, ETO blk bands on horiz. planes, no mirror.

44-14418   WD- 335-9/29/44—trfd 11/25/44.

44-14431   WD-Q 335-9/1/44—MIA 9/11/44-W. Groseclose.

44-14432   VF- *P. Morgan* a/c. CC-O. Garrison, ACC-M. Ferrell.

44-14435   WD-O 335-8/30/44—MIA 2/21/45-A. Rabe.

44-14438   WD-U 335-8/30/44—EOW. LITTLE NAN-L-M in 3/45.

44-14492   VF-G In 336-9/30/44—salv 3/2/45-W. Hastings, crashed at base at 0845 hrs, aborting mission.

44-14518   QP- *C. Beason*-4/45-NAD-L-M.

44-14527   VF-S MIA 4/16/45-M. Miller. MARY-L-M, dark name on light square, O/D canopy frame, 1 mirror.

44-14529   WD-X 335-9/23/44—MIA 11/18/44-R. Lewis.

44-14533   VF- MIA 1/16/45-F. Hall.

44-14537   QP-A MIA 2/27/45-R. Voyles.

44-14540   WD- 335-9/23/44—MIA 12/25/44-C. Poage.

44-14548   VF- D. Pederson-4/20/45.

44-14552   VF- W. Thompson-4/21/45.

44-14557   WD-B-Z 335-9/19/44—EOW. *W. O'Donnell*-THE DUCHESS-L-M, red name with yellow-orange shadow and blue outline on yellow engine cowl panel, 1 mirror, red canopy frame, blk ETO bands on horiz. planes, wht

rudder with red border. Z-5/45. CC-W. Gerth, ACC-M. Isaac, Arm-D.
Lambert.

44-14560   QP-V   *D. Malmsten*-CROTCH ROT-L-M, red name with blk outline. In
taxiing accident with 44-14142, on 1/6/45.

44-14570   WD-A-D   335-9/23/44—EOW. *P. McKennon*-RIDGE RUNNER-L-FW,
wild hog on dark panel, red canopy frame, blk ETO bands on horiz. planes.
CC-J. Sills. *R. Couse*-D-late 1945, a/c scrapped in junkyard with arrow
emblem-L-Ca.

44-14585   QP-   Code letter either G, O, or C.

44-14590   VF-   336-4/20/45.

44-14648   VF-H   336-4/45. Possibly H. Frederick a/c.

44-14772   QP-Z   MIA 11/6/44-J. Childs.

44-14787   VF-B   *F. Glover*-11/18/44, emblem-L-FW, eagle's head wearing infantry
helmet on U.S. flag shield, 12 kill crosses-L-canopy frame, fus. D-Day
bands, blk ETO bands on horiz. planes, lt. blue AG panel and canopy frame
with red edge. CC-Metcaffe, ACC-E. Marcotte.

44-14923   WD-   335-11/7/44—MIA 3/3/45-K. Green.

44-15028   WD-O-Y   335-10/25/44—EOW. *L. Norley*-O-10/44. *C. Willruth*-Y-
Spring, 45-DOTTY-L-FW, red canopy frame, no D-Day bands, blk ETO
bands except vert. stab., 1 mirror.

44-15054   VF-D   336-11/8/44—MIA 12/25/44-D. Emerson. *E. Quist*-11/44. CC-G.
Weckbacher, ACC-L. Brown.

44-15152   QP-T   JERSEY JERK-L-M.

44-15191   VF-C   336-12/26/44—EOW. *J. Hileman*-12/44-MARY BELLE-L-M, no
D-Day bands, ETO except vert. stab. *G. Ridler*-4/45. CC-J. Wilson.

44-15216   QP-F   334-1/45.

44-15291   VF-   336-EOW.

44-15324   QP-M   MIA 1/16/45-V. Rentschler.

44-15326   QP-H   334-12/44. *G. Montgomery*-SIZZLIN LIZ-L-M, red/blk name, 1
red mirror, 15 kill crosses-L-Co, ETO bands except vert. stab., no D-Day
bands. CC-E. Nelson.

44-15330   WD-   335-11/23/44—EOW.

44-15347   QP-J-O-V   MIA 4/25/45-W. Hoelscher. *H. Hively*-J-1/45, O/D upper-
sides/NMF undersides, blk ETO bands on mainplanes, red bordered codes,
red rudder/fin top. *L. Norley*-1/45-O, same scheme as J except code
change.

44-15350   VF-   MIA 12/11/44-P. Morgan.

44-15351   WD-   335-11/26/44—MIA 2/20/45-J. Fitch.

44-15375   VF-   12/28/44—EOW. F. Grove-12/28/44.

44-15381   QP-X   MIA 2/24/45-A. Hand.

44-15395   VF-   336-4/21/45.

44-15455   WD-   335-11/26/44—MIA 12/18/44-C. Hewes.

44-15531   VF-   Salv 2/4/45-A. Wallace.

44-15551   WD-   335-1/3/45—trfd 4/18/45-left in France by forced-down pilot.

44-15575   VF-

44-15613   VF-M   336-3/45—EOW. *H. Bousfield*-PEACHES-L-M, thin red script
letters, O/D canopy frame, blk ETO bands on horiz. planes only, slanted
serial on fin only.

44-15615   WD-   335-1/3/45—MIA 2/6/45-P. Santos.

44-15647   VF-I   336-4/21/45. JOHNETTA IV-L-M, baby angel with tommy gun in
light circle, 1 mirror, thin red edge to O/D AG panel and canopy frame
extended to antenna, thin dark edge to nose color.

44-17415   WD-   *R. Ackerly*-MAN-I-ACK-L-M. CC-E. Cool.

44-53223	QP-S *R. Bowers*-3/26/45-SWEET ARLENE-L-M, girl in undies-L-FW, 1 mirror, no ETO bands.
44-63166	WD-A 335-1/3/45—MIA 3/18/45-*P. McKennon*.
44-63223	QP- *K. Helfrecht*-Spring, 45-GEORGIE-L-M, little boy's face-L-FW, CC-W. Rushing.
44-63233	VF-D *G. Davis*-12/44-INKYS DINKY-L-M. MIA 2/11/45-H. Kaul. CC-G. Weckbacher.
44-63583	QP-T Salv 4/15/45-*E. Wozniak*. E. Wozniak-HELEN-L-M/FW, baby angel with tommy gun, ? blk and red swastika flags on L canopy frame. CC-W. Rushing.
44-63599	WD- 335-1/29/45—MIA 3/3/45-G. Davis.
44-63670	WD- 335-1/15/45—MIA 3/21/45-A. Davis.
44-63736	WD-M 335-2/22/45—EOW. *G. Green*-SUZON-L-M, girl reclining on dark background, red canopy frame, no mirror, no D-Day, no blk ETO bands, red and white rudder. CC-W. Schultz. 1945 nose style. Famous "piggy-back" a/c of McKennon rescue.
44-63831	VF- MIA 4/16/45-L. Carpenter.
44-64054	VF- W. Riedel-4/21/45.
44-64116	? Salv 4/24/45.
44-64142	VF-G Spring, 45. TIGER BABY-L-M, dark cat with light name over it, light panel background, 1945 nose style, O/D canopy frame.
44-64153	VF-B-P EOW—7/7/45. *F. Glover*-B-eagle's U.S. Army helmeted head on U.S. flag shield background-L-FW, 1945 nose style, light blue AG panel and canopy frame bordered red, 24 red/wht/blk. kill flags after pilot name on canopy frame, light blue rudder, no ETO bands, no D-Day bands. *VF-P*; 7/7/45, light blue AG panel/canopy/rudder edged with red (not rudder), red/wht/blk kill flags around canopy frame, crew of pilot and chief names-L-Co, dive bomb marks on wing, FOURTH FIGHTER GROUP-L-FW, facing boxing eagle emblem over name, REGGIE'S REPLY-R-M/FW. ACC and Arm crew names-R-Co. All art names red with blk outlines. Crew names blk. A/C not used by Godfrey, but marked for Paris display post-VE.
44-72053	VF-Y 336-Spring, 45. *H. Hagan* a/c. O/D AG panel and canopy, 1 mirror, shadow-edged codes. CC-E. Rowe.
44-72061	WD-N 335-3/23/45—EOW. No mirror, no D-Day bands, no ETO bands.
44-72151	VF- 336-3/21/45-D. Pederson, forced down in Belgium at 1130 hrs this date.
44-72155	QP-W *R. Buchanan*-THE COUNT, bleary pilot holding head and clutching beer mug at bar.
44-72181	VF-S 336-12/26/44—salv 5/29/45-H. Frederick. *E. W. Stewart*-SUNNY VIII-L-M, red name outlined blk, 2 mirrors, light blue AG panel/canopy edged in red, light blue rudder, crew names-L-Co, pilot name-fore canopy frame, aft canopy 10 red/wht/blk kill flags, no ETO/D-Day bands. CC-G. Weckbacher, ACC-L. Brown, Arm-V. Young.
44-72196	QP-O 334-Spring/45. *L. Norley*. 1 mirror, horiz. plane ETO bands.
44-72210	VF-S *E. Stewart*-6/15/45. Light blue AG panel/canopy edged red, light blue rudder, 2 mirrors, 2-seat a/c, 3-section canopy, no ETO/D-Day bands, radar antennas on top/bottom/front of outer wing. CC-G. Weckbacher.
44-72241	WD-W 335-2/28/45—EOW. No mirror.
44-72251	QP-A *S. Woods*. 6 Japanese kill flags on left canopy frame, 1 mirror, no D-Day/ETO bands. CC-R. Lonier, Arm-R. Easley.
44-72265	WD- 335-3/22/45—EOW.
44-72285	VF- Salv 4/6/45-G. Kesler, force-landed 7 mi. N/E of Aachen, Ger., at 1125 hrs.

44-72308   WD-A   335-3/20/45—EOW.   *P. McKennon*-RIDGE-RUNNER-III-L-FW, razorback hog in tan on blk panel with 2 parachute symbols, ?-red/wht/blk kill flags-L-M, red canopy frame, 1 mirror. CC-J. Sills.

44-72327   QP-   *P. Burnett*-MARJORIE-L-M, red name outlined blk, 1 mirror. CC-W. Rushing.

44-72340   WD-   335-3/6/45—salv 5/17/45-R. Tannehill.

44-72346   QP-K   334-Spring, 45. No ETO/D-Day bands, 1 mirror, no other marks.

44-72362   QP-J   334-4/16/45. No art.

44-72369   WD-   335-3/6/45—EOW.

44-72377   QP-*H*   MIA 4/16/45-P. Burnett.

44-72381   QP-J   334-5/8/45. No ETO/D-Day bands, 1 mirror, Tru-vue canopy.

44-72382   QP-H   *G. Montgomery*-SIZZLIN LIZ-L-M, red name outlined blk, 15 blk kill crosses-L-Co. CC-E. Nelson.

44-72416   WD-P   335-3/20/45—EOW. *R. Ackerly*-4/16/45-RITA MARIE, 6/45-MAN-I-ACK. CC-E. Cool.

44-72478   WD-I   335-3/20/45—EOW. *R. Mabie* a/c. CC-W. Behm.

44-72523   VF-   MIA 4/16/45-C. Alfred.

44-72767   VF-T   336-Spring, 45. *F. Grove* a/c. O/D AG panel/canopy with thin red edge, no ETO/D-Day bands, 1 mirror, slanted serial no. CC-J. Ferra.

44-72769   VF-   MIA 4/16/45-E. Gimbel.

44-72789   VF-D   336-7/8/45.

44-72816   VF-P-J   336-4/21/45. J-same date.

44-72863   QP-K   334-4/4/45-LIL AGGIE-L-M.

44-73021   VF-F   *D. Groshong*-4/20/45-CLARINE-L-M, red name outlined blk, O/D AG panel/canopy edged red, 1 mirror.

44-73043   VF-   336-4/21/45.

44-73061   VF-X   Salv Spring, 45, bellylanded on north runway? BLOOD AND GUTS-L-M, name formed by rope of intestines on wht panel, red edge to AG panel.

44-73097   WD-   335-4/17/45—EOW.

44-73100   WD-B   335-4/17/45—EOW.

44-731?6   QP-   334-Spring, 45. MY ACHIN BACK-L-M, girl in undies on dark circle.

44-73108   QP-O   Late Spring, 45. *L. Norley*-RED DOG XII-L-M, red name outlined in blk, 15 red and blk kill swastikas-L-canopy frame, no mirror, no ETO/D-Day bands. CC-V. Andra. Tru-vue canopy.

44-73112   WD-   335-4/10/45—EOW.

44-73141   QP-   334-Spring, 45. ANNE II-L-M, 1 mirror, no ETO bands.

44-73154   VF-

44-73155   VF-   336-4/21/45.

44-73218   VF-C   O/D AG panel/canopy, Spring, 45. No D-Day/ETO bands.

44-73304   QP-U   *M. Arthur*-BLONDIE-L-M/FW, girl in blk gown on red circle outlined blk, no mirror, no ETO/D-Day bands. CC-D. Allen, ACC-J. Byrge.

44-73843   VF-E   W. Hastings a/c.

4th Fighter Group Non-combatant and Special Aircraft

North American AT-6; serial no. 42-84602, no code letters, NMF a/c, colors as of June 1945: red nose cowl swept under to wing leading edge; red tips to wings, horiz. stabilizers, fin/rudder; red wheel covers; serial number below rear seat on middle of fus. side; a/c had D-Day bands in summer 44. It was maintained by the Flight Section of the 45th Service Sqd., M/Sgt. M. Markowitz, Line Chief. It was used for pilot blind-flying training and the pickup of repair parts and downed pilots.

Douglas A-20G-DO; serial no. 43-9202, codes 2A-B, O/D and Gray, later painted black (it is believed) in the spring of 1945, a 9AF 416BG a/c which damaged a wing and engine forcelanding at DB. Pilot wanted to declare it salvage, but 864th A.E.S. mobile units rebuilt it with depot parts.

Martin B-26G; serial no. 34195, no codes except QP-? under the lower left wing, NMF a/c, O/D glare panel, dark fin tip and full rudder, yellow serial no. on rudder above hinge, dark wheel covers, maintained by 864th AES Flt. Sect. in June 1945. A/C used for rum running to Paris mainly.

Noorduyn UC-64 Norseman; serial no. 44-70392, no codes, NMF a/c, red group nose color swept under in 1945 style in the spring.

Noorduyn UC-64 Norseman; serial no. 43-5257?, no codes, NMF a/c, noted on base, possibly not assigned 4FG.

Miles Master III; serial no. W8938, no codes, transferred to 4FG along with RAF Spitfires in 1942. AAF national insignia applied to RAF color scheme which later was repainted in AAF O/D and Gray.

Airspeed Oxford V; serial no. AS-728, no codes, O/D and Gray a/c, red engine cowlings in Aug. 1944. Used as utility transport.

Piper L-4 Grasshopper; serial no. 9628, no codes, O/D and Gray a/c, red group nose color on engine cowling.

Fairchild UC-61A; serial no. 43-4469, no codes, O/D and Gray a/c, yellow nose cowling, name WEE FLY on left cowling, broken landing gear in June 1945, 864th AES maintained.

Fairchild UC-61A; serial no. 43-14442, no codes, O/D and Gray a/c, red engine cowling, name ETO HAPPY in light color on left cowl under windscreen, red bordered star/bar insignia, 864th AES a/c in June 1945.

Supermarine Spitfire VB; serial no. P7965, no codes, O/D and Gray a/c, red bordered star/bar insignia on Oct. 19, 1943, Sky or white prop spinner; believed to be lone Spitfire retained by group out of nostalgia and to keep pilot's hand in on inline engine a/c.

de Havilland Tiger Moth II; serial no. DE-262, no codes, O/D and Gray a/c, yellow bordered star/circle insignia; a/c assigned to 335FS.

de Havilland Tiger Moth II; serial no. C-7237, no codes, RAF color scheme in the Fall of 1942, later changed to AAF O/D and Gray; 334FS assigned a/c.

de Havilland Tiger Moth II; serial no. ?, no codes, O/D and Gray a/c, yellow bordered star/circle insignia, name DOROTHY under aft windscreen on right side; 336FS assigned a/c.

65TH Fighter Wing A/C based on Debden.

Vultee Vengeance A-35B-VN; serial no. WW-131385 and FD196, O/D and Gray a/c, RAF roundel insignia, white 1' band around front of engine cowl, name MISS BEVERLY in light color aft of cowl flaps on left side, wheel covers halved in light & dark colors, light color 1' high "X" on tail fin tip, WW serial on tail fin and FD196 below on fuselage; a/c fitted with tow-target equipment.

Republic P-47D-22RE; serial no. WW 42-26059, coded A–J, NMF a/c, blue star/bar insignia, O/D glare panel, no other markings. Believed to be Gen. Jesse Auton's personal a/c (CG of 65FW), hence initials on a/c.

Piper L-4 Grasshopper; serial no. 656, no codes, O/D and Gray a/c, blue star/bar insignia, red nose engine cowl with two white rings around aft half of cowl, shark teeth/mouth painted under engine manifolds, name AH-OY in light color on left cowl below windscreen, Popeye style cartoon man below left front of canopy.

Cessna Bobcat UC-78; serial no. 42-58515, serial nos. 3 and 3 on fin and rudder, no codes, O/D and Gray a/c, red/white/red/white engine cowling bands, blue star/bar insignia.

North American P-51 B Mustang; serial no. 43-6542, NMF a/c, coded J-A, regular canopy, red/white/red/white nose cowl/spinner stripes, D-Day bands on undersides.

4th Fighter Group Aircraft Markings

Supermarine Spitfire A/C:

Upon the Eagles' transfer to the AAF and the 4FG, their Spitfire Vb a/c came with them. Only minor changes were made to the standard RAF Dayfighter Northern Europe camouflage finish. This scheme was Ocean Grey and Dark Green shadow-shaded on the upper surfaces with Medium Sea Grey on the bottom. The prop spinner, code letters, and the 18″-wide recognition band on the rear fuselage were colored Sky (duck-egg blue). Each wing leading edge had a 4″-wide yellow strip out to the tip. The national insignia was changed by overpainting the 36″ RAF roundels with the U.S.A.A.F. white star and dark blue background. A 2″ yellow ring was added as an outline. The RAF tail fin flash, right upper wing, and the left lower wing roundels were camouflaged over. Upper and lower wing roundels had no yellow outer rings, being 56″ and 32″ respectively.

The Eagle Squadron's code letters of XR, AV, and MD were retained on the a/c, although they were now the AAF numbered squadrons. No 4FG Spitfires were known to have carried the later 8AF assigned code letters, QP, WD, and VF. The squadron two-letter codes were forward of the roundel on both sides of the fuselage except for several odd a/c where it was aft on the right side. The a/c ID letter was normally aft of the roundel. Most code letters were 18″ high, but some varied to the 24″ height. The a/c ID letter sometimes appeared on the nose, behind and centered under the prop spinner. Usually it was a black block letter, but various colored and styled letters were seen. The position of the black a/c serial varied from forward of, onto, over, and high on the fuselage spine, on the recognition band. Serials were from 4″ to 8″ in height.

The wing machine gun and cannon were capped with red doped fabric tape prior to shows. Sometimes just a GI-issue contraceptive was seen on a cannon barrel.

Personal pilot artwork was evident, but nowhere as profuse as later in the P-47/P-51 era. These emblems, usually some form of the Eagle, or just a name, usually appeared below the manifold aft to the cockpit on the left side of the a/c. If wheel covers were used, various designs usually adorned them, the dominant one being the RAF roundel. The Spits carried the small rectangular rear-view mirrors, as the later and much-sought-after spherical type was not yet in service. 336FS Spits were crudely unit-converted to clipped wingtip models in late fall 1942. The wingtip was hack-sawed off on the panel line. Then wooden planks were pounded in the wing and fastened with screws to the skin. Next came a rough airfoil-shape carving and a coat of paint to finish it. At one time a problem of supply was manifest, due to rusting Spit tail wheels. However, an official VIII Fighter Command order soon stopped the pilots from taking their pre-show "Good-Luck Panic-Pee" on the wheel before they donned the parachute resting on the horizontal stabilizer.

While one or two Spitfire IXs were photographed on the base and flown by some 4FG pilots, it is thought these were just visitors the pilots were having a "try" with. None are documented as 4FG assigned.

Republic Thunderbolt P-47 A/C:

The P-47C made its debut in the 4FG on January 15, 1943. These a/c were in a color scheme of Dark Olive Drab No. 41 on the topsides with the undersides in Neutral Gray No. 43. Just aft of the fuselage intercooler doors appeared the AAF insignia in the same colors, size, and style as on the Spitfires. The wing cocardes were without a yellow border ring. The upper left wing cocarde was 45″ in diameter and there were two 59″ in diameter under each wing. A serial/Call Number in ID Yellow was positioned above the center hinge line on the forward tail on both sides.

While 335FS and 336FS fought on with Spitfires, 334FS took the first P-47s and went non-operational to serve as the Group OTU for the Jug. These OTU a/c carried a special code comprised of the last two digits of each a/c serial number. It was placed in the usual squadron code spot forward of the fuselage cocarde in white paint.

On Feb. 20, 1943, 8FC ordered the placing of a 24″ forward cowl-tip band, a 12″ tail band above the serial, and an 18″ band on each horizontal stabilizer. These "ETO" bands were in white. Their purpose was to avoid confusion of the P-47 with the FW 190 in combat.

One of the first unofficial unit markings was a repeat of the two-digit code/serial no. on the lower front nose cowl lip. This was usually in black and outlined yellow, but it also showed up in white on black or plain black. The purpose of this marking was to aid groundcrews in spotting their charge as it taxied towards them on the perimeter track. Then they would flag the pilot into the bay/hardstand.

The giant nose cowling quickly became a billboard of gaudy pilot personal art emblems. These were mainly on the left nose cowling and aft to the cockpit area. Some were on both sides of the a/c and one even turned up on the aft fuselage by the squadron code. Often a simple geometric design on the inboard wheel cover accompanied the nose art. Probably the main reason for such profuse 334FS artwork was S/Sgt. Donald Allen, a talented commercial artist turned crewchief. Much of the early 336FS nose-art was attributed to a Sgt. Hutton. Artwork flowered on the P-47 from moment of issue in 334FS and 336FS. 335FS artwork was slower to appear as their CO, Don Blakeslee, withheld it as a reward for achievement. 335FS art never reached the glory seen in 334FS and 336FS.

The 4FG was assigned a new set of squadron codes on April 3, 1943 for the introduction of the P-47 into combat. These codes had been used by the 52FG which had been sent to Africa. 334FS became QP, 335FS was WD, and 336FS had VF allotted. These white 24″-high codes were put in the usual position. Due to Donald Allen's talents, a number of 334FS a/c codes got a thin red outline shortly thereafter. Each a/c received a single plane-in-squadron ID letter aft of the fuselage cocarde as on the Spits. At least two a/c had all three code letters, with a dash after the squadron code, applied forward of the cocarde. But these were exceptions, not the rule. Upon the code change the a/c letter replaced the two-number digits on the cowl lip in most cases.

When the AAF insignia was revised on July 12, 1943, the a/c letters were moved further aft. A white bar was added to each side of the cocarde and all was bordered in red. Both underwing insignia remained throughout 4FG P-47 service. The red border was changed to a blue border on Nov. 5, 1943.

In July 1943 the 4FG introduced belly drop-tanks to the ETO ("babies"). These 200-gallon tanks as well as the follow-on 75-gallon tanks were painted Neutral Gray No. 43 with a red filler cap. Next came the paper-fabricated 108-gallon tanks finished in silver dope with red bands to indicate lift-strap positions.

The P-47s were transferred out of the 4FG in Feb. 1944 as the unit re-equipped with the P-51B Mustang. After VE-Day in May 1945, the 4FG again was given a small number of P-47s. These were ex-5th Emergency Air-Sea Rescue Squadron Jugs from Halesworth, UK. The war-weary status a/c were to be used in training 4th pilots to operate P-47Ns in the Pacific, but the idea was short-lived and they disappeared after some weeks. The a/c were finished in both Olive Drab and natural metal schemes. Their nose cowlings were given a coat of glossy Group Red aft to the cowl flaps. Squadron codes were white on Olive Drab and black on NMF. Either a/c letters or OTU a/c numbers were put aft of the cocarde on the fuselage. Being training a/c, most received the red/white/blue OTU (Operational Training Unit) rudder colors, tip to bottom order respectively in equal segments. Some had the rudder color of their assigned squadron. The W.W. denoting war-weary status was carried over or below the tail serial no. The Olive Drab/Gray a/c were much over-painted due to their long service in the ETO. It is believed that approx. eight of these Jugs were assigned to the 4FG, with several going to each squadron.

P-51B/C North American Mustang A/C:

Several P-51Bs were periodically attached to the 4FG for testing in the early fall of 1943, one of which involved the new G-Suit development. These a/c were in the brown-tone AAF Olive Drab and neutral Gray on the bottom. No markings were carried other than the national insignia and the serial no.

The first three group-assigned P-51s arrived on Feb. 14, 1944. They were in the brown-tone O/D and Gray with no ETO bands and the old red 1943 bordered Star/Bar remained on them. More 51Bs arrived in late Feb 1944. These were O/D and Gray, serialed yellow, and had white ETO bands of 12", 15" 2", and 15", on the nose, wings, tail fin, and horizontal stabilizer respectively. As on the P-47 a/c, the maintenance and specification lettering on O/D a/c was in black. The Blue/White AAF cocarde was outlined insignia blue. On March 23, 1944, the tail ETO bands and some of the serial nos. were painted out with camouflage to avoid confusion with the Bf 109 by improving the tail silhouette.

While the a/c were being inspected over March 15–18, 1944, the new 8AF Group nose marking was applied. The 4FG adopted a red spinner and a 12" red band ahead of the exhaust manifolds aft of the spinner. The color hue was a glossy warm red with an orange tinge to it. This paint was purchased from local civilian sources and had very little pigment content. From 4 to 6 coats were needed to coat well. There being no masking tapes available, the masking of most 4FG paintwork was done with greased newspapers. Group paintwork was done by the squadron hangar painter, often the least technically trained of personnel.

Soon after arrival, some of the 334FS A Flight 51s received a thin red outline to their code letters. No other 4th a/c had this marking until much later. In April–May, 1944, several 334FS 51Bs sported a red ETO tail fin band, the purpose of which is unknown, possibly as a Flight color ID. On approx. March 22, 1944, the first natural metal finish (NMF) 51Bs began to arrive for 4FG use. They were given to the rookie pilots, the veterans preferring the less visible O/D a/c. The entire a/c was NMF with black ETO bands (full tail) in the usual positions as on O/D a/c. The red Group nose band sometimes appeared to have a white border to it on NMF a/c, but this was just paint overspray of the masking.

Some 336FS 51Bs carried two types of extra squadron markings on O/D and a few NMF a/c during the early spring of 1944. The VF code was put in two colors, one light and one dark, aft of the nose band and centered under the carburetor air scoop in approx. 6" letters. The second marking on O/D squadron a/c was a NMF plate over the carburetor air filter on the lower nose cowl on both sides. These plates were outlined a dark color and inscribed with token "V-Mail" messages to Hitler and others.

The British-made clear bubble "Malcolm Hood" canopy conversions began to arrive during April 1944 as a remedy for the poor vision with the factory canopy. They were eagerly vied for, but rank usually won out, except in 336FS, where Lt. McDill got the first one to the chagrin of senior pilots. His crewchief Cardella was also able to wangle a scarce Spitfire cupped mirror, which added injury to insult. The Malcolm Hood also required the installation of a whip antenna on the 51B's rear dorsal spine. Some 51s, both

B/C and D-models, had a light color number "67" on the left side of the glare-panel ahead of the canopy. This indicated that grade 67 hydraulic fluid should be filled at that tank location. The red-doped gun tapings were continued on P-51 a/c.

In May 1944, prior to D-Day, the 8AF ordered that NMF fighters should be painted camouflage on the topsides. Only a few such paint jobs were done in the 4th's 334FS before the order was cancelled. 335FS and 336FS did not operate a/c in this scheme. These few 334FS a/c had O/D on the wing and horizontal stabilizer tops, full tail fin/rudder, with a narrow top profile strip on the rear fuselage.

In the late afternoon and through the night of June 5, 1944, the 4FG a/c received their "D-Day" stripes in wht/blk/wht/blk/wht order around the wings and rear fuselage. Each color stripe was 18" for a total width of 90". The a/c code letters were painted around and an O/D space was left around the letters on O/D a/c. These AEAF stripes were removed from all upper surfaces in late July 1944, completely from the wings in Sept. 1944, and from the lower fuselage in early 1945.

The 8AF set up a system of fighter squadron rudder color markings circa Oct. 10, 1944. 334FS rudders became Group red. 335FS used a white rudder with a thin red edge around it. One photo of a plain white rudder probably was of an a/c being painted. One known instance of a black edge was probably a short-lived experiment before the red edge was finalized. 336FS a/c received a blue rudder. The blue varied from dark insignia blue to an RAF Photo-Recon light powder blue. The black ETO band on the tail fin was removed when the rudders were colored. In the late fall of 1944, 334FS adopted a red border to all squadron a/c code letters. About this time 336FS began to put a red shadow/depth edge to the forward sides of their code letters, but not all a/c in the squadron displayed it. 335FS did not use a red code border until spring of 1945.

In the fall of 1944, the 4th squadrons each received 2 or 3 war-weary P-51B/Cs to use for their squadron OTU "Clobber Colleges." Instead of a letter, these a/c were given a number code of 2, 3, or 4. Their rudders were painted top to bottom in equal segments of red/white/blue. 335FS converted an OTU NMF 51B to a two-seat model in Nov. 1944. By VE-Day it was colored overall glossy red with a light blue A/G panel and an OTU rudder. On Feb. 18, 1945, 336FS completed a two-seat conversion which was colored light blue overall with red trim by March 1945.

Early in Dec. 1944 the Group nose cowl band of red was extended to 24". After Jan. 1, 1945 it was being swept down under the nose to a point which ended and centered at the lower wing leading edge.

51B/C models were scarce but still in combat into the late winter of 1944/45. However, none were noted on ops by Mar. 1945. By then they had too many hours on them and there were enough D-models to retire them. These older B/Cs had the fillet added to the front of the tail fin and Malcom Hoods.

When the squadrons had more than 26 a/c, the code letters were repeated. However, a second lettered a/c had either a bar under its letter or a dash after the letter. From late 1944 on, a second lettered a/c sometimes had a double letter, i.e., VV, Ss. The second code letter was either full or half-size.

NOTES: The new P-51Bs in Mar. 1944 were brought up to B-7 configuration soon after arrival. Many pilots repeated P-47 artwork emblems on their new 51s. Most art appeared on the left nose to canopy area. Victory "Kill" markings (more profuse on 51s) were usually just below and forward of the left canopy quarter panel. These were either swastikas, crosses, or flags combining the first two. Swastikas and crosses were black and white. Flags usually added a red field to the blk/wht of the preceding. The gas filler caps on all types of 4th a/c were red, as were the lined "No-step" areas on the wing flaps. A black dot near a gas cap was a ground point for the hose. Oxygen filler caps were green or black. Exhaust stacks were a rust brown color. There was always a stained oxidation trail behind the exhaust stacks. When the O/D a/c were in the hangar for checks or VIPs were around, the paint was touched up in spots till the weathered shades of O/D and Gray on them was considerable. Some a/c thereby resembled a mottled camouflage pattern. After rough weather flights the cheap red nose paint wore down to the white ETO underneath. It was not unusual to see O/D replacement panels on NMF a/c. Col. Blakeslee's NMF B-model once flew with the entire O/D wing mainplanes of a 334FS a/c because he wanted his damaged a/c on ops the next day. Tail serial numbers were both block & stencil styles. The right lower wingtip housed three identification lights (small) of red, green, yellow for the IFF colors of the day. The lower nose cowl carburetor air filters were plated up or not according to the weather and season. The use of exhaust plinths seemed to be a matter of choice. A good number of Mustangs sported red painted wheel disks.

The 75-gallon metal teardrop wing tanks used in early 1944 on the 51B/Cs were neutral gray with red filler caps. The 75-gallon tanks were in short supply by May 14, 1944 and the Group switched to 108-gallon cigar-shaped tanks by necessity. These were either metal or formed paper, colored neutral gray and silver respectively. They had two fastening bands of black or green with red taping wrapped over them. At first the 108-gallon tank was only filled to 75 gallons due to a 550-lb. limit on the bomb shackles, but two weeks prior to the Russia shuttle they were satisfactorily test flown at full capacity. On June 14, 1944, 19 a/c of the 352FG were fitted at Debden with 108-gallon kits for the Russia trip.

P-51D/K North American Mustang A/C:

The first 4FG-issued P-51D models with the new 360-degree-vision teardrop canopies arrived several days prior to D-Day on June 6, 1944. They were without the tail fin fillet modification later added to all Ds by Sept. 1944. All 4FG Ds were NMF except one later painted O/D on the topsides by Deacon Hively. There were two styles of D-model canopy: the rounding-curve top of the Inglewood, Cal., plant, and the Dallas, Tex., plant's flat-topped "Tru-Vue" style canopy.

The group, squadron, and national markings on the D's were the same as applied to the B/C's at the time periods both were in service in the 4FG. Additions to the D-model schemes were the following: 336FS painted some (not all) of their lower canopy frames in O/D after Nov. 1944. Several 336FS a/c had light-blue anti-glare panels and lower canopy frames, both edged in red. 335FS colored their lower canopy frames in red in the Spring of 1945.

Victory markings were moved to the lower left canopy frame on most 4th Ds. They also showed up under the left exhaust on several a/c. Pilot and ground crew names began to appear on the left cowl below the canopy quarter-panel and on the canopy frame. Usually they were in black. Some were white on 335s red canopy frames.

Code letters were block style unless the hangar crew hadn't touched up the stencil lines, but they were corrected on the next hangar visit. Tail serial numbers were black and positioned in either of three ways—3 digits each level on the fin and rudder; six digits level on the tail fin only; or all on the fin and slanted up towards the rudder. These were in both block and stencil style. The D-Day band was the same as on B/Cs. The last four digits of the serial number were often put on the engine cowl panels in small black figures. This was to avoid mixup in the crowded hangar at inspection time, etc. The two cowl panels around the exhaust manifolds were a heavier gauge heat-proof metal that always appeared darker than the rest of the a/c's lightweight skin.

Most D's had Spitfire mirrors, some even had dual ones, all being mounted on top of the windscreen in NMF, black, O/D, or red. Green, black or NMF oxygen filler caps were aft of the canopy on the left upper fuselage. The rear fuselage radio antenna was usually painted O/D.

In Sept. and Oct. 1944, a flashy scheme of dark green wavy stripes appeared on the topsides of Lt. Col. Claiborne Kinnard's P-51D. An oblique red band across the glare panel accompanied the stripes. After a few weeks the stripes were removed because they were attracting too much hostile attention from friend and foe.

The Spring of 1945 found black sighting angle degree marks for glide and dive bombing applied to the inboard left top leading edge of the wing. These approx. 1-inch-wide marks radiated at various angles from the wing root outboard and forward.

Several peacetime changes came with the arrival of VE-Day in May 1945. The a/c code letters were added to the lower left wing to thwart low level buzzing by pilots. These 36"-high letters were in black outboard of the bomb shackles almost to the wing-tip. They appeared as three spaced letters or as two squadron code letters with a dash separating the a/c letter. Night formation flying lights were also added to some of the squadron leaders' a/c. Two lights were installed on each side of the a/c, one just aft of the firewall above the specification lettering and one below the radio mast on the aft white bar of the national insignia.

NOTE: There is one steadfast rule in a/c markings: they are *never* uniform or exactly to specifications. Exceptions and irregularities abounded in the 4FG as everywhere.

APPENDIX XI

The 4th "Flying Eagles" Dance Orchestra

It is not known exactly when the band was formed, but it was some time in the first months of 1943. The guiding genius behind it was Maj. Edgar Levy, an intelligence officer in 4th Hq. Sq. He played an important role in the band's success by acting as their booking agent. Special appearances in London and elsewhere, and shows such as "Glad to See Ya," were his works.

When the band (17 pieces at its largest) hit off with its theme song, "Sophisticated Swing," these known 4th men were sitting behind the blue music-stands with the name Flying Eagles in the front bearing the Group's fighting eagle emblem: Chase Wilkins (band leader), Harold Goldblatt (hit singer of "Lilly" song), Jame Jordon (vocalist), Howard Crossett, William Brong, Charles Kirkpatrick, Hubert Schroeder (top pre-war pianist with the famous Bunny Berrigan Band in the U.S.), Dave Tucker, Charles Brashares, Frank Nowak, Clarence Wilcox, Eugene Baim, Clyde "Mac" Hayes (m.c. and electronics sound man), James Scharren, Joseph Lopez, William Avery, John "Jack" Loy, Anthony Fontana, ? Lattimore, Peter Miodaszewski (set-up and prop man), Andy Di Carlo, and Mickey Balsam (guitarist and songwriter). Of course all the preceding men did not play in the band at the same times, since there was a natural turnover during the war due to many causes. The band's composition was: 5 saxophones, 4 trumpets, 4 trombones, piano, bass, guitar, drums, 2 vocalists, prop man, and the manager/booker.

The band's activities were varied and exciting. They played for dances, athletic field days, stage plays (toured on the road with same for three weeks, made recordings, and broadcast to the U.S. and the ETO). One of the members, Mickey Balsam of the 52nd. Fighter Control Sqd. in Saffron Walden, wrote the words and music to the famous ETO tune, "Lilly from Piccadilly." This was a lyrical account of a GI's encounter with one of London's ladies of the evening, which included a second set of lyrics not suitable to publish. It was recorded in London and published by Harms Ltd. (they wouldn't put their name on it though) in 20,000 copies. This was all the paper the British would authorize for the printing and it was sold out within two weeks time. Mickey also wrote "Mama Listen to Me Now" from the stageshow "Glad to See Ya."

The Flying Eagles were in demand for the Wednesday night dances at the base E.M. Club and the monthly payday dances at the Officers Club which drew patrons from all over the European Theatre of Operations. Every type of aircraft flown in the ETO could be seen parked near the control tower on those nights. On days and nights when the field was socked in by bad weather, the band got up jam combos to entertain in the clubs.

Not only did the band play at nearby bases like Cambridge, Bassingbourn, Stansted, and at Hub Zemke's "Wolfpack" fighter base (one of the band members took advantage of the hospitality and "stole" Zemke's girl!), but their fame was well known further afield. The following is a short list of their appearances: The Stagedoor Canteen of the London American Service Club, from which they broadcast to the U.S. and the ETO Armed Forces; London Red Cross clubs such as Rainbow Corner on Piccadilly Circus, where they performed with the group stage play; Bournemouth, a coastal resort; several times at the Columbia Club in London; Covent Garden Royal Opera House; a large dance hall in London which held daily performances, where they may have been the only American band to play there in WW2; at parties of the Headquarters of SHAEF, Supreme Headquarters Allied Expeditionary Forces. They were also requested to appear at British Royal Birthday parties. On July 10, 1945, they went on a three-week tour of bases, hospitals, and staging areas with the stage play "Glad to See Ya." They flew to Bury-St. Edmunds airfield, which served as their tour headquarters, by B-17.

At one time the band joined a company of 32 American entertainers, dancers, singers, and comedians to help cheer the GI's, because the USO shows were not too good towards the end of the war. In these shows the jokes and skits were mostly about "Jolly Olde England," its customs, and how the GI's were trying to make out with the English girls.

One band member remembers, "There were occasions when we played for the VIPs. When they had a little too much to drink they would like to show off their dancing ability to their girl friends. They would approach the band with their girl and pull rank on the band. They would say to our leader, 'Soldier, this is an order. I want you to play these tunes'—usually a slow waltz or some slow tune which they thought they could dance to. Sometimes they were in no shape to sit, let alone do a dance. So the leader would call back to us and say, 'Men, this is an order.' We knew what he meant. We had a special list of tunes for such occasions, usually entirely different and with a fast tempo. It wouldn't take long before the VIPs would fall over each other and land on the floor. It would be bedlam, their partners trying to pick them up, and they in turn would fall down on them. This would create quite a commotion and fun for the others as they would mock each other out. It was a sight to behold when their dignity was hurt. Normally we would acknowledge any reasonable request, except when a joker would pull rank on us *artists!*"

Music at Debden was certainly not limited to the dance band. Many parties and dreary hours of boredom were brightened by such gifted pilots as Pierce McKennon, a collegiate classical pianist who could pop the top off a piano with his boogie-woogie tunes, and "Deacon" Hively launching into his slapstick routine of "The Red Ace's Demise." Another favorite was "Red Dog" Norley piping thru the choruses of numerous flying ditties during some post-mission "Mild & Bitters" session. Some of these ditties were 4th-authored and others were carryovers from RAF and training days.

4th Fighter Group Service Units

The AAF Service Units that served at different periods at Debden, Essex, 8AF Station No. 356-F, were: 33rd Air Service Grp.—438th Air Service Grp.—45th Air Engineering Sqd.—864th Air Engineering Sqd.—1770th Ordinance Supply & Maintenance Company (Avn.)—688th Air Materiel Sqd.—128th Army Postal Unit—18th. Weather Sqd.—24th Station Compliment Sqd.—546th Army Postal Unit—Detachment A, 1126th Quartermaster Company—1063rd Military Police Company (Avn.)—Detachment A, 33rd Air Service Grp. Headquarters Sqd.—Detachment A, 1030th Signal Company—2119th Engineering Fire Fighting Platoon (Avn.)—30th. Postal Regulating Section—102nd Provisional Gas Detachment.

On January 13, 1943, the 33rd ASG disembarked from the HMS *Queen Elizabeth* in Scotland and proceeded to Debden, Essex. Actually only half of the group went to Debden, because the group was split between two fighter groups with the other half being assigned to the 56th Fighter Group at Kingscliffe. The 33rd parts which went to the 4FG were: the 45th AES, the 1770th Ord. S&M Co., and the Det. A, Hqs. Sqd. of the 33rd ASG. The 24th Station Compliment Sqd. joined the service group at Debden on July 12, 1943. The various MP and Postal units were assigned as they arrived in the UK. These were the main 4FG service units during most of the war, until April 12, 1945.

The 45th AES and 24th SCS personnel provided the following services to the 4FG: personnel section, administrative section, finance, inspection depts., station defense, medical section, Post Exchange, enlisted men's club, officer's club, quartermaster section, chemical warfare section, a General Mess hall, motor pool, wreckage crew, photo lab, MP and prison detail, MP Alert detachment. The 45th AES operated the following shops: machine, electric, propeller, spark plug, paint, carpenter, engine, welding, parachute, sheet metal, instrument, aero repair section, and the Flying Control Section.

The 1770th Ordinance S&M Company supplied and serviced the following: technical items, communications items, ordnance items, and chemical items. It operated filling and distribution points for gasoline, oil, lubricants, and engineering supplies.

At the approach of VE-Day, the War Dept. activated a reorganization of the 8AF service groups (new type). Each base would now have a service group of its own instead of half a larger group. On April 15, 1945, the 33rd ASG, 45th AES, 1770th Ord. S&M Co., 1126th QM Co., 24th Station Compl. Sqd., 1030th Sig. Co. were all disbanded. In their stead was activated the 438th Air Service Grp., comprised of the 438th HQ & Base Services Sqd., 688th Air Materiel Sqd., and the 864th Air Engineering Sqd. The new group had 41 officers and 578 enlisted men. The entire changeover was conducted while continuing combat operations for the fighter group.

Thus the 438th ASG carried on the work thru the summer and fall of 1945, which the old 33rd ASG had done so well during the actual combat days of the 4FG. After VE-Day the work was the same, but the old *esprit* was gone as the units went through the changes of the boring wait to go home. The high point men went home along with the over-35 men, and the low point men went to other units destined for the occupational forces. This left the units filled out with transferees on the way home. While the fighter group personnel could sport decorations and citations, the service unit men who had worked side by side with the fighter crews could only take solace in their knowlege of a tough job well done. They were not given the recognition due to them for their faithful and superior works. The 4FG service units set many command records for achievement. Sic transit gloria!